WHAT MA
ALWAYS SAID

WHAT MA ALWAYS SAID

A Special Edition of the Bestselling Dublin Memoirs
What Would Ma Say? and *In Ma's Footsteps*

KATHLEEN DOYLE

POOLBEG

Published 2011
by Poolbeg Books Ltd
123 Grange Hill, Baldoyle
Dublin 13, Ireland
E-mail: poolbeg@poolbeg.com

1

A catalogue record for this book is available from the British Library.

ISBN 978-1-84223 491-4

Printed and bound by CPI Group (UK) Ltd, Croydon, CR0 4YY

www.poolbeg.com

About the author

Kathleen McGrath was born Kathleen Doyle in 1948. She is married to Alan, and they have three children (Martina, Alan Junior and Amanda), three granddaughters (Danielle, Jessica and Robin) and one great-grandson, Conor. Kathleen set up her own hairdressing business, eventually running three salons. She has now retired and lives in Tallaght. In 2009, her first memoir, the bestselling *What Would Ma Say?* was published, followed by *In Ma's Footsteps* in 2010.

WHAT WOULD MA SAY?

BOOK 1

1

From Jam Jars to China

The phone rang. It was my sister Clare. The call I was expecting but didn't want to hear.

'Kathleen, Ma is gone,' she cried. 'Ma's dead.'

I had only been down with Ma the day before. As soon as I'd walked into the house I could see how weak she looked. She was eighty-four and had been sick a lot over the past two years and her mind was starting to wander. There were days when I would go in to see her and she wouldn't know who I was. I'd get so upset when that happened.

I thought to myself, *This is it. Her time has come.* I could see in her eyes that she was ready to go. The life was gone completely out of her. She was like a little child sitting in her chair, helpless, unable to do anything for herself.

My sister Carmel, who lives in the family home and looked after Ma so well, tapped me on the shoulder.

'You're miles away there, Kathleen. Have you heard anythin' I've said?'

'Sorry, Carmel, I was thinkin'. Wha' did yeh say?'

'You'll have to try and get some food and water into Ma. She's eaten nothin' for me since yesterday.' Her eyes filled up as she spoke.

'Yeh look tired, Carmel. You go and have a break for a few hours and don't be worryin'. I'll take care of everythin'.'

It wasn't long before the house was empty and I was alone with Ma. I knew in my heart that there wasn't much time left and was grateful for the next few hours we were to spend together. Just the two of us. I sat there holding her hand, trying to get her to sip some water for me. But she wasn't having any of it. As weak as she was, she still put her hand up to stop me, shaking her head from side to side, saying, 'No'. She gestured for me to bend down.

'What is it?' I asked. 'Wha' are yeh tryin' to say, Ma?' It took her a minute or two of struggling in such a low voice to get the words out. But I was so happy when I heard what she had to say. 'Kathleen, make's a cup of tea.' I couldn't believe it. She knew who I was.

They were the last words that Ma spoke to me. I sat there for the next couple of hours, Ma sipping on her tea and me pouring my heart out at last, telling her all the things I had bottled up inside me all these years.

'D'yeh know, Ma, sometimes I used to think as a child growin' up, tha' yeh didn't love me. Yeh never said the words, ever.'

She looked at me the whole time I spoke, listening and giving me the nod every now and then.

'Ah, don't take any notice of me, Ma. I'm just rammagin' on here. They're just thoughts from a child, Ma, tha's all. Thoughts from a child, from long ago.'

She then gave my hand a little squeeze, and with the other hand pointed towards her eye and then to her heart, holding it there for a few seconds longer and then, last but not least, straight at me. Eye for 'I', heart for 'love', and 'you'.

I cried and cried as I spoke the words back. 'And I love yeh too, Ma.' I hugged and kissed her. The words had never been spoken, but they were there all this time, inside her head and mine. That was all that mattered to me.

* * *

The next day, when Clare told me Ma had died, I was sad but didn't cry at first. I knew she couldn't hold on any longer. She had done her time on this earth and what a great job she had done. She was at peace now. All her worrying was over.

In the days leading up to Ma's funeral, the whole family gathered in the house to support one another. There was myself, Carmel, Noel, Clare, Marion, Thomas, Jacinta, Patricia, Mano and Paul, remembering all the funny stories, laughing and crying at the same time. The only one missing was Phil, the oldest of all of us. He had been so young when he died, barely forty; such a character, always full of life. If he'd been here now, God only knows what antics he'd be getting up to. How I wished he could have been there. He'd have helped us get through a very hard time with his funny ways, just like he always did when we were growing up. We all missed him so much.

I could hear Noel and Thomas reminiscing about the day they robbed a dead pig with Phil and how they hid it in the wardrobe so Da wouldn't see it. Then Clare turned around and brought up the day that we all made a swimming pool in the kitchen. The other sisters got their spoke in straight away: 'Wha' are yeh talkin' about, Clare? At least the whole gang of us did tha' together. Remember when yeh went and painted the table and chairs, and every plate and jam jar in the house gold and silver – and yeh did tha' all on yer own!'

'Tha's because I was tryin' to keep meself awake,' said Clare. 'I was afraid to go asleep because of the ghost.'

On went the storytelling while all the grandchildren sat there in amazement listening to all the things that we had got up to! How Ma put up with us I will never know. We went on for hours, all of us going over events from so long ago.

Ma was laid out in the very sitting-room that she had spent

3

most of her life in, where all the bedlam and mayhem went on. Be it good, sad or funny, that's where it all happened. We all felt it was only fitting that she would leave from the home that she and Da had built around us so many years ago.

Down through the years, Ma had always spoken about having a big send-off when she passed away. I would tell her not to be talking about such things, as you never want to think of your parents dying. But no, Ma would never let it go. She made each and every one of us promise to keep her wishes.

'Remember tha' film *Madame X*?' she would say. 'There was these big black stallions and a glass carriage bringin' the woman to her restin' place. Well, tha's wha' I want and if I don't get it I'll come back and haunt every one of yiz. Oh, and another thing, yeh're to make sure the horses trot nice and slow, so as everybody on the road can see me. When me day comes, I want to go out in style. I might not have had much in me life, but by God, when I'm ready to leave this earth, I want everybody to remember the day tha' Lil Doyle died.'

And what a send-off she got. For the outspoken woman that she was, and for all her toughness, she was so well liked that people came from far and near to pay their respects. You couldn't put a price on all the flowers in the house. All Ma's favourites. She loved flowers so much she used to spend half of her pension every week doing the flowers for the church, telling us, 'Now tha' I'm able to, I want to thank the Holy Mother herself for all the years tha' she helped me through all me hard times.'

The day of Ma's funeral was such a lovely November day, the sun splitting the trees. We were all down in the house from early to say our last goodbye. I remember standing back and looking at all the family, from the youngest to the oldest, dressed in black as a mark of respect. I thought Ma would be well pleased with them all.

When the horses and carriage arrived at the house, we were all speechless. I had never seen the likes of it before at any funeral. It was everything Ma had wished for and more. The two black horses were groomed to perfection. They stood tall with their black plumes on the tops of their heads, waiting patiently. The coachmen looked so impressive dressed in traditional uniform – double-breasted coats with big silver buttons, expensive cravats, top hats, snow-white gloves and black leather polished boots. They stood silently on either side of the glass carriage, which was gleaming so beautifully. It was perfect.

It was now my turn to go in to Ma to say my last few words. As I stood there holding Ma's hand, I finally broke down and cried. Such a loss and emptiness came over me as I said goodbye. 'Yeh were a great Ma and will never be forgotten. Yeh'll live on forever in all our hearts. It's time to go now Ma, your carriage awaits yeh.'

My brothers placed the coffin into the glass carriage as Ma left the house for the last time. The horses trotted slowly up the road, while all the neighbours, young and old, stood still, the older men taking off their caps out of respect for Lil Doyle. When we got to the church I couldn't believe the number of people there. It was packed to capacity. We played Ma's favourite songs as the priest said Mass. I sat there listening to all the family as everyone broke down crying. They too were feeling the loss I felt inside.

Her cremation in Mount Jerome was so peaceful. There were no more words spoken. While the song 'In the Arms of an Angel' played, we all sat there in silence. As the curtains slowly closed, I felt Ma was at peace at last. I sat there on my own for a few moments, thinking, 'Well, wha' de yeh say, Ma? Is it everythin' yeh wished for? Did we do yeh proud? I think so, Ma; it was a funeral fit for a queen.'

* * *

The day slowly came to an end. I felt so tired and drained, I thought I would never get home to put my head down. Later, unable to sleep, I made my way downstairs. As I sat there drinking a cup of tea, I thought about the first time Ma sat in this very kitchen with me.

Over the years, Ma had been visiting myself and Alan every Sunday and sometimes used to stay for the weekend. We had bought a new house at the bottom of the mountains in Tallaght. I thought I'd never get her up to see it. We were only in the door and as usual the cup of tea and a smoke had to come first.

'Are yeh right, Ma? Come on and I'll show yeh around while the kettle is boilin'.'

As we went around the house, you could see she was surprised and well pleased, but didn't say it. She had mellowed a lot over the years and only now you could have a bit of crack with her. I laughed as we walked in and out of the rooms.

'Ma, which toilet would yeh like to use today? There's the blue one, the green one and there's the yellow one downstairs. Your choice.'

'Would yeh get away with yerself, Kathleen Doyle, I wouldn't be able for yeh with yer showin' off. There was a time yeh hadn't got a pair of knickers to yer name, and don't yeh ever forget tha', de yeh hear me now?'

In a way I suppose I was showing off. I wanted Ma to be so proud of me for what I had achieved throughout the years. As a child, I craved the slightest bit of attention. Even the tiniest bit of praise meant so much to me. But I rarely got it.

'All the same, Kathleen, did yeh ever think tha' yeh'd see the likes of it? Three toilets and all in yer own house, for only yiz to use and nobody else. Isn't it a far cry from the tenements and the shite bucket, and you know tha' more than the rest of the kids – helpin' me carry it down all them stairs to tha' filthy toilet in the yard. We've come a long way since then, so we have.'

'Yeh should be very proud, Ma. Yeh built a lovely home around yerself and Da over the years and look at the way all the kids turned out. Yeh did well.'

'I have to say – and I'll say it straight to yer face, Kathleen – it was a long, hard road, but yiz didn't turn out too bad for a shower of ticks.'

And by that she meant we had done well for ourselves, which we all did. Believe it or not, that was a big compliment coming from Ma.

'Kathleen, me mouth's waterin' here. Are yeh makin' me tha' cup of tea or wha'?'

I took out my special set of china cups and saucers as Ma sat there puffing away. 'Wha' de yeh say, Ma? Will we go all posh for the day to celebrate the new house or would yeh prefer a jam jar?'

The look on her face was priceless. I was still showing off and I didn't care.

'God be with the days, Kathleen, when we had nothin' else only jam jars to drink our cup of tea out of. Such poverty, how did we ever get through it all?'

I sat there listening to Ma while she reminisced about the past. I let my own mind slowly fade back to a time gone by so long ago.

2

The Tenement

My name is Kathleen Doyle. I'm one of twelve children, five brothers and six sisters. I was born in a tenement house – number 7, Cook Street – off the back of Christ Church Cathedral in Dublin City, in 1948.

Ma was small in height, about five foot, but she was heavily built. She had very dark skin and the most beautiful head of long black hair that you ever saw. An ordinary woman with very little education behind her, but maybe not so ordinary in the way she learned how to survive and handle life. She was so strong and tough, cunning, smart and very streetwise and that's how she was able to get through so much turmoil in her life.

She could be very witty in her own way. I laugh now when I think of the things she used to say with her friend Maisie. They were gas when they got together; that would be the only time Ma would let herself go and probably be the Ma that I didn't know but should have known.

Maisie was the complete opposite to Ma. She was very tall and thin, her blonde hair always tied back in a bun. When I think back to those times, she was some character and the only one who ever made Ma laugh. One day as they sat in the kitchen having a cup of tea and smoking their Woodbines, I heard Maisie speak to Ma.

'Lil Doyle.'

'Wha's tha', Maisie?'

'How come yeh nearly go like one of them Comanche Indians out of them cowboy pictures the minute the sun comes out? Would yeh have a look at the colour of yeh?'

Ma replied, trying to keep her face as serious as anything, 'Well now, Maisie, if the truth be told I think one of me grannies must have went off with a foreigner of some kind. Yeh know, when them big ships came here with them Vikings and Spaniards on board? Yeh know, years and years ago, when they invaded and pillaged the life outta everyone.'

'Jaysus, Lil, yeh were listenin' in school all the same. Yeh know yer bit of history and stuff. Good for you, cause I know fuck-all.'

'No, Maisie, I swear there's foreign blood flowin' through me veins, so there is. I'm tellin' yeh, there is.'

'Yeh mean one of yer grannies was, like, a bit iffy, Lil? Yeh know, yeh know?' she said, giving Ma the nod and a wink.

Ma couldn't keep her face straight any longer. She was bursting her sides with the laughing.

'Go away, yer a mad thing, Lil, pullin' me leg like tha'. If yer Ma heard yeh sayin' tha', she'd kick the fuckin' daylights out of yeh, so she would, talkin' about yer ancestral people like tha'.'

The two of them sat there laughing and joking, telling yarns to one another.

'Sure, wha' else have we got, Maisie, only a bit of a laugh to keep us goin'.'

'Yeh never said a truer word, Lil. An oul' laugh keeps the heart sweet, so it does.'

I loved when Maisie would visit. She brought out the best in Ma.

* * *

Da was eight years older than Ma, a slim man, about five foot ten in height, with fair hair going a bit bald on top. He was a very good man, quiet in his own way. He always helped around the house with the cleaning and cooking and never minded helping out with us kids while Ma was out and about.

Phil was his name. He loved the church, sang in choir, and would help the priest to serve Mass and do the collections. Anything that needed doing around the church, Da was there. Some say that he might have gone to the priesthood only he met Ma. You couldn't blame him for getting sidetracked – she was beautiful.

But he had his downfalls, as we were to learn through the years. Very early in our lives, Da turned to drink and gambling. He became weak and didn't face up to his responsibilities very well, which was the root of all the poverty and heartache in Ma's life and ours. Life would have been a lot easier, and so much better, if he didn't drink, but that wasn't to be.

My brother Phil was born first. He had the same name as my father – the first son always carried the name. I came along eleven months later.

Back then, most working-class people in the city lived in tenement houses, which were three or four storeys high with only one toilet to serve the whole house. We lived in one very small room at the top of the tenement house. There was a small table with two chairs, one wardrobe, a double bed for Ma and Da, a single bed which myself and Phil shared and an old chest that Ma used to keep a few sheets and clothes in. The gas cooker was by the window and candles were used for lighting. There was no electricity, or at least if there was, we didn't have it – probably because it had been cut off.

The fireplace was very big. At the side of the fire there would be a stack of turf or logs and if there were an extra few bob to spare, the black bucket would be filled with coal.

We had a big milk churn. Da filled it up with water from the tap in the yard every day. In the evenings when the fire would get going and the room warmed up, Ma would do her best, but the water was never very warm and we'd be shivering as we stood there, waiting our turn to be washed from head to toe. I dreamed of sinking into a hot bath filled with bubbles.

The room had two windows. Some of the glass was missing in one of them and when the wind would blow through the lace curtains, Ma would say, 'It's grand in the summer, yeh get plenty of fresh air, good for the lungs; but in the winter the arse is blown off yeh.' She was forever at Da to fix the window.

I didn't like living in the tenement; it was such a dark and dreary house. It wasn't too bad during the day when the sunlight shone through, but at night, as soon as you went in through the front door, there was complete darkness. Ma always carried a candle in her bag, to make sure that none of us would slip and hurt ourselves.

There was nowhere for us to play except the street around the tenements or sometimes the small park at Christ Church. It was the only place in the area with a few trees and a bit of grass. I used to love when we would go up there – we would play around for hours and have the best fun ever.

Da's family lived up the hill from us. There was Granny Mariah; she was very good to us. A big woman, tall and with snow-white hair, I never remember her smiling, but then again she hadn't got much to smile about living with Granda Phil. He was a pig and a mean old shitebag. He was a lot smaller than my granny, a frail little man who looked more dead than alive and was never out of the bed. Every time we saw him, he was giving out about one thing or another. He used to frighten the shite out of me.

Then there were Da's sisters, Maggie, Mary and Emmie. They loved Da to bits and, in their eyes and Mariah's eyes, he could do no wrong. He was the only boy. They were very funny. Maggie was very posh and spoke really well. She always had her make-up on and used to tell the other two they were so common. She'd say to me, 'Listen to yer Auntie Maggie, Kathleen, and you'll go far.'

Mary and Emmie would chime in, 'Who de yeh think yeh are, Maggie Doyle, callin' us common? Yeh'd think yeh had a bag of marbles in yer mouth! And as for yer face, yeh'd get yerself a job in a circus, so yeh would; it's a clown yeh look like, with all tha' muck yeh have on.' They would always be slagging each other, but not in a bad way; they were the best of friends.

On my Ma's side was Granny Kitty. God, she was a big woman; she must have weighed about twenty-five stone. There was talk in the family that she couldn't get a pair of knickers to fit her, that she had to make them herself, and I could well believe it.

My Granda John. He always had a big smile for us but didn't have much to say. He would sit there in his rocking chair smoking his clay pipe. He would give myself and Phil a penny or two to buy a few sweets. He was nice. I liked him.

They had this lovely little red-bricked house at the back of the fish and fruit market, off Smithfield. I loved going there; they had plenty of rooms and they had their own toilet, which only they used.

My brother Phil said to Ma one day when we were visiting, 'Hey, Ma, why don't we have nice shiny windows and a toilet like me granny?'

That was the first time I saw Ma give 'the look'. I thought she was going to kill him there and then for saying that in front of everyone. You could see her face change but she was trying to be nice at the same time as she spoke to Phil.

'Yeh know the window is too high and we haven't got a ladder to reach tha' far. As for the toilet, well, yeh'll just have to shit in the bucket for now, won't yeh, luv?' As she bent down pretending to fix his hair, she whispered in his ear, 'I'm goin' to give yeh such a kick up the hole when I get yeh home, yeh'll go flyin' through the fuckin' winda' for makin' a show of me in front of me family.'

We learned that day what the look meant and never, ever to say anything out of place in front of family or strangers again.

The bucket was kept out on the landing and was emptied a few times a day. I used to hate when we had to go down to the toilet, which was out the yard at the back of the house. At night, I had to carry a candle down three flights of stairs while Ma would be carrying the bucket. When we got down to the yard, the toilet was forever blocked. There would be bits of newspaper and shit floating around, right up to the top, while the piss would be overflowing down the sides. The smell was so bad, I'd pull my dress up to my mouth and cover my nose, while Ma would be fucking and blinding out of her, calling whoever had used the toilet last all the bastards under the sun for not cleaning up after themselves.

'Mark my words, Kathleen, some day we won't have to do this.' She would try to unblock the toilet with an old wire coat-hanger.

If he wasn't working, Da did the bucket run on the weekends with Phil. I remember one day Da and Phil were taking the bucket down to the yard to empty it. Phil slipped and knocked Da down the stairs; there was piss and shit all over the two of them. Oh my God, you'd want to have heard the roars of Ma when she had to clean it up. The whole of Christ Church must have heard her that day. The fucking and blinding would start all over again.

'Tha' brother of yers is a gobshite, Kathleen. If he's not trippin' up, he's droppin' things. Accident prone, so he is. Tha's it, you'll have to carry the candle every time.'

Phil was no more accident prone than I was. He was just a cute little fucker, to say the least. 'But tha's not fair, Ma,' I mumbled.

'Wha's tha' yeh said, Kathleen? Are yeh givin' me lip now?'

'No, Ma, I was only sayin' . . .'

'Well, *don't*.' She gave me the staring look that would nearly cut you in two.

I learned a very important lesson that day: keep your mouth shut and your thoughts to yourself. You could think what you liked, but you couldn't say it out loud, not to Ma anyway. That was the way I would have to behave all through my young life, always keeping everything bottled up inside me. Back then I was too nervous to speak out.

I looked up at Phil who was standing at the top of the stairs with a sly grin on his face. I swear the little bastard had tripped on purpose because he didn't want to go down to the smelly yard himself, knowing full well that I would have to do it. I was just sorry that I didn't think of it first; but then again I don't think it would have made much of a difference. If I'd been the one who'd tripped, I wouldn't have got off that easily. There would be no excuses made for me. Phil was always Ma's blue-eyed boy.

From then on, at such an early age, I became Ma's right arm. She depended on me for so much and forgot I was a child like the rest of the kids. As far back as I can remember, that's the way things were for myself, always: minding the kids, cleaning, and helping Ma.

3

Kidnapped

Ma couldn't stand being stuck in the room all day. It was so small and cluttered.

She wasn't one for lying in bed and made sure we didn't either. She would be up from early, getting us ready to take us off for the rest of the day. We would be out and about, rambling around a few of the shops in town, with Ma picking up a few bargains here and there, before going over to Granny Kitty's.

Granny Kitty had a lovely little donkey and cart from which she sold the biggest and tastiest fish on Wednesdays and Fridays and the freshest vegetables and fruit you ever saw the rest of the week, all around Smithfield and the back of the quays. They came from near and far to buy from her. She was one of the best-known traders in the inner city. Kitty always had plenty of money tucked away in her apron and she was very good to us. Some days, if the weather wasn't too bad, she would take us with her. I loved when that would happen. We would have the best fun ever. She'd have me roaring as loud as I could:

'Get yer fresh fish straight from the sea today.'

And my brother Phil would shout, 'Cabbage and spuds straight from the farm.'

Some days we'd head off to Howth with Granny Kitty. It would take us a long time to get there. Granny always tried to be there as early as she could to catch the first trawlers docking. All the fishermen knew her very well and she knew every one of them by their first name.

'There yeh are, Kitty, first as usual.'

'Well, Johnny, doesn't the early bird always catch his worm.'

'Kitty, not a truer word could yeh say.'

She'd be asking them if they'd got a good catch and they would go on about how rough the water was. Granny would pick every piece of fish herself and made sure she got the best for all her customers.

'Kathleen, Phil,' she would say, 'come over here and count the fish with me and make sure I'm not doin' meself out of a penny.'

We would sort the fish out into different boxes, then she'd start the haggling.

'Johnny, I've twenty-five smoked cod here, thirty fresh cod, twenty mackerel, fifty of them whitin' – they went very well last week. The ray looks very big, so I'm takin' only twelve pieces. Wha' will yer price be today? Now, before yeh say a word, don't be gettin' into me with yer high prices. Yeh know I'm yer best customer.'

'Ah now, Kitty, don't I work hard out on them high waters, with the wind batterin' the face off me. You'll get rid of tha' lot in no time, you bein' one of the best fishmongers in the city of Dublin.'

As soon as they agreed on a price, there would be the spit and a shake of the hands. Only then would the deal be sealed.

Granny Kitty was great at selling. On a Friday morning the bells for twelve o'clock mass would only be ringing out, with not a fish left in sight, every box empty. She had the gift of the gab.

We would get a penny each and we would be straight down

to the shop for some clove rock and a few bulls eyes. Kitty always handed Ma a little parcel of food and a half crown when we were leaving, giving Ma the nod and the eye at the same time, saying, 'Put tha' by for a rainy day, Lil, de yeh hear me now? None of us know wha's ahead of us.'

Of course, Ma never did this, as she always needed a few bob for one thing or another; if she didn't owe it to somebody it would be spent straight away.

* * *

On the way home from town with Ma, we would drop into the small park in the grounds of Christ Church. Sally, Mary and Kathleen, Ma's sisters, would be there with their kids. The sisters were very close and would meet up every chance they got. We would play around, climbing the trees and chasing one another. Ma and her sisters always brought their knitting with them; they would be sitting there, backbiting everyone who lived on the Hill while they smoked their Woodbines.

One day I heard Mary say to Ma, 'Are you gone again, Lil Doyle?'

'For fuck's sake, Mary! Will yeh be quiet, the kids will hear yeh.'

I cocked my ears up when I heard that.

'Ma, are yeh goin' somewhere?' I asked.

They all laughed and told me not to be listening. 'Get away with yerself, Kathleen. Go and play with the rest of the kids and don't be always ear-wiggin'.'

A few months later my sister Carmel was born. That was the start of me minding Ma's babies; I was about four years old at that stage.

It was around that time that I was kidnapped.

* * *

I remember the day so well; Ma was in the best of form.

'Wha' a lovely day it is, Kathleen. The sun is splittin' the trees out there. It's a great day to get the washin' dry. Come 'ere and hold these pillowcases for me while I fill them up.'

'Okay, Ma.'

'It's a right load of clothes I have to wash. I wonder would oul' Granny Mariah keep an eye to yiz while I slip up to the wash house?'

Ma had no washing machine in those days; she had to wash everything by hand. The wash house had a dozen or more sinks but you had to bring your own washboard, which was made of wood with a metal-ridged front. It was back-breaking work and wasn't easy for her.

Ma was rammaging on, talking away to me like I was a grown-up. I was standing there listening to all she was saying, shaking my head up and down, not saying a word back to her, while Phil was grinning over at me, knowing he was never made do anything, and all the while all I wanted was to play with him.

'Right, tha's done, Kathleen. Hold this washboard for me while I settle Carmel into the pram.'

One of my aunties helped her carry the pram down the stairs. Phil was a lazy little fucker who was always falling and crying, so she put him sitting on the pram with the washing and off we walked up the Hill to Granny Mariah's, which was just around the corner from us.

As soon as we got there, Ma shouted up the stairs to Gran, 'Mariah, will yeh keep an eye to the kids for me? I'm just goin' up to the wash house in Francis Street.'

'Is tha' you, Lil Doyle?' Mariah looked down at us from the top window. 'Wha' was tha' yeh said?'

Ma mumbled under her breath. 'Deaf oul' fuck.' Then out loud, 'I said, would yeh mind keepin' an eye on the kids for me.'

'I will, but yeh better not be long, Lil, I have to get oul'

Phil's dinner ready and yeh know him – there'll be blue murder if it's not sittin' on the table waitin' for him.'

'I know wha' he's like, Mariah, so I'll be as quick as I can.' As soon as Mariah popped her head back in the window, Ma muttered, 'The oul' shite bag.'

'Come 'ere, Phil, sit with yer sisters. Kathleen, keep an eye to Carmel. If she cries, stick the soother in her mouth and rock the pram. Mariah will make her way down to yiz in a while. I won't be long. And wha'ever yeh do, don't move from the front of the house – de yeh hear me now? Are yiz listenin' to me? Don't move!'

We were playing around the steps, me with my skipping rope and Phil with a few marbles, when this man came along on a pushbike and stopped right beside us. He looked straight over at me and asked, 'De yeh know where the shops are, luv?'

'There's one, mister, right beside yeh.'

'No, I'm not lookin' for a sweet shop; I want one tha' sells hammers and nails.'

'Them ones are over there, around the corner.' I pointed down the road.

'I'm not from around here so I don't really know where yeh mean. Will yeh be a good little girl and show me and I'll give yeh a few sweets all for yerself?'

'Did yeh hear tha', Phil? I can get us a few sweets for nothin'. Will yeh watch Carmel for me while I show him the shop? It won't take long. I'll be back in a few minutes.'

Phil pulled at my dress. 'Kathleen, don't go. Ma will kill yeh. She said we're not to move.'

'Don't be a sissy. I won't tell if you don't.' I was a brazen little bitch and wouldn't take heed of what Phil was saying.

So off I went on the crossbar of this man's bike, not realising the danger that was ahead. As he went cycling down the Hill, we passed by Mrs Maguire, Gran's friend. I could hear her in the distance, calling out, 'Mariah, yer Kathleen's on a fella's bike. He's seems to be headin' for the Forty Steps.'

The Forty Steps was an old ruin that was used when the boats used to dock along the canal for people making their way from Cook Street up to High Street. Later on, through the years, part of it was turned into a small school for the children of the area. There were two rooms – one for the boys and one for the girls.

With the shops being only around the corner, I wasn't too long on his bike. He stopped and lifted me off, putting the bike against the wall at the entrance to the Forty Steps, which is across the road from where I lived.

'Hey, mister, the shops is not here.' I pointed across the road. 'It's over there, around the corner. Now, can I have me sweets?' I stuck my hand out.

'They're in my bag up here, luv. Come on with me and I'll get them for yeh, and if yeh're a good little girl there might be a bar of chocolate as well.'

My eyes lit up when I heard that. Chocolate was something we rarely got and I knew Phil would be chuffed when I got back, so off I went, skipping along, holding his hand – too innocent to know or understand the danger I was in. That was, until I heard Ma's voice calling out to me, over and over.

'Kathleen! Kathleen! Where are yeh? Answer me!'

I felt afraid then; I knew there was something wrong. Ma kept calling me.

'Kathleen! Kathleen!'

I shouted down. 'Ma, Ma, I'm here!' I was getting more frightened by the minute.

By this stage the man was dragging me along the steps, telling me to be quiet as he slapped me in the face. My knees were all torn and scratched. I kept telling him as I cried and sobbed, 'Please, mister, I want to go home now. I don't want any of yer sweets. Please!'

He wouldn't listen.

I was nearly up the top of the steps when Ma and a few of the men off the Hill reached me. The man pushed me to the ground and tried to run, but there was only one way out and that was through Ma and, believe me, there was no way he was getting past her. Nobody asked any questions. They went and kicked the living daylights out of him. He had his hands up to his face and kept shouting as he fell to the ground, 'Stop, stop, I didn't touch her!'

Ma was on top of him, screaming and punching.

'Touch my Kathleen, would yeh? Yeh dirty fuckin' bastard of a man. By the time I'm finished with yeh, yeh won't be using yer balls ever again. I'll kick them so far up into yer stomach tha' yeh'll be pissin' out of yer mouth, yeh pig!' She roared as she put the boot in once more.

I kept trying to tell everyone that he was giving me sweets, not balls, but nobody would listen to me.

The men had to drag Ma off the man. 'Stop, Lil, you've done enough damage. Now take Kathleen and off home with yeh. We'll take care of him.' And that they did.

While Ma made her way over to me, I could see the man move as the men from the Hill carried on finishing what Ma had started, kicking the shit out of him again and again.

I kept saying, 'I'm sorry, Ma, I'm sorry.' She picked me up. I waited to get a dig for not doing what I was told. I thought she was going to bash me also, but no, to my surprise she cried, hugged and kissed me so hard I could feel her tears against my face.

'Kathleen, Kathleen,' she kept saying. 'Thank God yeh're safe. Did he touch yeh? Did he do anythin' to yeh? Tell me, tell me!'

'He slapped me face, Ma, and dragged me along the steps. Look at me knees. They're all cut and bleedin'.'

'Don't worry, I'll look after them as soon as we get home,' she said, hugging and kissing me again and again. It felt good.

We made our way down the steps. The bike was lying on the ground. Ma picked it up. 'He won't be usin' this again in a hurry, the pig! I'll sell this on and make meself a few shillin's.'

23

Ma held on tight to me with one hand as she pushed the bike with the other. As we made our way back up the Hill, Mrs Maguire and a few of the neighbours came running over to us.

'Lil, it was meself tha' told Mariah. I knew tha' fella was up to no good, with him not bein' from around here. Is she all right? Did he harm her?'

'Just a few cuts and scratches when he was pullin' her up the steps.'

'God luv her, the poor little mite.' One of them rubbed the top of my head.

'Thanks to the Holy Mother I got to her on time. God only knows wha' would have happened,' said Ma as she blessed herself, launching into telling them the ins and outs of what had gone on at the top of the steps.

'I hope yeh kicked him good and hard,' all the women chimed in.

'Well, let's just say he'll be findin' it very hard to walk for a good while.'

'Good for you, Lil, and no better woman to do it.'

'I'll be on me way now, and thanks for askin' about me child. Oh, another thing; if anyone asks yeh tha' doesn't live on the Hill, yeh know nothin'. Keep yer mouth zipped.'

'Yeh don't have to worry there, Lil. Mum's the word.'

When we got to the top of the Hill, I could see that Carmel and Phil were crying. Gran was sitting on the steps with them. Ma got into one of her mad rages again and didn't half lash Gran out of it for not looking after us kids.

'Holy Jaysus, Mariah, why didn't yeh try and stop him?'

'I was still upstairs, Lil, how could I?'

'Yeh stupid fuckin' oul' wan! You were supposed to be keeping an eye on the kids for me. I trusted yeh with them. Only I got meself there when I did, God only knows wha' could have happened. Kathleen could have been destroyed for life.'

'Don't talk to me like tha', Lil Doyle! The cheek of yeh. Yeh'll mind yer own kids in future. Anyway, didn't I get a few of the men to help yeh? An' I thank each and every one of them for tha'.'

'But I didn't need anyone to sort tha' bastard out for me, I can well take care of meself and me family, yeh can be sure of tha'. And I won't be askin' yeh for any more help, I can tell yeh tha' for nothin'.'

She bundled Phil into the pram on top of Carmel, took me by the hand and we made our way back down the Hill. When we were walking away, I looked back. I could see Gran was real upset, but Ma didn't care. That day she had herself so worked up and she soon let Da know that too when he came home from work.

Well, you'd want to have seen the shock on Da's face when Ma told him the goings-on of the day. He picked me up and put me sitting on his lap and held on to me so tight as he listened to the story unfold. I didn't realise the seriousness of all this. I was just enjoying all the attention I was getting for a change.

'We'll have to go to the police, Lil, and let them know wha' happened.'

'There will be no police brought into this, Phil. Tha' bastard got wha' was due to him today and won't be botherin' any little children for a long time, and I mean a long time! So we'll leave it at tha'. Right Phil? And say no more.'

Da knew not to argue with Ma. Once she had her mind made up about something, there would be no going back.

'Anyway, Phil, I have something else on me mind I want to talk to yeh about. I have been thinkin' about this for a while. Me mind's made up now after wha' happened to Kathleen today. We're movin'. I'm puttin' in to the Corporation for a house. The kids are not safe around the Hill any more. I'll put our name down first thing in the mornin', then I'll go on over to see me father. He might be able to put in a good word for us, with him workin' there. Maybe he'll get our name moved up the list. Tha' way we might not be waitin' too long for a house.'

* * *

Ma stuck to her guns as always and had her name on the list the following day, with Granda doing his bit on the side.

Things were never the same for us or Ma after that day. She wouldn't let us out of her sight. Before that, we used to play around the Hill with all our cousins, getting up to all sorts, having the best of fun ever, but that all stopped after that day.

I didn't understand what all the fuss was over. I was just happy that Ma kicked the shit of that man and not me. From that day on, I always listened to what she had to say.

4

Da Sacked

Da had a very good job, working in a factory that made chocolate, among other things. He was so religious and honest that he wouldn't take a sweet for love nor money. We were often watering from the mouth for the want of a bit of chocolate. I heard Ma say so many times, 'Go on, Phil, get us a few bits of the broken chocolate; sure nobody will miss a few squares.' His answer was always 'No!'

But, after the shock of me going off with the stranger on his bike for a few sweets, he was so afraid that Phil or I would do the same thing again. So what did he only go and do? He took a few bars of chocolate. He got himself caught and they gave him the sack. It nearly killed him, everybody knowing that he was after robbing from the factory, him always helping the priest and all.

Da was out of work for months, so Ma got herself a job patching the old potato sacks from the Daisy Market. Herself and her friend Maisie would sit at home for hours sewing by hand, while they tore the back off everyone on and off the Hill, drinking tea and smoking their few Woodbines.

I loved my Da being at home with us. He was so good, always helping Ma with cleaning and tidying around. He

27

would be up from early looking after us kids, keeping us busy and out of harm's way. While Ma and Maisie would be working away on the sacks, Da would tell us the best stories ever.

The one we all loved the best was 'The Jelly Mountain'. He told us that story over and over and over again. Da would sit there with Carmel on his lap while Phil and I would sit on the bed.

'I have a new story to tell yiz today, and if yeh're good and do wha' yeh're told, I might even bring yeh to the Jelly Mountain. I was there many times when I was a little boy – the nicest place you ever saw in the whole world. Very deep in the forest it is, where only good children can go.'

That's when Phil and I started jumping up and down, one shouting over the other, 'I want to go, take me, Da! I'll be good, I'll be good!'

'Right, then. It's settled. Yiz can come with me the next time I'm goin'. But in the meantime, I'll tell yiz all about it. Be quiet now and listen. The first thing yeh see as soon as yeh get there is this big red jelly mountain, wobbling all over the place. Now, yeh have to make yer way up to the top first. An' when yeh're doin' tha', yeh can eat as much jelly as yeh like. And that's only the start. Now, when yeh're ready to slide down, guess where yeh splash and land.'

'Tell us, Da, tell us!' we kept shouting.

'Only into a pool of custard. And when yeh're finished there, isn't there only a river of chocolate across from the mountain, and yeh can swim away there to yer heart's content, drinkin' as much chocolate as yeh can for as long as yeh want.'

We would sit there with our mouths wide open, wishing we were in Jellyland.

'Now, after tha' yeh head over to the lemonade waterfall. Yeh have to make sure and drink plenty of it while yeh're washin' all the chocolate off yerself, before yeh go over to Lollypop Land where all the trees have every kind of sweets tha' yeh ever wanted growin' out of them. Oh, I nearly forgot. It never rains there; the sun shines there all day long. So yeh will be able to play in the golden cornfields until we're ready to come home. Now, who's goin' to be good?'

We would jump up, screaming, '*We are, Da, we are!*'

* * *

Ma didn't seem to mind Da being around in the beginning but, after a while, you could see that it was starting to get on her nerves.

She was in a right mood one day and didn't half let rip at Da.

'Phil Doyle!' she roared at him. When Ma said the second name, I knew: *here we go, trouble again*. I would take my brother Phil and sister Carmel and sit out on the landing, and then all hell would break loose. 'Phil Doyle, yeh can't keep hiding yerself up here in the room. Fuck everybody out there, who cares what they think.'

'I do, Lil, I care. How can I hold me head up knowin' everybody knows I did a bit of robbin'.'

'Ah, for Jaysus' sake, Phil, will yeh give it over. A few bars of chocolate, tha's all it was. Now yeh'd better get up off yer arse and get yerself a job. The blood's drippin' from the tops of me fingers from sewing these bloody sacks. And on top of all tha' I'm fallin' behind with me bills.'

Da just kept reading his paper, not taking any heed of what Ma was saying.

'Phil, I'm talkin' to yeh. Are yeh listenin'? Jaysus, Maisie, I think he's goin' deaf, or is he ignorin' me?'

'Phil ignore yeh? Are yeh mad, Lil? Not at all, look at him, he's away with the fairies, Lil. In another world, so he is.'

'Well, I won't be long bringin' him back into the real world.' She shouted at the top of her voice, 'Phil Doyle! Did yeh hear wha' I said?'

'Right, right, Lil. I heard yeh the first time. There's no need to be shoutin'. And de yeh have to talk to me like tha' in front of Maisie?'

'Then why didn't yeh *fuckin'* answer me if yeh heard me, lettin' me go on and on?' roared Ma.

'Don't mind me, Phil,' said Maisie. 'This is nothin' to wha' goes on between me and Jojo Murphy. Yeh're only in the ha'penny place here.'

Da would never curse or take the Lord's name in vain, not like Ma. He just took his cap and coat, passing us on the stairs, giving Ma a staring look for a change.

'I want yiz to keep out of yer mother's way for a little while. Kathleen, will yeh mind yer brother and sister out there on the front steps; get yerselves a bit of fresh air at the one time. I'm off to try to get meself a bit o' work. Anythin' to keep yer mother quiet and off me back. Come on while I carry the pram down the stairs. Hold on to Carmel for me. Are yeh right then, Phil – move yerself. Now promise me, Kathleen, tha' yeh won't move or talk to anybody tha' doesn't live around here. Remember wha' happened to yeh only a while ago.'

'I won't, Da. I'll never do tha' again.'

'Tha's a good girl. I'll be on me way, and if it's not too late when I get back, we'll go up to the park. Yerself and Phil can have a bit of a play around before it gets dark.'

* * *

We were playing around outside when Granny Mariah came over to us.

'Kathleen, where's yer father gone? I saw him headin' up towards Thomas Street.'

'He went out lookin' for a job, Gran.'

'Thanks be to God he's after gettin' himself out and about. I have meself sick worryin' about him. I'm prayin' mornin' noon and night to the good Lord, hopin' he'll help yer father get a bit of work for himself.'

'So is me Ma, Gran.'

'Hmm, is she now, Kathleen?' She rolled her eyes in the air. 'Where is yer mother anyway?'

'Sewin' up in the room with Maisie.'

'Go up and tell her I want her.'

I ran straight up the stairs. 'Ma, me Granny Mariah wants yeh.'

'Wha' does tha' oul fuck want now, Maisie? She has a nerve comin' around here. I haven't seen her in months since the big row I had with her about Kathleen and the kids.'

I shouted down, 'Gran, me Ma said wha' de yeh want?'

'Ask her can yeh go down to the butcher's for a bit of tripe for yer Grandad's tea. Me legs is very bad today, I can't walk very far.'

Ma opened her mouth, but Maisie cut across her. 'Before yeh say any more, Lil, and yeh know I'm not one for interferin', but don't be too hard on Mariah, she's not the worst. Tha's probably just an excuse about her legs . . . for her to come around and talk to yeh. After all, Phil's her only son and yeh know she loves to drop in every chance she gets to see him. Blood is blood, Lil, and yeh know he loves his mother.'

'Ah, I suppose yeh're right, Maisie. If the truth be known, I shouldn't really be askin' her to mind the kids. She is gettin' old and a bit forgetful.'

'Now, I'm only sayin', Lil . . . I hope yeh don't mind.'

'No, no. Yeh're a good friend Maisie. It's not everybody tha' I'd let put me in me place. But I have to agree, yeh're right. Kathleen, I see it's startin' to rain out there. Bring Carmel and Phil back up. The pair of yiz push the pram under the stairs. Yer Da can bring it back up later. Tell yer Gran to come up and have a cup of tea. I'll slip down in a little while to the shop and get the few bits for her.'

When I told Gran what Ma said, I knew she was happy by the smile on her face, which you didn't see very often.

I thought I'd never get to tell Phil that Gran and Ma were friends again.

'Tha's great,' says Phil. 'I missed her comin' around with the little bags of sweets.'

I had to agree, so did I.

* * *

Ma was talking away to Gran and Maisie when Da burst in the door. 'Lil, I've got great news. I got meself a job on the docks. It's just day-by-day work.'

'Oh my God, tha's great, Phil. Now, isn't it better than sittin' around here all day. I'll be able to pay me few bills again.'

You could see Ma was well pleased with the news and Da was even happier when he saw Gran sitting there with Carmel in her arms.

From then on, Da left the house at six o'clock in the morning to make sure he was at the top of the queue, hoping each day to get some work – which he always did. Ma only had to sew the sacks a few days a week, which meant we were able to go down to my Granny Kitty's again, my favourite place to go.

Everything was great for a while until one day Da was carrying a heavy sack of flour off the boat. He slipped and fell in the water, and sure he couldn't swim. Only that one of the fellas jumped in after him, he was a goner. He lost his nerve and no way would he go back to work on the boats again and was out of work once more.

Ma was on his back all the time about getting work, telling him he should have stayed in the job until something else came up.

'Lil, don't yeh care what happens to me? De yeh realise tha' I almost drowned? I was nearly out to Dollymount before they got me out of the water.'

'Go 'way, yeh shaggin' eejit, Phil. Yeh would have been dead ten times over with you not bein' able to swim.'

'Did yeh hear tha', Kathleen? Would I lie before the holy mother of God's statue standing there in the corner?'

'No, Da, yeh wouldn't.'

Ma just looked over at us and shook her head.

'Sure, when I was goin' up and down in the water I thought I saw Moby Dick swimming away from me with the big harpoon stuck in his back.'

'Ah, for fuck's sake, Phil, will yeh stop. Kathleen, don't be mindin' yer Da. Some of the water must have got into his brains. Moby Dick, me arse!'

'Da, who's Moby Dick?' says my brother Phil.

'Did I never tell yeh tha' story? Come over here, the pair of yiz, and sit down beside me. Well, wasn't he only the biggest fish tha' yeh ever saw in yer whole life, the length and width of the hill out there, so it was. Isn't tha' right, Lil?'

Ma just looked over and shook her head, once more not saying a word.

'Righ' then, gettin' back to me story. There was this man called Captain Ahab, who owned his own ship called *The Pequod*. He spent most of his life out on the open sea; a whale-catcher he was. He kept hearin' about this big white whale from all the other fishermen and about how nobody could ever catch him. Well, didn't he go an' get it into his head tha' he was goin' to be the one to capture Moby Dick. Which he did. Himself and the whale got into a fierce fight one day, with the whale bitin' one of the captain's legs off.'

'Wha' happened, Da? Did he die, did he die?' I asked.

'De yeh know wha' kept him alive, Kathleen? Hate and revenge. He became obsessed with Moby Dick and spent years roamin' the sea lookin' for him until one day he finally caught him with one of his big harpoons. He lodged it deep into the whale's flesh. He struggled and struggled for God only knows how long. Wha' de yeh think happened then?'

At this stage, Phil was jumping up and down on the bed with excitement. 'Quick, Da, tell us, tell us!'

Even Ma stopped sewing, waiting to see what was going to be said next.

'Ahab, the bloody eejit, went and got the good leg caught in his own harpoon's rope and, unable to free himself, was dragged out to the cold sea by the whale and was lost forever.'

Da told the story of his own encounter with 'Moby Dick' many times over the years, with the waves getting higher and the fish getting even bigger.

* * *

So Ma was back to sewing the sacks every day. Granny Kitty knew a woman who was selling a little sewing machine cheap. She bought it for Ma, so the blood wouldn't be dripping from her fingers from the big needles. That kept Ma happy and off Da's back.

Da got himself a few hours' work up in the Phoenix Park picking the papers up and emptying the small bins. He didn't get paid very much but what he did get he gave to Ma. He was so good back then, never keeping a penny for himself. Everything was always for Ma and us kids.

'Lil, it's not much, but every little helps. It's the best I can do for now.'

'Tha's grand, Phil. Sure won't it keep our heads above water.'

'Don't be mentioning water to me, for God's sake, Lil! I'll be bringing a panic attack on meself.'

They both laughed as Ma went back to her sewing, while Da took Carmel in his arms and we all went up to the Christ Church park to play.

Da went out every day looking for work. He put his name down everywhere. Then, one day, two letters came. Ma and Da looked at one another. We never got letters, never mind two at the same time.

34

'Jaysus, Phil, wha' could they be for? You open them; yeh know I'm not good at the oul' readin'.'

He sat there for a minute looking at the letters.

'Will yeh open them, for Jaysus' sake, Phil!'

Da sat there reading away to himself, not saying a word to Ma. Then he jumped up off the chair.

'I don't believe it! The Lord answered me prayers, Lil.'

'Will yeh tell me wha' they say? The suspense is killin' me.'

'I'm after gettin' offered two good jobs – one in the Corporation and one in Guinness.'

'Tha's great, Phil. We'll have a steady wage comin' in. Me mind will be at ease at last. I won't have to worry any more.'

'Wha'll I do? I don't know which one to pick. Wha' de yeh think, Lil?'

'I don't know, Phil, I'm not sure. Go over and talk to your Da, see wha' he says.'

Off Da went to Granda Phil and they made their way down to the Irish pub at the bottom of the Hill to make the big decision.

Back then it wasn't very often Da took a drink, but when he did you always knew. You could hear him singing at the top of his voice, from one end of Christ Church to the other. He thought he could sing like an opera singer. He'd make up all of his own words, pretending he knew how to sing in Italian. That night, the whole of Cook Street was awake, including Maisie, who opened her window and roared at the top of her lungs.

'Is tha' you Phil Doyle? Who de yeh think yeh are, Mario Lanza, yeh fuckin' eejit? Wakin' us all up! I won't be able to go back to sleep now, I'll be fallin' out of me standin' tomorrow, yeh bloody gobshite.'

With a struggle Da finally got up the stairs and into the room.

'Jaysus, Phil, yeh have the whole house awake with the roars of yeh.'

'I've made up me mind, Lil. I'm takin' the job in the Corporation.'

My brother Phil and myself were under the covers laughing our heads off at Da swaying from one side of the room to the other. We had never seen him that bad before.

'Lil, I've made up me mind. I'm takin' the job in the Corporation.'

'I heard yeh the first time,' whispered Ma. 'Now, shut the fuck up and get into the bed. The whole Hill will be talkin' about us tomorrow.'

'Let them talk. I'm a happy man tonight.'

And so he was; he never had to go out looking for work again.

* * *

Da was up early the next morning. He was green in the face and as sick as anything.

'I'm dyin', Lil. Me head's burstin'.'

'And so yeh should be, yeh fuckin' eejit. Makin' a show of me!'

'It's not every day a man gets offered two jobs. Yeh should be pleased and proud, not givin' out to me.'

'Ah, I suppose yeh're right, Phil. To hell with everybody! Now drink tha' sup of tea and get yer arse down to the Corporation before they give the job to somebody else.'

He was up and on his way out before Ma could say another word.

Maisie was standing at the door as Da was walking out.

'Tha's a lovely voice yeh have there, Phil. Yeh had the whole house awake last night with the roars of yeh.'

'Sorry about tha', Maisie.' Da gave her a nod of the head, tipped the peak of his cap and kept going.

'Jaysus, Lil, he looks a bit rough around the edges. He must have had a right sup on him last night.'

'He's not used to drinkin', Maisie, I can tell yeh. He's in a right state. Anyway never mind all tha', come in, come in. I've great news. Sit down there and we'll have a cup of tea. Phil's after gettin' offered two jobs – Dublin Corporation and Guinness – but he's takin' the one in the Corporation.'

'Tha's great news, Lil. Is tha' wha' all tha' singin' was about last night? I never knew your Phil could sing. He hasn't got a bad voice there at all.'

'It's only when he takes a few pints, Maisie, which doesn't be very often, I can tell yeh tha' for nothin', thank God. He starts with all tha' opera stuff. I don't have a clue wha' he does be sayin' and neither does he. Anyway, I was thinkin' to meself last night, why don't yeh tell your Jojo there's a job goin' in Guinness?'

'Ah, for fuck sake, Lil. Are yeh serious or wha'? Yeh couldn't give him a job there. Sure, yeh'd find him dead after a week, he'd be after drinkin' tha' much of the stuff. And if tha' didn't happen they'd go bankrupt in no time.'

'I wasn't thinkin' there, Maisie, I forgot about his drink problem.'

'Would yeh mind, Lil, if I told me brother Jimmy about the job?'

'Not at all, Maisie, tell him I think the job in Guinness is only temporary, tha's why Phil went for the Corporation. Sure wouldn't it do him for a while, Maisie and yeh never know, he might get himself a full-time job out of it after a while.'

'Thanks, Lil. Yeh're real good thinkin' of me and all. I'll run down to me Ma's and tell Jimmy to go up straight away. Put the teapot on there, I'll be back in a few minutes with a packet of Woodbines for yeh and a few jam doughnuts to celebrate.'

Da was never out of work from that day on.

5

The Fever

Da was working away in his new job and delighted with life and Ma was as happy as Larry, with not a worry in the world. Until one morning my brother Phil woke up with spots all over him.

'Wha's wrong with yeh, Phil? Yer face is full of freckles.'

His hair was wringing wet and he didn't answer me. I kept nudging him. 'Are yeh after pissin' on yerself, Phil?' I whispered in his ear. 'If yeh did, Ma will kill yeh.'

'Wha's tha' yeh said, Kathleen?' Ma shouted over. 'Did he piss in tha' bed again? Phil, didn't I tell yeh to go in the bucket last night before yeh went asleep? Kathleen, I'm still feedin' Carmel. Will yeh get him up for me and while yeh're at it, strip the sheets off the bed.'

'Okay, Ma.'

I tried to push him out of the bed but he just lay there lifeless, with not a sound coming from him.

'Ma, he won't move for me. Look at him. He's messin'.'

She took one look at Phil and screamed.

'Holy Mother of God! Quick, Kathleen, take Carmel,' she said. She wrapped Phil in a blanket. 'Go down to Maisie. Tell her I think young Phil has the fever. I have to go to the doctor quick. Ask Maisie if she will keep an eye to yiz 'til yer father comes home.'

'Wha's the fever, Ma?'

'For God's sake, Kathleen, just do wha' I tell yeh. This is no time to be askin' me twenty questions. Move now. Go on, go on.'

I ran down the stairs as quick as I could, with Carmel in my arms roaring and shouting as I banged on the door. 'Maisie, Maisie, open up quick!'

'For Jaysus' sake. Wha' the hell is goin' on with yeh, Kathleen, with all yer screamin' and shoutin'?'

'Phil has marks all over him and he's after pissin' on himself. Ma said he has the fever.'

'Holy Mother of God,' she said, blessing herself. 'Come in, come in, Kathleen.'

'Maisie, wha' does the fever mean?'

She kept blessing herself. I was afraid to tell her I was after wetting my knickers with the fright of Ma turning green in the face and running to the doctor's place.

'Here, give me Carmel. Sit down there, Kathleen. Did yeh have anythin' to eat?'

'No, Ma just ran with Phil.'

'I have a drop of porridge over, yiz can have tha'.'

'Wha's wrong with Phil, Maisie?'

'Yer brother is a very sick boy if he has the fever,' she said, as she blessed herself another dozen times. 'All we can do now is pray and hope the Holy Mother herself is listenin' to us.'

* * *

When Da came home from work, Maisie told him about Phil. He too turned green in the face.

'Quick, Maisie. Give me the kids and thanks for lookin' after them. I'll leave them with me mother. I'll have to get over to Lil as quick as I can. She'll be frantic on her own.'

'Da, Da, I want to go with yeh, please, I want to see me brother.'

'Shush, Kathleen,' says Da.

'She's cryin' all day, Phil. Let her go with yeh. I'll come and look after her while yeh're in with Lil.'

Da dropped Carmel off at Granny Mariah's. As soon as she heard the word 'fever', the rosary beads were taken out and she too blessed herself a dozen times. Maisie took me by the hand as Da took us over to the doctor, who told us Ma had gone on to the fever hospital.

There we found Ma sitting outside the door, crying her eyes out.

'Lil, wha' did they say?' asked Da.

'He's bad, Phil, the water's drippin' outta him. His temperature's sky-high. Me child's rantin' and ravin' all over the place.'

'Try and calm down, will yeh, Lil. It might not be tha' bad.'

'Don't tell me to be calm, me child's fightin' for his life in there.'

'Shush, Lil, here's the doctor.'

The doctor looked serious. 'I'm afraid your son has scarlet fever. We have to try and keep his temperature down and hope the fever breaks. I have to be honest with you, your son is a very sick child.'

'Holy Mother of God, Phil. There's children dyin' from tha'.' The tears rolled down her face.

Maisie stepped in straight away, trying to calm down both of them. 'Now, now, Lil, the Holy Mother herself is lookin' down on him. Don't be thinkin' like tha'. Gettin' yerself into a state. We'll drop into the church on the way home and light a few candles,' said Maisie, giving Da the eye to try and get Ma to leave the hospital, which she did, after a lot of persuasion.

'Is Phil okay, Ma?'

'He's real sick, Kathleen. They have to keep him in hospital,' she said, bursting out crying again.

We picked Carmel up from Gran's and headed home. As soon as she got through the door, Ma lit up a Woodbine, her hands shaking. 'I'll have to get a bit of heat into this room. God love yiz, yeh must be freezin'. Phil, get tha' fire goin' as quick as yeh can and I'll make a bite to eat.'

Carmel and I were fed, stripped and in the bed in no time. Carmel was asleep as soon as her head hit the pillow, as usual, with her thumb in her mouth and a finger up her nose. I cried myself to sleep that night because I missed Phil so much. I always slept at one end of the bed while he slept at the other. We were like two peas in a pod. At night, I used to rub my feet on Phil's to heat them up. Now, I was worried that there would be no one to keep him warm that night.

I woke up and could hear Ma crying and talking to Da.

'Lil, yeh'll have to be strong and try to keep yerself together. Yeh have the other two kids to take care of.'

I lay there thinking to myself, *What does Da mean? My Ma's real strong. She can bash anybody.* I was too young to understand the seriousness of Phil's fever.

* * *

Ma and I went to the hospital every day to see Phil, stopping at the church on the way to light a few candles. Then, on the way home, we would light more candles. At the hospital, we weren't allowed into Phil's room, so we had to stand outside the door and look through a small pane of glass. We stood there for such a long time. Every now and then Ma would pick me up in her arms to let me have a look at him. He lay there looking lifeless.

'Kathleen, look at his little face. He's gone so thin, the flesh is walkin' off him.'

One day we went up to Granny Kitty's from the hospital. Ma cried uncontrollably, telling all the family, 'It's touch and go. They'll know tonight if he'll pull through.'

They all started crying and took out the rosary beads and prayer books. They sat there for hours on end, praying, praying and praying again. I looked around at all the grown-ups, not understanding what all this meant. I asked Ma if it meant that if they all touched Phil and then go, that he would get better. I could hear a few of my aunties in the background giggling and praying at the same time. Ma couldn't answer me. She walked away, not saying a word.

We all went to the church that evening. Everybody was putting money in the candle box. I sat there looking at all the money God was making out of my brother being sick. I told him that night that unless he made Phil better, every chance I'd get I'd be robbing all his candles, and he wouldn't be making money any more.

God must have had a good think about what I said that night because Phil pulled through and everything was great again. I didn't tell Ma what I'd said in the church. It was my secret.

After Phil's fever broke, we were allowed to go in to sit with him. Ma hugged him so tight I thought she was never going to let him go. After a while, the doctor came over and was talking away to Ma, so I jumped up onto the bed.

'When are yeh comin' home? I missed yeh. Did yeh miss me, Phil?'

He just smiled, not saying a word.

'I was here every day with Ma. We were standin' over there behind the door. See tha' one with the bit of glass? Well, I was lookin' in at yeh all the time. The nurse kept washin' yeh cause yeh were sweatin' and she even washed yer bum cause I think yeh pissed on yerself again.'

Phil started laughing and showing off his pearly whites. I knew then he was okay and would be coming home to me soon.

* * *

43

He was skin and bone for a long time. Ma treated him like a God from then on. He was her blue-eyed boy and that was that. In her eyes, he could do no wrong – and he didn't half milk it.

'Kathleen, hand yer brother his dinner . . . Help him with his shoes . . . You carry the bags, yeh know Phil's legs are weak, he's not able.'

When she wasn't looking, the little fucker would be getting me back up and giving me the sly grin, but when Ma wasn't around and when I got the chance, I'd give him a good kick up the hole. That would soon knock the grin off his face, but deep down inside me I was so happy he was better.

* * *

Phil was home from hospital a good few weeks now, getting stronger and stronger by the day and starting to look more like his old self again, which made Ma very happy. But he wasn't talking very much.

One morning we were sitting at the table eating our porridge when Ma let out an unmerciful scream.

'Jaysus, Kathleen. Wha's tha' walkin' down Phil's face?'

'Where, Ma?'

'There! For God's sake, Kathleen, look – it's after movin'.'

Of course, Phil jumped up and started crying as usual.

'Christ, come over to me till I check yer head. It's walkin'.'

'Walkin', walkin' where, Ma?'

'Never mind, Kathleen. Run downstairs and ask Maisie for a lend of her fine comb.'

I was down the stairs in seconds, banging the door and shouting. 'Maisie, Maisie, me Ma wants yeh. Phil's head is movin' and walkin' as well. Have yeh got a fine comb?'

'For Jaysus' sake, Kathleen, will yeh keep yer voice down, the whole house can hear yeh.'

Maisie followed me back up to Ma. 'Wha's wrong with yeh, Lil?'

'Would yeh have a look at the state of his head.'

Maisie had a quick look. 'Jaysus, Lil, how did his head get so bad? They're like a herd of buffaloes runnin' around. They're tha' big. How did he catch them?'

'I bet yeh he got them off tha' scaldy-eyed young wan who lives down the bottom of the Hill. Yeh know who I'm talkin' about. I don't think she gets washed from one end of the week to the other. The hum off her would turn yer stomach. Will yeh check Kathleen's hair for me? I'll go crazy mad if her head is the same. Her lovely long black plaits, she'll have to get them cut off.'

'Don't be panickin', Lil. It's only a few fleas. Here, give me a bit of newspaper. Bend yer head over, Kathleen,' she said, and began combing through my hair. I thought my brains were going to come out, she dug the comb in that hard.

'There, yeh see, Lil. There wasn't tha' many. Only a dozen or so. Now have yeh got a bottle of vinegar, Lil?'

'Vinegar? For wha'?'

'Did yeh never hear about tha'? I can't believe nobody ever told yeh. Just in case we miss any fleas, the vinegar will smother any little bastards tha's left.'

'Maisie, I'm ashamed of me life. I'm sewin' them bloody sacks from mornin' 'til night. I didn't think to check their heads.'

'Will yeh go away, Lil. Everybody gets fleas and hoppers.'

'Ma, where do they come from?' asked Phil.

'Yeh get them from somebody tha's not clean, or it could be the dust from the sacks or the turf,' said Ma as she sat there combing Phil's hair back. 'Would yeh have a look at him, Maisie? De yeh know who young Phil always reminds me of, with his hair combed back off his face and all curly at the back?'

'Who's tha', Lil?'

'Ah, yeh know yer man tha' does be in the films. Wha's this his name is? It's on the tip of me tongue. I have it. Errol Flynn, the movie star, tha's who.'

45

'I wouldn't be able for yeh, yeh're a scream, Lil. Movie star, me arse.' She stood back from me. 'There. The plaits are done now. Wha' de yeh think?'

'God, Maisie, I'd be lost without yeh.'

'Don't be gettin' all sloppy on me now. Put the teapot on the fire there and give me a Woodbine.'

'I've none, Maisie. Phil will be in from work soon. We'll get one off him. Kathleen, Carmel's asleep, so take Phil with yeh and sit at the front steps so tha' vinegar can dry well into yer hair. And don't move, de yeh hear me?'

'Right, Ma.'

We made our way down the stairs and were sitting on the front steps when Phil turned to me. 'Yeh know wha', Kathleen, I'm goin' to get me Da to make a sword out of this bit of wood I found under the stairs and if anybody starts pickin' on us again I'll give them a bang on the head and then stick it up their arse.'

'Jaysus, yeh're talkin', Phil! Don't let anyone hear yeh, for fuck's sake, or yeh'll be gettin' yer own arse roasted, especially if Ma hears yeh.'

Scaldy-Eyes and her friends came over to us. They started jeering, calling us 'lousy heads'.

'Yeh have fleas, Kathleen Doyle. I know yeh have. Yiz are rotten. Yeh can smell the stuff in yer hair.'

I jumped up.

'Who de yeh think yeh are, with yer scaldy eyes and yer smelly knickers? Me Ma said tha' yeh could do with a good wash.'

All her friends started laughing at her. She ran off crying, with Phil fucking and blinding as he chased her with his plank of wood.

It was starting to get dark so we made our way back up the stairs. Carmel was at the age where she was starting to talk so I had to keep telling Phil to stop saying 'fuck' in front of her. Or in front of Ma, for that matter.

'If Da hears yeh, he'll be lightin' candles for a month. I'm tellin' yeh, Phil, Ma will ram a bar of soap in yer mouth. Yeh'll be sick as anythin'.'

I think I was better off when he was crying all the time and not talking.

* * *

It was starting to get cold so Da fixed the panes of glass that were broken. Granny Kitty bought herself new curtains so she gave us the old ones. Ma said that they were nearly new.

'Come on, the three of yiz, we'll go up to the Iveagh Market in Francis Street and see if I can get a cheap tablecloth to go with the curtains. When we're there we'll have a root through the second-hand stuff and see if I can get some boots for yiz.'

We used to love going to the market. Ma would be yapping for ages while the three of us would be off dressing up in all sorts of clothes, me with a straw hat and flowery dress, while Phil would have a bowler hat and a coat down to his ankles. Carmel was small and still sucking her thumb, so we would stick a wig on her or any oul' hat to keep her happy. We'd have great fun. They were happy days.

* * *

It wasn't long after Phil's sickness that I heard Ma telling my Aunt Emmie, 'I'm gone again.' By this stage, I had learned what these words meant: another baby on the way. This time it was to be my brother Noel.

6

Noel's Birth

It was Christmas Eve and it was very cold outside. The snow was thick on the ground. Da lit the fire early that morning and kept an eye to Phil and Carmel while myself and Ma went for the last of the Christmas shopping. We met Maisie up Thomas Street. She was carrying a big Christmas tree.

'Howyeh, Lil. Where are yeh off to?'

'Just gettin' the last few bits in, Maisie.'

'I'm half-dead carryin' this tree. Tha' bastard of a husband of mine, Jojo Murphy, is down in the pub, pissed drunk after spendin' all me wages on drink – didn't give me a penny, Lil. He's only a bollocks, I swear he is, a pig if yeh ever met one.'

Jojo was a very big man, well over six foot and built like a lion. Da always said that he had hands like shovels – 'If yeh got a dig off him, sure yeh'd be dead.'

Ma wasn't saying much. Maisie was still going on and on and on . . .

'I had to go down to me Ma and borrow a few bob to get me over the Christmas. Thank God, I had the kids' things in.'

At this stage Ma was bent over, holding herself. She was nearly on her knees.

'Jaysus, Lil, are yeh all right?'

I could see a big gush of water pouring down Ma's legs.

'Me waters are gone, Maisie, I've started.'

'Christ, Lil, here's me givin' out like fuck and you in the height of labour! Let's get yeh back home.'

'Wha's wrong, Ma?' I asked.

'I'm okay, Kathleen; just a few cramps in me stomach. I'll be all right when I lie down.'

Maisie was dragging the Christmas tree with one hand and trying to help Ma with the other. It took us ages to get back home, with Ma stopping every few yards, bending over with the pain.

'Kathleen, run on down the hill and tell yer Da I'm on me way with yer mother. Tell him she's started.'

I was gasping for breath as I got to the end of the stairs, screaming my lungs out.

'Da, quick, Da, come down! Ma is all bent up and she's after pissin' on herself and Maisie said she's after startin' somethin'.'

Da came running down the stairs. 'Jaysus Christ, Kathleen, will yeh watch yer tongue. If anybody hears yeh. Yeh're startin' to sound more like yer mother every day.'

'I think Ma is sick. Sorry, Da.'

Da only had the words out of his mouth when we heard this unmerciful roar from Maisie: 'Phil Doyle, come down here quick! Lil's started.'

Da went running ahead of me. 'Wha' are yeh sayin' Maisie? Started wha'?'

'For fuck's sake, Phil, yeh know wha' I mean. Do I have to spell it out for yeh? Sure she didn't even get to the top of Thomas Street. Will yeh look at her, the child is on its way.'

'Christ, Lil, I thought yeh said tha' it wouldn't be happenin' 'til after Christmas?'

'Will yeh shut the fuck up, Phil, and just get me up the stairs. I must have got me dates mixed up.'

With Maisie in the front and Da at the back, after a

struggle, they finally got Ma up the stairs and into the bed.

'Phil, yeh better get the doctor here quick,' said Maisie. 'I'll stay and look after Lil and the kids until yeh get back.'

My brother Phil and myself just stood there, while Carmel slept in the pram. Ma was twisting and turning, screaming and shouting, as Maisie wiped her face with a towel.

'Lil, try and keep yerself calm. Phil is on his way with the doctor.'

In the middle of all this mayhem, I could hear Ma tell Maisie, 'Their few bits is under the bed, wrapped in one of the oul' sacks.' Ma was in the height of labour and she was still worrying about us and Santy.

It wasn't too long before Da walked in with the doctor and nurse.

Maisie told Da to take us downstairs to her place.

'I'll be down in a couple of minutes meself, Phil.'

'Wha' about Santy?' he whispered in Maisie's ear.

'It's okay, Phil, Lil told me where everythin' is. I'll take care of all tha', you've more to be worryin' about tonight. Go on over to yer Ma's. It'll be well into the morning before the child's born.'

Da told us the fire had to stay lit because Ma was sick. 'And we have to stay with Maisie for the night as Santy won't be able to come down our chimney.' The look on our faces told Da what we were thinking. 'Don't be worryin', the pair of yiz, I'll let Santy know where yeh are.'

* * *

The three of us slept in Maisie's bed that Christmas Eve. I was awake first. Santy left me a lovely doll, Phil a truck and Carmel a teddy bear.

Maisie had four kids herself. We were all running around like lunatics while she made us something to eat. Jojo was lying across the kitchen table, still drunk from the night before.

Maisie burst open the door and let out her usual scream, 'For fuck's sake, will yiz be quiet! Everybody on the Hill will think I'm murderin' yiz. Kathleen, when yeh're finished tha' bit of bread get the other two and go up to yer Ma. She has somethin' to tell yiz.'

'Is me Ma better, Maisie?'

'There's not a bother on her, Kathleen. Now, run along; she has a nice little surprise for yiz.'

We got our toys and went up to Ma, who was sitting up in the bed, with Da standing beside her. She had this little bundle in her arms, which I thought was a doll, until it started to cry.

I got such a fright, I jumped. 'Ma, is it real?'

'Of course, Kathleen. Isn't he lovely?'

'Where did it come from?' Phil asked.

'Santy left him.'

'I thought he couldn't get down the chimney with the fire, Ma.'

'Tha's right, Kathleen, but wasn't the door half-open? Santy popped his head in to see who was here and, this bein' his last stop, he said tha' he had one more parcel left. Would I like it? Sure, I couldn't say no to Santy, could I?' She pulled the blanket back to show us. 'This is yer new brother. I'm goin' to call him Noel. The three of yiz come over and sit up here beside me.'

Da lifted Carmel up and put her under the blankets with Ma.

Phil was jumping up and down on the bed – 'A brother for me to play with!' He was well pleased with himself.

I just smiled as I looked down at Noel. 'He's nice, Ma.' But, as young as I was, what was really going through my head was, 'Here's another little fucker for me to mind.' I rolled my eyes up to the ceiling.

'Right then, Lil, we better start gettin' the Christmas dinner ready,' said Da. 'Kathleen, get the spuds out of the bag. Phil, bring tha' head of cabbage over here. Where's the chicken, Lil?'

'I think Maisie left the bag out on the landin'.'

'Are yeh sure tha' it'll be all right now? Yeh should have brought it in – yeh wouldn't know wha' would be crawlin' around out there in the depths of the night.'

'Well now, Phil Doyle, I wasn't thinking of chickens last night, was I, with me waters broke, and the child halfway into the world? Yeh fuckin' eejit, yeh're gettin' me all worked up now and me tryin' to get me milk goin' to feed the baby.'

'Holy Mother of God, Lil, could you please, on Christmas Day, of all days, not curse.'

Ma was mumbling to herself and we all knew when she started fucking and blinding, you'd best be quiet.

'Kathleen, get Phil and Carmel, put their coats on and I'll bring yiz to Mass first. We'll let yer mother get a bit of peace and quiet, and maybe then she might calm herself down by the time we get back.'

We dropped in to see Granny Mariah to tell her about the new baby and to wish her a Happy Christmas. While we were there, Da asked if she had a spare bar of soap.

'Wha's tha' for, Da?' I asked.

'To wash yer mother's mouth out – a terrible woman she is, Kathleen, with that tongue of hers.' He gave me a little smile, so I'd know full well that he was making up a yarn.

Little did he know that it should be two bars of soap he should be getting.

One for Ma and one for me.

7

The Move

Ma roared down from the top of the landing.

'Maisie, will yeh come up to me for a minute? I've somethin' to tell yeh.'

'Okay, Lil. I'm after makin' a lovely pot of stew – will I bring yeh up a bowl?'

'Tha's great, Maisie. Are yeh sure yeh don't need it for yerself?'

'No, my lot's fed. Anyway, wouldn't you give me some if yeh had it over?'

'When have I ever got anythin' over?'

Ma was a bit quiet and not her usual self that day.

'Wha's wrong with yeh, Lil? I never saw yeh down in the dumps as bad as this before. Have yeh got tha' thing where all yer bits inside go a bit mad after a baby and have yeh cryin' and all? Jaysus, wha' the fuck is it called?'

'Maisie, wha' are yeh talkin' about?'

'I have it Lil – hormones. Tha's it, hormones. I hear they can make yeh go crazy mad.' She was trying to put a smile back on Ma's face.

'Go away, yeh mad thing. It's nothin' to do with me hormones. I was dreadin' havin' to tell yeh this, bu' . . . I'm goin' to be leavin' the city. I've put in for a house.'

Maisie kept talking, not taking any heed of what Ma had just said. She didn't want to know.

'I'm just windin' yeh up, Lil. I'll heat this bowl of stew; yeh need all yer strength after bringin' tha' Noel fella into the world. He must have been at least twelve pounds the night he was born; sure look at the size of him now for three weeks old! Yeh could nearly put a bag on his back and send him to school, he's tha' big.'

'Maisie, will yeh shut the fuck up and listen to me? Please! Me Da knows someone in Dublin Corporation; he's goin' to see if he can pull a few strings and get me name moved up on the list. Tha' way we won't have to wait years for a house.'

Maisie just sat there with the tears falling down her face; she couldn't stop crying.

'Lil, yeh don't have to move. One of the houses up the Hill has a few rooms goin' cheap. I'll see if I can get them for yeh.'

'No, Maisie, I'm sick to death goin' down to tha' bloody yard, cleanin' tha' filthy toilet. Anyway, me mind's made up after wha' happened to Kathleen. All I want is a house with me own toilet and garden for the kids. At least I know they will be safe. The traffic around here is gettin' worse. Only yesterday mornin' I couldn't keep count of the cars goin' up and down Christ Church Hill; me nerves were gone watchin' and worryin' about them. There's a place called Crumlin . . .'

'Ah, for fuck's sake, Lil! Tha's out in the wilderness. Yeh know tha' young wan, "Scaldy-Eyes", who lives down the Hill? Well, they're after gettin' a house out there. I met her Ma and she was tellin' me they haven't even got proper shops, only a little bit of a one, and they're robbers with their prices. And tha's not all; there's cows lookin' in yer back garden at yeh. Jaysus, Lil, it's in the arsehole of the country. Yeh'll go mad out there on yer own.'

'Maisie, don't be gettin' yerself all upset; yeh'll bring on an asthma attack. I'll make yeh a cup of tea and we'll have a smoke. Come on now, stop cryin'.'

'I can't help it, Lil, yeh're me only friend. Tha' Jojo Murphy doesn't give two fucks about me. Have yeh seen him lately? He's pissed drunk every night, the pig.'

'Sure haven't yeh got yer Ma, Maisie?'

'I know I have me Ma, and she's real good and all, but it won't be the same. If I slip up and say "fuck" or "piss" in front of her, she starts chasin' me with the holy water. And who's goin' to lend me a cup of sugar or a Woodbine when I've none? There's only yerself, Lil. I've nobody else.'

'Why don't yeh come down to me Da's with me and see wha' he says? Maybe he could put yer name down on the list with mine; we might even get a house beside one another. Jaysus, Maisie, I'd love nothin' better than to have yeh with me. Tha' would be all me dreams come together.'

'No fuckin' way, Lil. Yeh wouldn't get me out there for love nor money, not even for yerself.'

'Wha' are yeh goin' to do when they start pullin' down all the tenement houses? It's goin' to happen, Maisie – mark my words, it's on the cards.'

'I don't care, Lil, I'll get meself somethin' – one or two rooms over a shop. I'll never leave. I love the city too much.'

'Come on, Maisie, walk down to me Da's. We'll have a yap on the way. We'll worry about it when the time comes.'

* * *

Noel was nine months old when the letter finally came about the house.

'Phil, you open it. I can't look; if they turn us down I'll go mad. Hurry up and tell me wha' it says.'

'Lil, will yeh stay quiet and let me read it first.'

Da stood up and blessed himself as he read down the page.

'Will yeh tell me wha' it says, Phil!'

The suspense was killing Ma; it seemed to take ages for Da to read the letter and then there was a scream out of him.

'Yes, yes! We got the house in Crumlin!'

'Jaysus! Oh my God, I can't believe it.'

We kids were jumping and screaming. We knew something good was happening. Da picked up myself and Carmel and swung us around. Ma was jumping and dancing with Phil. Everyone was happy that day.

'Lil, yeh'll have to go over to yer Da and thank him for puttin' a word in for us. Tell him I'll buy him a pint when I get paid.'

'Yeh're right, Phil, I will. Kathleen, get the pram ready.'

The pram was more like a small bus. It was huge and the wheels were so big you could put them on one of the horses up the lane and use it as a cart. Carmel was put up the top of the pram, Noel down the other end and Phil, with his weak legs, was put in the middle. As usual, I was left running after Ma.

When we got down to Granny Kitty's, Granda John was there.

'Ah, Lil, come in and sit down. Have yeh heard any word about the house, luv?'

Ma threw her arms around him. 'Here's the letter, Da – it came this mornin'. I can't believe it, a house of me own. How will I ever thank yeh?'

'Shush . . . Now, Lil, don't be lettin' anyone know I put a word in for yeh. There's people years on the housin' list. Yeh'd be gettin' me into trouble, so say no more about it.' He went back to reading his paper.

'Lil, let me know when yeh get yer key and wha' day yeh're movin' and I'll come over with Fanny and the cart to give yeh a hand,' said Granny Kitty. Fanny was her donkey.

'Tha'll be great, Ma. Now, I'll just have a quick cup of tea with yeh and then I'd better be on me way home. It's gettin' late.'

Over the next week there was great excitement around the area. A good few people had got letters saying they'd got houses too. Ma was happy about that.

'At least we'll know a few families from town, Phil. It won't feel so lonely.'

* * *

The day finally came to move. My uncle Billy, who was married to Da's sister Emmie, said he could get a loan of a small wagon for ten shillings. Da gave him the money and they shook hands on it.

'Tha's grand, Billy, we'll be able to do the trip in one go, 'cause we've Kitty's cart as well.'

While all the running up and down the stairs was going on, Maisie made over to Ma.

'So, yeh're really goin', Lil. I still can't believe it.'

'Yeah, I am, Maisie. I'm goin' to miss yeh.'

Maisie was sobbing like I never saw before. Ma put her arms around her.

'Please don't cry, Maisie, you'll start me off. Sure I'll be back in to see me Ma and Da every week and I'll come over to see yeh. I promise. And yeh can even come out for a day with the kids and we can catch up on all the gossip. Won't it be like an outin' for yeh, comin' out to the country. Wha' de yeh say?'

'We'll see, Lil. I'm goin' down to me Ma now; I can't stand here and watch yeh go. It's too hard. Me heart is broke.'

They cried, hugged and kissed one another and said their goodbyes.

Da turned to Ma. 'Lil, there's no room for the pram. It's too big.'

'Okay, Phil, you go ahead with the wagon. Put the oul' chest on the cart with Kathleen and young Phil and I'll walk with the pram and the two younger kids.'

Sitting on top of the cart, Phil and I waved goodbye to all the neighbours as Ma started the long walk to Crumlin.

* * *

I thought we were never going to get to the house. It seemed to be taking forever, between Granny stopping and talking to half of Dublin on the way, Fanny having a shit every few minutes, and Phil crying in my face that he was going to piss on himself.

'Here yiz are now,' said Granny. 'There's yer new house; I can see yer father and Billy. Hold on to young Phil and don't let him move, Kathleen, while I settle Fanny down.' She pulled the reins in. 'Slow down girl, slow, slow.'

We were here at last. Myself and Phil stood there beside Granny, looking at our new house. We couldn't believe our eyes. It was huge; we had our own front gate with a long garden and a path in the centre leading to a red hall door, with '51' in brass number plates and a brass letterbox. It looked ever so posh, just like my Granny Kitty's house.

Phil tipped me. 'Kathleen, look at tha' gate over there at the side of the house. Let's see wha's behind it.'

It was the back garden, which was three times bigger than the front garden.

'Ma will be over the moon when she sees this, Phil. Tha's all she talks about – the garden and the toilet. Come on, let's go and check out the rest.'

When we went inside, we looked at one another in amazement. There were rooms everywhere. Downstairs we had a kitchen and a parlour. After living in one room, this looked like a mansion to us. We ran upstairs, each trying to get in front of the other. To our surprise, there were two bedrooms with small fireplaces and a bathroom off the landing.

'Da, did yeh see this?' I roared. 'We have a bath and it's in the same room as the toilet!'

'Tha's right, Kathleen; yer Mother will be well pleased when she sees tha', like I am with the garden. Wait and see, I'll soon have vegetables growin' the length and breadth of it. Enough of all tha' now; come and help me get these few bits in before yer mother arrives.'

Da was struggling in with the beds, giving us the small stuff, when a man came over to him.

'Can I give yeh a lift with tha'?' He put his hand out. 'I'm Mr O'Brien from next door.'

Phil and myself looked at each other. 'There's goin' to be a fight, Kathleen. I'm off.'

'Where are yeh runnin' to, Phil? Come back here, yeh eejit; just wait and see wha' happens. I keep tellin' yeh, always listen first.'

'Yeh told me to run for cover when yeh hear the second name being mentioned.'

'Tha's only when it's between Ma and Da. Now shut the fuck up and listen.'

Da put his hand out.

'I'm Phil, pleased to meet yeh. We're movin' from town. Lil the wife is on her way with the rest of the family.'

Da was shaking his hand so hard I thought it was going to fall off. He was delighted with himself to meet a friendly face. It looked like a good start.

'I'd better get the furniture in quick. It looks like there's rain on the way.'

Da and Mr O'Brien were talking away as they carried everything in. He told Da they were living there a few years and that it was a grand new house we got.

Phil kept tipping me. 'There's no fight, Kathleen. It must be different out in the country.'

'You're right there, Phil, it must be.'

We ran around pressing all the switches on and off, even though there were no bulbs yet. Granny Kitty let out such a scream that Mr O'Brien nearly dropped the one and only wardrobe we had.

'Stop tha' now, the pair of yiz! You'll break them,' she roared.

'Is it true, Gran?' I asked. 'Da says the lights are magic and there'll be no more candles ever again.'

'Tha's right, Kathleen. Now, come 'ere, young Phil. Help me get the fire goin'. We'll have to get a bit of heat into this house. Yer Mother will be cold and tired by the time she gets here. And when yeh're finished tha', there's a box of food on the back of me cart. Go out and get it while I talk to yer father.'

Gran wasn't long sorting out the food into the kitchen press and getting a fire going. 'Phil, the gas is turned on. I checked it meself. Will yeh make a bit of dinner for Lil and the kids? There's a grand blazin' fire on in there. I can't wait any longer. I'll have to be on me way before it gets dark. I've to get Fanny back to the yard; she has to be fed and bedded down for the night.'

'I'll take it from here, Kitty; and thanks again. I'd have been lost without yeh.'

'Isn't tha' wha' families are for? To be there when it's needed.'

'Yeh never said a truer word, Kitty.'

* * *

We were standing at the front door waving Granny off when I saw Ma coming up the road. 'Ma, Ma! Up here, we're up here, Ma!'

Myself and Phil were jumping up and down, screaming our heads off.

'Ma, Ma, wait 'til yeh see the house! It's huge!'

'Phil, Kathleen, for God's sake will yiz be quiet!' roared Da. 'Wha' will the neighbours think?'

'Sorry, I was afraid Ma couldn't see us.'

'Well, she certainly heard yiz, tha's for sure.'

Ma stood at the front gate, worn out from the long walk to Crumlin. Well, you'd want to have seen the look on her face – it was priceless. Suddenly, she started to cry.

'I can't believe it, Phil; me own house at last.'

She pushed the pram through the side gate and into the kitchen.

The first thing she did was to go straight upstairs and look for the toilet, with myself and Phil running behind her.

'Wha' did I tell yiz? Didn't I say we'd have our own toilet one day?' Ma smiled at us through the tears running down her face.

'Ma, why are yeh cryin'?'

'Because I'm happy, Kathleen. Now, come on, help me make the beds and sort some of the stuff out while yer Da makes a bit of dinner. Young Phil, will yeh go down and keep an eye to Carmel and Noel.'

Ma went on talking about all the things she was going to do with the house as soon as she got a few shillings behind her.

'Ma, we've been up here ages. I'm starvin'; can we go downstairs now?'

'Okay, Kathleen, we'll finish this tomorrow. Anyway, me diddies are full to the top. I'll have to go down and feed Noel before he starts screamin' the house down. I swear, Kathleen, I never saw a baby drink so much on top of his dinner; he'll have me two diddies worn out in no time.'

When we came down, Da had a blanket spread out on the floor in front of the fire.

'Now, sit down there, the three of yiz, and eat yer dinner. I'll ask around tomorrow and see if I can pick up a few chairs, now tha' we have somewhere to put them. Lil, are yeh ready for yer dinner?'

'No, not yet, I have to feed Noel.'

'Okay, I want to talk to yeh anyway.'

'Yeh do? About wha', Phil?'

'Hold on a minute, Lil – Phil, Kathleen, Carmel, come over here and listen to wha' I have to say as soon as yeh're finished.'

Da started telling Ma all about Mr O'Brien helping him and how nice he was.

'Wasn't he very good to do tha', Phil, and him not even knowin' us. I'll go in tomorrow and thank himself.'

'Tha's grand, Lil. Now, when yeh go into him, I'd like yeh

63

to say tha' you're Mrs Doyle – will yeh do tha' for me?'

'Wha' the hell are yeh goin' on about, Phil? I'll say tha' me name is Lil; everybody calls me Lil.'

'I know, I know, but it seems to be different out here. When I was goin' in and out with the furniture, a few people was goin' by and they were all callin' one another Mr and Mrs. They don't seem to call yeh by yer first name. We don't want to be lettin' ourselves down, do we?'

Everything went real quiet. Ma just sat there with her diddy stuck in Noel's mouth, thinking for a minute and giving the look at the same time.

'Right then, if yeh say it's the proper thing to do. Yeh heard yer Da – from now on, all grown-ups outside the family will be called by Mr or Mrs and I'll do the same – BUT! . . .' Ma looked across at Da. '. . . I'll be gettin' called Lil and tha's the end of tha' and there'll be no more talkin' on the matter.'

'Okay then, Lil. But there's just one more thing – will yeh try and keep yer voice down and stop the cursin'? We don't want people thinkin' we're a shower of bowsies.'

Well, when I heard that, I nearly choked on the bit of sausage that was still in my mouth. I gave Phil and Carmel the eye and we ran out and sat on the stairs. All hell broke loose. Ma was screaming at the top of her voice.

'Would yeh ever go and fuck off! Don't start goin' all high and mighty with me, Mr Phil Doyle. If I want to say "fuck" I'll say "fuck" and I'll raise me voice as high as I want when it suits me. I'll not put any airs or graces on for nobody. Yeh take me as I am, and you should know tha' more than anybody.'

'See wha' I mean, Kathleen, Phil? Are yiz listenin' to yer mother? I'm just tryin' to get yeh to be a bit quieter, Lil, and not be losin' yer temper so quick and easy. Will yeh even try and cut the bad language out? I don't think tha's too much to ask.'

Da was running around the house at the same time, closing

all the windows and doors, while Ma was still shouting at him, making sure she got her point across.

That was our first night in Crumlin.

* * *

The next morning there was a hard banging on the hall door.

'I'll get it, Ma,' I roared with excitement. We had never had our own front door before.

'No,' said Phil, 'I'm doin' it.' He tried to push me out of the way.

'Yeh little bastard.' We nearly killed each other trying to get to the door first, but I won.

'Hello, mister, wha's yer name?'

'I'm Paddy and I'm here to switch the lights on.'

'Who's tha', Kathleen?' Ma roared out to me.

'Ma, it's Mr Paddy. He's goin' to switch the lights on.'

Da came running out of the kitchen, 'Come in, come in! Will you two move out of the man's way. Kathleen, take Carmel and go out and play in the garden.'

You could see that Da felt great saying that. We had a garden at last.

'Sorry about tha'. They're just excited about the new house. Yeh know yerself; kids, they're always under yer feet.'

'I've got a few meself; they drive yeh round the bend half the time.'

Da stood there talking away to Mr Paddy while he got on with the job. He had the work done in no time. Ma made him a cup of tea and chatted with him about what it was like living in the country.

As soon as Mr Paddy left, Da called us in from the garden.

'Okay, in with the three of yiz. I have a surprise for yeh. Now, just stand there and watch.'

We waited with excitement while Da ran around the house, putting bulbs in every room, pressing on all the switches as he went along.

65

'Now, wha' did I tell yeh – didn't I say the lights were magic?'

We never saw the likes of it before, the whole house lit up like a Christmas tree.

It really was magic.

8

On the Mitch

I didn't start school until I was six years old and I hated the place from the first day I walked into it. As I stood there with Ma waiting in the long cold corridor, all I could see were these huge big statues with vases of flowers at their feet.

Two nuns were walking towards us. It was my first time ever to see a nun, and from day one they frightened the shit out of me. I hid behind Ma's back, peeping out all the while. Their long black habits flowed down to their ankles, the black and white veils clinging tight on their heads. All I could see were these faces glaring at me, with not a smile. They wore giant rosary beats, tied around their waists like belts, with big crucifixes on the end. I could hear the beads swishing from side to side as they made their entrance, letting me know with the full tone and force of their voices who was boss.

Then one of them stepped out in front of the other. 'My name is Sister Joseph.' She went on talking away to Ma, setting down all the rules I was to obey, which I very seldom ever did. I was so afraid that the first day; when the nun tried to pull me from behind Ma's back, I held on so tight to her dress, hoping she wouldn't let the nun take me away.

'I don't want to go, Ma,' I cried. 'Please don't make me stay.'

'Come on now, Kathleen, yeh're not to carry on. Yeh're a big girl now,' said Ma. 'Yeh have to go with the Sister.'

The Sister was starting to look very annoyed at this stage. She gave my hand a nice little squeeze, pulled me away from Ma and walked me firmly down the corridor, putting me into line with all the other kids. They were all standing there with one finger pressed against their lips, not a whisper or a sound coming from any of them. As time went on I would soon learn what that was all about. If any of the nuns caught you speaking to one another, you would get lashed across the legs with the cane that was strapped beside their beads, or a box in the head that would nearly knock you to the floor. I was an awful chatterbox and got the cane more times than not.

I always seemed to be one of the kids picked out of the line and put cleaning the toilets or scrubbing the marble corridors. They would pick two of us out at a time, hand us our scrubbing brushes and tell us they would be back to inspect our work later. We would be down on our knees, scrubbing and cleaning away, along the edges and in and out of all the corners, making sure not a scrap of dirt was left. If there was, you'd know what to expect – another lash of the cane. One or two of the bigger girls would follow us with a bucket and mop.

This was always done during school hours, when you were supposed to be learning. When you would eventually get to your class, you were expected to be able to catch up and know what the teacher had been talking about while you weren't there, and if you didn't know that, you were in trouble again. You couldn't win; their rules were impossible at times, for me anyway.

* * *

I haven't got many good memories of school. But one day in particular sticks out in my mind.

Sister Carmel – that was her name. She was very kind and

so different from the rest of the nuns. One morning, she came over, took me out of the line and told me to stand to one side. I was shitting myself, not knowing what to expect. While she walked me down to her office, to my surprise, she started asking me about Ma and Da and how many brothers and sisters I had.

'Right, Kathleen,' she said as soon as we got to the office. 'Sit down.'

I was starting to panic at this stage.

'Am I in trouble, Sister? Wha'ever it is, I didn't do it. I swear it wasn't me.'

'It's all right, Kathleen, there's nothing wrong.' She handed me this lovely red jumper. 'Now, try that on. I think it's your size. And here's some shoes and socks. Take those runners off, they're falling apart. Your poor feet are purple with the cold. After school, come back down to me. I'll have a parcel for you to bring home to your mother. Hurry along there and get down to your class as quick as you can.'

'Thanks, Sister,' I said. I ran down the corridor, somewhat confused in my mind as to what had just happened.

I thought I'd never get home to tell Ma. As soon as I got in from school, I handed her the parcel.

'How come tha' nun was so nice to me, Ma, and the others are so mean?'

'Isn't it obvious, Kathleen? It's as plain as the nose on yer face. She must be happy and contented with wha' she's doin' with her life. See the way she was able to stand back and have a look at yeh, and see tha' I needed a bit of help? Not like half of them other nuns. Miserable, they are. With their serious faces, lookin' like they hate themselves and everythin' around 'em. The likes of them should be tucked away behind closed doors in the convents, prayin', and not lookin' after little children.'

* * *

Down through the years, Sister Carmel often helped me and my sisters, giving us parcels of clothes or food to bring home to Ma.

About the rest of them, I think Ma was right. They were so strict and serious all the time. And the teachers weren't much better. It didn't have to be such a miserable time for us kids, but they were hell-bent on making it so. The school was ruled with an iron fist, which there was no need for. It could have been such a happy time in us kids' lives.

So, is it any wonder that every chance I got to avoid going there, I took it? If Ma wasn't keeping me out of school to help her with one thing or the other, I would be off mitching with my brother Phil. And believe me, he didn't need much coaxing. His school was across the road from mine. It was run by 'the Brothers', and they were even worse than the nuns.

Little did Ma realise the goings-on that we got up to behind her back. I remember the first time we scarpered off 'on the mitch'. It was a freezing cold day, in the depths of winter. There we were, rambling around the streets, in and out of the shops every now and then, trying to get a bit of heat, not knowing half the time where we were.

That's when we stumbled onto the dump for the first time. We couldn't believe our eyes. We were like two pickaroonies, rummaging through all the rubbish.

'Kathleen,' shouted Phil, 'would yeh have a look at this?' He held up a small truck with one of the wheels missing. 'De yeh know somethin'? I could fix this.'

I stood there laughing over at him, 'Did yeh see wha' I found?' I held up a doll with half a leg and one eye missing. 'Can yeh mend her for me, Phil?'

'For Jaysus' sake, Kathleen, can yeh not have another root there, and see if yeh can find somethin' a bit better.'

Which I did – a big lump of chocolate, and plenty more on the ground where I was standing. I didn't realise that the rats had probably been having a good piss on it before we got there.

'Come 'ere Phil. Yeh're not goin' to believe this.' I handed him some chocolate. 'De yeh think it's okay to eat?' I asked.

'Who gives a fuck, Kathleen, I'm starvin'.' He rubbed away at it with the sleeve of his jumper.

The two of us sat there in the middle of all this rubbish, eating away until we made ourselves sick, me screaming and jumping on top of Phil every time I saw a rat. We were green in the face when we finally decided to make our way back. On the way home, Phil came up with another one of his bright ideas. We were wondering where we were going to clean the chocolate and dirt off ourselves. Where did we go, only into the church, to the holy water font! We stood there, letting on to be saying a few prayers, dipping our hands in and out of the water, splashing our faces at every chance we got, hoping at the same time that the priest wouldn't catch us. We just about made it home in time, with Ma being none the wiser.

The dump was to be a hideout for all of us down through the years whenever we would scarper off on the mitch from school.

The Drink

There were seven of us kids now and another baby on the way.
Ma was finding it very hard to make ends meet. Da would
always make a few bob here and there, on bits of scrap and old
furniture which were left outside the houses where he and the
other Corporation workers went to collect the bins. He would
then sell the various bits and pieces to the shops in and around
Portobello Bridge. The money would be divided equally
between them. He always gave his share to Ma, which just
about helped us to keep our heads above water.

As soon as Da finished work, he would be home straight
away. There was never a bother on him when he had to get in
and help around the house. Be it cleaning or cooking, he would
always get stuck in and give Ma a dig-out. His favourite part
of the day would be when he was out the back garden, digging,
weeding and planting his veg. He would spend hours out there,
especially in the summer. We'd all be gathered around him.
He'd have Phil digging the long trenches, getting it ready for his
potatoes. He would show me and one or two of the younger
kids how deep to make the hole for his veg.

Ma would sit there with the babies beside her, looking
pleased with herself about the few shillings that Da had just

73

given her. She never looked for much for herself. Neither did Da, for that matter. They lived from day to day, as most people did back then. Once the few bills were paid, and there was a bit of food each day, Ma was happy.

I remember Da coming home late one evening, which was very unusual for him; he was like a clock, always there at four on the dot.

'Don't be mindin' me bein' a bit late, Lil. I slipped in for a quick pint with the men. I can't keep sayin' no every time they ask me. They'd think I'm being stand-offish, not mixin'.'

'I suppose it's all right the odd time, Phil, once yeh keep it at tha'.'

* * *

Which, of course, he didn't. Da started coming home more than the odd day with a sup on him. Ma didn't say anything in the beginning, but you could see her giving 'the look'. None of us were any the wiser. I thought it was great when Da would start with the singing. He would break into a few of his usual pretend-opera songs with one or two of the little ones sitting on his lap. Then he would start with the storytelling. He had a few great classics, which he would tell over and over again, each of us asking for our favourites.

Slowly but surely, the 'odd day' became every second or third day, and in no time at all he was coming home with more than a sup on him. And into the bargain, he took to the gambling. Not only was he losing his own few shillings, but Ma's wages also.

Things went from bad to worse, so much so that Ma couldn't pay the bills. The lights were cut off, and the glimmerman wouldn't be too far away to knock off the gas. It was back to the candles again. The young kids thought it was great sitting in the dark. There would be a few candles on the mantelpiece, one or two over at the kitchen sink. We'd sit there for hours, telling ghost stories, frightening the shite out of one another, not realising the trauma that was going on around us.

That's when all the fighting started.

When Da won on the horses, he'd be in the front door singing his head off with a big bag filled with chips and a juicy fish for Ma, thinking that would make everything okay.

'Isn't this a grand supper I have for yiz all? And for yerself, Lil. There's the wage packet with an extra few bob to help yeh with yer bills.'

She'd snap it out of his hand. 'Wha' de yeh mean my bills? They're yer fuckin' bills as well.'

She was always so angry. Da thought that once he handed his money up his job was done. Even at that, it still wasn't enough to go around.

But when he lost money gambling, which was a lot of the time, he'd slip in the side gate and try to get up the stairs without Ma seeing him. Either way – upstairs, downstairs – it didn't matter; she'd be after him like a light. Her words were always the same.

'Is tha' you, Phil Doyle? Jaysus Christ, yeh're drunk again. De yeh not realise the kids are hungry? I'm waitin' all day on yeh to bring the few bob home. Where is it? Where's me money?'

That would be Friday, wages day. They were the worst.

Da would launch into how he was waiting on the last horse to come in.

'It was a cert, Lil, a sure winner. I could smell the money, it was nearly in me hands. The tip was tha' good, so it was.'

'It's in my hand I want the money, not yours, yeh bloody waster of a man.'

His excuses were always the same.

'Wha' am I to do, Phil? Wha's after happenin' to yeh? Yeh used to be such a good man. Don't yeh care any more? There's not a crust of bread in the house. If yeh keep this up, we'll be out on the street.'

We were often hungry for days on end, with very little food to go around.

She might as well have been talking to the wall. As soon as his head hit the pillow, he'd be out like a light, snoring away without a care in the world. If he stayed asleep, things wouldn't be too bad, but if he shouted back and called her 'woman', all hell would break loose.

One night in particular, Ma completely lost it. Da kept saying, 'Woman, get yer hands off me and leave me alone.' He was so drunk that night. I went upstairs to see if I could get them to stop fighting. When I went into the room, Ma was sitting on top of Da on the bed, shaking the living daylights out of him, screaming into his face at the one time, 'Yeh're only a drunken bastard, so y'are, de yeh hear me?' She gave him a fist in the face.

'Please, Ma,' I roared, 'come on down, leave him.'

'I'll leave him all right, Kathleen.'

Before I could say another word, she jumped up off the bed and pulled our one and only wardrobe down on top of Da. That soon woke him up. Well, you'd want to have heard the screams. The whole road must have heard him. 'Me nose is broke,' he kept roaring. I could see the blood pouring down the side of his face as I tried to move the wardrobe. My brother Phil flew up the stairs to help me, but with all our efforts, we couldn't get it to budge, it was so heavy.

'You stay here, Phil, I'll be back in a minute.'

'Right, Kathleen, but hurry, will ya?'

'Come on, Ma, please. Can yeh not hear the kids? They're upset. Come downstairs with me.'

'I can't take any more of this, Kathleen,' Ma screamed, holding on to her head with her two hands. 'Me brains is goin' to burst with the worry of everythin'. Look at him, he doesn't give two shites about us.'

'Leave it, Ma. Come on,' I said as I coaxed her back down to the kids.

In I went next door to get Mrs Kennedy's son, Peter. He was very good to us. He was always there with his little medicine box. If any of us fell, got a nosebleed or cut ourselves, he was there. We called him our chemist. A small man he was, very neat and tidy, his hair combed tight into his head with a half-jar of Brylcream in it. He always wore his braces out over his jumper. As for his shoes, you could nearly see your face in them, they were so clean. Ma always said, 'Peter Kennedy's a gentleman. He should have been a doctor; he has the gift, so he has.'

I knocked on the door, screaming in the letterbox at the same time.

'Peter, Peter, quick.'

When he opened the door, I was jumping up and down.

'Now, now, Kathleen, calm down. Wha's this all about?'

He spoke slowly and in a low voice; you really had to cock your ears to hear him.

'Ma's after smashin' the wardrobe on top of Da; there's blood everywhere. Quick, quick!'

'Hold on now, Kathleen, wait a minute until I get me little box.'

I ran back into the house with Peter right behind me. Ma was still in the kitchen with the kids. They were crying; she was crying. I followed Peter up the stairs. Phil was still struggling with the wardrobe.

'It won't move, Peter. I've tried everythin'. I can't get it to budge.'

'Stand back there, the two of yiz. I'll manage it on me own.'

Up he pushed it, back against the wall. Then he brought Da into the toilet.

'Wha' have yeh been up to, Phil, for Lil to get all fired up and do this to yeh?'

'A few drinks, Peter, tha's all I had, a few drinks.'

Da was lying through his teeth. We knew it and so did Peter.

'Me nose is broke. Would yeh have a look at the size of it?

It's all over me face.'

'Now, now, Phil, stay quiet and let me have a look.'

He cleaned the blood off first. Then he pressed around his face. Da let out an unmerciful roar.

'Jaysus, Peter, will yeh take it easy, yeh're killin' me.'

'Well now, Phil, yeh're a lucky man. It's just a bad nosebleed, tha's all. But I tell yeh one thing, yeh're goin' to have two nice black eyes over the next few days. Just to be on the safe side, when yeh go into work tomorrow, get the Corporation doctor to have a look.'

'How can I go into work lookin' like this? I'd be the laughin' stock of the place. No, I'll take some of me sick leave, tha's wha' I'll do. Tha's a mad woman I'm married to, Peter, mad so she is.'

Peter wasn't having any of it. He didn't half let Da have it right, left and centre. There was no way he was letting Da say anything about Ma. Raising his voice slightly, he told him, 'Now, yeh listen to me, Phil Doyle. Tha's a fine woman yeh have down there and yeh want to start takin' care of her, de yeh hear me now?'

Da just stood there. He couldn't believe his ears – quiet Peter lashing out at him like that.

'Yer best bet now is to sleep them few drinks off and sort things out with Lil tomorrow. I'll be on me way now. Kathleen, come on down with me, make yer Ma a cup of tea and help her settle them kids down.'

When we got to the end of the stairs, Ma was standing there.

'Peter, I'm sorry for all this trouble we're givin' yeh, but the man is breakin' me heart. I don't know where to turn to any more.'

'Now, now, Lil, try and talk to Phil tomorrow, when he's sober. He's not a bad man.'

'I know tha', Peter. It's a curse, the drink, it'll be the ruination of us all.'

'De yeh want me to come in and have a chat with him? Maybe I can get him to take the pledge and keep him away from the stuff altogether. Wha' de yeh think, Lil?'

'Would yeh, Peter? Tha' would be great, if yeh could do tha' for me.'

'Right then, I'll be off now – and, Lil, leave the wardrobe where I left it, standin' against the wall. See yeh tomorrow.'

'Thanks again, Peter.'

Ma turned to me. 'Kathleen, get Phil; yeh'll have to go in and ask tha' oul crank of a Granda of yers for a lend of a few pound. Tell him yer Da lost me wages on the horses again. I'll try and pay him back when I get me children's allowance.'

'Please, Ma, don't ask me to go in there. He screams and shouts. He frightens me.'

'De yeh think I like sendin' yeh in to tha' oul fuck? Wha' am I to do, Kathleen? The kids are hungry. I know he's a crank but there's nothin' I can do. Yiz have to go. Now hurry up and get yer coats on. Carmel, ask Mrs Kennedy for a loan of the bus fare. Tell her I'll give it back tomorrow.'

Carmel was gone and back in two seconds.

'Mrs Kennedy says yeh're not to worry, Ma, it'll do when yeh have it.'

'Tha's grand. Off yiz go. Try and get back as quick as yeh can before the shop closes. I'll give Mr Green a few bob off me bill. Hopefully, he'll give me enough messages for a few days anyway.'

'Ma, wha' if Granda doesn't give us the money? Wha' will we do?'

'Just tell Mariah things are really bad and don't leave until youse get somethin' off him. I'm dependin' on yeh, Kathleen. I've nobody else.'

* * *

We got off the bus at Christ Church and walked down the Hill towards the tenements, where Granda Phil and Granny Mariah lived.

'You can ask him, Kathleen. I'm not. I asked the last two times.'

'Phil, tha's not fair.'

'I don't give two fucks. I'm not askin' him for anythin'. I'll go in with yeh, and stand there, but I won't be sayin' nothin'. I hate tha' oul' shitebag.'

When we got to the door, I gave a little knock, half-hoping they wouldn't hear us, but Phil soon fixed that. He gave the door a right bang with the back of his hand.

Gran answered the door, as usual. Granda never did; he was always sick. There was only one room, so as soon as you walked in, there he'd be in your face. You wouldn't have time to take a breath.

Coughing and choking, he let out a roar, 'Who's tha'?'

'It's young Phil and Kathleen. They've come all the way in from the country to see us.'

He was still coughing, waving his hand in the air for us to come over. I looked up at Gran, half-afraid to move.

'I suppose yeh're hungry. I'll get yeh some bread and sugar. His chest is very bad today, Kathleen,' she whispered in a low voice. 'Go on over and sit beside the fire, get yerselves a bit of heat.'

Granda was turning purple at this stage. He picked up this metal bowl and started choking and spitting in it. My stomach was turning inside out at the sight of it; I felt sick.

'Well now,' said Gran. 'How's tha' son of mine, yer father?'

'Drunk,' Phil said, real cheeky-like.

'Yeh mean he has a sup on him. A man's entitled to a drink after a hard day's work.' She never wanted to believe that Da, her only son, would do anything bad. She looked at Phil, and gave him the bad look, and then turned around to me. 'Right, Kathleen, now tell me wha's goin' on out in tha' God-forsaken place.'

I said in a low voice: 'Ma has no money to buy food, the kids are starvin', the lights were turned off and the glimmerman is on his way, Gran.'

She put her hands up to her forehead and blessed herself.

'Holy Mother of God, wha' way is me son livin'?'

Granda finally got his breath and sat up in the bed. He was very small and thin – as Ma would say, 'a bag of bones, tha' oul' fella, so he is.'

'I heard tha', Mariah. Spent the wages again, did he? Wha' did I tell yeh? A bad crowd tha' son of yours got himself in with, and tha' Lil wan out there havin' all them children. Is it any wonder they're starvin'? Yeh'd need a job in the government to be able to keep all them goin'. I suppose it's money yeh're in for, the pair of yeh? Well, yeh won't be gettin' any, so off with yiz now!' He pointed over to the door.

'Now, oul' Phil, don't be gettin' yerself all worked up like tha'. Somethin' must have happened. Phil wouldn't do such a thing.'

'Would yeh stop and listen to yerself, Mariah? Always makin' excuses for him. Why don't yeh face it, yer son is after turnin' into a waster. Now, you two get yerselves home. Yeh'll be gettin' no money offa me. And tell tha' mother of yours, she's not to send yiz in here again.' With that, he went into another frenzy of coughing and spitting.

It took all my strength to hold onto Phil and stop him from running out the door on me. I wanted so much to shout at Granda, 'Yer only an oul' fuck and I hate yeh.' But I knew Mariah would have a heart attack and Ma really needed the money, so we stood there and let him go on and on and on.

'Come here, the pair of yiz,' said Mariah, 'an' get yer coats on. Wait at the end of the stairs, I'll talk to him.'

'Will yeh, Gran? Thanks.'

We made our way out of the room. We sat there listening to him ranting and raving, with Gran trying to make the peace.

She came out after a while with some messages in a bag and the money.

'Why does he always do tha', Gran? He frightens the shite out of us, and then he gives the money. Why?'

'Don't be mindin' him, Kathleen, he's sick and old. Now run along and get home before it gets dark. Tell yer mother to send tha' money in as soon as she gets her allowance or I'll have to listen to him. I'll be out to see yiz next week. Tell yer father I said so.'

'Right, Gran, thanks,' I said, as we went running up the Hill.

* * *

Just as we got to the top, I heard a familiar voice. I turned around and who was it – only Maisie, Ma's best friend.

'Would yeh have a look at the two of yiz? When I saw tha' head of blond hair, and them long black plaits, I knew, I just knew yeh were Lil's kids. The pair of yiz have got so big.'

She rubbed Phil's hair, tossing it like mad.

'Jaysus, Phil, the last time I put me fingers through yer hair it was like chasin' a herd of buffaloes, the fleas were tha' big.'

'Wha' de yeh mean? There nothin' in me head.' He walked off, all annoyed with Maisie for saying that.

'Cranky little fucker, isn't he, Kathleen?'

'Ah, he didn't mean it, Maisie, he's just a bit upset.'

'Anyway, wha' are yiz doin' in here? How is yer Ma? I haven't seen her in ages.'

'She's at home with the kids.'

'Jaysus, Kathleen, let me see yer face. Were yeh cryin'? Wha's after happenin'? Is Lil all right?'

I told Maisie everything. 'I tried to tell Granda how bad things are at home, but he wouldn't listen and told us to get out.'

'Don't mind tha' oul' fuck, Kathleen. He's on his last legs, tha's wha's wrong with him. I hope he dies roarin'. Men, they're all the same – a shower of bastards, so they are. Look at me with tha' Jojo Murphy, the life he's after givin' me, the pig. I never thought I'd see the day tha' Phil Doyle would turn to the drink. Come on, luv, I'll walk yiz up to the bus stop. Tell yer Ma I'm goin' to make me way out to see her. I don't care if it's in the arsehole of the country. God help her, she must be in an awful state.'

'Will yeh really come out, Maisie? She'd love tha'.'

'I give yeh me word, Kathleen. I'm goin' straight up to the church now and light a candle to our Blessed Lady askin' her to help yer Ma get back on her feet.'

With that, Phil made his way back over to us.

'Don't you be so touchy, Phil, de yeh hear me?' She tossed his hair again. 'Sure, I'm only windin' yeh up. Yeh should know me by now. I was just havin' a bit of a laugh with yeh, tha's all.'

Phil stood there with a sulky face on him, mumbling under his breath, 'Sorry, Maisie.'

Just then the bus came. Maisie hugged and kissed us. She stood there waving and shouting. 'Tell yer Ma I'll be out to see her as soon as I can.'

We were halfway up Thomas Street and could still hear her voice.

* * *

As soon as we got off the bus, we ran all the way to Mr Green's shop. He was getting ready to close. Phil asked him would he hold on because Ma was on her way. I fell in the front door, gasping for breath.

'Quick, Ma, here's the money. Mr Green has the gates on the shop and all – hurry up, he's closin'!'

'Kathleen, you stay here and watch the kids, make sure they don't go near any of them candles.'

'Okay, Ma.'

She stood there and looked at me for a second.

'Yeh're a good girl, Kathleen.'

Hearing her say that made it all worthwhile. Those few words meant so much to me.

It wasn't long before Ma was back in the house with Phil and herself carrying a right load of messages.

'Tha's great, Ma, yeh made it in time.'

'Just about, Kathleen. The only thing is, the glimmerman was here when yiz were in town. The gas was cut off.'

'Wha' are we goin' to do now, Ma?'

'The same as always, Kathleen.'

'Ah Jaysus, Ma, not out the back yard again! We'll freeze to death and to top it off, it's lashin' rain out.'

'Wha' else can I do? Yiz have to be fed. Come on, yeh all know the drill. Young Phil, gather the big rocks I have out there against the wall.'

Ma made a circle with the rocks, filled it up with turf and sticks and got a right blazing fire going. She took one of the grids from inside the oven, placed it on top of the rocks to make sure the pots wouldn't tip over. She sat there muttering to herself, 'Typical timin'; fuck tha' glimmerman anyway, me with all these mouths to feed.'

I stood over her with a big umbrella while dinner was cooked.

Sometimes that went on for a few days, or maybe for a week or two depending on how quick things could be sorted out. Although we didn't know it at the time, I suppose we were one of the first families around Crumlin to have our own barbeque.

* * *

Da was in a bad way the next day. He had pains everywhere. We were all sitting around the table when he came down. Noel started laughing first, then Phil, and that got them all going. Ma just glared at everybody, which soon put a stop to the laughing.

'Jaysus, Lil, wha' did yeh do to me last night? I'm in bits.'

'Yeh pushed me too far this time, so yeh did, Phil Doyle.'

You could hear a pin drop. There wasn't a sound out of any of us. We all knew that if Ma gave the look and used the second name, there was big trouble on the way.

'Yeh left me with not a penny in me pocket, and me havin' to send them two kids into tha' oul' fella of yer's, beggin' for a few shillin's, so tha' I could feed them, and him treatin' them like dirt.'

She was really screaming loud at this stage. There was a plate of fried bread in one of her hands and a jam jar of tea in the other. I thought she was going to throw them at Da. Instead, she bashed them on the table. The bread and the tea went everywhere. None of us moved. She stood face to face with Da. He never said a word.

'I'm not puttin' up with yeh any more. De yeh hear me?' She pushed her fist into his face. 'Yeh can go back to yer oul' wan. I'm sure she'll be glad to have her precious son back. I'll get help somewhere. A waster yeh're turnin' into – and you were a man of the cloth for years. Yeh should be ashamed of yerself.'

Da said nothing. He just got himself a cup of tea and sat by the fire, thinking, knowing full well that Ma was right.

* * *

Peter came in that evening and Da went up to the church with him and took the pledge. He promised Ma the sun, moon and stars, and swore that he would never set foot inside a pub or bookies ever again, and that he really meant it this time. That's the way things went over the years with Da: on and off the drink, in and out of the bookies. He tried really hard, but he always fell off the wagon. For him it wasn't worth it. He always came out the worse in the end. Ma made sure of that.

'From now on, Phil Doyle, Kathleen and young Phil will be at the wages office every Friday, bang on the dot of four. As soon as yeh get paid, yeh can take yer own few bob first. Then yeh'll be handin' them over me wages.'

Da jumped up off the chair. 'There's no way I'm standin' for this, Lil – sendin' the kids down to the yard, makin' a show of me! Yeh're not doin' tha', I don't care. I'm off the drink, for God's sake, Lil. Wha' more de yeh want?'

'No! I heard all tha' before. Tha's all I ever get, just words tha' mean nothin', broken promises. I'll be takin' no more chances. Yeh won't put me through this ever again. The next time yeh hit the bottle, at least I'll have me few bob to get me through.'

'Jaysus Christ, woman!'

'Don't *woman* me! It's either the kids or me goin' down to the yard, and by Jaysus, Phil Doyle, if yeh make me go down to tha' Corporation yard, and go down I will, yeh won't hold yer head up for a long time. I'll go crazy mad, so I will.'

Da wasn't long backing off. He knew better.

* * *

The first wages day came. Ma had her plan all ready to go into action.

'Kathleen, take tha' dress off yeh. Go upstairs and put on a skirt and jumper.'

'Why, Ma?'

'Just do wha' yeh're told. I have me reasons. Hurry up now, and come straight back down.'

I was up and down the stairs in a jiffy. Ma was sitting by the fire pushing the pram, trying to get Jacinta asleep.

'Pull yer jumper up, Kathleen.'

'For wha', Ma?'

'Just watch, listen and learn.'

She had one of the baby's big nappy pins in her hand and fastened it to the top of my knickers.

'Wha' are yeh doin' tha' for, Ma?'

'Kathleen, when yeh get to the yard and get the wage packet off yer Da, turn around and face the wall. Have young Phil standin' beside yeh. Make sure nobody is lookin'. Put the wage packet inside yer knickers and pin it to them; tha' way there won't be a chance in hell of yeh losin' it, or for tha' matter gettin' robbed. Now, when yiz get on the bus tell the bus conductor to let yeh off at Rathmines, beside the big buildin' with the clock on the top. There's gates at the side of it; go through them, and tha's were yer Da will be standing with all the men, waitin' for the wages office to open. Just go and stand over at the wall, smile and give a big wave to make sure yer Da sees yiz. He should come over to yiz. Now, if it's a thin' tha' he doesn't come near yiz, tha's when I want yeh to call his name out. Scream and keep screamin' until he does. Tha'll soon put a stop to him sneakin' off. Are yeh listenin' to me?'

'Ma, will Da not get annoyed with us?'

'Fuck 'im, Kathleen, he doesn't be worried if I'm annoyed when he's spendin' his wages. Kathleen, I'm dependin' on yeh to do this for me. I've nobody else.'

Those words were said to me so many times over the years.

'Yeah, Ma, I know wha' to do.'

'Take Clare with yeh. She's a cheeky little bitch. There'll be no problem for her to scream her brains out if she has to.'

As soon as we got to the yard, I stood at the wall with my brother Phil and sister Clare, all the while keeping an eye on Da. You could see he was uneasy as he walked up and down, fidgeting with his hands while he spoke to the other men. Phil gave a little wave over, making sure Da saw us.

'Tha's lettin' him know we're here, Kathleen.'

'I think he already knows tha', Phil. Shuss . . . say nothin'. Here he is over.'

Da was fuming as he made his way across to us.

'Did the three of yiz have to come down? Would one of yiz not have been enough? Tha' mother of yours is hell-bent on makin' a show of me. I'll be the talk of the yard tomorrow. There's no need for this. No need at all.'

The three of us stood there, not moving, waiting on Da to hand over the wage package.

'I'm sorry, Da, Ma says we're to stay here until yeh give us the money.'

That's when Clare got her spoke in. 'Will I scream now, Kathleen, will I?'

'Stay quiet, Clare, I'm talkin' to Da. Please, Da?' I put my hand out.

He gave a quick look around, checking to see if anyone was watching him as he slipped the wage package into my hand. Then he walked away from us without another word spoken. He was all agitated and annoyed. I watched him make his way down through the yard, all the while keeping his head down as he passed by the other men, not knowing for sure if any of them saw what was going on over at the wall.

* * *

Ma never had to go without her part of the wages, ever again. Every Friday on the dot of four, there would be two of us standing at the wall to meet Da. She always had to be two steps ahead just to get by. And get by she did.

But Da never gave up the drink.

10

Ma Starts Work

There seemed to be no end to Ma having babies. They kept arriving, one after another. Thomas was less than two when Jacinta arrived and then, two years later, there was Patricia. I never seemed to get a chance to mix with the other kids or to play outside. By the time I was twelve, there were nine of us kids.

Ma was finding it very hard to make ends meet and was on Da's back all the time to hand up more wages. But there was no way he was handing over his drink money. They seemed to be at one another's throats all the time. I would sit there listening to them going on and on, Da lying through his teeth, Ma giving out about this and that, which she had every right to.

As a child I longed for a happy home. I was always daydreaming, letting myself get lost in my thoughts, wishing and hoping things would be different. I wouldn't be long being pulled back from my dreams with the roars of Ma.

'How in the name of Jaysus am I supposed to manage on seven pound a week, Phil? I've too many mouths to feed now. If yeh're not goin' to give me more money, I'll have to get meself a job.'

'Yeh can't go to work, Lil. Who'll mind the kids?'

'*You* will, Phil.'

'Are yeh mad? *I can't mind babies!*' he roared.

'Well, yeh better start learnin', because if we don't do somethin' soon we'll be out on the street. I haven't paid the rent in six months.' She handed Da a letter. 'There, read it yerself. It came this mornin'. Tha's the final warnin'. If we don't give a few bob soon, they're goin' to evict us.'

'Good God, Lil! Why didn't yeh say somethin' sooner? Yeh shouldn't have let it get to this.'

'And would it have made any difference? *Would it?*' she screamed into his face, one of her mad rages coming on. 'Yeh'd only be tellin' me I'm naggin' yeh again. I'm robbin' Peter to pay Paul. Every time I try to give a few bob off the rent, one of the kids needs somethin'. If it's not them, it's the gas or the lights. Can yeh not see wha's goin' on around here, Phil? Ah, maybe it's easier for yeh to turn a blind eye.' She went over to pick up one of the babies.

'Lil, de yeh have to keep puttin' me down all the time in front of the kids? I'm not tha' bad.'

'So tha's wha' yeh think I'm doin'? Right then! Have a look at this. Come 'ere, Noel, Phil, Carmel, Clare! Show yer father yer shoes. Go on! Lift yer feet up.'

One by one, the kids showed Da their shoes.

'Jaysus, Phil, will yeh have a look and open yer eyes, *for God's sake!* Look, a bit of plastic and cardboard in the soles of the shoes. There's tha' many holes in them I have to try and do somethin' to keep the rain out. They haven't got a pair of stockin's between them.'

Da stood there, looking at each and every one of us, not saying a word. How could he? Ma was right and he knew it.

'I'm borrowin' a few bob all the time just to keep them in food. Somethin' has to be done, Phil.'

'Lil, we'll talk about this later.' He was trying to gloss things over as usual. It was always the same with Da, putting everything on the long finger. He wouldn't face up to his responsibilities, leaving it all up to Ma.

'No, Phil, it's gettin' sorted out now, once and for all. Me mind's made up. Mrs Reilly up the top of the road – she works in O'Connell Street in some fancy restaurant called the Paradiso. They're lookin' for a woman in the evenin's to take over when she's finished work, for washin' up and keepin' the kitchen clean. It's from five in the evening until three in the mornin'. She's goin' to put in a good word for me. Tha' way I'll have a good chance of gettin' the job and, if I do, *I'm takin' it.*'

'And how are yeh supposed to get home at tha' hour of the mornin', Lil?'

'I have it all worked out, Phil, and don't yeh be tryin' to put obstacles in me way. It's happenin', so yeh better get used to it. One of the women tha' does nights all the time has a friend who owns a taxi. He collects a few of the women every night and drops yeh straight to yer door. He gets ten shillin's for the week off each of them. If I get the job, he said tha' he'd squeeze one more in. I'll be left with three pound after tha' and, by God, tha'll go a long way to helpin' me with everythin' around here.'

'But, Lil . . .'

'There's no buts about it, Phil Doyle! Did yeh not hear a word I said? They're goin' to kick us out on the fuckin' street. Is it not sinkin' into tha' head of yers?' she shouted.

'I'm sorry, Lil, I'll change me ways. I promise I will.' Da would really mean what he said at that moment in time, but he never changed. They were only words.

'Yeh'll have to, Phil, there's no two ways about it. I'm at me wit's end.'

In the middle of all this mayhem, Ma took out a small white clay pipe.

'Wha's tha', Lil?'

'Can't yeh see it's a fuckin' pipe! Tha's wha yeh drove me to.

I have to do somethin' to settle me nerves. Me father gave this to me today. I'm not able to buy me few Woodbines, I'm not like you. I wouldn't spend me last few shillings on meself knowin' tha' I needed it for the kids and the house. Yeh're a fuckin' waster of a man, tha's wha' yeh are. No good at all.'

'For God's sake, would yeh ever cut yer language out, Lil? There's no need for it, no need at all.'

'Is there not now? Well fuck, fuck and fuck again. Wha' de yeh think of tha'? Ah, me arse. Don't be annoyin' me, would yeh. The only thing I have to keep me sane is me few cigarettes and I can't even have them now.'

'Yeh're not goin' to start smokin' tha' pipe. Yeh'll be makin' a holy show of me altogether. Wha' will people think if they see yeh?'

'If tha's all yeh have to worry about now, Phil Doyle, yeh can count yerself lucky. Anyway, I don't give two shites wha' you or anybody else thinks. As a matter of fact, I'll start smokin' right now. Where's tha' bit of tobacco me father gave me?' She rummaged through her pockets. 'Ah, here it is.' And up she lit the pipe. She was puffing and puffing for a few minutes before she got it going. After that, she was away in a hack. Da just shook his head and started reading his paper. The kids all thought it was great.

'Hey, Ma,' Clare laughed, 'yeh're like one of them Indians out of the cowboy pictures.'

'Tha's right, Clare. They used to smoke their pipes before the war, or was it after the war? I'm not too sure. Isn't tha' right, Phil?' She raised her voice once more.

Da just sat there, shaking his head and not answering.

'Phil, I want yeh to listen to me. Take yer face out of tha' paper when I'm talkin' to yeh.'

'Jesus, Lil, I heard yeh the first time. I *am* listenin'.'

'I'm goin' to make me way down to Mr O'Keeffe, the councillor. He has a shop down Sundrive Road. Mrs Reilly told me she got into a bit of bother with her rent. He went into the

Corporation with her and got an arrangement set up.'

Da wasn't long putting the paper down and cocking up his ears to what Ma was saying.

'Tha' would be great if he could do tha' for us, Lil. Go on, go ahead, meself and Kathleen will watch the kids.'

'Oh, so I have yer attention now, have I?' She made her way out the door.

* * *

Ma saw Mr O'Keeffe that night. I was walking the floor with Patricia, who was going mad for the diddy, when Ma finally got back.

'Yeh were gone ages, Ma. The baby is starvin'.'

'I know, I know, Kathleen, give her over here to me, quick! Me diddies is burstin'. Tha's a filthy night out there. I'm soaked into the skin. Grab tha' towel Carmel and dry me feet before I catch me death of cold. Clare, make me a cup of tea, I'm gaspin'.'

'Well, Lil, how did it go? Did yeh get to see him?'

'I did, Phil, I did. The nicest man you could ever meet. You want to see all the women down there. Tha's why I was so long. All as bad as meself, not a shillin' between any of us. I showed him the letter and told him how bad things were. He said if the Corporation agree and yeh let them take the rent out of the wage packet and a few pennies of the arrears every week, tha'll settle it. I've to meet him at twelve o'clock tomorrow outside the rent office.'

Da didn't say much but you could see the relief on his face. He was well pleased with the news.

The rent was taken out of Da's wage packet every week and sent into the Corporation. From that day on, Ma never again had to worry about being put out on the street.

Ma kept up the pipe over the years after that when the money was scarce. You always knew she had an extra few shillings when you saw her smoking the Woodbines again.

* * *

A few days later Mrs Reilly dropped in to see Ma on her way home from work.

'I've good news for yeh, Lil – I got yeh the job.'

I thought Ma was going to burst out crying. 'The blessin's of God on yeh,' she said, nearly taking the hands off Mrs Reilly, she shook them that much. 'Come in, come in. Sit down there. Kathleen, make a cup of tea for Mrs Reilly. I'm prayin' to the Virgin Mary herself every night, askin' her to help me. Now me prayers is answered. She never lets me down. I'll be lightin' a candle first thing in the mornin'. Thankin' herself.'

'Does Phil mind yeh goin' to work, Lil?'

'Don't yeh know he does, Mrs Reilly? Mind you now, when it comes to them kids, he's an awful worrier. He'd never leave them on their own once he knows I won't be here. I won't let yeh down. I give yeh me word and tha's me bond.'

'I'll have to run now, Lil, so I'll tell me boss tha' yeh'll start at five o'clock tomorrow. I'll drop in in a day or two to see how yeh're gettin' on. Cheerio now and the best of luck to yeh!' Off she went.

Ma was thrilled with herself. As well as making the extra money, you could see she was looking forward to getting out of the house. Even though the work was going to be hard and the hours long, she didn't seem to mind.

'Yeh know wha', Kathleen? This could be the makin's of yer father.'

'How de yeh mean, Ma?'

'He'll have no time to go to the pub and I have to say, when he has an extra few bob and not spendin' it on the drink, he's very good to me. Things could be startin' to take a turn for the best around here.'

'I hope so Ma. I really do.'

'I'll start gettin' a bit of dinner ready now. Kathleen, gather them small ones up and put them sittin' down at the table. When tha's done, tell Carmel to call the others in. A half an egg, a slice of bread with a few chips will have to do; tha's all I have. Things is really bad this week.'

The kids would be all trying to get the plate that Ma cut the eggs on. That way yeh got the extra bit of yellow to dip yer last bit of crust in.

'Phil, run upstairs and tell yer father to leave readin' tha' paper. There's a bit of dinner ready. He's to come down straight away or there won't be a chip left on the plate. Every time I turn me head there's a few more chips gone. I can't catch which one of the kids is takin' them.'

Da came over and sat down beside me. Thomas jumped onto his lap. I had Jacinta in my arms and Patricia was asleep in the pram. Phil, Carmel, Clare, Marion and Noel were finished their dinner and were getting ready to go upstairs, when Ma called out.

'Hold on there a minute, I've somethin' to say.'

Clare jumped. 'It wasn't me, it was him,' she said, pointing over at Noel.

'Yeh're a liar, Clare! You went into the garden first,' Noel answered.

'You robbed Mrs Kennedy's apples first.'

'No, I didn't.'

'Yes, yeh did.'

The two of them started scrapping, Clare spitting and kicking, Noel pushing and shoving.

Bloody eejits, I thought. *I keep telling them, always wait and listen to what's going to be said and say nothing. But do they listen? Never!*

Ma put her hands on her hips. 'So tha's wha' yeh're up to when me back's turned. I'll sort you two out later.'

'No, Lil, it'll be done now.' Da got Noel by the ear. 'Kathleen, grab Clare and follow me, before she runs off. In yeh go, the two of yeh, and tell Mrs Kennedy yeh're sorry. I

95

wouldn't mind but yeh only have to ask the woman and she'd give yeh any amount of apples yeh want.'

We marched them in next door to Mrs Kennedy's. I stood there holding onto Clare while Mrs Kennedy told Da, 'I know Clare is only a skinny little thing, Phil. But yeh'd want to see her climbin' the tree. She does be like a little monkey, swingin' with one hand and throwin' the apples over to yer garden with the other. Tha's a wild one yeh have there.'

'Sure, don't I know it? We'll have to keep an eye on her, Mrs Kennedy. Tha's for sure.'

It wasn't long before we were back in our own house with a big bag full to the top with the loveliest apples you ever saw, all red and shiny.

'It's the tree Mrs Kennedy is worried about, Lil, in case they break any of the branches.'

'Right, right, Phil. Tha's enough about the apples. Are yiz all here? Now listen to wha' I have to say.'

'Lil, wha's so important tha' yeh have us all gathered here like the twelve apostles at the Last Supper?'

'I said, are yiz all listenin'? Right then, I got the job.'

Da's face dropped but he said nothing, because he knew it had to be done. The kids just stood there listening, not really understanding what this was all about. Not that it would change much for any of them. They'd just carry on as usual. It was up to myself and Da to look after things from now on.

'Phil, yeh have to make sure yeh're home every day at four o'clock. I have to start at five. Tha'll give me plenty of time to get into town. Mrs Reilly told me tha' they're very strict about being late, so yeh can't let me down.'

Da just nodded his head. I think he was still in shock.

'Kathleen, you'll have to take over the two small ones. Make sure they're fed and yeh change their nappies. Yer Da's no good at tha', but he'll help yeh with feedin' the rest of the kids. Young Phil, you make sure the others give themselves a wash every night.'

That's a joke, I thought. *Phil can't wash himself right, never mind look after the kids. That'll be left to me as well.*

'Everybody has to pull their weight around here now. I can't do this on me own. There's no two ways about it. This has to be done.'

* * *

There was loads of hustle and bustle the next day, with Ma trying to get everything sorted before she started her first day at work. I never saw her in such a tizzy, rushing all over the place: 'Do this . . . fix tha' . . . hold him . . . feed her.'

'Ma, will yeh sit down for a minute? I'll make yeh a cup of tea. I want to ask yeh somethin'.'

'Wha', Kathleen, wha' is it? I haven't got time to sit. We have to get the washin' done and then there's the dinner.'

'It's about Patricia, Ma. Wha' am I goin' to do when she's hungry and lookin' for the diddy, and yeh're not here?'

'I know, I know. I've already thought about tha'. I've two old baby bottles here. I'll squeeze me milk into them through the day and I'll feed her just before I go. But yeh have to make sure she gets her last feed before eleven, because me diddies will be burstin' with milk and I'll need her nice and hungry to empty them out. Now, de yeh understand tha', Kathleen?'

'I think so Ma,' I said, not realising I'd be walking the floor every night with Patricia screaming with the hunger, waiting for Ma to come home.

'Kathleen, look after the little ones there. I'll try and get a bit of dinner started before yer father comes home. Come 'ere, Carmel, take Clare with yeh and go down to Mr Hogg the butcher, tell him I sent yeh. Ask him will he give yeh a pound of rashers and two pound of sausages. Can he put them on me bill? I'll give him a few shillin's at the weekend. Then, go over to the corner shop. I have a half a crown here. Give it to Mr Green off me bill and say yer Ma is sorry it took so long to pay.

97

Then ask could yeh have a few messages until next week. Tell him I got meself a job and tha' I'll be in as soon as I get me first wage packet. They know me word is good. Tha's grand, Kathleen. As soon as they get back, I'll make a coddle. Tha'll be easy for yiz. Yer father just has to heat it up when he comes home.'

Ma was running around like I don't know what, half talking to me and half talking to herself.

She was so excited her first day, heading off to work. I stood at the front door with little Patricia in my arms and Da standing beside me, waving and waving until she got lost in the distance, thinking to myself, *Will we be able to manage?*

* * *

The following morning, Ma was up bright and early, making the breakfast. She was really on a roll, talking and talking like I never saw before. We were all gathered around the table when she started launching into the goings-on of her first night at work. 'The nicest people yeh could meet. They made me very welcome, so they did. I was only in the door when the chef came over to me, fillin' me in on wha' me jobs were, and I can tell yeh, there was a lot for me to do. I never stopped from the minute I went in, washin' delph, cleanin' pots and scrubbin' floors. I had the kitchen gleamin' in no time. Yeh'd want to see the amount of food tha' goes to waste in there. Some of the plates had half of the dinners still on them, and me havin' to scrape it out into the bin. I could have fed the lot of yiz today with wha' I had to throw out. A mortal sin, tha's wha' it is.'

'Ma, why didn't yeh ask if yeh could bring all the bits home to us?' I asked.

'Jaysus, Kathleen, I couldn't do tha'. Well, not on me first night anyway. Let me get meself in there for a little while first.'

And no better woman to ask, which she did after a few days. And it wasn't a problem. Anything that was left on the plates, Ma could have. Believe me, that went a long way with us kids. There would be pieces of chicken, halves of chops, bits of meat, rashers and sausages, all heated up together to make a dinner the following day.

* * *

Ma settled really well into her job and seemed to be happy in herself, heading off every day to do her ten-hour shift in the restaurant while I got ready to do mine.

Da was great the first couple of weeks. He was on time every day, but wasn't long slipping back into his old ways. Each day he got later and later. Ma would have herself in a right state, she'd be walking the floor, fucking and blinding, waiting on him to come in.

'You go ahead, Ma,' I would say. 'Yeh're only gone out the door when he gets here.'

'Are yeh sure about tha', Kathleen? Yeh wouldn't be tellin' me lies now, tryin' to keep yer father out of trouble?'

'I'd never do tha', Ma. Honest, I swear.' I made the sign of the cross on my chest. Once I did that Ma would believe me, or pretend to. I had got so tired of all the fighting between Ma and Da that it was easier to tell a few lies; it made life a bit better for everyone.

Most days I would manage the kids with the help of my brother Phil, and Carmel was starting to get a bit of cop-on, so she gave a dig-out as well. But there were days when I would be frantic and up the walls with worry, especially when baby Patricia was teething and crying all the time. And little Jacinta missed Ma terribly at first. It took me all my time to comfort her, but after a while she settled in with the rest of the kids. We all looked after one another. That's the way it had to be.

Da would always go on with one yarn or another as to why he was late. And no matter how much of a sup he had on him, he'd always say, 'Now, Kathleen, I don't think yer Mother needs to know tha' I fell a little bit behind with the time. We don't want her gettin' all fired up now, do we? I'll give yeh me word tha' I'll be here on the dot of four tomorrow.'

'Of course yeh will, Da,' I would say, as Phil and myself would help him up the stairs to sleep it off, knowing full well that not a word of what he was saying was true.

* * *

That was the start of Ma working for many years to come, and me taking on an even bigger role in rearing the family.

11

Maisie and Ma

A good few months went by before Maisie finally made her way out to see Ma. I was in the garden with a couple of the kids when I heard a scream.

'Kathleen, Phil! One of yiz come down here to me and give me a hand with these heavy bags.'

When I looked down the end of our road, there she was.

'Ma, quick, look who's comin'!'

Ma rushed out to the front door. 'Wha' the hell are yeh gettin' yerself all worked up over, Kathleen?'

When she looked down the road, she let out such a roar. 'I don't believe it – Maisie, Maisie!' Ma ran down the road to her. The two of them just kept crying and hugging each other. 'After all this time, yeh finally came out to see me, Maisie.'

'Holy Jaysus, Lil, how in the name of God de yeh live out here in this God-forsaken place? It's in the middle of nowhere.'

'Would yeh stop, Maisie, it's not tha' bad. Yeh don't be long gettin' get used to it. All the kids love the open space. They can go mad up in the fields. It's great for them, and it gives me a grand break.'

'All the same, Lil, there was no stoppin' yeh once yeh got goin'. Yeh can make babies quicker than anybody I know.'

'Didn't I tell yeh before, Maisie? Phil Doyle only has to hang his trousers at the end of the bed and I'm gone again. Every time he knocks he gets an answer,' she said, giving Maisie a nod and a wink.

'Yeh're a mad thing, Lil, de yeh know tha'? Jojo Murphy could be bangin' the door down all night long and he wouldn't be gettin' any answers off me, I can tell yeh tha' for nothin'. Put the teapot on there, Lil. Me mouth is dried up to nothin' here. And we'll have a smoke.'

'I haven't got one to me name. I only have me oul' clay pipe.'

'Ah for fuck's sake, yeh're not smokin' a pipe?'

'I do, Maisie. When I've no smokes I put a bit of turf in the pipe and have a few puffs.'

'Here yeh are, Lil, I picked up a few loose Woodbines in Meath Street before I got the bus. And there's a few messages. It'll make a bit of dinner for yiz. So, fill me in on wha's happenin' with yeh.'

'I wouldn't know where to start, there's tha' much gone wrong in me life.'

'I'm not rushin' anywhere, and if I make me mind up and if yeh have somewhere for me to put me head down, I'll stay the night. We might even go to the pictures, wha' de yeh say?'

'Would yeh really stay, Maisie? Wha' about Jojo?'

'Fuck him. And the kids are big and hairy enough to look after themselves.'

'Yeh can sleep in the bed with me, Maisie.'

'With yerself and Phil? No, thank yeh very much. He might get himself all confused and throw his leg over the wrong way. I swear, Lil, I'd piss on meself with the fright, so I would. I'll stay in with the kids, if tha's okay with yeh.'

'No, yeh won't, I'll push the two chairs together. Phil can sleep there. It won't do him any harm for one night. Anyway, I'm dyin' to tell yeh, Maisie — I got meself a job. Tha's how I haven't been able to come in and see yeh for so long.'

'And I thought yeh just forgot about me, Lil.'

'Never in a million years, Maisie, would I ever forget yeh.'

'Tha's it, Lil, we're definitely goin' to the pictures tonight. This calls for a celebration.'

'I haven't got a shillin' to spare, Maisie, never mind go out.'

'Don't yeh worry about tha', I have a few bob. I rifled Jojo's pockets last night when he was asleep.'

'Jaysus, Maisie, yeh never!'

'I did; I do it all the time, Lil. Sure he wouldn't know. He'd think he was after spendin' it on the drink the night before. Yeh learn a few tricks as the years go by. Fellas like Jojo only think of themselves and tha's wha' I'm doin' from now on, lookin' after me. The only way I know how. Yeh're as strong as an ox, Lil, and well able to take care of yerself, but me with me six and a half stone, if a gust of wind blew up now, it would pick me up and fuck me through tha' winda in seconds. It would, Lil, I swear it would.'

'Yeh're a scream, Maisie. I haven't laughed this much in years.'

'Lil, would yeh ever give us another drop of tea? Me throat feels like I'm after swallowin' half of Sandymount Beach.'

'I don't like the sound of tha', Maisie. Yeh want to go to the doctor and get tha' checked out.'

'Would yeh stop yer fussin', Lil, it's just a few swollen glands – nothin' to worry about. Kathleen, come 'ere, I have somethin' for yeh. Take tha'.' It was a big green pound note. 'Yerself and young Phil go down to tha' chip shop at the bus stop and get about ten singles of chips and two nice fresh fish for meself and yer Ma.'

'Jaysus, Maisie, yeh don't have to do tha'. It's too much.'

'I know I don't have to. The thing is, I *want* to. Isn't tha' wha' friends are for? Now, run along the pair of yiz and wha'ever change is left, pick up a few sweets for later on.'

I chatted away to Phil as we made our way down the road. 'Wouldn't it be great if Maisie lived out here all the time? Did yeh see the way Ma is all happy in herself? She's laughin', messin' and actin' the eejit since she arrived.'

'Well now, Kathleen. She hasn't exactly got much to be laughin' about with Da comin' in most of the time mouldy drunk and hardly ever a shillin' in her pocket, scrimpin' and scrapin' all the time.'

'Yeh don't have to tell me, Phil, I know all tha'. I'm only sayin', tha's wha' I would love.' I was getting myself all worked up.

'Ah for Jaysus' sake, Kathleen, will yeh not be gettin' yer knickers in a knot. The way I see it, everythin' is okay tonight, so enjoy it when it's goin'. Now, come on, let's get the chips, I'm starvin'. Maybe we'll fiddle an extra single in and eat it on the way back. Wha' de yeh say?'

'Ah, I suppose yeh're right, Phil. Don't be mindin' me. I do be just daydreamin'. We'd better hurry.'

* * *

We were only in the door with the fish and chips when the front door opened again.

'Maisie, here's Phil comin' in. He's after been in with his mother. He goes in every Sunday to see herself and his three sisters. Him being the only brother, they think there's no one like him. Now, sayin' tha', they're all very good to me. He never comes home without a few messages and somethin' thrown in for the kids. Credit where it's due, Maisie.'

'Shush . . . say nothin', Maisie, here he is.'

In came Da. 'Well, well. I haven't seen yeh in years, Maisie. Wha' brings yeh out to this neck of the woods?'

'I had a bit of time on me hands and I thought, who better than Lil and yerself to visit? It's well yeh're lookin', Phil.'

Da looked at the table full of food. 'Wha's this, Lil?'

'Maisie's treat, Phil.'

'Tha's right, a few of me numbers came up on the bingo last night, isn't tha' right, Lil?'

The pair of them laughed themselves silly, not letting Da know the truth.

We all sat there, delighted with ourselves, getting a full bag of chips for our tea instead of a slice of bread and dripping, and there were a few sweets for afterwards. To us it was like having a party.

* * *

Maisie and Ma went out to the pictures while I minded the kids with Da. And by the sound of them when they came home, they had the best night ever. They fell in the door laughing.

'You'll never believe wha' happened to us, Phil,' said Maisie.

'Well, by the sound of the pair of yiz, it was a good night.'

'Kathleen, love, get me a cup of tea there 'til I get meself together and fill yer father in with the goin's-on of the night. There was this fella sittin' next to me and when it was comin' near to the end of the film, he went and offered me a few sweets. I didn't want to be rude, him bein' so nice and all, so I went and put me hand into the bag, which was on his lap. There's me thinkin' I was takin' a few sweets for meself and Lil, and wha' de yeh think was in the bag? Yeh're never goin' to believe me, Phil. He had "down below" sittin' there, waitin' on me hand to come in! A heart attack I thought I was goin' to have. The whole picture house heard me screams – *and* his. I jabbed me favourite hat pin straight into the top of his leg. He was up and gone like Flash Gordon before the lights were put back on.'

Da looked over at Ma, saying, 'Lil, the kids. Yiz have to watch wha' you're sayin'.'

Ma was still laughing away at Maisie, saying to Da, 'Give it over, Phil. They don't know wha' we're talkin' about.'

I didn't, but as I looked over at my brother Phil, with a sly grin on his face, *he knew*.

'Phil, wha' is Maisie talkin' about?' I whispered.

'I'm not sayin', Kathleen. Ma would kill me if she knew I talked about stuff like tha'.'

'Ah, go on, tell me. I swear I won't say anythin'. I'm dyin' to know wha' they're laughin' at.'

'Right then, yeh'd better not say I told you. Yer man is one of them dirty fuckers Ma is always warnin' us about. They sometimes call them flashers. They open their coat real fast and show off their mickey and run. Don't ask me why they do it, I don't know. Well, tha's wha' yer man was doin' with Maisie, only *his mickey* was in the bag.'

That soon took the smile off my face and stopped me asking any more questions.

* * *

Maisie stayed the night and slept in with Ma. You could hear the two of them talking and laughing away into the early hours of the morning. Da slept on the two chairs and didn't mind a bit.

Maisie visited Ma a few times after that day and always had her laughing. From the time she walked in, Ma would be at her happiest. Until one day she told Ma the bad news.

'This will be me last time comin' out to see yeh, Lil. The bus run is gettin' a bit too much for me now.'

'Holy Mother of God, yeh don't look well, Maisie, wha's wrong with yeh? Sit down, sit down.'

'It's me oul' glands again. A bit of an infection went astray, Lil.'

'Didn't I tell yeh to get tha' checked months ago? Maisie, I told yeh.'

'I did, Lil. It was already gone too far. The doctor said a couple of months at the most. Sure I already knew meself.'

Ma burst out crying, she was so upset. I had never seen her like that before.

'Yeh should have said. Why didn't yeh tell me, Maisie?' She

was crying and hugging her like she never wanted to let her go.

'And have yeh cryin' every time yeh looked at me? Sure, look at yeh now. It's a bit of laughin' I need, Lil, not cryin'. Tha's why I made it me business to come out to yeh. We had some great times over the years.'

'We did, Maisie, we did.'

'Go on, Lil. Put the teapot on and we'll have a smoke and an oul' yap.'

They sat there for hours crying, laughing and smoking, both of them going back down memory lane.

* * *

That was the last time I saw Maisie. But Ma made sure she got in to see her as often as she could in those last few months.

I'll never forget the day the news arrived.

Da had been in to see Granny Mariah and when he came home, he was pale in the face and had such a worried look on him.

'Sit down there, Lil. I have something to tell yeh. I didn't want to be the bearer of bad news, but I suppose it's best tha' I be the one to tell yeh. Poor Maisie died early this morning.'

I got such a fright when I heard those words. The tears flowed down my face as I watched Ma fall to pieces in front of me. She cried and cried. You could have filled a river with the tears she shed.

Da took the day off work to look after the kids so that I could go to the funeral with Ma. She never spoke the whole time we were there – not that there were many people to talk to, with only a handful having turned up.

Ma put me sitting to one side as she stood by the coffin. I felt sad that Maisie was gone but I was more upset looking over at Ma saying her last goodbye to her one and only friend.

* * *

Ma wasn't herself for a long, long time after. All the life seemed to go out of her. She went into herself, barely speaking to anyone, just going through the motions of looking after us kids. She'd sit there in the chair, feeding the babies, staring out the window, not minding anyone or anything around her. I didn't know how to comfort her, being too young to understand the hurt and loss she was feeling inside.

One day, on my way down to the shops I bumped into Mrs Kearney. I told her about Maisie dying and Ma not being herself.

'Don't worry, Kathleen. It'll be all right. I'll talk to yer Ma. She'll be fine. Wait and see.'

Mrs Kearney was so good; she dropped in every day after that. She'd sit there for hours on end trying to cheer Ma up. Slowly but surely, Ma started to come round and get back to her old self again.

12

The Cane

Because Ma had been sick, I had been out of school for months on end and I really hated going back. I was so far behind the rest of the class, there was no way I could keep up with them. I used to feel such a fool, sitting there knowing nothing. I suppose if I had been in all the time and knew some of the lessons, it might not have been so bad. The odd time that I was sent to school I was always late, so straight away I was in trouble.

Ma got free milk from the clinic because she had so many kids. I had to collect the milk every morning before I went to school. The clinic didn't open until half past nine, so by the time I had queued and got the milk, it would be nearly ten o'clock by the time I reached school. I'd be falling up the long marble corridor with my schoolbag over my back and ten bottles of milk banging and clattering all over the place. No matter how hard I tried to sneak in as quietly as possible, I always got caught.

One morning, I was nearly at the classroom when a voice called out. I knew it was one of the nuns. I could hear the sound of heavy rosary beads swishing against her black habit. I was so afraid of those nuns!

109

'Kathleen Doyle, is that you again? What did I tell you about being late and bringing that milk into the school? Do you ever take any notice of what's been said to you, child?'

I looked around and there was Sister Norma, the ugliest woman you ever saw on two feet. She had a big fat face pushed out from under the veil on her head, and this big red lump of flesh hanging under her chin in what passed for a neck. I swear, the cock Ma had out in the backyard with the chickens was better looking than that nun.

'Sorry, Sister. There was loads of people on the queue. I hadn't time to go home with the milk. I would have been more later.'

'And what time do you call this, you God-forsaken child?' I bit my lip and said nothing. 'I'll be giving you a note. And tell your mother I want to see her about you not being in school. The inspector will be giving her a visit.'

I wanted to say, *I don't care and I don't want to be here, so fuck you, Sister, and fuck Speckie the Inspector*, but instead I stood there listening to her go on and on about how close I was to being put into a home for not going to school.

When she was finished giving out to me, I smiled and asked, with a sly grin on my face, 'Sister, can I bring the milk down to me Ma on the lunch break? She'll be waitin' on it for the babies.'

'This is the last time, do you hear me, Kathleen Doyle? Now get into your classroom before I change my mind about letting you go home with that milk.'

I was trying to slip into the classroom unnoticed, but the noise of the bloody milk bottles gave me away. The teacher turned around and caught me. Twitchy Maher. That was her nickname and it suited her so well. She had a face like a rabbit; if she wasn't twitching her nose, she was picking and flicking it.

'Well now, Miss Doyle, you've decided to make your entrance, have you?'

'Sorry I'm late, Miss,' I said, thinking to myself, *for fuck's sake, tha's twice I'm after gettin' the second name, first off Sister, now Twitchy*. I knew, I just knew it – there was going to be big trouble for me today.

'Who do you think you are, Miss Doyle? You seem to think that you can wander in and out of school when you feel like it. Do you think you know more than the rest of the class?' Her voice rose into a high-pitched squeak.

'Sorry, Miss. I don't. It's just tha' me Ma . . .'

'Be quiet, child, when I speak to you.' She banged her fist on the desk.

Good Jaysus! Now she's callin' me 'child' as well. Tha's it, I'm dead. She's goin' to fuckin' kill me.

'Get up to the blackboard and let's see if you can do that sum. Then we can all see how smart you are.' A few of the kids giggled. 'Be quiet down there!' she roared at the top of her voice.

I was shitting myself walking past her. I stood there with the chalk in my hand, shaking. I hadn't got a clue what to do and she knew it.

'Sorry, Miss, I don't know it. I'm sorry.'

She pulled me by the plaits over to where she kept her long skinny bamboo cane, which had tiny pieces of wire wrapped around it. She swished the cane up and down, banging it off the desk, getting ready to give me a good lash.

'Hands out, you good-for-nothing child!'

I slowly stretched my hand out with fear. Down came the cane, with an unbearable sting to follow.

'That's for being late, Kathleen Doyle. Now, out with the other one.' I looked and stepped back. 'I said the other one!' She lashed out in temper and the full force of the cane came down, again and again. 'That's for answering me back.'

'But, Miss, I didn't . . . I wasn't . . .'

'More cheek, is it, from you? Hands out again!' she roared. I stretched my hands out once more.

'Now, tell the class you're sorry for all this delay.'

I was very stubborn and wouldn't say sorry; so she just kept slapping me. She wasn't about to let me get the better of her in front of the class. You could hear a pin drop as the kids watched in horror. I lost count of how many times the cane came down. I could feel the blood drain from my face and my legs starting to wobble.

'I'm goin' to be sick, Miss.'

'You're a weakling as well as stupid! Now get outside of my class and sit on the bench until I say you can come back in.'

When I got outside, I cried and cried from the pain and the stinging in my hands. Every finger was cut and bleeding. *Tha's it! I'm gettin' outta here. Tha' fuckin' bitch is mad. She'll kill me before the day's over with the mood she's in.* I was down the stairs and heading for home before I knew it.

When I got to the house and Ma saw my hands, she went crazy mad. She ran out to the back yard, roaring up the gardens for Mrs Kearney.

'Mrs Kearney, quick! Quick, come down here to me. Would yeh have a bandage and a bit of cream?'

'Give me a minute and I'll be down, Lil.'

There was no way you could call Mrs Kearney by her first name; you had to give her the full title. She was very tall and thin, with long red hair all wavy and curly. She spoke real posh and always had her full make-up on. She was a really kind person and very good to Ma.

Ma lit a Woodbine and put the kettle on, pacing up and down in one of her mad rages.

Mrs Kearney made her way into the kitchen. 'Now, Lil, what's this all about?'

'Kathleen, come'ere! Look wha' she's done, look at her hands.'

'Who, Lil, who are we talking about here?'

'Tha' fuckin' teacher, tha's who. I'm goin' to fuckin' kill the baster'n' bitch when I get me hands on her.'

'Now, Lil, stop that cursing in front of the children. Come over to me, Kathleen. Oh my God, look at the state of your little hands, you poor child. There is no need for this, no need at all. They're not allowed to do the likes of this to any child.' She put some cream and bandages on my hands. 'Right, Lil, get your coat; we are not letting this go, but you have to promise me one thing.'

'Wha's tha', Mrs Kearney?'

'You'll keep that temper of yours under control.'

That was like asking for a miracle. You could see Ma was getting all riled up more and more as the minutes went by.

'I'll ask Mrs Kennedy next door to watch the children for you until we get back, Lil.'

Up to the school the three of us went. We were only in the door when we met two of the nuns, one of them being Sister Norma. She stood there with her chicken neck hanging out, looking down on us.

'Can I help you, ma'am?'

'Yeah, just tell me where tha' Twitchy Maher wan is,' said Ma.

'I beg your pardon? Twitchy? Twitchy who?'

'Twitchy fuckin' Maher. Are yeh deaf or wha'?'

I tipped Ma. 'Ma, it's tha' room at the top of the stairs, just up there.'

She took the stairs in twos, with the nuns running after her.

'Lil, come back,' Mrs Kearney shouted. 'You promised to keep your temper.'

Ma banged and kicked the door as she screamed for Twitchy to come out. I thought it was going to come off the hinges.

'What on earth is going on here?' Twitchy said, opening the door. She only had the words out of her mouth when Ma gave her the fist straight in the face. Twitchy fell to the floor. Ma was on top of her, pulling the hair out of her head.

'Beat my Kathleen, would yeh, yeh fuckin' bitch? No

wonder he left yeh standin' at the altar – with a face like tha' any man would run a mile.'

Sister Norma eventually managed to pull Ma up off Twitchy.

'Take yer hands off me! I'm warnin' yeh! You're just as bad for lettin' this happen, and don't pretend yeh don't know wha's goin' on around here! Why don't yeh get up off yer big fat arse and see wha's goin' on in this school, and the world out there for tha' matter. Yeh frustrated oul' fuck.'

Sister nearly fainted when she heard what was coming out of Ma's mouth. 'Mrs Doyle, how dare you speak to me in that manner!'

'Don't "Mrs Doyle" me, I'm tellin' yeh!' Sister couldn't get a word in edgeways; Ma was on a roll. 'Everybody around and in the school knows, Twitchy Maher's fella went off with another wan.' Ma roared into Sister's face. 'And tha's why she's a moody fucker. She won't be takin' her moods out on my child. I'll kill her first. Did yeh see wha' she done to my Kathleen?' She took the bandages off my hands.

When Sister Norma saw my hands, her face changed colour. She didn't know what to say or where to look. Then she tried to switch the blame from Twitchy to Ma.

'Now, Mrs Doyle, this is all down to you keeping Kathleen out of school and coming in late, upsetting the class and teacher.'

'I'm tellin' yeh, tha' Twitchy wan will never lay a finger on my Kathleen again or she'll have me to answer to.'

Ma just gave the look and shook her head, as she took me by the hand to bring me home.

* * *

Da was only in the door when Ma launched into the goings-on of the day. The first thing out of his mouth was, 'Lil, yeh didn't make a show of me in front of the nuns, did yeh?' The priests and nuns could do no wrong in Da's eyes.

114

'Fuck yeh, Phil Doyle, and them nuns – look at the state of Kathleen.' She held my hands out. He wasn't long pulling his words back.

Da brought me to school after a few days. He spoke to the Principal about what happened. He said the matter would be dealt with and there would be no charges brought against Mrs Doyle for attacking the teacher.

I was put back into Twitchy's class. Ma tried to send me to school as much as she could, which wasn't very often, but it didn't make any difference. Twitchy put me down the back of the class and taught me nothing. I never said anything to Ma or Da. It wouldn't have made any difference anyway – Da always had a sup on him and Ma was too busy with the babies. Sure, I thought, it was great not having to worry about doing schoolwork.

I'd take out a book the odd time and try to read it and sometimes I'd put up my hand in class to answer a question, but Twitchy would just pass me by, giving me the sly grin. That was her way of getting her own back on me for the day Ma went crazy mad.

Ma might have won the fight that day, but in the end Twitchy really won because when I left school I had little or no education at all. I couldn't read and was just about able to write my name. But what I did have, which Ma instilled in every one of us, was an inner strength and determination to make something of myself in life and never, ever to be as poor as I was as a child.

13

The Swimming Pool

Little Patricia was nearly a year old and not a bit of trouble. She'd sit in the pram, laughing and farting out at everyone. She always had a smile. Unlike Jacinta – you could see that she was going to be wild.

It was summer. I was sitting on the steps outside the front door rocking Jacinta in my arms trying to get her asleep. She was two years old and a desperate whinger. You wouldn't have a minute's peace, between her eating muck, climbing the garden walls and demolishing the few flowers we had left in the garden. You couldn't watch her.

I can't believe this, I thought. *It's bad enough that Clare is as mad as a hatter, but I now have another wild one to mind, one more to drive me nuts altogether, and it won't be too long before Patricia is handed over to me as well.*

Ma called out to me. 'Kathleen, I'm goin' out to do a bit of shoppin', see if I can pick up a few bargains. I'm takin' Patricia with me.'

'Sure, that's grand, Ma.' *You take the quiet one with you, and leave me with all the head-bangers.*

'I've to go down to the clinic. Patricia has to get one of her needles, so I'll be gone a while. Keep an eye on the rest of the

117

kids and don't let them carry on. They're not to *move* outside tha' gate! De yeh hear me, Kathleen? I'm dependin' on yeh to look after things for me. I've to get all this done before I get meself off to work.'

'Right, Ma, wha'ever yeh say.'

'Oh, Kathleen, I nearly forgot. There's some drippin' in the dish in the oven for when they get hungry. Get Carmel to put it on some bread. Tha'll keep yiz goin' until I get home.' *That's right, Ma, give Carmel the easy job to do. Don't ask her to do anything. Leave it all to me. Why can you not depend on her for a change, or Phil for that matter?*

Off Ma went with not a notion of what was going on inside my head. I was still giving out like mad to myself. *Dripping again,* I thought. *Jaysus, will we ever see a bit of real butter in this house? God, what's wrong with me? I'm doing nothing but giving out since this morning. I'm starting to sound like Ma. I'll have to stop.*

It was really hot that day. The kids were running around in their knickers out in the back garden. The two basins and buckets from the kitchen were brim full of water and the kids were having great fun splashing and trying to drown one another. After a while, they started whispering and giggling. I always knew when they were getting up to something.

'Wha' are yiz up to?' I shouted out at them.

'We were just sayin', Kathleen . . .' piped up Marion.

'I'm sorry I asked. Whatever it is, I don't want to know!'

'Will yeh just listen to us?' the rest of them shouted in.

'Right then. Go on. I'm listenin'.'

'Wouldn't it be great to have our own swimmin' pool, Kathleen?' says Clare, trying to suck up to me.

'Don't be stupid, Clare; only rich people have things like tha'.'

'We could make our own,' Marion and Noel roared at me.

'Are yiz nuts? Will yeh get away and leave me alone, the lot of yiz,' I shouted back.

I wasn't in any humour to listen to them. I was fed up; I wanted to go out, swing on the lamp-post and play with the rest of the kids on the street, playing beds, skipping, marbles, all the things they were doing. I didn't want to be always looking after babies.

Just then Phil came in. 'De yeh hear wha' them eejits are sayin', Phil? They're talkin' about makin' a swimmin' pool. Did yeh ever hear anythin' so stupid?'

'Wha' have yiz got in mind? I could do with a dip meself. I'm sweatin',' said Phil.

'We could get loads of clothes and block around the doors in the kitchen, then fill the room up with water,' said Clare and Noel.

That got Phil thinking: 'Could be done, Kathleen, could be done.'

'Are yiz all gone mad? Ma' would kill us stone dead. It's not goin' to happen, go away.'

I stood up and went into the kitchen with Jacinta in my arms, the rest of them all trailing behind me.

'Ah, go on, Kathleen,' they chimed in. 'Let's do it.'

'No, no, forget it, it's not happenin'.'

'Yeh're just like Ma,' says Clare. 'We're never let do anythin'.'

'No, I'm not like her! I'm me, I'm meself, I'm Kathleen.'

'Yeh are, yeh are,' they all roared.

'Fuck off, the lot of yiz, and leave me alone.'

'See. Yeh even curse like her,' said Carmel.

Phil took up the cry. 'Why don't yeh prove it then and let them? Ma does be gone for ages when she goes to the clinic. Sure we'll have it all brushed out the back yard by the time she comes home,' he added reassuringly. 'Come on, Kathleen, do it. Let yerself go for a change.'

Thomas was going mad, jumping up and down at the thought of a swimming pool. In fact, I must have gone a bit mad myself that day, because they finally got around me and I said 'yes'.

Before I knew it, they had blankets, coats, sheets and anything else they could get their hands on blocking every door in the kitchen. All the furniture was pushed into one corner of the room and then the basins and buckets were filled up right to the top with water, which was lashed all over the floor. We all took turns blocking the doors by lying against the coats and blankets, doing our best to keep the water in. We didn't get up off the floor until the water was way up past the skirting boards.

I got stripped down to my vest and knickers, and then stripped little Jacinta, leaving her with only a nappy on. We all jumped around like lunatics, while Phil kept lashing the buckets of water onto the floor. I was laughing and playing with the kids for a change and it felt good instead of giving out and always telling them what to do, which shouldn't have been left up to me. It wasn't fair.

Next thing, Noel got the kitchen table, tilted it against the wall and made a slide. We put the youngest ones onto the top of the table and then pushed them into the water. You'd want to have heard the screams of us! We had a great laugh, the best fun ever. The whole road must have been listening to us.

'Kathleen, yeh know the way yeh're always sayin' some day yeh're goin' to have a lovely bubble bath all to yerself?' asked Clare.

'Yeah. So? Wha's tha' got to do with all this?'

'Well, yeh're goin' to have one with all of us now!' she screamed, wheezing with the laughter. Then, before I could open my mouth, she shook half a box of washing powder into the water.

'Right, Marion, will yeh splash? Thomas, come over here and start kicking the water to make the bubbles.'

I couldn't stop them. They were all at it. Within minutes, the bubbles were nearly up to the ceiling. We couldn't even see one another. *Holy Jaysus. What am I after getting myself into?*

'Yeh stupid little fuck, Clare Doyle, we'll never get rid of these bubbles. Tha's it, we're all dead. Ma will be back soon. She'll kill us all first and then we'll be put in a home.'

Jacinta started crying. The suds had got into her eyes. Then the rest of them started whingeing. 'Me eyes, me eyes! They're burnin' me.'

With that, there was a big bang on the front door and everybody went really quiet.

'Who's that?' I asked.

'It's Mrs Kearney, Kathleen,' she called out in her posh accent. 'What is going on? Is Lil there? I can hear you from my garden. You're all being very boisterous.'

I opened the window. 'Ma brought Patricia to the clinic for her needles, Mrs Kearney.' I whispered in a low voice, 'Jacinta is asleep.' I was hoping she would just leave and not hear the mayhem going on behind me.

'You must have a burst pipe or something, Kathleen. There's water pouring down the three steps out here. Open the door. I'll get Jack to have a look.'

Oh Jaysus, how did the water get out the front? 'Ah, it's okay, Mrs Kearney, one of the kids knocked over a bucket of water.'

'There's a lot of water out here, Kathleen. Are you sure it was just a bucketful?'

As I kept Mrs Kearney distracted, the older kids were trying to get as much of the water out to the back yard as quickly as they could. But it was very hard, having only the one brush to do the job. Phil came up behind me.

'It's no good, Kathleen. The more I brush, the worse it's gettin'. Tha' tick Noel was dyin' to have a shite. Wha' does he only go an' do? Open the kitchen door to make a dart up to the toilet and now the suds are all over the hall.' By now, I was hanging out the window, smiling down at Mrs Kearney while Phil was roaring in my ear: 'Did yeh hear me, Kathleen?'

'Shut the fuck up until she goes,' I snarled at Phil over my shoulder.

Mrs Kearney was droning on. 'Make sure you dry that lino well, now. If a drop of water gets underneath, it will smell something terrible. And we can't have that, Kathleen, now can we?'

'No, Mrs Kearney. Thanks for knockin'.' I gave her a big smile.

Just as she turned to walk out the gate, I looked down the road and there was Ma puffing on her Woodbines, pushing the pram with one hand and waving to Mrs Kearney with the other. I ran into the kitchen shouting, 'Ma's at the corner.' There were suds and bubbles everywhere, bursting out all over the hall, on into the kitchen and out into the back yard.

'Wha'll we do? Wha'll we do, Kathleen?' the kids kept saying, looking at me and hoping I was going to fix the problem.

'I'm outta here,' said Clare.

She went to make a run for it but I grabbed her by the plaits. 'No, yeh're not, yeh little bitch. Now, get them towels off the line and start dryin' yerselves, de yeh hear me? Phil, the hall is burstin' with water. Wha'll we do?' I was frantic at this stage.

'Well, Kathleen, there's no two ways about it. We'll just have to open the front door, whether we like it or not. There's no other way.'

We tried to pull the door inwards to open it, but it wouldn't move. Phil took Noel and Thomas around to the front of the house so that they could help him push the door in while myself and Carmel pulled on the other side.

'Are yeh ready, Kathleen?' said Phil. 'Pull the door when I tell yeh to. Are yiz pullin'?'

'We are, Phil, but we keep slippin'.'

'Push, yiz lazy bastards. Noel, get yer fat arse up against the fuckin' door and push.'

'I am pushin' and don't call me fat.'

'Yeh are fat.'

By now, I was screaming through the letterbox at the lot of

them, telling them to stop fighting. All I could see was Noel's face going purple with temper. Phil knew how touchy Noel was and could get him going in no time. Phil kept up the stream of abuse: 'Yeh're just a big heap of shite, Noel. I've more strength in me little finger.'

'You fuck off, Phil Doyle.' Noel was like a bull, pushing like mad, and in seconds the door was open.

The water gushed down the three steps and out the front gate. Phil turned to Noel, giving him a good pat on the head and saying, 'Sure, I didn't doubt yeh for a minute, Noel. I knew once I got yeh goin' with tha' temper of yours, yeh would do all the work for me in no time.'

Phil didn't keep the grin on his face for long. I tipped him on the back and gave him the nod to look. When he turned around, there was Ma standing at the gate, the water gushing down through her sandals.

I was covered in suds and green in the face with fright. Carmel and Noel had vanished. Phil's face was as white as a sheet. We just stood there. Everything was quiet for a few seconds and it seemed to take ages for Ma to react. She looked at Phil and then back at me. We were sick in the pits of our stomachs. Mrs Kearney was standing beside Ma, saying, 'Now, Lil, let's not lose control here,' knowing full well the mad temper Ma had.

Ma looked down at her sandals and then straight back at us again. I must have suddenly gone deaf because I could see her mouth moving, but I could hear no sounds coming from her. I could feel Phil pulling at my vest, trying to get me to run with him. I was stuck to the ground. My feet wouldn't move; it was like Ma was moving in slow motion, coming towards us. Phil didn't run.

Mrs Kearney tried to pull Ma back, yanking at her cardigan. As Ma's arms came out of their sleeves, Mrs Kearney went flying back and landed on her arse. Ma didn't even notice that she had fallen as she charged at us, screaming. I jumped out of her way and landed on the only rose bush in the garden. That soon brought my hearing back! I was still in my vest and knickers, and now I had cuts all over me, with thorns stuck everywhere.

Phil went flying in the other direction and landed on the big black pram, or 'the bus', as we used to call it. As the two front wheels collapsed, all I could hear from Phil were the words 'holy fuck'. Within seconds, he too had gone missing with the rest of the kids. I got such a box in the head off Ma as she made her way into the house. As I pulled myself from the thorn bush, I could see Mrs Kearney struggling on the ground.

'Oh, Kathleen, love, come over here and help me up before anyone sees me,' said Mrs Kearney.

'Look at the pram. Ma uses tha' at night for the babies. She'll really go crazy mad when she sees the state of it. She'll kill us, Mrs Kearney, she will, I know she will.' I stood there trembling with fright.

'And what do you call that, Kathleen? Just listen to her. If that's not your mother going mad, I don't know what to say. You have really pushed her too far this time.'

Ma stood in the kitchen, screaming out the window. 'Bad cess ta yiz. When I get me hands on yiz I'm goin' to fuckin' kill yiz all. Me house is ruined. Wha's tha' on the floor? Me blankets, yeh shower of bastards! Holy Jaysus – wha's this? The only coat I have to me name. It's all tha' keeps me warm in the winter. Ah for Jaysus' sake, will yeh have a look at the bit of fur on the collar? It's like a dead fuckin' rat, so it is.'

I quickly went around the side of the house to see where the rest of the kids were hiding; they were up Mrs Tully's big tree, which was at the end of our back garden.

Ma ran out of the kitchen and spotted them in the tree. Mustering up every ounce of strength that she had, she started throwing stones, bricks and anything she could get her hands on. I didn't know if I was safer on the ground or up in the tree with the rest of them.

All the saints and scholars, popes and any statue that had a name in the Catholic Church got a mention that day. Then, after all the shouting and roaring, Ma walked up the garden, tears rolling down her face. Finally, after five or ten minutes, she remembered that she had left Patricia in the pram around the front of the house. Only now did she finally get around to spotting the unfortunate Mrs Kearney sitting on the steps, her two hands cut to bits.

'Holy Mother of God, Mrs Kearney. Wha' happened to yeh? Are yeh all right?'

'You knocked me flying in the air with that temper of yours, Lil Doyle!'

Ma starting crying again. 'I'm sorry, I'm sorry. Let me get yer hands cleaned up.'

Just then, Phil popped his head around the corner. 'Ah, Ma, I'm really sorry.' Ma would neither look at him nor answer him.

Mrs Kearney stepped in straight away.

'They're a wild bunch, Lil, there's no doubt about that. Now, I know the house is ruined, but if we all get stuck in, we'll have it back to normal in no time.'

Mrs Kearney stared straight at Phil, trying to get his attention.

'Phil, go up to my house and get Jack. Tell him to come down here and check the plugs. Lil, it's just to make sure it's safe to go back into your kitchen.' It wasn't long before Phil was up and back with Mr Kearney.

'Sorry, Ma. Sorry, Ma,' I kept saying.

But she wasn't having any of it. She just sat there with a stern look on her face, telling me that since I was the one who had been left in charge, I should have had more sense. I wanted to tell her that I didn't want sense. I wanted to be just like the rest of the kids. I didn't want to be in charge, I didn't want to be a Ma. But no time was ever the right time to say that to her.

Mrs Kearney asked for a glass of water and a damp cloth to wrap her cut hands in.

Well, you never saw Phil run as quick. He was in that kitchen and back to her in a flash, and was in there straight away, licking up to Ma.

'There yeh are, Mrs Kearney. We've no glasses, will a jam jar do? And one for yerself, Ma.' He smiled from ear to ear.

Mrs Kearney sat with Ma for ages, trying to keep her calm as she wrapped her hands in the sheet that Phil tore up in the kitchen. The rest of the kids slowly made their way down the garden to see if it was safe, one after the other mumbling, 'Sorry, Ma', 'Sorry, Ma'.

Ma sat there with the stern look still on her face, saying nothing.

* * *

Da was home early that day, with not a sup on him, thank God, and was in shock when he saw the state of the house. He stood there listening to Ma telling him all about what we kids had got up to. When she mentioned how there was a swimming pool made in the kitchen, he tried hard to keep a straight face. He knew that Ma was after giving all of us a lash and there was no point in him starting on us, because that would only get Ma going again. Instead, he tried to fix the situation, telling Ma not to be getting herself into a state. Amazingly, he wasn't long sorting things out. I stood there and listened to Da and thought to myself, *Why can't you be like this all the time? Then maybe things would be different for all of us.*

'Phil, lift this pram into the house with me, then get yerself and Noel out to the back yard and bring me in them two concrete blocks and put them under the pram. When I'm down in the scrap-yard tomorrow I'll pick up a couple of wheels. Now, hurry up. There's a lot to do. Kathleen, get yerself dressed and make yer mother and Mrs Kearney a cup of tea while I sort out this house.' He gave me a wink while Ma wasn't looking. I felt a bit better. 'The rest of youse girls get them coats and blankets, give them a good twist and throw them over the clothesline. Lil, the lino will have to be taken up off the floor. There's no savin' it.'

Ma looked at Da. 'Jaysus Christ, Phil! We're back to bare floorboards again!'

'It can't be helped, Lil. It'll stink us out of the house if I don't take it up.'

Ma glared at us kids and all she could say was 'Bad cess ta yiz all.'

'Come on now, Lil,' said Da, 'don't be keepin' it up. Wha's done is done. Anyway, yeh're runnin' late for work as it is. Yeh best be on yer way.'

'Phil is right, Lil,' says Mrs Kearney. 'You run along. I'll give a hand here.'

'Right then, Phil, I'll leave it to yiz. I'll only end up goin' crazy mad again if I stay here.'

Usually I would be giving out like mad to myself about having to mind all the kids when Ma went to work, but I was never as happy to see her head off that day, knowing that by tomorrow she would have calmed herself down, as she always did.

* * *

It took days for the coats and blankets to dry. The weather was good, so every door and window was open for a week to air the house. Da asked Mr Kearney to rig up a hose out in the back yard.

'Thanks, Jack. If it keeps them mad kids of mine happy and it stops me house floatin' down the road like Noah's Ark, sure wouldn't it be worth it, Jack, to give them a hose each?' said Ma, once again giving us kids the stern look.

You wouldn't even have the word 'warm' or 'sweating' out of your mouth when one of the kids would turn on the hose and drown you. We all made sure to be on our best behaviour, for a few days anyway, and nobody mentioned the word 'swimming pool' again.

Well, not for a long time anyway. We all knew better.

14

Chocolate and Turf

'Kathleen, go out the back yard and bring me in two heads of cabbage. I'm after gettin' a lovely bit of bacon and two sheets of ribs. Carmel, come 'ere.'

'Wha', Ma?'

'Put them bloody dolls away and start peelin' tha' small sack of spuds there. I'll try and get this dinner done before I get meself off to work. Tha' should keep yiz goin' until tomorrow. Kathleen, make sure when yeh're washin' tha' cabbage yeh check it well for maggots and flies. Tha's only fresh ou' o' the ground. It'll be crawlin' alive with them.'

'Did yeh have to say tha' Ma? Yeh'll be puttin' me off me dinner before I get it, for God's sake.'

'Don't be so bloody squeamish.'

'Oh God! There's loads of them. I'm not eatin' any of this.'

'Hold on a minute there, Kathleen. Who's tha' after comin' in?'

She caught Noel and Clare sneaking up the stairs.

Gobshites, I thought, *if they charged in like they always do, she wouldn't take any notice, but when they sneaked in she smelled a rat.*

'Wha' are yiz up ta?' she roared. 'Come down here, you two.'

'Hold on, Ma,' Noel said. 'I'm doin' me toilet.'

'I'll give yiz two seconds to get yer arses down here. If I have to go up them stairs after yeh, it's the back of me hand yeh'll be gettin'.'

The two of them made their way down and walked into the kitchen.

'Holy divine Jaysus! Would yeh have a look at the cut of them, Kathleen?'

I had to put my hand up to my face to stop myself laughing or Ma would end up killing us all.

Noel was around seven years of age by this time. He was a big heavy young fella, with slanty eyes, his hair shaved, skin tight into his head. 'Jap-head', we used to call him. Clare was a year younger, as skinny as ever, with her long black plaits and the biggest green eyes you ever saw. She was trying to hide behind Noel, but he kept pushing her to the front. They were covered from head to toe in muck, except for their faces; that was full of chocolate.

'Yiz were up in tha' dump again!' shouted Ma, running at the two of them. Noel got a right box in the head. Clare must have run around the table a dozen times. Ma couldn't catch her; she was like lightning.

'Wha' did I tell yiz about goin' up to tha' fuckin' place? A disease yeh'll get! Tha' chocolate's dumped because it's gone off. There's rats pissin' and shitin' all over it. Can I not get tha' into tha' tick skull of yers?' She gave Noel another box. 'As for you, Clare, yeh skinny little fuck, if I get me hands on yeh, I'll redden the arse off yeh for not listenin' to me.'

Clare was like a hare, running around the table, in and out the back yard before Ma could catch her. She dragged the pair of them by the scruff of the neck up the stairs.

'Yiz'll be eatin' soap for a week by the time I'm finished with the two of yiz. I'll be the talk of the road with this carry-on; makin' a holy show of me, so yiz are.'

I'm sure the people at the top of the road could hear the

roars of them and Ma as she scrubbed them in a bath of ice-cold water.

'I haven't got time to start molly-coddlin' yiz, heatin' pots of water. *Think* the next time. This is wha' yiz'll have to face, if yeh go near tha' dump again. Are yiz listenin'?' And the pair of them got another box.

Ma made her way down the stairs, breathless from all the running around.

'Tha's the two of yeh sorted out. Now sit at the fire, the pair of yiz, and heat yerselves up there before yeh freeze to death. Right then, Kathleen, is them spuds and cabbage done?'

'They are, Ma.'

Carmel always took half the day to do anything, but by God those spuds were peeled in record time.

'I hope the rest of yiz don't go near tha' dump.' She looked over at me.

'No, Ma. We wouldn't do tha'. Would we, Carmel?'

'Never, Ma, honest to God. We don't.'

'*Hmm* . . . I hope not.'

If she only knew the lies I told for them; the half of what they got up to when her back was turned! Not a day went by that two or three of them weren't up in that dump, rooting out old bits of scrap, never mind the chocolate. They got cute and stopped eating the chocolate themselves, copping on that it was giving them the shites; but they didn't care who else ate it or what state their arse ended up being in. They'd clean it and break it up into squares, put it into a bit of paper, pretending that one of our aunties worked in a sweet factory, and sell two or three pieces for a penny. Any bits of scrap would be brought around to Wally around the corner. He'd buy anything for a shilling or two.

In the middle of all this mayhem, Phil walked in with a smile stretching from ear to ear.

'There yeh are, Ma. There's a few shillings. Help yeh with the messages.'

131

'Where did this money come from, Phil?'

'Sure, I was up helpin' Paddy load the turf into his van, up there in the turf depot.'

'Who's this Paddy fella?'

'Yeh know him. He lives down Sundrive Road. Everybody knows Paddy, Ma. He's always up there gettin' the turf for the old folks. Isn't tha' right Noel, Clare? Tell 'er, didn't yeh see me?'

'Yeah Ma, I did.'

'I can't place him at the minute but he sounds like a good man. Phil, I hope yeh thanked him now.'

'Course I did, Ma.'

'I'll go out meself tomorrow and tell him any time he needs a bit of help, just knock here. There's always one or two of yiz around to give him a hand.'

You could see the panic on Phil's face, knowing he'd been lying through his teeth to Ma; he had really been up in the dump with the other two. They didn't know where to look. Noel wouldn't look at Phil, because they'd start laughing, and then Ma would smell a rat once more, so they just kept looking at me. I just gave them a little grin, thinking: *Nice one – I'll have these in me grip for a little while anyway. They'll jump any time I need a bit of work done.*

Phil chimed in, 'No, Ma, don't do tha'; don't go out to him. I want him to think I'm all grown-up and can get me own work.'

She thought for a minute. 'Hmm . . . right then, I'll leave it with yeh.'

He was nearly fourteen and just about ready to start work anyway.

* * *

Phil was outside the turf depot as soon as he got in from school the next day, waiting on Paddy to come along. And, sure enough, he got himself a job.

When Phil came home that evening after finishing work with Paddy, he was telling Ma all about how he was able to lift the sacks of turf onto his back and carry them into the back yards for the old people.

'You'd want to see the money tha' he makes! A wad of notes in his pocket, he had.'

Ma sat there and listened, taking it all in and saying nothing.

The next morning we were all eating our breakfast when Ma turned around to us.

'I want yiz all to listen to wha' I have to say.'

Everyone looked at one another with panic on their faces, wondering if they were after getting caught for whatever they'd been up to the day before.

'I got a bit of a brainstorm last night after listenin' to yeh, Phil, about all the money yer man Paddy is makin'. I wonder, does he deliver the turf around here?'

'I'm way ahead of yeh, Ma. No he doesn't, I already asked him tha'. He goes all around Sundrive, Walkinstown, Drimnagh and Kimmage, he said. He never does around here; the houses are too close to the turf depot and it wouldn't pay him.'

'Right then, tha's all I wanted to hear.' She rubbed her two hands together. 'When yiz come home from school today I want a couple of yiz bigger ones to go knockin' on the doors. Start with Mrs Kennedy next door and every house after tha', right up to the top of the road, all the houses at the back of us and right down onto Cashel Road. Ask around and see if they would like the turf delivered for as little as a shillin'. No roarin' and shoutin' when yeh knock. See wha' they have to say – and one more thing, make sure yeh smile. Yeh're bound to get a few jobs outta tha'.'

The kids were all tryin' to get their spoke in.

'I want to get the turf, let me go.'

'Ma, how are we goin' to get the turf to the people?' Phil asked.

133

Ma put her hand on the big black pram. 'I'm goin' to give yiz the bus. I think it's seen its day as far as puttin' me babies into it goes. There's nothin' only tears and rips everywhere. But the frame is still very strong. It'll do the job.'

I was so happy when I heard Ma say that. *Could this mean she's finished having babies? I hope so.*

* * *

It didn't take long for us to build up a turf round. People were well pleased with the price and so was Ma with the extra money. Phil was great; as soon as they were old enough, he taught all of the kids how to lift the sacks and tip them into the back yards. When they would be standing there waiting to get paid, he would be twisting the ear of whoever was with him.

'Remember now wha' Ma said – show yer pearly whites and smile. Yeh never know, we might get an extra penny.'

As Ma always said, a smile never cost anything but could make you plenty in life. She was right; it always did.

That was the start of the turf round. It was handed down to each and every one of us and went on to make a few shillings for Ma.

15

The Rat and the Sword

Da stayed off the drink for a good few months this time. He got himself back into the garden. There were rows of cabbages, spuds, lettuce, onions and scallions. You name it, he planted it. The back garden was very big and he would spend hours out there in the summer. Ma even made herself a few bob, selling the vegetables to some of the neighbours.

Ma was standing at the back door with Jacinta in her arms, as proud as punch. It was great to see her smile and be happy for a change.

'Would yeh look out there at yer father, Kathleen. He's as happy as Larry, diggin' and weedin'. I swear tha' man has green fingers. Look at the size of them heads of cabbage; yeh could feed an army, they're tha' big.'

I thought to myself, *Wouldn't it be great if things stayed like this forever?*

But that wasn't to be.

Word got around the road: the best of veg at number fifty-one. When any of the neighbours knocked, they would get a right load of stuff for little or nothing.

'How much do I owe yeh, Lil?' they would ask.

'Just give me a few bob when yeh get yer allowance, and

don't forget now. God is good – isn't he keepin' tha' man of mine busy and off the drink.'

'It's a curse, Lil, a bloody curse!'

Peter next door and Mrs Kearney up the road never had to knock. Every week Ma would make up a parcel for each of them with everything that Da grew. Ma always told whichever one of us was bringing the bag into them not to take a penny, no matter what they said, because they were very good to us. Ma drilled it into each and every one of us. 'When yeh can, it's nice to be able to give and not always be takin'.'

* * *

In the summer Ma would have all of us up from early morning. She would never let any of us stay in the bed.

'It's not good for yeh, makes yer brain lazy. There'll be no wasters in my house, not if I have anythin' to do with it.'

Ma would call once, then twice, and if you were not halfway down the stairs the third time you would get a box in the back of the head or a good root up your arse.

'Phil, Kathleen, Carmel! Get yerselves washed first, you go first, Phil; as soon as yeh're finished, get back down here and start dishin' out the porridge with Clare. Kathleen and Carmel, start cleanin' out the bedrooms while yeh're waitin' to get washed. Open all the windows, pull back the blankets and check and see if anyone pissed in the bed last night. And when yeh're at it, give them blankets a good bang and shake – make sure there's no hoppers in them. Shake the DDT powder in – tha'll kill the little fuckers.'

There was a double bed in the back bedroom for Ma and Da, and a cot for the new baby, Patricia.

'Wha' are yeh doin' Carmel?'

'I'm checkin' the beds, like Ma said.'

'Carmel, don't be such a gobshite. Yeh hardly think Ma and Da piss on themselves, for Jaysus' sake! She was talkin' about the two beds in our room.'

The four girls slept in one double and the three boys slept in the other. I pulled the blankets off the bed and as usual it was always the girls' bed with the pissy stains. I took the sheet off, went down to the kitchen and slipped it in the washing machine.

Ma was feeding little Patricia. 'Wet again, Kathleen.'

'Just a bit, Ma.'

I went over to the table where Marion and Clare were sitting, stuffing their mouths with porridge.

'Right, which one of yiz is pissin' in the bed? I'm sick of wakin' up every morning with a smell on me. It's not me or Carmel so it has to be one of yiz.

Clare jumped up with embarrassment. 'How de yeh know it's not one of them?' She pointed at Phil, Noel and Thomas, who were laughing and whispering to one another. 'They could easily come over in the middle of the night and do a sneaky piss. Phil Doyle would make them do it for a laugh.'

Before I could say anything, the three boys started singing, 'Smelly knickers, Clare, piss in the bed Marion, pissy, pissy, pissy!'

Marion started crying. Clare made a run at them. Phil jumped out of her way. Thomas was only four, so she left him alone. She knew Ma would kill her if she punched him, so she dived on Noel. She was a wild little bitch and afraid of nobody.

'Kathleen, wha's goin' on? The noise of yiz!'

'Ma, they're only messin'.'

'Well, let them get out the back yard and do their messin'; I'm tryin' to get the child asleep.'

Noel shouted, 'Get her off me, Kathleen, she's a head-banger.'

'Clare, will yeh stop, for God's sake.'

'They started it, Kathleen.'

'I don't care who started it. It's bad enough I have to drag Ma off Da when she's all roused up without me havin' to do it with yiz as well. Now stop it!'

Carmel just sauntered out to the yard, not giving too shites who was killing who. Phil was sitting on the kitchen sink,

137

turning blue he was laughing that much, and Thomas was dancing on the table, cheering.

'Clare won, Clare won.'

Noel stretched out and gave Thomas a right kick in the leg.

'Shut the fuck, yeh little turncoat.'

'Right! Out the back yard, all of yiz, before Ma comes in.'

Marion was still sitting by herself, crying. 'It's me, Kathleen, wettin' in me knickers. It just happens, I don't know I'm doin' it. I'm sorry – don't tell Ma.'

'Marion, it's okay, Ma won't fight with yeh. She'll get yeh checked and make sure yeh're all right.'

Clare came over. 'Don't cry, Marion.'

'I told her it was me wettin' the bed.'

'De yeh want me to batter Noel again? I will, I'll kill him for yeh.'

Marion just laughed, she was an oul' softy. Clare always looked after her; they were great pals. 'You two go in and clean the kitchen, I'll talk to Ma.'

Tha's them sorted for a while, anyway, I thought.

* * *

Every morning Da pulled up outside our house in the bin truck, ten o'clock on the dot, for a cup of tea with the other men. There was Ronnie the driver, Jembo, Blinkie and Mickey. They'd all worked together for years and were the best of friends.

During the summer holidays, us kids loved to see them stopping for the cup of tea. They would have a right load of sandwiches with them. I think they used to get their wives to put an extra bit in just for us. The minute they sat down we'd all stand around the table looking into their faces to see what we could get from them.

'You lot get yerselves out the back yard and play! Yeh're makin' a show of me,' Ma shouted.

Ronnie laughed, 'Not at all, Lil, sure I think tha' woman of mine thinks I'm eatin' for half the Corporation.'

Blinkie and Mickey chimed in with the same response: 'Mine too, Lil.'

'Lil, it will only be thrown out. And anyway, sure don't yeh make us our tea every mornin'? We all live too far to go home for a break.'

'Ah, here now, yeh can't be throwin' out good food like tha', and I couldn't let yeh sit out in tha' smelly bin truck now, could I, Mickey?'

Ma was a very proud woman and tried to hide how bad things really were at times, which was most of the time for her. As soon as Da and the men would leave to go back to work, Ma would call us in.

'Sit down at the table, the lot of yeh, and we'll see wha' we have here.'

The sandwiches would be cut to a finger size; Ma made sure every one of us got a taste. Sometimes if we were lucky we would get two or three each. There could be a bit of egg in one, cheese in another, but the ones we all loved the best were the sausage and rasher sandwiches; your mouth would be watering and you'd wish you had more.

* * *

One day, it was only nine o'clock when the bin truck pulled up.

I was sitting on the front steps, with Patricia in my arms, trying to get her asleep.

'Kathleen, is tha' yer father I hear out there?'

'Yeah, Ma, they're early today.'

Ma came out to see what was going on.

'Holy Jaysus, wha's after happenin' to yeh, Phil?'

Da was limping up the garden path; he had only one boot on and one of the legs of his trousers was ripped right up to his waist.

'Lil, yeh'd never believe wha's after happenin' to me. I'm lucky to be standin' here alive. Isn't tha' right', Blinkie?'

'He's not tellin' a word of a lie, Lil, I was nearly a goner meself.'

139

'Hold on a minute until I put the teapot on.'

'Are yeh listenin', Lil? Wha' are yeh doin'?'

'I'm lookin' for me Woodbines, Phil, will yeh hold on. Righ', I have them – go on now, tell me wha' happened.'

'We went down to the flats our usual time, eight o'clock. I was pullin' out one of the large bins from the chute. It was full to the brim, overflowin' with rubbish, so it was, when I felt somethin' runnin' up me leg. I let out such a scream then, I couldn't talk. I just stood there with me mouth open, holdin' the top of me trousers, pointin' down between me legs.'

'Ronnie roared over, "Jaysus, Phil, wha's wrong with yeh? Yeh're gone an awful bad colour – are yeh alrigh'?"

'"It's . . . it's . . . it's a fuckin' rat! It's between me legs. Get it out, get the fuckin' thing out!" I was roarin' all over the place.'

'Phil, yeh never said "fuck" – you don't curse! I don't believe yeh,' Ma said.

'Believe him, Lil, the whole of the flats heard him screamin'.'

'Such a day I'm after havin', Lil.'

'Did it bite yeh?'

'How the hell do I know if it bit me or not? Wasn't I bangin' and punchin' down there tha' hard, I don't know whether the rat or meself done the most damage.'

'Well, yeh better keep yerself to yerself, Phil Doyle, and not be comin' near me until the doctor has a look at yeh.'

Ma was laughing and giving the men a wink.

'Will yeh watch wha' yeh're sayin' in front of the men, for God's sake, Lil.'

'Don't be so fuckin' serious, Phil, will yeh!' She walked into the kitchen to make the tea for the men. 'I'm afraid yeh'll have to settle for yer tea in jam jars today. There's not a cup left in the house with them kids.'

'We don't mind, Lil, a cup of tea out of a jam jar is the tastiest yeh'll get,' Jembo answered.

'Lil, are yeh goin' to stay quiet and let me finish?'

'Go on, go on, Phil, I'm listenin'.'

'Ronnie put me lyin' down on me back while Mickey pulled me boot off. He had to slit the leg of me trousers with his penknife. He grabbed the rat by the throat and choked it to death there and then, right in front of me.'

Ma screamed with fright. 'For fuck's sake, Mickey, yeh didn't! How could yeh do tha'?'

'I did, Lil, I did. There's nothin' to it. I live along the canal and the rats come up to the bins all the time. Mind you now, yeh have to be very fast – grab and twist the little fuckers' necks or yeh'd never catch them.'

'Mickey, will yeh stop, for Jaysus' sake, yeh're makin' me sick.' She lit another Woodbine.

'I swear, Lil, it was the size of a cat. Jembo, back me up, tell 'er.'

'Phil's not tellin' a word of a lie.'

'There's more, Lil,' Da went on, getting more worked up by the minute. 'I hadn't even got the colour back in me face when this fella hangs out over the top balcony of the flats and starts threatenin' us. "Will yeh ever keep quiet down there," says he. "I'm tryin' to get some sleep up here! Now, fuck off or I'll come down and sort yiz all out."

'"Who the hell de yeh think yeh're talkin' to?" Ronnie roars up at him. "Yeh'll be sortin' nobody out – an' serve yeh better to get up off yer arse and get yerself a job, yeh lazy heap o' shite."'

Ronnie was well over six foot tall and as broad as an ox; he had a big porter belly. Ma was forever slagging him. 'I don't know who looks like they're havin' the babies around here, Ronnie, you or me.' Ma was the only one who could get away with sayin' things like that to him.

Da went on. 'I was bendin' down, Lil, just about to put me boot back on, when yer man from the top flat comes chargin' down at us with a samurai sword. "I'll show yiz who's a heap of shite," he roared as he swung the sword all over the place. "Talk to me like tha', will yiz, with the wife and kids listenin'? I'll fuckin' kill one of yiz first." He was lashin' the sword against the walls, and takin' lumps out of the bin truck at the one time. There was no talkin' to him, Lil. He was full of the whiskey – yeh could smell it a mile away.'

Ronnie took up the story. 'I meself like a sup now and again, but yeh never saw the likes of it, Lil. His eyes were roarin' red in his head. He was out for blue murder, so he was. I'm afraid of no man, I'd take the best of them on. I think yeh know tha' yerself, Lil.'

'I do, Ronnie, no better man than yerself.'

'But a man with a sword, now tha's a different kettle of fish altogether. We were runnin' all around the flats, up and down the stairs, tryin' to get away from him. He was out of control. I thought he was goin' to take Blinkie's head off. He missed him by an inch – am I right there, men?'

'Yeh are, Ronnie, not a word of a lie.'

'Only Mickey jumped over the railin's, run and got the police, God only knows wha' would have happened,' said Da. 'It took us all our strength to hold him down until he was taken away in the police wagon. Sure, look at me, I hadn't even got time to get me other boot back on, Lil.'

'It sounds like yiz were lucky to get out in one piece, Phil.'

'I'm tellin' yeh, it was touch and go there for a while. I tell yeh one thing for nothin', Lil, yeh won't be seein' me in them flats again, not unless tha' maniac is sorted out. I'll give the job up first, and we'll be sayin' the same,' said Ronnie. 'The funny thing about all this, Lil, when he sobers up tomorrow he won't remember a thing and one of us could have been lyin' in the city morgue, dead as a dodo.'

'I know somebody like tha', Ronnie.' Ma looked straight over at Da. 'Remembers only wha' he wants to, when it suits him. Isn't tha' right, Phil Doyle?'

'For God's sake, Lil, I've had a bad enough day without yeh rubbin' and clippin' at me and in front of the men.'

'Hurry up and get changed, Phil,' Ronnie said, giving Da the eye. 'Yeh'll have to get yerself looked over by the doctor, and we've to get the bin truck back to the yard to be checked and tell the foreman wha' happened. Thanks for the tea, Lil.'

After they'd left, Ma sighed. 'Isn't tha' terrible, Kathleen?'

'Wha's tha', Ma?'

'The men didn't have time to even open their sandwiches, and all over tha' gobshite in the flats carryin' on like a madman.'

'They'll be able to have them later on, Ma.'

'Tha's not wha' I mean, Kathleen. I was dependin' on them few bits they leave me every day to make some lunch later for yiz. There's hardly anythin' to eat. Ah well, nothin' I can do about it now.'

* * *

Da came home early that day.

'Wha's wrong now, Phil Doyle, was there trouble over this mornin'? Is yer job safe?'

'Will yeh stop worryin' all the time, Lil. I'm home because the doctor said so. He gave me a shot in the arse.'

'Why's tha', Phil?'

'Tha' bastard of a rat gave me a nick down there. I was screamin' and bangin' meself tha' much I didn't feel it. He gave me a sick note for a few days; he said I'll be rightly swollen by tomorrow.'

'Phil, wha' de yeh mean "down there"? Is it yer leg or wha'?'

'Yeh know wha' I mean, Lil.' He rolled his eyes in the air, getting himself more worked up by the minute.

'Oh, I see, yeh mean yer balls, Phil, is tha' wha' yeh're tryin' to say?'

'Jaysus, Lil, will yeh watch yer mouth in front of the kids? It's a bar of carbolic soap yeh need to clean out tha' mouth of yours.'

'Are yeh goin' to tell me or wha', Phil? Yeh're turnin' yer eyes crossways in yer head. I don't know wha' yeh mean.'

'Right then, it seems yeh're goin' to keep it up until I tell yeh. Yes, yes, yes, I'll say it – balls, balls, balls – me balls! Is tha' enough for yeh, Lil? Are yeh happy now tha' I said it. I can't get a bit of privacy around here with yeh. I'm goin' upstairs.' He slammed the door behind him.

Ma roared up the stairs after him. 'Yeh're a cranky fuck, Phil Doyle, tha's wha' yeh are. I was only askin' wha' happened.'

'Well, now yeh know, Lil. Are yeh happy? Yeh'd bring out the worst in anybody, so yeh would.'

I was in shock when I heard Da roaring and cursing, as you would never hear him speak like that or be rude to anybody.

'Ma, Da's real annoyed, I never saw him like tha' before.'

'Never mind yer father, Kathleen, he can be a bloody crank at times. Gather the kids up and put them sittin' down at the table. A half an egg and a slice of bread will have to do; tha's all I have. We missed out on our sandwiches today.' She mumbled to herself as she cooked the eggs.

'Are yeh talkin' to yerself again, Ma?'

'Well then, I'll say it out loud and clear for yeh. There's just one thing I have to say about the goin's-on of the day, Kathleen.'

'And wha's tha', Ma?'

'Fuck yer man with tha' sword, and fuck tha' rat.'

* * *

Da was out of work for the next two weeks because 'down below' was swollen so bad and he had himself in a terrible mood with Ma because she had made him say 'balls' in front of us kids. He kept himself busy out the back garden, digging, weeding, and planting a few seeds, keeping out of Ma's way. And the pubs, for that matter. For a little while anyway. Da thought he would never get himself back to work quickly enough, away from Ma's watchful eye, so he could get back to his old ways again.

I loved my Da so much, but I would get so angry with him at times, but only ever in my thoughts. *Does he care about us?* I would wonder. *If I can see what is happening, why can he not?* I should have said something. Why didn't I speak out and try to make him see sense? But they weren't the ways back then. Children were seen and not heard: that's what we were told. Speak only when you're spoken to, and never answer back.

16

Fish and Chips

'Kathleen, where are yeh?'

'I'm upstairs, Ma.'

'Come down here, I want yeh to do somethin' for me. I was talkin' to one of the Caffola sisters down there in the chip shop earlier on. I want yeh to go down around three o'clock, take one or two of the kids with yeh. She was tellin' me tha' she does have bits of broken fish left over from the night before and, if I'd like, she'd keep them for me. Now, when yeh go into the shop, tell 'er Lil sent yeh and don't forget to use yer manners. Oh, and another thing – make sure to give her a big smile. Tha' way she might throw in a few chips. If she does, don't touch even one, or I'll take the hand off yeh, de yeh hear me now, Kathleen? Tha'll help me make a bit of dinner for tonight with a few mash potatoes.'

I arrived on the dot of three with Carmel and Clare, calling across the tall counter: 'Hello Missus, me Ma Lil sent us for the bits of fish and a few chips.'

Carmel nudged me. 'Kathleen, yeh were only supposed to ask for fish.'

'Shut up, will yeh, or she'll hear yeh! Tha's wha' Ma meant

when she told us to smile. Have yeh not got any cop-on at all, Carmel?'

The three of us stood there with smiles on our faces the length of the shop, hoping that she would put more than a few chips in the bag, so we could nick one or two on the way home and, to our surprise, she did. On top of all that, she handed each of us a chip bag full to the top with all the bits of crisps that she had taken from the bottom of the pan. We were over the moon.

'Now, girls, tell your mother to send you down every day to me and I'll keep any bits I have for her.'

There was no end to the smiles on our faces as we left the shop and Ma was well pleased with the news.

We went down to the chip shop over the following weeks and were standing outside one day waiting for the queue to empty, when this woman on her way out of the shop put a bag of chips into one of my hands and a shilling in the other. I stood there and looked at her, not knowing what to say or do.

'Share them with the other two little ones and bring that money home to your mother.' And off she went about her business with not another word spoken, leaving me standing there with my mouth open, not understanding what it was all about.

'Kathleen, why did tha' woman give yeh money and chips?' Clare and Carmel asked.

'How do I know? I don't know everythin', do I! We'll ask when we go home. Now, come on, we'll go in and get the bits of fish for Ma.'

The three of us devoured the bag of chips on the way home, only telling Ma about the shilling.

'Now why did tha' woman give yiz this shillin'? Wha' were yiz doin' when she handed it to yeh, Kathleen?'

'Nothin', Ma, we were just standin' there, I swear.'

She stood back and looked at the three of us. Then out of the blue she burst out crying.

'I'm sorry, Ma. I thought yeh'd be glad. I promise I won't take money off anyone again.'

'It's not tha' Kathleen, I'm only glad of the shillin'. Tha'll get me a loaf of bread and a drop of milk. I'm cryin' over the fact tha' yiz look so poor. Is it any wonder the woman gave yeh money? Look at the three of yiz – yer dresses are fallin' apart, and the shoes on yer feet are barely holdin' together. Pity tha's wha' it was, pity.' She broke down crying again.

The three of us stood there looking at one another, not knowing what to do or say.

'This is not the life I wanted for any o' yiz, but it's the best I can do for now.'

None of us cared or took much notice of what state our clothes or shoes were in. The only thing that would have been on my mind from day to day was whether we were going to get any dinner or would it be bread and dripping again.

Ma finally calmed herself down and got on with checking out what was in the bag, hoping there would be enough to go around all of us. It wouldn't matter how little you got; she always made sure everybody got a taste.

* * *

I was dying for Phil to come home so that I could tell him what had happened and to see what he thought. He stood there listening to me, taking it all in.

'Well, wha' de yeh think, Phil?'

'We could be on to a good thing here, Kathleen.'

'How can it be a good thing? Ma was real upset and all.'

'Yeh're an awful gobshite at times, de yeh know tha'? Can yeh not see further than yer nose? We could make ourselves a few shillin's out of this.'

'But how, Phil, wha' de yeh mean?'

'I'll go down with yiz the next time. If yer wan thought yiz looked bad, wait 'til she sees me. Would yeh have a look at the state of me shoes? And with not an elbow left in me jumper, sure they'll be throwin' the money at me.'

I looked down at Phil's feet and, right enough, his stockings were sticking out from the toes of his shoes and his jumper was in a bad way.

Sure enough, Phil was standing outside the chip shop the following day when I arrived with Clare.

'Right then, Kathleen, show me wha' yiz were doin' just before tha' wan gave yeh the money.'

'We were doin' nothin', only standin' like the way we are now. I told yeh all this last night, so wha' are yeh shitin' out of yeh for?'

'Wha' I'm tryin' to find out off yeh is, were yiz jumpin' around laughin' and playin', or were yiz standin' there all serious and miserable.'

'We were talkin', tha's all, I keep tellin' yeh.'

'Good, tha's wha' I wanted to hear. Tha' means yeh were a bit serious. Right – are yeh listenin' to me, Kathleen? – if yeh see anybody goin' to pass by us, put a real sad face on, tha' way they might pity us and give us a few pennies, or maybe a shillin' or two.'

'Phil, if we do get money, how are we goin' to give it to Ma? We can't say somebody gave it to us; she'd smell a rat, or get upset and start cryin' again.'

'Kathleen, don't yeh know I always have a back-up plan? I'll tell her the turf round is doin' well and she'll be none the wiser. And I have another little scheme goin' around in me head if this doesn't work.'

I was soon to learn Phil's other little scheme. Myself and Phil, with a couple of the little ones, would stand at the bus stop, lying through our teeth, telling people as they got off the bus that we lived in Walkinstown, which was a good distance from Crumlin, too far for the small ones to walk, and that we'd lost our bus fare. That got us loads of pity and plenty of pennies in our pockets. Outside the chip shop didn't work too well, so it was the bus stop every time, until one day we were standing there with our sad faces on us when Mrs Kearney tipped me on the shoulder. I nearly wet my knickers with the fright. Phil scarpered and left me to face her on my own.

'Kathleen Doyle, before you start telling me a string of lies, I have been standing over by the chemist for the past ten minutes, watching you and Phil. Do you realise what you are doing? You are begging, that's what you are doing – begging!'

'No, we're not, Mrs Kearney. The people are real nice; they were just givin' us a few pennies.' I hoped I could pull the wool over her eyes, but she wasn't having any of it.

'Well then, Kathleen, you won't mind me telling your mother how kind all these people have been to you.'

'No, no, Mrs Kearney, please don't! We're tryin' to make some money for Ma. Things are really bad; some days there's not enough money to buy any messages. Ma thinks we're makin' extra money on the turf round. Please don't tell her, she'll get all upset and cry, then she'll kill us.'

Her voice softened. 'Do you not think I know that? I have no intentions of telling on you. Your mother is a very proud woman and if she got the slightest inkling of this it would kill her, never mind all of you. Now, Kathleen, I want you to promise me that none of you will ever do this again.'

'I swear we won't.' I made the sign of the cross, knowing Mrs Kearney was really religious, hoping that she'd believe me even more.

'Right then, Kathleen, we'll leave it at that; but I will still be keeping an eye on you, so pass that message on to young Phil.'

I was so glad it was Mrs Kearney who tipped me on the shoulder that day and not Ma. We still went down to the chip shop for the bits of fish, but we didn't hang around there too long, and the only time after that day we went near a bus stop was to get on a bus.

* * *

Phil wasn't long coming up with another of his little schemes.

'Kathleen, come 'ere, I want to talk to yeh.'

'Fuck off, Phil; wha'ever it is, I'm sayin' no. I don't care, yeh do nothin' only get me into trouble. Yeh left me standin' on me own with Mrs Kearney the other day at the bus stop, scampered off, so yeh did. She gave me a right mouthful, yeh know wha' she's like; there was no end to the threats I got from 'er.'

'Would yeh give it over, Kathleen, yeh're well able to handle her and anyone else around the road. Anyway, never mind all tha' shite, tha's over and done with. It's now we have to worry about. Did yeh see the few scrappin's tha' Ma was tryin' to make a dinner from? There's not enough food to go around. Wha' she has will have to do the little ones. Come on with me, Kathleen, we'll have to do somethin'. Get yer coat and while yeh're in the house grab the net bag Ma gets the messages in. Tell 'er yeh're comin' with me to deliver a few sacks of turf; tha' way she won't smell a rat.'

We weren't long dropping the turf off to a couple of houses on Cashel Road, making ourselves a shilling or two. Phil left the big pram at the side of one of his customers' houses, saying he would pick it up on the way back. Off we headed down towards the Old County Road shops, with Phil filling me in on his plan as he tied the net bag on the belt around his trousers, which was well covered up with his jacket.

'Kathleen, before we go into the shop, take this shillin'. Now, wha' I want yeh to do is pick somethin' out to buy, then change yer mind a few times. Tha'll get up yer wan's back tha's servin' yeh and have her all annoyed and worked up. Now when yeh're doin' tha', first chance I get, I'll grab anythin' I can tha' we can eat. I'll give yeh the eye and the nod tha' I'm finished, but wha'ever yeh do, don't leave the shop without buyin' somethin'. Tha' way we won't look too sussie. And whatever yeh do, get somethin' we can eat – don't go spendin' the shillin' on soap or powder. Yeh know wha' a cleanin' freak yeh've turned into, always moppin' up around yeh.'

'Oh, I don't know, Phil, robbin' out of the shops! No, I'm too afraid, I can't do it. Anyway, it's a sin and I'd never be able to tell the priest I was out robbin'.'

'For Jaysus' sake, just say an extra few Hail Marys tonight when yeh're sayin' yer prayers! Now, will yeh give it over, I need yeh to keep nicks for me.'

I still wasn't moving.

'Right then, don't help me. I'll do it on me own, but if I get caught it'll be all yer fault. Anyway, it's Ma yeh should be thinkin' about, not yer bloody sins.'

'Okay, okay, I'll do it. But yeh have to promise me, Phil, yeh'll say nothin' to nobody, ever.'

'I don't think this is somethin' I'll be goin' around braggin' about. Now, will yeh shut the fuck up, Kathleen, and get into the shop.'

'There's just one more thing, Phil. If we're goin' to be robbin', will yeh try and get a bit of real butter? It's so long since we had some.'

'Tha's more like it, Kathleen.'

He gave me a sly grin, pushing me into the shop ahead of him. I got the poor woman behind the counter so confused she was nearly tearing her hair out by the time I was finished, giving Phil enough time to get as much as he could into the net bag.

Ma couldn't believe her eyes when we handed her the bag of messages. Of course, the first thing she did was to ask where the money came from. As always, Phil had all the answers, telling Ma that he collected bits of scrap and copper off the people while he was doing the turf round and selling it on to Wally, a scrap merchant down the road. Ma looked down at the bag checking out all that we had 'bought'.

'Yeh must have had a right load of scrap to be able to buy all of this.'

As she looked at the two of us, I kept my head down, trying not to look her straight in the eye. The rest of the shite that came out of Phil's mouth was a string of lies – and Ma knew it. He came up with one of his classic stories as usual.

'Sure, haven't I been savin' it up for the past few weeks? How else would I be able to get the few messages for yeh? I wanted to surprise yeh, Ma.' He smiled, showing off his pearly whites.

'Hmm . . . I see then . . . and you were there when he was sellin' the scrap, Kathleen?'

'I was, Ma.' I was still too afraid to look at her.

'Tha's okay, then. The blessin's of God on the pair of yiz; the Holy Mother herself is lookin' after me again.'

And that's all that was said on the matter.

* * *

As kids, each and every one of us would always be scheming, coming up with one idea after another. If we weren't out robbing from the shops, living next door to the turf depot came in very handy. We'd be up there after it was closed, filling the sacks up and selling it on cheap the next day; or Phil would be out with me or one of the other kids as soon as it got dark, a screwdriver in his pocket, unhinging any wooden side gates he could get his hand on. Himself and Noel would chop them up, making up bundles of sticks, selling them on the following day with the turf. If the truth be known, some of the neighbours were actually buying back their own side doors.

I would say an extra few Hail Marys every night, trying to convince myself it was okay to do what we were doing. Back then, we weren't thinking about doing harm or wrong. In our minds, we were helping our Ma, and that's all that mattered to us. She never would have survived otherwise.

That's the way things went, on and off, over the next two years, until Phil went out and got himself a proper job, delivering messages for the local shops, passing the turf round on to Noel, teaching him all the tricks he had learned. He would drill it into his head how important the big smile was. That's when we decided to give up the robbing.

'Kathleen, me face will be too well known around here now. We best stop while we're ahead.'

'Oh, thank God! I'm only too happy to stop.'

For once I didn't argue with Phil.

* * *

Before I knew it, I was thirteen years old and Ma was getting ready to have her tenth baby – my little sister Mary. Although I didn't realise it at the time, it was to cause so much sorrow and heartache for Ma.

17

Baby Mary

At this stage I definitely knew that babies were not delivered in Santy's bag, or found in a head of cabbage, or that the stork dropped one in on his way to Africa. I was as usual out of school, cleaning and looking after the kids.

'Kathleen, will yeh go upstairs and get the sheets off the beds, and any other bits lyin' around, and bring them down to me. I have to try and keep the washin' down before I go away for a few days.'

I knew what she meant: into the hospital. The rest of the kids had been told that Ma would be going to the Isle of Man to do a bit of shopping with the other women on the road, for the Christmas clothes.

The local nurse had just been in to see Ma on one of her routine visits. She was one large woman, with her arms crossed under her diddies, pushing them nearly up into her mouth. As for her arse, it was so big, I thought when she sat on the chair that the legs were going to fold in.

'Lil, you'll have to have this child in hospital; you're not getting any younger.'

Ma had had the first seven of us at home and the rest in hospital. She wanted to have this baby at home, but the nurse wasn't having any of it.

'There are too many children in this house anyway. You can't be jumping up a few hours after the birth – and knowing you, Lil, that's what you will be doing. Your husband is well able to make babies, so he should be well able to mind them for a few days.'

Ma would usually have put up a fight and not let anybody tell her what to do. But she looked so drained and tired, she just sat there and said nothing. I think she was glad to be getting a bit of a break for a few days away from all the mayhem and worry that surrounded her.

After the nurse left, we were sorting out the washing. Ma was telling me all the things I was to do while she was away. She had this little electric washing machine which had a mangle attached; it was great for squeezing the heavy water out of the clothes.

'Kathleen, yeh know yer Da hates doin' the washin'. He'll do anythin' else, but don't ask him to wash. Now, where's tha' Carmel wan? She should be in from school by now.'

'She's out the back yard, Ma.'

'Tell her to peel the spuds for the dinner.'

Carmel? Tha's a joke, I thought to myself. *Ten years of age and all she wants to do is play with her dolls. She lives in her own little world.*

'And when yeh're finished there, Kathleen, go up the road and see if Clare is on her way home. Check with one of the other kids and see if she was in school today. Yeh know her, she's a little fuck on the mitch, any chance she gets. Yeh'll have to keep an eye on her for me as well.'

'Right, okay, Ma.'

I was glad to get out of the house for a while, even if it was only to look for Clare. I would get so fed up; there was always something for me to do or someone for me to mind.

I laughed to myself while I walked up the road; as if any of the kids would tell on Clare! She'd kick the living daylights out of them.

There she was, running down the road, a skinny little

thing and black as the ace of spades, covered in muck.

Oh my God! Look at the dirt of her. She's making a holy show of us. 'Clare Doyle! Look at the cut of yeh. Have yeh been up in tha' dump again? Ma will fuckin' kill yeh. She told yeh if yeh went on the mitch again wha' she'd do to yeh. It's bad enough Speckie the Inspector knockin' on the door for me. If he finds out yeh're not in school, he'll fuck the two of us in tha' home for them delinquent young wans.'

Clare was like a gypsy, always rooting out old bits of things, fixing them and trying to sell them on to the other kids on the road.

She tried to suck up to me now. 'Look wha' I found, Kathleen.'

I gave it a quick look. 'Wha' is it, Clare?'

'It's a brooch, Kathleen. Wha' de ye think?'

'Tha's no good, Clare; the pin is gone off the back.'

'Sure, I'll get a small safety pin and put it through the holes. Teresa Kearney said she'd give me three pence for it. I'll give yeh half, if yeh don't tell Ma . . . ah, Kathleen, don't tell, she'll kill me. One more chance, please?'

'I swear this is me last time, Clare. I'm not coverin' up for yeh any more.'

'Ah, thanks, Kathleen.'

'Right then, get yer arse down tha' road. When yeh get to the house, slip in the side gate and, quick as yeh can, wash tha' dirt off yeh. I'll tell Ma one of the young wans up the road is helpin' yeh with a few sums. Now whether she believes me or not is another thing, but I'll try anyway.'

Ma asked as soon as I walked in the door. 'Kathleen did yeh find Clare?'

'Yeah, Ma. She'll be here in a minute; she's doin' a bit of homework with one of her friends.'

'Jaysus, tha' has to be a first, Clare doin' homework without bein' made to. Are yeh sure, Kathleen?' She gave a bit of a stern look.

'I am, Ma, I am.'

* * *

Noel and Marion were running around the kitchen playing chasing. Jacinta was out the back yard making muck pies with Thomas. Patricia was asleep on the chair and Phil was delivering the messages for the shops down the road.

'Kathleen, help me hang the sheets on the line. I'm not able to stretch.'

We were just about finished with the washing when Noel roared out with panic. 'Ma, Ma, quick, there's fire comin' outta the wall.'

'Holy Jaysus, let me in.' Ma pushed past me, nearly knocking me to the ground.

The kids were running around like lunatics, screaming, 'The house is on fire, the house is on fire! Wha' will we do, Ma?'

Ma ran over to the washing machine. I could see the plug sparking and smoke coming from the socket. Ma wrapped a small cloth around her hand, not realising it was wet, and pulled the plug out. She got a terrible shock and fell to the ground.

All the kids just stood there. I was hysterical. I ran up the road to Mrs Kearney. I tried to keep myself calm but I couldn't.

'Quick, quick, Mrs Kearney! Ma needs yeh. She's on the floor, she's bad, she's really bad.'

When we walked back into the kitchen, I got the fright of my life. Ma was as white as snow and out cold. I thought she was dead. I didn't know what to do. The kids were all crying. Noel and Marion kept saying, 'Ma is dead, Ma is dead, Kathleen, she's dead!'

Mrs Kearney bent down and felt Ma's wrist. 'Lil, Lil!' she called out as she stroked her face.

Ma started to move and slowly came around.

'Noel, quick, go upstairs and get me a pillow for your mother, and bring down a blanket as well. Kathleen, try and settle down the children. They have themselves in an awful state.'

I got them all to sit on the floor and be quiet. It all happened so fast I didn't know what to be doing.

With all the commotion going on, a few neighbours had gathered outside. One of the women got the ambulance; somebody else sent for the ESB. Ma was taken straight to the hospital. Word was sent down to the yard where Da worked to come home urgently. Mrs Kearney stayed with us until Da came home.

In the meantime the men from the electricity board had arrived and they told Da, 'The wires were live; your wife is lucky to be alive.' I'll never forget the look on his face when they said that to him. He turned green with fright and went straight to the hospital, not knowing what to expect when he got there.

Mrs Kearney turned to me. 'Kathleen, I'll have to go home to make Jack's dinner, he'll be in soon. Will you be all right? I'll check with you later, to make sure you are all okay and to talk to your father to see how Lil is.'

'Thanks, Mrs Kearney, we'll be fine. I'll take care of things here.'

Phil came in and helped me with the kids. Jacinta was pulling at the end of my dress. 'I'm hungry, Kathleen.' That started them all off.

'Carmel, butter some bread. Tha'll keep them quiet for a while. The spuds are peeled, so we'll fry a few sausages. Clare, go down to the corner shop with Noel, ask Mrs Green will she give us a few messages on the bill. Tell her Ma is sick. She'll pay her back next week, when Da gets paid.'

If I hadn't sounded like Ma before, I certainly did now.

When they'd all finished eating, we got the younger kids washed and up to bed while the rest of us waited on Da to come home from the hospital. I was sitting there giving Patricia a bottle of tea, when he walked in. I knew something was wrong. His eyes were all red and swollen. He'd been crying.

159

'Where's Ma? Where's Ma? Is she with yeh?' the kids asked.

He sat down. I could see that his lip was trembling, as he tried not to cry. I thought my heart was going to burst.

'Yer mother is all right. She'll be home in a few days. She just got a bit of a fright.' He looked over at Phil and myself with sadness in his eyes and shook his head.

The kids were jumping up and down. 'Ma's okay, Ma's okay!'

'Will yeh have a cup of tea, Da?' I asked.

'Tha'll be grand, Kathleen.'

Phil jumped up. 'I'll get it. Yeh're lookin' after Patricia.'

When the rest of them fell asleep, Da told us what happened.

'Yer mother had a little baby girl, but the shock went through her and she died; her little heart gave in. The doctor said yer mother was a very strong woman; they don't know how she is still alive.'

I couldn't believe or understand the words that were coming out of Da's mouth. *How can this be? Ma's baby, my little sister, dead. Why did this happen? WHY?*

* * *

Da took a few days off work to help with the kids and go up to the hospital. The next day Phil and Carmel minded the kids. I went up with Da to see Ma.

We were only in the door when she told him, 'Phil, I'm goin' to call our little baby Mary. I want yeh to get the priest and make sure she gets the blessin' and when yeh're there ask if they'll let yeh see her. Yeh can tell me who see looks like.'

Back in those days, when your baby died, you weren't shown or allowed to hold her. It was wrong, but that was how it was.

'Jesus, Lil, please don't ask me to tha'. It'll kill me. I can't, please.'

160

'I swear, Phil Doyle, 'til the end of me days, if yeh don't do this for me, I'll never forgive yeh.'

Da wasn't very good at dealing with anything like this but he went along with Ma's wishes. The whole time Da was gone, Ma sat in the bed, crying her heart out, not saying a word. All I could do was hold her hand.

When Da came back up to the ward, he looked so distressed his lip was trembling as he spoke; he told us she was lovely.

'She has a head of black hair, just like you, Kathleen.' Ma got so upset when he said that and so did I. 'Lil, the sister said it would be cheaper to get her buried from the hospital, costing only a few shillings. She would be taken to the Holy Angels in Glasnevin.'

Mrs Kearney came down to the house the day before Ma came home. She told me to go upstairs and see if there were any new clothes put by for the baby. I found a little brown parcel in the back of the press. In it were two vests, two cardigans, three little blankets and a half-dozen nappies. I cried as I came down the stairs with the parcel.

'Give that to me, Kathleen. It's better not to have them in the house; your mother will only break her heart every time she looks at them. And not a word about the baby when she comes home. You're a big girl now, Kathleen, you understand?'

I wanted to scream out loud: 'No, Mrs Kearney, I don't understand. All this is grown-up stuff. I don't want to know. Why can I not talk about my little sister?' But no, as usual I just kept my thoughts to myself and said nothing. I worried so much that it was all my fault, because I was always giving out about minding babies.

Ma was home the following day. She was so quiet for such a long time. All the kids thought it was great, her not chasing them around or getting a dig for one thing or another, but I knew the truth. I wanted so much to ask her, 'Are yeh all right, Ma? They should have let yeh see little Mary.' I wanted so much to speak out, to say how I was feeling, but I never did.

That wasn't the way back then.

Nobody spoke about little Mary ever again.

* * *

The next year seemed to take for ever to go by. Ma slowly started to come around and get back to her old self. I wasn't sure if that was a good thing; then again, it was better than looking at her being so sad all the time.

18

Going to the Hop

The day finally came when I officially left school and was off Speckie the School Inspector's list. At least now I would be able to go down to the shops and not have to look over my shoulder for Speckie, who used to come up behind me on his bike, stop and tell me I was going to be sent away to a home for delinquent girls.

He was one tall man. He must have been about six foot three and not a bit of flesh on him. I don't know how he used to ride that bike with those long legs. I think he must have been deaf as well, because he was always screaming into my face. 'Speak up girl,' he would roar. I would be shitting myself, telling him all the lies under the sun as to why I wasn't in school.

I suppose he wasn't all that bad, especially when I think back on all the lies Ma used to tell him too. According to her, I had every sickness going. He probably took one look at Ma and her clatter of kids and felt sorry for her. Or maybe giving out just made him feel better.

I was only fourteen and dying to get out into the big world. After all the years being stuck in the house, minding kids, I was raring to go.

'Ma, I want to go out today and get meself a job.'

'Tha's right, Kathleen. Yeh're a big girl now. It's time yeh started makin' a few shillin's for me and start earnin' yer keep.'

Jaysus, Ma, I thought, *haven't I always been a big girl as far back as I can remember? And I think I well earned my keep.*

'Well now, Kathleen, wha' would yeh like to work at?'

'I want to be a hairdresser, Ma.'

I was always messing about with the kids' hair, trying all sorts of hair-dos out on them and on myself. I was really good at it. But it wasn't to be.

'Jaysus, Kathleen, they don't get paid hardly any money. Yeh'd be better off gettin' yerself a job in one of the factories. Just go around and see wha' wages they offer yeh.'

I went around a few hairdressers. The most they were paying was ten shillings a week, so that was hairdressing out the window. The factories, on the other hand, were paying three pounds five shillings a week. Ma was delighted when I told her. But I wasn't.

'Tha's great money, Kathleen. I know yer brother Phil is workin', but yeh wouldn't see wha' he brings in, with him servin' his time at the paintin'. Tha' takes seven years. Sure he'll nearly be a married man himself by the time he gets a decent wage. So, you'll have to go where the money is. I don't know how I'm goin' to keep up with everything. These kids are eatin' me outta house and home.' And that was that. I had no say in the matter, as usual.

* * *

My first job was in a sewing factory but I didn't last long at that because I was afraid of my life of the needle.

I ended up in a sweet factory in Tallaght called Urneys. When I brought my first wage packet home, Ma was well pleased, handing me back five shillings for myself.

'Now, Kathleen, outta tha' yeh have to pay yer bus fare.

And whatever else yeh have left, yeh have to put by and try to dress yerself because the rest has to go on food and bills.'

'Talk about trying to perform a miracle! But that is exactly what I did. I saved every penny and if it took me six months to get myself a skirt or a jumper, I wouldn't touch a penny of it in the meantime.

* * *

I was on my way home from work one day when I heard a shout.

'Is tha' you, Kathleen Doyle?'

I looked across the other side of the road. It was Breda Murphy. She was as blind as a bat; you'd nearly have to be right on top of her before she could see you. She was much taller than me and had a waxy white face. Her hair was a coal-black fuzz-ball; you'd think somebody was after putting a plug up her arse and giving her an electric shock. If you saw her in the dark, you'd get the fright of your life.

I made my way over to her. 'Yes, Breda. It's me, Kathleen. Wha' de yeh want?'

'There's a hop on Sunday night up in the boys' school. Are yeh comin'?'

My ears cocked up when I heard that. 'I'd love to Breda, but I'll have to ask me Ma and Da.'

'Tell them I'll mind yeh and tha' the Brothers do be walkin' around and all, makin' sure nobody does be wearin' or anythin'.'

'Yeh mean kissin'?' I thought I was real grown-up saying that to her.

'Nobody says kissin' any more, Kathleen. Tha's real old fashioned. It's a wear, righ'?'

'Okay, Breda. I'll come up to yer house and let yeh know if I can go. See yeh.'

It was Friday night and I always had a few bags of broken chocolate for the kids. I used to buy them for five pennies in the factory. I needn't tell you, they would be sitting in the garden watching out for me to come up the road. You'd want to have heard the screams and shouts of them whenever they saw me coming!

'I knew tha' was you, Kathleen, as soon as I heard them kids roarin'. I says to young Phil, so I did, "here she is with the sweets",' Ma said as she shared out the chocolate. 'Yer Auntie Mary was here today, Kathleen. She left a bag of clothes. Have a look and see if there is anythin' there to fit yeh.'

Auntie Mary was very good to us. She was always bringing stuff down – food, clothes, shoes, bed sheets, you name it. Anything her family was finished with and didn't want, we got it.

Da also sometimes brought us home parcels of clothes. He worked all around Rathgar and Rathmines, lovely big houses, really posh areas. If you lived there you had money. All the ladies thought Da was a proper gentleman – and he was, only for the drink. He always wore a cap, a heavy tweed one in the winter and a light beige cotton one in the summer. He knew everyone from working the streets; he'd pass nobody by without tipping the peak of his cap and wishing them all a good morning.

One day one of the ladies whispered to Da, so as not to let any of the other neighbours hear her, 'Philip, could I have a word with you if you don't mind?' He always got his full title off them, and he loved that. 'Would you be very offended if I left a parcel of clothes out now and then for you? I know you have lots of children and it is such a shame to throw them in the bin. Some of the clothes are practically new.'

'Jaysus, missus, yeh can offend me anytime yeh like. The wife will be delighted.'

The word got around that Da wasn't offended, and so a couple of times a year when the posh ladies would be kitting out their kids with all new clothes, we'd get the old ones. We used to be like vultures; Da would only be in the door with the brown parcel under his arm and not a crease in the paper, tied real neat with a bit of twine and a proper bow. We would kill one another fighting over who got what. Ma always made sure that everyone got something out of each parcel.

Anyway, I had a good root through Auntie Mary's bag that day.

'Ma, would yeh have a look at this? Sure it's nearly new.'

'Let's see, Kathleen. Jaysus, tha's lovely. Go on upstairs and try it on.'

It was a tight green skirt with a waistcoat and brown polo neck jumper. *I could wear this to the hop,* I thought to myself. Up the stairs I went and tried it on, with Ma following behind me.

'Tha' looks nice, Kathleen, but I think it's a bit too tight around yer rear end.'

'No, Ma, it's not. Tha's the way they all wear them now — skin tight. It's all the fashion.'

I was poured into the skirt; my arse was bursting at the seams. But I didn't care. I thought I was lovely. I was definitely keeping this for myself.

'Ma, I met Breda Murphy when I got off the bus tonight. She asked me to go the school with her on Sunday night. There's a hop on.'

'Hop wha', Kathleen?'

'Jaysus, Ma. Tha' means they play music and all.'

'Yeh mean a band?'

'No, Ma, records! So can I go?'

'Oh, I don't know, Kathleen. Wha' time is it on 'til?'

'Ten o'clock, Ma. The Christian Brothers and all will be there. Ah, go on, Ma. Let us go, please! I never go out anywhere. It'll be me first dance.'

'Hmm . . .' she thought for a few moments. 'I suppose tha's true, Kathleen. Right then. Yeh can go. Once yer father hears tha' the Brothers are keepin' an eye on yiz, he won't mind.'

I jumped up with excitement and threw my arms around

Ma, with no response back, of course. 'Would yeh give over yer molly-coddlin', for God's sake, Kathleen.' She got herself together and went back downstairs.

* * *

I thought Sunday would never come. I had my rollers in all day. I cleaned the house from top to bottom and helped get the kids washed and ready for bed. I didn't want anything to stop me from going to that hop.

I went upstairs to get ready. Phil and Noel were lying on one bed, Carmel, Clare and Marion on the other. Jacinta and Patricia were asleep on the chair downstairs and Thomas was in the kitchen playing with his soldiers. The girls thought it was great, me going to my first dance. As usual, Phil had to start with his messing and getting my back up.

'Noel, would yeh have a look at the state of her! Kathleen, I'm tellin' Ma yeh're puttin' lipstick on.' I ignored him and tried to give him the look, just like Ma did when she was raging.

'Wha' will yeh do if yeh're asked up to dance?' asked Marion.

'I'll get up and dance, tha's wha' I'll do.' I was showing off because I knew Phil was listening. With that, he burst out laughing.

'Who'd ask yeh up to dance? With tha' big fat arse on yeh and yer smelly breath.'

'Wha' de mean? There's nothin' wrong with me breath.'

'Yeah, there is, Kathleen, it's rotten. Yeh wouldn't know if yeh were talkin' to yer face or yer arse half the time.'

Phil was nearly on his knees with laughing, with Noel joining in, as they watched me getting myself into a state, knowing full well I'd lash back at him.

'Tha's it. I'm goin' to fuckin' kill yeh, Phil Doyle,' I roared.

I was on top of him like a flash, beating the head off him with my hairbrush. The bastard pulled every roller out of my hair, and me after spending ages putting them in. The girls were all jumping up and down on the bed, cheering me on to win the fight. With that, didn't the bed only go and collapse, and that soon put a stop to our fighting.

Ma was up the stairs in seconds.

'In the name of Jaysus, wha's goin' on up here? Yiz are like somethin' out of a madhouse with the carry on of yiz. Yeh're after wakin' up the little ones – and look at the bed, look at the fuckin' bed.' She was screaming her brains out. 'Who started all this?'

'It was Phil, Ma. He wouldn't leave Kathleen alone.' The girls took up for me straight away.

I was sitting on the bed with my hair standing to attention, not a curl left in sight, lipstick all over my face, with a hole in the knee of the stockings I had only bought the other week.

'I have a good mind not to let yeh go out tonight, Kathleen.'

'Ah, Ma! I didn't do anythin'. It was Phil. He started it.'

There were tears and snots running down my face. Phil was standing behind Ma, laughing and sticking out his tongue at me. With that, Ma turned around and gave him such a box in the head I thought he was going to go flying out the bedroom window.

'Get down them stairs, yeh long skinny fuck. I caught yeh. Laugh at me when me back's turned, would yeh? I keep tellin' yiz, I have eyes in the back of me head.'

He nearly died on the spot. *Jaysus,* I thought, *Ma hit Phil!* I couldn't believe it; it was a first, her hitting her blue-eyed boy like that.

'Kathleen, get yerself ready before I change me mind. Look at the state of the bed. I'll have to wait until yer Da comes home from yer Gran's to see if he can fix it. If not, the four of yiz will have to sleep on the floor until I get a new spring, and God only knows when tha'll be.'

I didn't give two shits who was sleeping on the floor and for how long, once she let me go to the hop. I ran into the toilet like a light to fix the mess I was in. I back-combed my hair, smoothing it out, trying to make some sort of a flick.

'Run downstairs, Clare, an' see is me bottle of lacquer in the press.'

She roared back up to me, 'Kathleen, it's empty!'

'Wha' am I goin' to do, Ma?'

'Don't worry, Kathleen, I'll make yeh some lacquer.'

'How, Ma? Out of wha'?'

'Come down and watch this.'

She filled the empty bottle with warm water and poured in some sugar.

'Now, Kathleen, let tha' cool down for a few minutes. Tha'll keep yer hair in for a week. The only thing is the flies, they like the sugar.'

'Wha' de yeh mean, Ma?'

'Well, if yeh see any flies around the top of yer head, yeh'd better run because if one of them gets into tha' nest on yer head, we'll have to shave all yer hair off.'

I looked at Ma, then at the bottle, then back at her. I wasn't sure if I was supposed to laugh or not. With that, all the kids started laughing like mad.

'Kathleen, yeh're an awful gobshite at times. Yeh'd believe anythin'.'

It wouldn't be very often Ma would crack a joke or for that matter say anything that you would giggle about.

I ran back up to get ready. Just then there was a knock on the door. It was Breda Murphy.

'Is tha' you, Breda?' I roared down. 'Come on up.' I gave her a little twirl in my green suit. 'Well, wha' de yeh think?'

'Kathleen, tha's a massive suit. Where did yeh get it?'

'Me cousin Marie gave it to me. Yeh don't think it's a bit tight? Me Ma said it was.'

'Don't mind yer Ma, sure wha' would she know.'

'Ah Jaysus, Breda, look at me stockin'. The hole is gettin' bigger. Wha' am I goin' to do?'

'No worries, Kathleen, I'll fix tha'.'

'How, Breda? There's no time.'

'With nail varnish, of course. Yeh just put a bit around the hole – tha' stops the ladder goin' up yer leg. I do it all the time. There's some up in me house. I'll go and get it. I'll be back in a few minutes.'

I gave my hair a little tip up with my steel-tail comb, sprayed on the sugary water and made my grand entrance into the kitchen. All the kids started cheering and clapping.

Ma gave me a little smile. I thought, *this is great – Ma's in good form.*

'Enjoy yerself, Kathleen, and make sure yeh come straight home, as soon as the dance or wha'ever it's called is over.'

'I will, thanks, Ma.'

Breda came back with the nail varnish, fixed my stocking, and off we went to the hop. When we got there we went straight to the toilets to put on our lipstick.

'De yeh want some eyeliner, Kathleen?'

'Sure, I don't know how to put it on, Breda.'

'I'm great at doin' it – now hold yer head back.'

Good God, she'll blind me, I thought, *she can't see a fuckin' thing.* 'I'll leave it alone, Breda. It's okay.'

'Would ye give it over, Kathleen. Yeh have to have a bit of eyeliner. Now, hold yer head back against the mirror and close yer eyes.' She began painting my eyes. 'Good Jaysus, Kathleen, wha' have yeh got in yer hair? It's like a rock. Yeh're nearly after crackin' the glass.'

'Me Ma made it out of water and sugar because I didn't have any lacquer.'

'Wha' did she do? Put the whole bag of sugar in? Tell her yeh only have to put in one or two spoonfuls in the water. Tha's wha' my Ma does. Now. Wha' de yeh think, Kathleen?'

I stood back and looked in the mirror, hardly recognising myself. 'Oh, I don't know, Breda. Does it not look like I've two black eyes?'

'Would yeh go 'way, Kathleen. It's all the fashion. Sure doesn't Dusty Springfield have her eyes like tha'?'

'And who is she?'

'Jaysus, Kathleen, de yeh not listen to the radio or anythin'? She's real famous. She sings an' all. Oh, I keep forgettin' – yeh're only fourteen and I'm sixteen, I know much more than you do. Now stand back and let's have a look at yeh. God, yeh're very flat. Have yeh not got on a bra?'

'I have, but me diddies is not growin'. Every night I pray to the holy statue in me Ma's room and ask her to make 'em bigger. But I think she's gettin' herself all mixed up and puttin' them in me arse instead of me chest.'

'Kathleen, didn't I tell yeh I know everythin'? Come 'ere, watch this.'

She took some toilet paper and stuffed it into my bra.

'Now. Yeh look better already. Yeh haven't got a big arse, Kathleen. It's just when yer diddies are small it makes yer arse look big.'

'Are yeh sure, Breda? It's just tha' Phil said . . .'

'Don't mind him. He's a fuckin' eejit.'

As we were walking down the corridor to the big hall, I could see a few fellas standing around, smoking on the sly. I saw one or two of them nudging each other as we passed by. I looked over and gave them a little grin. Breda pushed me and gave me a thump in the back.

'Wha' did yeh do tha' for?'

'Yeh never look at them, Kathleen!'

'Why not, Breda?'

'Because they'll think tha' yer interested in them, tha's why. I know wha' I'm talkin' about. I've been here a few times and tha's wha' all the girls do. Yeh just give them a look.'

I thought, *I don't want to give them 'the look'. I get enough of tha' at home with Ma.*

'Now, when we get into the hall, and if a young fella asks yeh up, yeh're to say no and turn away.'

'Why, Breda? I want to dance. I've been practising ever since yeh asked me to come to the hop.'

'Will yeh listen to me, Kathleen? If yeh smile and get up straight away, they'll think yeh're real easy.'

'Easy for wha', Breda?'

'Yeh know wha', Kathleen Doyle, yeh're a fuckin' eejit! De yeh not know anythin'? First of all, they'll be lookin' for a wear. Then, they'll ask yeh to go outside. Make sure tha' yeh don't do tha' because if yeh go outside with them, before yeh know it they'll be pullin' the diddies out of yeh and feelin' yer arse. Now, de yeh see wha' I mean? Are yeh takin' all this in? Me Ma always says yeh have to play hard to get.'

'Well, Breda, me Ma said tha' I was to have a great time and tha's wha' I'm goin' to do. And if any young fella tries to feel me diddies he'll be in for a shock because I've none, only toilet paper. So I don't care – the first one who asks me up, I'm gettin' up. So there.'

'Suit yerself then, Kathleen Doyle, but I'm tellin' yeh, they'll all think yeh're real easy.'

So Breda was standing there giving the looks and turning away with her head in the air, but whenever she wasn't minding me I was smiling and showing my teeth to the whole hall. I wasn't leaving that hop without a dance, and that was that. That's when a slow dance came on. All the Christian Brothers started walking around in between the couples, making sure that they weren't standing too close to one another or trying to get a wear. It was just as well Phil told me what a wear meant. Breda would have really killed me because I would have thought it meant something to do with wearing my clothes.

'Kathleen,' said Breda, 'we're standin' here long enough. If anybody comes over now we'll get up.'

She was making faces and rolling the eyes in the air all the time, so it wasn't any wonder nobody was coming near us. Just then, I saw two young fellas looking across at us. I tipped Breda.

'Breda, Breda, there's one on his way over.'

'Wha's he like?'

Her being half blind and all, he could have looked like something from Mars but she wouldn't have known that until he was nearly on top of her.

'Kathleen, I said wha's he like?'

'He's about yer size; wait, hold on. Oh Jaysus, Breda, he has millions of pimples.'

'At this stage I don't give two fucks, Kathleen. The night is nearly over.'

Before I could say anything, she pushed me out of her way and stood in front of me, grabbed his hand and started dancing. She was one sly bitch.

I stood there mumbling and fucking to myself. Then I turned around, and there he was.

The love of my life.

Alan.

'De yeh want to dance?' he asked.

He was the same height as myself, small and stocky, with dark blond curly hair combed back with a half tub of Brylcream in it, with a kiss curl flicked down on his forehead. Just then, 'Jailhouse Rock' came on and he gave me this big smile.

'Can yeh jive?' he asked as he took my hand.

'I can a bit.'

My brother Phil had shown me a few steps that he learned from some young wans he was hanging around with, so I wasn't too bad. I was on that floor like Flash Gordon. After a few minutes we were flying. He was doing backhanders, side-steps and double twirls – you name it, he was great. After the first dance he told me his name was Alan and that he was from Walkinstown.

I was shitting myself, my voice shaking with excitement. 'I'm Kathleen. I live down the road from here.'

He gave me that big smile again. The next song came on. It

was a slow set, so I didn't know what to do – Phil had only shown me how to jive. Alan just slid his hand around my waist, put my right arm around his shoulders, and held my left arm against his chest. I pulled back real quick.

'Wha's wrong?' he asked.

'Ah, it's just the Christian Brothers. They'll give out if yeh stand too close.'

To tell you the truth, I didn't give two fucks about the Christian Brothers. I was just worried that the toilet roll would make a dinge in my bra and Alan would know that I had no diddies.

'Well, Kathleen, are yeh still in school?'

'No, I left a month ago. I'm workin' in a sweet factory.'

'So how old are yeh, then?'

'I'm fourteen.'

'I'm fifteen and I work for me Da. He has a shoe repair shop.'

And it went on like that. We seemed to be talking for ages.

'Can I walk yeh home, then?'

I was just about to say 'yes' when Breda pushed my coat in between Alan and myself.

'Are yeh righ', Kathleen? Come on. We're goin' home.'

'Wha's wrong, Breda?'

Alan was still standing there.

'Kathleen, yeh know the fella with the pimples? Well, I went outside for a bit of fresh air and before I knew it, he was like a lizard. He stuck his tongue so far down me throat I nearly choked.'

'Just wait a minute, Breda, I won't be long.'

'I said we're goin', Kathleen, *now*, come on.'

With that, she stormed off.

I turned to Alan. 'Will yeh wait?'

'Yes,' he said, giving a big laugh.

'Breda, come 'ere. I thought yeh said not to go outside.'

'I know, I know. I was just standin' outside the door. I didn't go around the back of the hall.'

'Why, Breda? Wha's around the back of the hall?'

'I was just gettin' a wear, Kathleen, but the fucker wanted more.'

'More! More of wha', Breda?'

'Jaysus! De yeh know anythin', Kathleen Doyle? Yeh're as tick as shite. Ah, yeh're gettin' on me nerves. I'm goin' home.'

Off she went, leaving me standing by myself. Just then, Alan came over to me.

'Are yeh all righ', Kathleen?'

'Breda said tha' fella tried to choke her.'

'Don't mind her. Tha's me pal. He was just tellin' me he was only tryin' to give her a French kiss, tha's all.'

'Wha' does tha' mean? Is he from France?'

Alan fell around the hall laughing.

'Yeh're very funny, Kathleen.' He went on to explain to me that it was a new way of kissing. I thought my face was going to burst it got so red.

'I feel really stupid. I'm an awful tick, Alan.'

'No, yeh're not. We only found out about it last week. Tommy found a magazine under his Da's bed. It was all about kissin' and other stuff.'

Little did he know, I didn't even know how to kiss the old way, never mind the new way. And now, as I was discovering, there were other things as well!

When we got to the end of the road, Breda was standing there with a big serious puss on her.

'Yeh're a real sleeveen, Kathleen Doyle, lettin' me walk down tha' road on me own.'

'No, I'm not, Breda – yeh ran off on me.'

'Well, yeh should have run after me!'

I wanted to punch the head off her, she was making such a show of me. I was trying to be real nice in front of Alan but at the same time, I had to keep licking up to the bitch because I had no one else to go to the hop with, and Ma wouldn't let me go on my own.

176

'Breda, this is Alan.'

'Hello,' she said, rolling her eyes in the air and turning to walk away. 'Are yeh comin' or wha', Kathleen?'

'Walk on up, Breda, I'll be with yeh in a minute.' *Yeh bitch,* I thought to myself as I smiled at Alan. 'I'd better go, Alan, she's already annoyed.'

'De yeh want to go out tomorrow night? Maybe we can go and see a film.'

'I'd love to.'

'The Star picture house is just up the road from where yeh live. So, I'll be across the road, at the candy corner shop at half-past seven, if tha's all right with yeh, Kathleen?'

'Okay, I'll meet yeh there, Alan.'

He bent over towards me. *Oh Jaysus, he's going to kiss me,* I thought. I held my mouth closed real tight in case it was one of those French ones. I opened one eye and caught him laughing.

He just kissed me on the cheek and off he went. Breda was still giving out when I caught up with her. She went on and on and on . . . but I didn't care.

I was on cloud nine.

I had a date with Alan.

19

The Date

I was up bright and early the next morning. I stuck a few rollers in my hair. As a factory worker, I had to wear a turban on my head for hygiene reasons; so nobody ever noticed my rollers.

'Is tha' you, Kathleen?' Da whispered up the stairs.

'Yeah, Da.' I slipped out of the room, stepping over the four kids sleeping on the floor. It was only half past six, far too early for them to get up.

'Pour yerself a cup of tea. I have the fire lightin'. Will yeh have a bit of toast?'

I sat down with my cup of tea while Da knelt in front of the fire with the fork stuck in the bread, holding it against the flames.

'Yer mother told me wha' happened last night. Phil should have more sense. He should keep his fightin' for the boxin' ring and not his sister. I'll talk to him tonight.'

'Sorry about the bed, Da. I just lost me temper with Phil.'

'Well now, Kathleen, yeh didn't lick it off a stone; yeh take after yer mother for all tha'. There's one or two scrap-yards on me route today. I'll drop in and see if they have an oul' spring lyin' around. Tha'll solve the problem.'

'Da, can I ask yeh somethin'?'

'Course yeh can, wha' is it?'

'Ma said, if it's all right with yeh, I could go out tonight to the pictures. I met this lovely fella; I've a date with him. His name's Alan.'

'And how old is this young fella?'

'He's fifteen and he's from Walkinstown.'

Da looked at me for a minute, thinking to himself, but before he could say anything else, I got in there straight away. 'He has a job working for his Da, mending shoes.'

I had my coat and scarf on by the time I told him everything and was nearly out the door, rushing for the bus, with still no answer.

'Ah, Da, go on, let us go, please?' I put my arm around him. 'Go on, Ma will let me go if yeh say yes.'

'Are yeh sure yer mother said it's okay?'

'I swear, Da, on the Holy Bible she did.' I blessed myself.

'Now, yeh wouldn't say tha' if it wasn't true, would yeh, Kathleen?' He looked at me with a little grin. 'Right then, yeh can go. I'll see yer mother when she gets up.'

I gave him a big hug. 'Thanks, Da.'

* * *

The bus was just pulling up to the stop when I got to the corner. I fell onto the seat soaked to the skin; the heavens were open and me with not an umbrella. I kept saying that I'd buy one, but I never seemed to have the money.

My friend Rosie Delaney got on the bus at Walkinstown. I'd met her the first day I started work; she came over to me in the locker room and told me not to be nervous. She sat beside me on the bus every morning from then on and we'd be chatting all the way up the Greenhills Road.

'I was dyin' to see yeh, Kathleen. How did yeh get on with yer first hop?'

I launched in, telling her all about Breda and the fella with the tongue. She nearly fell off her seat laughing. She was seventeen and probably knew all about these things. I let on I knew too.

Then I told her about Alan.

'Yeh mean Alan McGrath?'

'De yeh know him, Rosie?'

'Yes I do, Kathleen, he lives up the road from me house, so he does. He's a really nice young fella.'

'Well, I have a date with him. We're goin' to the pictures tonight. Look, I have me rollers in and all.'

'Tha's great Kathleen. The only thing is . . . Molly O'Brien . . . she's a bitch, she works in the factory too.'

'*Who's she?*'

'Her and Alan were goin' together for about six months and they only broke up about two weeks ago. I'd say she'll go mad when she finds out he's goin' out with somebody else already.'

'Oh, maybe I won't go then.'

'No, don't be stupid, Kathleen, you go. Serves her right anyway; she used to treat him like dirt and he was mad about her, always buyin' her presents and things.'

We were outside the factory before I knew it.

'Rosie, wha' does tha' Molly wan look like? Tell me before I go in.'

'Don't be worryin' yerself, Kathleen, yeh won't even see her. She works up in Dolly's room – tha's miles away, yeh're at the other end of the factory. Jaysus, look at the time! It's nearly eight o'clock, we'll be late for clockin' in. I'll meet yeh on the bus on the way home; see yeh later.'

I made myself sick worrying and looking over my shoulder all day. Every girl that passed by, I jumped. I thought the day would never end so I could see Rosie and find out if she'd heard any news. She was on the bus before me and had plenty to say.

'Kathleen, I'm up here! I kept a seat for yeh,' she shouted down to me. When I went upstairs, Rosie was sitting on the front seat waving and shouting. 'I've loads to tell yeh. Molly heard all about yeh.'

The blood started to drain from my face. 'Oh shite, did she? Who told her?'

'Well, it wasn't me, I can tell yeh tha'. Sure wasn't half of Walkinstown at the hop Sunday night, Kathleen. Girls, they're all the same, they're right bitches. I was watchin' them all day, fillin' Molly in on everythin'.'

'Does she know I have a date with Alan?'

'Yeah, she does, Kathleen. Yeh know tha' young fella you were tellin' me about – Tommy, with the tongue.'

'Oh yeah, I forgot about him.'

'Well, his sister works with Molly; Alan told Tommy, and he told her, and tha's how the word got around. Are yeh with me, Kathleen?'

'For fuck's sake, Rosie, me head's all over the place. I can't think straight.'

'Yeh'd want to see the face on Molly. She was real sick, jealous as anythin'.' She glanced behind her. 'Oh' shite, Kathleen, I'm scarleh! She's at the back of the bus!'

'Good Jaysus, Rosie, wha' will I do? I'm dyin' to turn around.'

'No, don't turn around, Kathleen. Tha's why she came up the top of the bus – she wants to see wha' yeh look like. I'll be gettin' off at the same time as her. I bet yeh she comes over and tries to pick out of me. Don't worry, I won't tell her anythin'.'

'Wha' de yeh think I should do, Rosie? Will I not go?'

'Don't mind her, Kathleen, just go out tonight with Alan and have a great time and stop worryin'. Right then, here's me stop. See yeh in the mornin'.'

I turned around as Rosie walked towards the back of the bus, two girls looked down at me, nudging each other. I still didn't know who Molly was but she knew me now. I was in such a trance, wondering what I was going to do, that I nearly missed my stop.

I was halfway up the road when I saw Breda Murphy. She called out to me, 'Is tha' you, Kathleen Doyle?'

'Yeah, Breda, it's me.'

I wasn't in any humour for her and I didn't feel like listening to a load of scutter and shite; that's all you'd ever get out of her.

'Well, wha' happened? Did yeh get a wear or wha'?'

'*No, I didn't.*'

'Wha' are yeh lyin' for, Kathleen? I saw yeh; he was standin' real close and all.'

Yeh blind fuck, yeh can't see the hand in front of yeh, never mind me standin' down at the corner. 'He just gave me a kiss on the cheek, Breda, tha's all. He's real nice.'

'Kiss on the cheek, me arse, Kathleen Doyle, yeh fuckin' liar.'

I could feel my temper starting to rise. 'I have to go, Breda, I'm in a hurry. I have a date with Alan.'

'Yeh're not serious? With tha' teddy boy – sure they're all real slags. The first fella asks yeh out and yeh go runnin' after him. Yeh're an awful tick, so yeh are.'

'Don't be sayin' tha', Breda, he's not a teddy boy or a slag.'

'Yes, he is – did yeh see him when "Jailhouse Rock" came on? He was like a ravin' lunatic, dancin' and jumpin' around like a mad thing. I thought at one stage he was goin' to fuck yeh out the top window, he was liftin' yeh up in the air tha' much. And one other thing, every time the dance was over, he took his comb out to fix tha' kiss curl of his. They all do tha', me Ma says; all them teddy boys are the same, just after one thing. They'd have yer knickers off in a flash if yeh let them.'

I felt like saying, *Fuck yeh and yer Ma with her gammy leg; she's just a jealous oul' cow, because she can't dance. Call me a fuckin' eejit, will yeh? I'll put the eyes crossways in yer head with a good punch one of these days. It won't be glasses yeh'll be needin'; it'll be a pair of binoculars by the time I'm finished with yeh. Bitch.* But of course I didn't say anything; I just bit my lip and ran off before she could say another word.

I had myself in a state by the time I got to the house. My face was roaring red with temper. As usual, the kids were all running up to me to see if I had a few sweets in my pocket. I sat on the steps playing with them for a few minutes, calming myself down. If Ma saw me all worked up, she'd be asking what had happened.

'Is tha' you, Kathleen?' Ma roared.

'Yeah, Ma, I'll be with yeh in a minute.'

'Wha' kept yeh?'

'I was talkin' to Breda Murphy.'

'She's a nice young wan, very well mannered, and her mother's a lovely woman, so she is.'

'I know, she's real nice.' I thought I was going to choke on the words.

'Kathleen, sit down there and eat yer bit of dinner. Sure it's nearly cold as it is. Well, yer Da said yeh can go to the pictures with tha' young fella – wha's his name again?'

'Alan.'

I was getting butterflies in my stomach just saying his name. That was it, I made up my mind there and then: *I'm goin' to meet him, so fuck tha' Molly wan.*

After dinner I went upstairs to get ready. It didn't take long to make up my mind what to wear – either the green suit with the brown polo neck or the beige pleated skirt with the brown polo neck, both hand-me-downs from my cousins. I wished for once I had something new to wear that was just mine. I was giving out to myself like hell at this stage and was getting in a right tizzy.

Carmel was sitting on the bed playing with her dolls, not doing a bit of harm to me or anyone around her. I lashed out and took my bad mood out on her.

'Are yeh ever goin' to grow up, Carmel? Every time I look at yeh, yeh're dressin' up or playin' with them bloody dolls.'

'Wha's wrong with yeh, Kathleen? Yeh never fight with any of us.'

184

Granny Kitty and Fanny the Donkey

Granny Kitty and Granda John

Da and Ma on a rare day out in town

Ma and Da having a good day

Carmel, Phil and Kathleen

Da and Carmel

The little ones, Patricia and Jacinta

Dad, Noel and Phil with Jacinta
and Patricia

Marion and Clare, the best of buddies

Clare – the dog lover of the family

Phil Doyle, All-Ireland
Middle-Weight Champion

Patricia, Clare and Jacinta

Alan and Kathleen (sweet sixteen)

Thomas and Speedy the dog

Kathleen and Alan – at the Hop

Alan and Kathleen at their first dinner-dance

Kathleen and Alan on a date

Alan and Kathleen on their Wedding Day

Ma, Patricia and baby Paul

Mano and Paul, last of the babies

Da and Ma with Mano and Paul

'Ah, Carmel, I'm sorry. I didn't mean to loose me rag.' I put my arms around her. 'It's just, loads happened to me today. I don't know if I like bein' out there in the big world. Everyone keeps talkin' about things I don't know much about. It frightens me a bit tha's all. I'm afraid to ask Ma or Da about wha' they mean in case I shouldn't know, and then if I ask the girls in work they'd probably laugh at me because I should know. Ah, maybe yeh're better off in here with yer dolls, Carmel. Anyway, I didn't mean to give out to yeh.'

'Kathleen, Da brought home one of the parcels today. There was a nice yella cardigan in it. Ma gave it to me but yeh can have a lend of it if yeh like.'

'Ah, go on then, Carmel, give us a look. Jaysus, tha's lovely, tha'll go with the pleated skirt. Thanks, Carmel, yeh're a star.'

I went downstairs and got a pot of warm water to have a good wash. I was back up the stairs like a light before anybody else could get into the bathroom. As I was pouring the water into the sink, I looked down at the bath and thought to myself, *I'd love it to be filled up with hot water and loads of lovely fluffy bubbles. I could just slip in like yeh see in the films. But tha'll never happen, not for a long time anyway.*

Ma had always promised she'd try to get one of those new geysers that would heat the water, if she could ever get her gas bill straight. When we first got the house she used to fill a big pot with water and heat it on the gas cooker. Da would then carry the pot up and down the stairs a couple of times, but even then there'd be barely enough water to wet your arse, never mind have a good splash. As more babies came along, it became too much for him. That's when Ma came up with one of her bright ideas; it was a classic.

'Phil, we'll have to find some other way for washin' the kids. Somebody's goin' to get scalded goin' up and down them stairs with pots of boilin' water. I have meself a plan – we'll wash them in the machine.'

'*Wha*'? Yeh want to put the kids in the washin' machine?!

Are yeh gone stark ravin' mad altogether, Lil?'

'Jaysus, will yeh listen to me? We'll heat the water first, then take the plug out. I'll stand them in one by one and you'll dry them off. Right?'

Da thought to himself for minute. 'Now, Lil, I have to say, tha' deserves a pat on the back. A master brainwave if I ever heard one; only yerself would think of tha'.'

Da was delighted; the days of running up and down the stairs with boiling water were over. But as we all got older and our bits were starting to spring out, it was back to the bathroom sink with pots of warm water.

Ma would always tell us, 'Make sure yeh wash yer three bits where the smell comes from – yer feet, under yer arms and down below.'

For the boys, 'down below' was called the usual – 'willy' – but of course Phil and Noel had something to say about that.

'Ma, why can't we call ours "mickey" like all our pals.'

'There'll be no mickey talk in this house and if I hear any of it, yiz'll get the back of me hand.'

Us girls had to call ours 'Mary'.

'Why "Mary"?' I asked.

'Well, Kathleen, most women call theirs "fanny", but we can't do tha', because yer granny Kitty's donkey is called Fanny. Sure I wouldn't know if yeh were talkin' about yerself or the donkey; so "Mary" it'll be.'

And to the present day we still call 'down below' 'Mary' in our family.

I had just started washing myself and was bending down to put on clean knickers when the door was nearly kicked in on top of me.

'Who's in there?' Noel shouted.

'It's me – Kathleen. Go 'way, I'm gettin' ready.'

The door got another kick. 'Let me in before I piss on meself!'

'Go away, Noel,' I said. 'I'm not finished yet.'

'Kathleen, Thomas is out here too and he's goin' to shite all over himself.'

'Let me in, quick, me gick's comin' out,' roared five-year-old Thomas.

I opened the door slightly and peeped out, at the same time trying to cover myself. I had one leg in my knickers, with my arse still wringing wet.

'I'm not lookin' at yeh, Kathleen,' Noel mumbled. 'Will yeh let us in?'

'Yeh better not, I'm warnin' yeh.' I wrapped the towel around myself.

Just then Thomas pushed his way past me with his trousers around his ankles, 'Quick, Kathleen, it's nearly out!' I grabbed him and put him sitting on the pot.

'Jaysus, am I ever goin' to get peace in this mad house?'

I turned around and there was Noel, getting ready to piss in the bath.

'Noel, wha' the hell are yeh doin', yeh dirty little bastard?'

'I can't hold it any longer, Kathleen, let me go. Ma will kill me if I piss in me trousers – they're the only pair I have.'

'*I'll* kill yeh if yeh piss in the bath, never mind Ma.'

'Anyway, they all do it, Kathleen.'

'*Wha' de yeh mean "all"?*'

'Whoever doesn't make it to the pot has a piss in the bath.'

'Oh my God, who started all this?'

'Phil – but don't tell him I said; he'll kill me. I was havin' a shit one day when he pushed the door in and roared at me. "Right, Noel, get off the toilet pot, I can't wait any longer."

'"But, Phil, I'm halfway there – wait, it's nearly out."

'He walked up and down for a minute. I was turnin' purple in the face, tryin' to finish as quick as I could, but because he was standing there lookin' at me, everythin' stopped. It wouldn't move. "Tha's it," he said, "I can't hold it", and he went and pissed in the bath. He gave me a box in the head and told me he'd batter me if I told Ma or Da, but I told all the others. We only do it when somebody's havin' a shit and they're takin' ages. It's only piss, Kathleen; yeh turn the taps on and it washes away like the pot.'

'Well, now, Noel, seein's tha' yeh think it's okay, yeh won't mind if I tell Ma then, will yeh?'

'Ah, Jaysus, Kathleen, don't tell her. There'll be blue murder; yeh know wha' she's like. She'll batter me.'

'Right, then, I'll see Phil later.'

Noel started balling his eyes out.

'Tha's it, Kathleen, I'm dead. He said he'd kill me if I told on him.'

'Don't be such a fuckin' whinger, Noel, will yeh? He won't touch yeh because I'll tell him tha' if he goes near yeh, I'll tell Ma and Da he started it. Now get down them stairs and tell the others I want to see them.'

Noel gave them all the gypsy's whisper before they came up the stairs to me. They were all blaming one another, shoving and pushing at the same time. 'Kathleen, it wasn't me it was her'; 'She did it first, then I did it'; 'Noel said it was okay.'

In the middle of all this bedlam, Thomas, who was still sitting on the pot, called out, 'Kathleen, Kathleen, Kathleen.'

I turned around. '*Wha*? Wha's wrong with yeh?'

'Will yeh wipe me arse, Kathleen?' I couldn't keep my face straight and started laughing and of course everybody else chimed in.

That's when Da came to the end of the stairs. 'Wha's goin' on up there, Kathleen? Yiz are makin' a fierce racket.'

'It's okay, Da, they're just helpin' me get ready for me date.'

I told them, 'I'm warnin' yiz, I'll be watchin' out for yella stains in the bath. And if I see the tiniest bit of rust – I don't care, yiz can all blame one another – every one of yiz will get it from me and Ma. I didn't wait all these years to have me bubble bath, when Ma is finally ready to get the hot water, only to find out I can't sit down because it's rusted to fuck from yiz pissin' in it.'

Clare always had to get her penny's worth in. She was as

cheeky as hell. 'Wha'll we do if there's a few of us waitin' to go? We can't wet our knickers now, can we, Kathleen?'

'Tha's right,' Marion joined in, 'I won't be able to hold it.'

'Then there's Jacinta and Patricia,' Carmel said. 'It won't be long before they're on the queue with the rest of us.'

Noel came up with what he thought was a good plan. 'Wha' about the shore in the back yard? It's not too close to the house. Now, I'm only sayin', only if yeh're really stuck, we could piss in tha'. Wha' de yeh say, Kathleen?'

'Tha's not a bad idea and it has an open grille, too. Ma could pour a drop of bleach and hot water to make sure it doesn't smell. Right then, off yiz go, I'll talk to Ma and Da about it.' They all finally left me in peace. 'Jaysus, look at the time! It's nearly seven o'clock. I'll be lucky if I make me date with all this goin' on.'

On with the pleated skirt – *Oh, thank God, this cardigan buttons right up to the neck. I won't have to worry about wearin' anything underneath. Oh shit, wha' about me diddies? I'll just put a bit of toilet paper in me bra; tha' Breda wan must have put half a roll in last night. I must have looked a right eejit. I better not be thinkin' about her or I'll just get all worked up again.*

'Ma, will yeh send one of the kids in next door and ask Mrs Kennedy will she lend me her umbrella? It's lashin' out; I don't want me hair goin' all flat, I have it just right. And can I put some lipstick on?'

'Yeh can put on a little bit, but yeh're not to put tha' black stuff on yer eyes. I got a fright last night when I opened the door; I thought somebody was after beatin' yeh up.'

'Yeh know wha' else I need, Ma? A bit of talcum powder – I can feel under me arms sweatin' already.'

'For Christ's sake, Kathleen, will yeh stop gettin' yerself all worked up? Yeh're an awful young wan for worryin'.'

Worked up? If she only knew what was goin' on a few minutes ago, we'd see who'd be worked up.

'Anyway, Kathleen, yeh're better off bein' a few minutes late. Yeh don't want him thinkin' yeh're too anxious.'

'Okay, Ma, yeh're right, I will.'

Clare handed me the umbrella before I left.

'Mrs Kennedy said yeh've to bring it straight back when yeh come home.'

'I will, I will. Right then, how do I look?'

Da smiled at me. 'Yeh look great.'

'Yeh're grand, Kathleen,' said Ma. 'Yeh've plenty of time; the picture doesn't start until eight o'clock. Off yeh go then and mind yerself crossin' tha' main road. And don't be late – make sure yeh're in here at a proper hour.'

* * *

I took my time walking up Kildare Road so I wouldn't have a red face when I got there. I looked across at the Candy Corner Shop. There was nobody there. *Tha's great*, I thought, *gives me a chance to fix me hair and lipstick.*

The rain was bucketing down that night and I could feel the cardboard inside my shoes starting to crumble. I seemed to be standing there for ages. I hadn't got a watch, so I went in and asked the women behind the counter the time.

'It's eight o'clock, luv. De yeh want to stand inside the door? Yeh're gettin' soaked out there.'

'I'm grand, thanks.'

I was afraid I'd miss Alan if I stood in the shop. *He must have missed the bus, tha's wha' happened, and he's walkin' down. Tha's it, I'm sure of it.*

I waited for another half hour, blue in the face with the cold, before I finally got the message. He wasn't coming. I cried all the way home, thinking to myself, *I'm such a gobshite, standin' there all tha' time, makin' a fool of meself. He was probably laughin' at me all the time; and I thought he liked me.*

By the time I got home, the side gate was locked, so I had to knock on the front door. Da opened it.

'I thought yeh were goin' to the pictures, Kathleen.'

'I changed me mind, Da. I was up talkin' to Breda.'

'Women! I'll never understand yiz, always changin' yer mind at a blink of an eye.' He shook his head as he made his way back to the telly.

I held my head down and passed him by. He had a sup on him, so he didn't notice that I was soaked to the skin and my eyes were swollen from crying. But Ma did. She handed me a towel.

'Dry yerself off there, Kathleen, and I'll make a cup of tea.'

The young kids were in bed asleep, the other half were looking at the telly, not minding me. I followed Ma into the kitchen.

'Well, wha' happened?'

I looked at Ma, trying to hide my red eyes and I thought for a minute about what she always taught us: *Never tell me lies, any of yiz, I'd trust a robber first before I'd trust a liar.*

'He never turned up, Ma.'

'Yeh mean yeh've been standin' out in tha' rain all this time? Jaysus, Kathleen, I thought yeh had a bit of sense. Could yeh not see after a few minutes he wasn't comin'?'

'I know, I know, Ma. He was so nice. I didn't think he'd do tha' on me.'

'Well, Kathleen, yeh have an awful lot to learn about men and life.'

I started balling my eyes out again. Ma put her arm around me.

'Come on now, stop tha' cryin', Kathleen. Yeh'll wake the kids up, and if tha' brother of yours Phil gets a whisper of this – and yeh know wha' he's like with his messin' – yeh'll never hear the end of it.'

Ma wasn't one for showing her feelings. I suppose she was always too busy looking after us to think that we might need a hug or a kiss now and again. But that night it felt good with her arm around me.

'Right then, Kathleen, get them wet stockin's and shoes off. Take a lend of Carmel's shoes and her raincoat. We're goin' out.' She roared into Da, 'Phil, as soon as tha' film is over, put the rest of them kids to bed. I won't be long.'

'Lil, where are yeh off to at this hour of the night?'

'I'm just goin' out for an hour with Kathleen.' She turned to me. 'Come on, yeh got ready to go to the pictures and tha's where we're goin', I have a few bob put by off the gas heater. We'll use some of tha'. If we hurry up we'll make the second film and we might have enough to get a single of chips on the way home.'

'Are yeh sure, Ma?'

'Just get tha' coat on. We're goin' and tha's tha'.'

We had a chat on the way up the road. I told her about the kids getting stuck waiting to use the toilet and nearly wetting themselves and the idea about the shore – 'Now, only if they're really stuck, Ma, tha's all.' I never mentioned the bath.

'We'll see, just enjoy tonight. We'll worry about tha' tomorrow.'

I suppose that's how she got by – there we were with a twenty-six-inch telly on tick, and not a drop of hot water in the house and barely enough food to go around. But does Ma worry about it? *No.* She would always say, 'Yeh deal with each thing as it happens; take each day as it comes.' That's what I was going to do from then on.

* * *

The next morning Rosie sat down beside me on the bus as usual. She was itching to know how I'd got on. She nearly died when I told her.

'Tha's not like Alan McGrath. Somethin' must have happened.'

Just then I heard giggling up the front of the bus.

'Did yeh hear tha', Rosie? They know.'

'No, they don't, Kathleen, how could they?'

'Look at them, they're all laughin' and lookin' down at us.'

'Tha's her, Kathleen.' Rosie whispered, pointing out this wan to me. 'Tha's Molly.'

She looked straight down, laughing at me; I stared right back. *Bitch.*

I learned the truth as the day went by, with Rosie slipping over to me every chance she got, filling me in on everything. It seemed Molly had sent a note to Alan telling him she was still mad about him and wanted to see him. Little did he know that while he went to meet her, she was standing across the road from the Candy Corner Shop, watching me. She thought it was great fun, telling everybody how long I'd been standing there and how she had made a fool out of the two of us.

'I'll bash her brains in, I swear I will, Rosie. The bitch, to do something like tha'.'

'She's not worth it, Kathleen. Just ignore her, I think she's sick in the head and hasn't got a brain anyway. Wait until I see Alan McGrath; I'll tell him wha's been goin' on.'

'Rosie, leave it, don't say anythin'.'

I just wanted to run out of the factory, but I didn't. That skinny little two-faced fuck Molly would have loved that.

I thought the day would never end; all I wanted was to go home and hide.

When the buzzer went off at six o'clock, I rushed to get my coat, trying to get ahead of everybody. Rosie caught up with me.

'Are yeh okay, Kathleen?'

'I just want to get out of here, Rosie.'

Just before we got to the main gate, I thought I was seeing things. Alan was sitting there on his Honda 50. Talk about rubbing my nose in it. I held my head down, hoping he wouldn't see me. *I'll never live this down, him comin' up to pick tha' Molly wan up. They'll really have somethin' to laugh about tomorrow.*

Just as I walked out the side gate, he got off his bike and walked towards me. He had on a pair of skin-tight blue jeans, a black leather jacket and a pair of black 'Beatle' boots. *Jaysus, he's gorgeous,* I thought. My face got so red it could have lit up the whole road. Rosie was linking me and had one of her hands in my pocket. She squeezed one of my fingers so hard she nearly broke it.

Alan stopped right in front of me.

'Can I talk to yeh, Kathleen, please?'

I looked behind me and I could see all the young wans coming out the gate including, Molly. Then I looked at Rosie; she gave me a nod and a wink and left to get the bus. I thought to myself, *even if it's only to get up tha' Molly wan's back, I'll talk to him.*

'Okay, Alan, but not here.'

'Right, Kathleen. Hop on the back of the bike and I'll bring yeh home.'

I jumped on, gave Rosie a big wave and, to the rest of the bitches, the biggest smile you ever saw. The look on Molly's face was priceless.

Alan stopped down the road from my house. I got off the bike and faced him.

'Yeh never turned up last night. I waited for ages.'

'I'm sorry, Kathleen, let me explain.' He went on to tell me how he used to go with this girl. 'She works in the same factory as you. De yeh know her? She's called Molly.'

'Does she?' I pretended I knew nothing.

'Well, she sent me a note askin' me would I meet her, tha' it was real important, tha' she wanted to get back with me. We were goin' together for six months. I was all mixed up, I thought I still liked her, but when I was waitin' on her, I kept thinkin' about you. Tha's when I made me mind up; I was goin' to tell her it was over, but she didn't turn up. I knew it was too late to meet yeh, yeh'd be long gone. I had great crack the other night with yeh, I laughed more with you than I did with her in the last six months. Kathleen, will yeh give me another chance?'

He didn't have to ask me twice. The butterflies were doing somersaults in my stomach.

This was the fella for me.

20

Alan Meets Ma and Da

I was going out with Alan only a few weeks and was as happy as anything. He was spoiling me rotten. I wasn't used to getting all this attention, but I was loving every minute of it.

Until Da turned around one night and asked me: 'Kathleen, when are we goin' to meet this young fella of yours?'

Straight away, I looked across at Ma, who didn't say anything for a minute or two. She just stared over at me and then came out with the words I didn't want to hear.

'Your father is right, Kathleen. Bring him home. Let's have a look, see wha' he's like.'

'I told yeh, he's real nice, Ma.'

'It doesn't matter wha' *you* think; yeh're only a child, barely fourteen.'

For a split second I was back inside my head, thinking, *I'm only a child, am I? Well, how come I've been grown up all these years when it suits yiz all? All I ever wanted was to be a child like the rest of the kids, but I couldn't because youse wouldn't let me.*

'He could be a right bowsie, for all we know.'

'No, he's not, Ma.'

'Are yeh givin' me back lip now, Kathleen?'

'No, Ma. It's just tha' . . .'

'There's no just about it. Kathleen. Yeh bring him home to meet us, and tha's tha'.'

Da put his arm around me. 'Wha' are yeh worryin' about Kathleen? We won't bite him.'

You might not, Da, but I don't know about Ma. She'll still have it in her head over me standin' in the rain tha' night after Alan stood me up. I'll go mad if she says anythin' to him, I will, I don't care. Wha' am I going to do when he comes into this mad house: the little ones crying, the other kids running all over the place? He'll run a mile.

* * *

Alan didn't talk much about his family; everything seemed to be very quiet there. He had only one sister and a little brother.

'How come there's only three of yiz?' I asked him one night.

'Me Ma died when I was thirteen.'

'Oh my God! I'm sorry. I shouldn't have asked yeh.'

He could see I was getting all flustered and didn't know where to look.

'It's okay, Kathleen, it's all right. I can talk about it. Me Da worked away in England for a long time. We used to see him only a couple of times a year.'

'Did yeh not miss him?'

'Yeah, I did, but Ma wouldn't move over there.'

'And who looks after yiz now?'

'Da and Auntie Connie, me Ma's sister.'

He went on talking about her for ages. I thought, *she sounds real posh. I'll shit on myself if he asks me to meet her.* And I did meet her after a couple of months. Alan went out and bought me a lovely pink coat with a leopard-skin collar, new shoes, a handbag and a pair of white gloves. He thought I didn't cop on to what he was doing and I never said; he was dressing me up to impress his Auntie Connie. He wanted so

198

much for her to like me. You'd swear I was going to meet the Queen; I was only short of getting a crown on my head. It was my first set of clothes that weren't hand-me-downs. I looked and felt great when I went to meet her.

I could tell straight away that she didn't take a shine to me, as she thought I was beneath her and wasn't good enough for Alan. I hadn't got much in the way of reading and writing but I was years ahead with the teaching from Ma about life and people. I was well able to read Alan's aunt to a T. She was a bitch to me, but not in front of Alan, and I was always one step ahead. I would smile and agree with everything she said and she didn't like that one bit. I made it my business to keep out of her way, so she couldn't make any trouble.

As for my lovely pink coat, I only got to wear it twice. Ma asked me, 'Would yeh mind if I pawned it, just until Friday, Kathleen? I have electric and gas bills well overdue. I'll get it back out as soon as I get me wages.' But that never happened. She couldn't make the payment, so it was sold on to somebody else.

The pawn office was part of a lot of people's lives back then. If you had any clothes that were halfway decent, they would be brushed, pressed and folded up neatly, and brought to the pawn office on the Monday. You would try to get as much as you could from the pawnbroker, having to pay some interest on your return, which would usually be on the Friday. Ma didn't have much to pawn, but when she did, that would the ritual. It was more like robbing Peter to pay Paul.

'Kathleen, yeh don't realise how lucky yeh are, comin' from such a big family. Always somebody around and plenty goin' on.'

'Yeh can say tha' again, Alan; there's never a dull moment in my house.'

Little did he know he would be meeting them in the next few days; that might change his mind about big families.

* * *

199

Alan got a fright when I told him Ma and Da wanted to meet him.

'Why do they want to see me?'

'To make sure yeh're not a slag or a bowsie, Alan.'

'But I'm not!'

'I know tha', but please, Alan, they won't let me go out with yeh again if yeh don't. They just want to see yeh. Go on, Alan, please, just for me.'

'Okay, Kathleen, I will. Yeh know I'd do anythin' for yeh.'

* * *

'Ma, I told Alan to come down on Saturday night. Is tha' alright?'

'Good, Kathleen, yeh won't be in work. It'll give yeh a chance to get the place tidied up.'

'Ma, promise me yeh won't curse or smoke yer pipe, please?'

'I won't be puttin' any airs or graces on for anybody, yeh should know tha' by now. I'll just be meself.'

Jaysus, tha's wha' I'm worried about.

'Kathleen, if I've no Woodbines, I'll be smokin' me pipe; and as for me sayin' "fuck", I only say tha' when I'm all riled up. So yeh better talk to yer brothers and sisters, make sure they behave themselves. And tell yer father not to come in this house full of drink. Then I won't get all fired up now, will I?'

'Jaysus, Ma, tha's like askin' for a miracle. Yeh know all tha' won't happen at the one time and all in the one night.'

'Ah, yeh worry too much, Kathleen. I keep tellin' yeh.'

I suppose I didn't want Alan to see how poor we were and how little we had.

* * *

I thought Saturday night would never come and go. I had myself up the walls with worry.

I warned all the kids that if they started messing and making a show of me, I wouldn't bring home any chocolate ever again.

'And you, Phil, don't come in here with yer smelly stockin's on, stinkin' us all out of it.'

He smiled and gave me a sly grin.

'Did yeh see tha', Ma? Did yeh see him?'

'See wha', Kathleen? Wha' are yeh goin' on about now?'

Phil's laughin' at me! Did yeh not see him? Tha' means he goin' to mess and make a show of me in front Alan. Talk to him, Ma.'

'Phil, will yeh stop getting up her back, for God's sake? Yeh know wha' she's like for worryin'.'

I was cleaning all day, trying to make the place look something, which was nearly impossible. There were the two armchairs beside the fireplace: they had more footprints of muck on them from the kids jumping up and down. *I know wha' I'll do: put two blankets on them, tha'll clean them up a bit. Then there's the blue tubular table and four chairs, which were all covered in rips. I'll make sure the kids are sitting down on them; tha' way Alan won't see how bad they really are. There's nothin' I can do about the push chairs they'll just have to stay where they are. Ma likes to have the little ones beside her at the fire. Anyway, if they cry she just has to rock them to keep them quiet. I hope.*

'Ma, I'm goin' to get ready now. Will yeh make sure the kids take off their mucky shoes? I'm after scrubbin' every one of them floors. Alan will be here in half an hour. I told him he could bring his bike in the front garden. Is tha' okay?'

'Yes, yes, Kathleen. Will yeh stop fussin', for God's sake. As I said before, he'll just have to take us as he sees us, and tha's tha'!'

Da came in just then. 'The place looks great, Kathleen.'

'Thanks, Da.' *Tha's grand*, I thought, *he only has a small sup on him. At least there won't be a digging match tonight.*

I was just about ready when Carmel, Clare and Marion burst in the door, with little Thomas trailing behind them.

'Alan's here, Kathleen.'

Phil and Noel went out to look at his bike.

'Has Phil got his shoes on? Please tell me he has his shoes on.'

'How would we know?' Clare answered. 'We weren't lookin' at his smelly feet.'

'Yeh're a cheeky little fuck, so yeh are. I'll sort you out later.'

I peeped out the window. *Good, he has his shoes on.*

'Quick, the three of yiz take Thomas, get down and sit on them chairs and stay there until we go. I'll get extra sweets on Friday for all of yiz. Tell the others to be good.'

I got to the door just as Alan was walking in. He gave me a big smile and Phil gave me one of his sneaky grins. I could see how nervous Alan was, twirling his motorbike helmet around in his hands. Da put his hand out and they both shook.

'So, yeh're Alan.'

'Tha's right, Mr Doyle.'

'Mr Doyle, me arse,' Phil mumbled.

I knew it, I knew it – he's goin' to try and make a holy show of me, I thought to myself. *He's a pig, tha's wha' he is, a pig.*

I looked at Da and gave him the eye and the nod. He knew full well what I meant.

'Phil, be quiet there.' He turned back to Alan. 'We've been hearin' a lot about yeh around here. It's all Alan does this and Alan says tha'.'

I went as red as a tomato; all the kids start giggling. *Jaysus! Wha' did Da have to say tha' for?* I was mortified.

That's when Ma stood up and walked over to Alan. You could see the blood draining from his face. I was shitting myself, never mind Alan. She turned around and looked over at Da. He gave her the nod. She stood there with not a smile on her face.

'Right then, Alan, de yeh smoke?'

Alan looked over at me, not knowing what to say. I had told

him how Ma was if any of us ever lied to her. He looked Ma straight in the eye.

'I do, Mrs Doyle.'

'Tha's good, then, because we've none. Now give us a few, I'm gaspin'!'

Alan was so relieved, he gave her the whole packet. That was it: he was in Ma's good books from then on.

Phil kept his shoes on and the kids sat on the chairs just like I asked them. The little ones didn't cry too much. Ma had a few smokes in her pocket so there was no fucking and blinding out of her. Da was sober. All went well. I was happy that night.

They all did me proud.

21

The Strongest Finger

My brother Phil was so funny at times – a bit of a lunatic, to say the least. You never knew what he was going to do or say.

Alan had been coming down to the house a good few months now and I was always trying to impress him; making sure the kids were on their best behaviour, promising them the sun, moon and stars to be good for me, if that was at all possible. But Phil always had to get up to something.

I was sitting there one night, chatting away to Alan. Ma was in the kitchen with the babies. Da was upstairs reading his paper. Phil was sitting on the chair across from me and the rest of the kids were sitting on the floor, watching the telly.

I looked over and I could see Phil giggling and laughing away to himself. *Tha's it,* I thought to myself, *he's up to something*. Sure enough, a few minutes later he came out with it.

'De yeh know somethin', Alan? I bet tha' I could lift you, Kathleen and every one of them kids up off yer arses with just one finger and all at the same time.'

'Don't be so stupid, Phil, would yeh?' I said. 'Nobody could do tha'.'

'I have to agree with Kathleen,' says Alan. 'I think yeh'll be losin' yer bet on this one, Phil.'

'No, I won't, Alan, because I have the strongest finger in the world, and I'll prove it.'

All the kids started butting in, 'And wha's yer bet? Come on, tell us, Phil.'

'I know I'm goin' to win this bet, but if for some reason I leave even one of yiz sittin', well then, I'll make the tea and a heap of fried bread for yiz all. But when I win – which I know I'm goin' to – every one of yiz has to kiss me hand and say, "Phil's the Champ".'

We were breaking our hearts laughing at the thought of Phil having to make the supper, which would be a first.

'Right then, Phil, yeh're on. Let's have it,' I said. 'Let's see this famous finger work.' I was showing off in front of Alan, thinking Phil was going to make a thick of himself. Little did I know I would be the one with egg all over my face by the time he was finished.

'There's just one more thing I have to say, Kathleen. Whoever doesn't kiss me hand – and I mean this – gets the finger stuck up their nose. Tha's the deal, so does everyone else agree?'

'Right, right,' says Noel. 'The bet's on, now will yeh come on and let's see wha' yeh're made of.'

'Remember those words in a couple of minutes, Noel, when yeh're kissin' me hand,' said Phil, a big dirty grin on his face.

That's when he stood up off the chair and started bending up and down, flexing his muscles, pretending he was warming up like a body-builder and laughing all the while. I couldn't believe what he did next and was as sorry as hell I'd taken up the bet. He bent down, got his finger and stuck it between the crack of his arse, breaking his heart laughing all the while.

'Right,' he said, standing up and pointing the finger in the air. 'Who's first for a sniff?' And he made a run at us.

Well, you'd want to see the scatter from all of us. We were up off the chairs and the floor in seconds, running around, trying to get away from him. Half the kids ran screaming into the kitchen and hid behind Ma's back, shouting out, 'Phil has a smelly finger. He had it up his arse, Ma!'

At this stage, Phil was standing in the middle of the room, the tears running down his face with the laughing. I was over at the front door with Alan, and the rest of the kids were getting ready to run if he started again, when Ma shouted out to him: 'Phil, are yeh up to yer antics again? Wha' did I tell yeh about chasin' them kids around? Yeh have them all roarin', makin' a holy show of me. Wha' will the neighbours think? Yeh bloody eejit. Now get in here and wash tha' finger or I'll give yeh a clip around the ear.' Of course, she'd never carry through that threat.

'Five more minutes, Ma, tha's all I need,' said Phil. 'Right then, I think I won the bet. Now it's payback time.' We all knew that if we didn't honour the bet, Phil would get us back one way or the other and that the finger would be stuck up our noses somewhere along the line. Knowing him, he'd wait until we were asleep, so it was easier to get it over with.

'Noel, I'll let you be the first to kiss me hand,' said Phil, holding the smelly finger to one side and the other hand in front of Noel. There was nothing else he could do but kiss the hand. He just gave Phil's hand a quick bang of his mouth, muttered 'Champ' and walked away. We each did likewise, with me murmuring under my breath, so Alan couldn't hear me, 'Yeh dirty bastard.'

There was no way Alan was kissing Phil's hand, so he made his way in to Ma, laughing and shaking his head at the one time, probably wondering to himself, 'Wha' a load of head-bangers I'm after gettin' involved with here.'

Phil sat there with the biggest smirk on his face, as the last of the kids went through the ritual.

'Well,' he said, making his way over to the sink to wash his hands, 'Didn't I tell yiz all I had the strongest finger in the world? And did yiz believe me? No – but yeh have to admit it, tha' was a classic.'

'Well, yeh certainly got all of us up off our arses, and tha's for sure,' said Alan.

'De yeh know somethin', else, Kathleen?'

'Wha' are yeh on about now, Phil?'

'I must remember to keep this little episode in mind for any bits and pieces I want doin' for meself around here.' He grinned as he looked over at Noel.

'Yeh can fuck off, Phil Doyle,' answered Noel, who was still sulking over losing the bet.

We all settled ourselves back down, me sitting with Alan and the rest of the kids spread out all around the floor, when Ma walked in with a plate full of fried bread.

'There yiz are, now,' she said. 'Get yer teeth into tha' and make sure yiz all learned somethin' from tha' mad brother of yers tonight. Don't put yer mouth out there unless yeh know where it's goin', because it'll always bounce back into yer face when yeh least expect it, and tha's wha' happened here tonight. Yiz didn't think it through.'

Off she went back to the kitchen, leaving all of us with our mouths open. Ma should have given Phil a good box for what he had just done, instead of giving us a lesson.

He really got one up on us this time. He was one cute hoor, and that's for sure.

22

The Pig and the Fight

I was sitting in the kitchen putting a few rollers in my hair when I heard a tapping on the window. It was Phil, giving me the nod to come out to the back garden.

'Wha' de yeh want?' I yelled.

'Come 'ere, will yeh?' He was whispering, so I knew he was up to something.

'Who's tha' out there with yeh?'

'It's Noel and Thomas. Will yeh keep yer voice down, for Jaysus' sake, Kathleen? Just open the door.'

'Right, I'm comin'.'

Well, when I saw what they had I couldn't keep my face straight. I burst out laughing. Standing up between them was a dead pig.

'Well, Kathleen, wha' de yeh think? We got this for Ma.' He stood there with a grin on his face from ear to ear.

'It's a pig.'

'We know it's a fuckin' pig.'

'Yiz are after robbin' tha'. I know yeh have. Wha' are yiz goin' to do with it?'

'We didn't rob it, like breakin' into the butcher's shop or anythin' like tha'. Go on, Noel. Tell 'er.'

'Wha' de yeh mean *me* tell? I'm sayin' nothin'.'

'Yeh'd better tell me before Ma comes out,' I threatened. I folded my arms and stood there looking over at Thomas, who was picking his nose as usual and wasn't minding what Phil was saying. He gave Thomas a right box in the head.

'Wha' did I tell yeh about pickin? If the snots is not hangin' out, yeh're always pickin' and flickin' them, yeh dirty little fuck,' he roared, hitting him again. Thomas started crying.

'Leave him alone, Phil,' I yelled. 'Yeh're always hittin' him.'

'Ah, for fuck's sake, Kathleen, he's turnin' me stomach; he's always at it.'

That's when Ma came out.

'Wha's goin' on here, Kathleen?' I stood there with my mouth open, not saying a word. 'Well, Holy Mother of Divine God! A pig. Where did tha' come from? Who gave it to yeh? Did yiz rob tha'?'

'No, Ma. We swear, don't we?' the three of them answered, looking and tipping one another. Ma stood there with the arms folded, the froth slowly building up in her mouth, her temper starting to rise. That's when Phil stepped in with a classic of a story.

'Now, Ma, before yeh get yerself in a state, we were just walkin' up the road when this pig came flyin' outta the back of a lorry at us. Isn't tha' right, Noel?' he added, giving him a kick in the ankle.

'Tha's right, Ma. It nearly landed on me head, so it did.'

'Get yerselves into tha' kitchen before any of the neighbours sees or hears yiz.' She stood looking at the three of them for a few seconds, twisting the wet teacloth in her hands. 'Now, wha' I want to know – and yiz had better think hard before yiz answer me – was this lorry stopped or movin' when the pig landed on yeh, Noel?' She twisted the cloth tighter and tighter. We all knew what that meant – stripes on somebody's legs if the wrong answer was given. Poor Noel. His face was turning purple as he looked over at Phil for help. Phil stepped in straight away.

'Movin', definitely movin' Ma. Flyin' it was.'

The penny finally dropped with the other two.

'Yeah, Ma, tha's right. He was goin' up on paths, hittin' gates and all, could have killed us all.'

Shut the fuck up, will yiz? I thought. *Yeh're overdoin' it now.*

'Are yeh sure tha's the way it happened?'

'Ma, I swear, not a word of a lie,' Phil answered, making the sign of the cross, knowing full well Ma would be pleased – the crafty little fucker bringing in a bit of religion just at the right time.

'Well, tha's all right then,' said Ma.

I couldn't believe what she came out with next.

'All the same, Kathleen, isn't it strange?'

'Wha's tha', Ma?'

'The way the Holy Mother works. I'm sittin' here worryin' meself sick as to how I'm goin' to get through the next few days, with not a penny in me pocket for a bit of food, and wha' does she go and do? Only makes sure tha' the three boys are standin' in the very spot where tha' pig landed. I'll be up first thing in the mornin' to the church and light a candle, thankin' herself.'

I thought I was hearing things. I was afraid to look at Phil; he'd only make me laugh. The relief on Noel and Thomas's faces. She knew full well the little bastards had robbed the pig, but this was her way of glossing things over – when it suited her, of course.

'Clear tha' table, Kathleen. You three, carry the pig in.'

They were only in the door when the back gate opened.

'Tha'll be yer father. He must have a sup on him. Quick, quick hide the pig.'

'Where?' says Phil.

'Anywhere. Just don't let him see it; yeh know wha' he's like.'

They grabbed the pig and ran upstairs, with a couple of the smaller kids running after them.

'This is mental, Ma. Where'll they put it?'

'Say nothin', Kathleen. Here he is.'

Da had a right sup on him that night and Ma didn't half lash him out of it.

'Full of drink again, I see, Phil Doyle, and me with not a shillin' in me pocket.'

'Now, now, Lil. Not a penny did it cost me – sure, didn't I only go and meet Jimmy tha' I used to work with on the docks. I haven't seen him in over ten years. I couldn't stop him buyin' the Guinness for me.'

'Is tha' right?' said Ma, making her way over to the cooker.

'Lil, yeh'd want to see the wad of notes he took out of his pocket. Makin' a fortune over there in England, so he is.'

Da staggered over to sit down on the chair.

'Well now, yeh know wha' yeh can do with yerself, Phil Doyle.'

'Wha's tha', Lil?'

'Fuck off back over there with him and give me a bit of peace. It's Jimmy this week, Paddy the week before and God only knows who next week, yeh lyin', connivin' bastard! A waster of a man so yeh are.'

Oh my God, all hell is goin' to break out here, I thought. I decided to move little Jacinta and Patricia, who were sitting together with their arms around one another, terrified with all the shouting going on. I put my arms around them. 'Everythin's fine, girls, don't cry. Come on, sit on me lap.'

'Kathleen, is Ma' goin' mad again?' Jacinta asked, sobbing as she held on tight to Patricia. I looked in at Ma, who was really worked up at this stage.

'It's just a mad temper she has, brought on by lots of things tha' yeh're too young to understand. Now, why don't I get yiz a slice of bread and drippin'. Don't move, I'll be right back.'

As I walked into the kitchen, Ma lifted the pot with Da's dinner in it. Da just about saw what was coming and went to run. She caught him on the shoulder. The stew went everywhere. Da slipped and fell. Ma stood over Da and was getting ready to belt him on the head. I jumped in front of her and screamed, '*Stop!* Please, stop! The kids are cryin'! Yeh're frightenin' the life out of them.'

'I can't help meself, Kathleen. When I hear the string of lies tha' comes out of tha' man's mouth, I want to fuckin' kill him. Look at the two little ones with not a pair of shoes between them. I can't let them out the front to play for fear the neighbours will see them. I still have me pride, Kathleen. And there's yer brothers – cardboard inside all their shoes, tryin' to hold them together. Does yer father see any of this? *NO!*'

'Ma, calm down, please. Just let me get Da up to bed. We'll have a chat and sort things out when I come back downstairs. Make a cup of tea and just sit down. Now, give us the pot, will yeh?' She wasn't budging, still holding on tight to the pot. 'Please, Ma.' I put my hands over hers and eased the pot out of her hand.

'All right, Kathleen. I don't know wha' I'd do without yerself and young Phil.'

'Phil, come down and help me with Da,' I roared up the stairs.

Da had fallen asleep on the floor in the middle of all this mayhem. As we were lifting him up, he slipped and slipped again. As Da was starting to come around, I saw Ma coming at him with the pot again. I started to scream, 'Ma, stop,' as I tried to get her back into the kitchen once more. 'Let us put him to bed, please, Ma.' She reluctantly went back in and sat down.

Some of the pig's blood had got on to Da's hands as he lay on the floor. When he woke up all he saw was this blood and he started screaming, 'Jaysus, I'm open. Yer mother's after openin' me head. Look at the blood.'

Phil was great; he could make a story up in seconds. 'Will yeh get away, Da. Tha's just a bit of jam one of the kids must have dropped early on.'

213

'Is tha' wha' it is?' He was so drunk he couldn't tell the difference.

On the way up the stairs, I whispered to Phil, 'Where's the pig?'

'In the wardrobe.'

'*Wha*'? Yeh stupid tick. Wha' did yeh put it in there for?'

'Well, I didn't get much time, did I? With all hell breakin' out downstairs, I couldn't put it in the other room now, could I? The kids were all startin' to scream. They were afraid of their shit of it. I was goin' to put it in the bath in the first place, but I thought tha' the oul' fella would be goin' in for a piss. Kathleen, there was nowhere else.'

'There'll be blood everywhere, Phil.'

'Ah, here, give us a bit of credit, will yeh, Kathleen? I wrapped an oul' blanket around the head. Come on, help me get Da into bed. He'll be out cold in a few minutes. We'll take the pig back down the stairs first chance we get. I'll stay up here on the landin'. You go back downstairs to Ma before she gets all fired up again and starts wreckin' the kip.'

Downstairs, the two little ones were still sitting on the chair, cuddled together and sobbing their eyes out. I'd forgotten all about them. 'I'm goin' to get yiz tha' nice piece of bread tha' I promised yeh. I'll be straight back.'

Ma was eating the Woodbines.

'Ma, this'll have to stop. I'm nervous enough meself when all this starts, never mind the rest of the kids. Look at the little ones, afraid of their lives to move. It's not righ', Ma. It's just not righ'.'

'I know, I know, Kathleen.'

She was crying really hard at this stage. I called in Jacinta and Patricia.

'Ma just has a bad pain in her head; she'll be okay tomorrow. Now, here's yer bread. Go up to Carmel and Clare. They'll look after yiz. Say goodnight to Ma.'

The two of them looked over, said nothing and ran.

'Only I stopped yeh there Ma, Da would've been dead or hurt really bad. Did yeh see the pot yeh had in yer hand? The heavy iron one. His brains would have been all over the place.'

'I don't care, Kathleen, I just don't care any more.'

The words were only out of her mouth when we heard Da screaming. 'Lil, Lil, quick! Come up, come up to me, quick!'

'See wha' I mean, Kathleen. This is me life. This is wha' I have to put up with. Tha' man makes me go crazy mad.'

'Lil, Lil!' Da roared down again, but there was no moving her.

* * *

At this stage, Da was out on the landing. 'Lil, there's a pig in the wardrobe.' He shouted at the top of his voice.

Ma was out of the chair and up the stairs before you could blink an eye, with me running behind her. Da was standing on the landing with Phil behind him. Phil gave Ma the eye and the nod, pointing in towards the bathroom at the same time. She knew straight away what Phil meant. I took a quick look and there was the pig lying stretched out the full length of the bath, with Noel standing beside it, pointing to himself, letting me know that it was him who had helped Phil to make the big move. Phil, as usual, had a grin on his face, his pearly white teeth showing from cheek to cheek as he whispered in my ear.

'As soon as Da had his back turned, I had it out in seconds. I'd say tha' should get us back in Ma's good books. Wha' de yeh think, Kathleen?'

'Ah, I don't know, Phil. Is there such a thing?'

Ma pushed past Da, nearly knocking him back down the stairs. She went straight over and opened the door of the wardrobe.

'Well, Phil Doyle, wha's all the roarin' and shoutin' about? The wardrobe is empty. I don't see anythin'.'

Da looked in, 'There *was* a pig in tha' wardrobe, as true as all the saints are up in Heaven. I know I saw it.'

'Are yeh sure it wasn't an elephant yeh saw? Isn't tha' wha' drunks see? Not tha' I would know, seein' as I'm not a drinker meself,' she added, starting to raise her voice again. We all started laughing. She looked out at us and gave us one of her dirtiest looks that would cut you in two. That soon put a stop to our laughing.

'Maybe now yeh'll start listenin' to me when I tell yeh yer brains is gettin' damaged from the drink. This is only the start of it, mark my word, Phil Doyle.' Out she stormed past us down the stairs, lying barefaced through her teeth. Only that we knew the truth, we would have believed every word she spoke.

'Right, Phil. I'll get the kids settled into bed. You go in and get Da sorted. And wha'ever yeh do, make sure he's asleep this time.'

'Okay, Kathleen, I will.'

I was only in the room two seconds when I got twenty questions thrown at me from all the kids.

'Kathleen, who owns it? Where did it come from? Is it alive? Can it bite?'

'Shush . . . keep yer voices down. Now, all yeh need to know is, don't mention this in front of Da or yeh'll have Ma to answer to. The good news is, there'll be a nice bit of food for the next couple of days. Now off to sleep, the lot of yiz. Oh, and another thing, not a word about this outside the house.'

I thought, *tha' will give them somethin' to talk about; keep them out of Ma's hair for the night.*

As I closed the door behind me I heard Da ask Phil to check the wardrobe again and again. 'I keep tellin' yeh, Da, a bad nightmare it was, tha's all.' It took a good half hour before Da finally went off to sleep, and we got the pig back downstairs and into the kitchen.

By this time Ma had calmed down. She had the table cleared, a knife in one hand and a hacksaw in the other.

'Right, the pair of yiz, put tha' pig on the table. Young Phil, go next door to Peter and ask him would he lend me tha' hatchet of his.'

'Ma, tha' pig is huge. How are yeh goin' to cut all this and where will yeh put it?'

'Let me worry about tha', Kathleen.'

'There can't be any of tha' pig here when Da wakes up, Ma. Yeh know wha' he'll do. The priest will be brought down. We'll be told tha' yeh're after lettin' the devil get into us. There'll be more trouble.'

'Don't you worry about yer Da, Kathleen. The only devil he has to worry about is me and the only sight tha' will be seen of this pig by the time I'm finished will be the lumps of juicy bacon fryin' in the pan first thing in the mornin'. Now get yer arse up to Mrs Kearney and ask her could I put a bit of meat in tha' fancy fridge of hers and there'll be a free parcel in it for herself. And Kathleen, while yeh're at it, knock on a few of the neighbours' doors and tell them there's some cheap meat goin'. They can pay me next week when they get their children's allowance. Oh, and another thing, make sure and tell them to say nothin' about where it came from and not a word to yer father when they see him.'

Not many people had fridges back then. There wasn't much point having one, not in our house anyway. What was bought on the day was eaten and not a crumb would be seen anywhere.

Nobody asked too many questions that night as I knocked on the doors. They were all glad to be getting something for half nothing. 'Tell yer Ma we'll see her tomorrow, Kathleen, mum's the word.'

Ma was well pleased when I told her. 'Tha's grand, Kathleen. The rest is easy; this is no different to any of the fish tha' I filleted over the years with me mother. It's just bigger. The skin and guts are all gone, so tha'll make it easier for me.'

Down came the hatchet, off came the head.

'Phil, out the back yard with tha'. Them dogs will think all their birthdays came in one. As for the rest, I'll just glide me knife slowly through. It'll be done before yeh know it.'

And sure enough it was. Mrs Kearney got her parcel and held onto a few for Ma. Myself and Phil dropped off the rest to the neighbours while the dogs chewed on the bones for the night.

* * *

When Da came down the next morning, the only trace of the pig, just as Ma had said, were the lumps of juicy bacon frying in the pan.

'They're grand rashers yeh have there, Lil,' said Da.

Ma turned around and looked over at us. 'Thanks to me family. Not tha' yeh would've noticed, Phil Doyle, yeh drunken bastard, with the carry on of yeh.'

Da just gave a little cough and sat down at the table. He went on to tell us about the nightmare he'd had and how real it seemed to be.

'I'll have to give up the drink; it's startin' to make me see things, Lil.'

She just gave him the look and carried on cooking. The little ones sat and listened to Da's story, the others laughing and nudging one another, not saying a word.

* * *

Ma made herself a few bob from that night and was able to clear some of her bills. How she kept a straight face the day we went into the butcher's shop, I'll never know.

'Yeh must have had a windfall, Lil, clearin' the whole bill in one go,' smiled Mr Hogg, the butcher.

'Let's just say somethin' fell me way. Yeh know me, always pay me bills when I'm able. Tha' way yeh can knock again.'

'Yeh never said a truer word, Lil.'

And on they went, chatting away about the goings-on in the world. By this time, Ma was convinced the pig had been sent to help her and I suppose it was in a way. There would always be something or someone, just when she would be on her last legs. That's how she survived.

That was Ma.

23

The Ghost

After little Mary died, I really thought Ma was finished having babies. I was shocked when she told me there was another one on the way and a couple of months later little Paul arrived.

I was seventeen and I still had half of the kids sleeping in the bed with me. I woke up one night to the screams of Clare, who was around eleven years old. She was climbing all over me.

'Jaysus Christ, wha's wrong with yeh, Clare? Yeh're after frightenin' the shite out of me.'

'There's a ghost in the room, Kathleen,' she screamed hysterically.

At this stage she was nearly on top of my face.

'For fuck's sake, Clare, will yeh get off me and calm yerself down.'

She got under the covers and held the blanket over her head, screaming, 'It's at the end of the bed.'

I sat up in the bed and looked down. 'There's nothin' there, Clare.'

'There is, Kathleen. I saw it, I swear.'

With all the commotion going on, all the kids woke up.

'Wha's goin' on in there, Kathleen?' Ma roared in from the other room.

221

'It's okay, Ma. Clare is just havin' a bad dream.'

'Tell her to shut up. She has the whole house awake.'

'It's not a dream,' Clare shouted from under the covers. 'It's real. I'm tellin' yeh, I saw him.'

When she said *him*, a cold shiver ran right through me. I could feel myself slowly slide down in the bed as I pulled the blanket right up to my face.

'Right then, Clare. Tell me, wha' did it look like?' I said, trying to calm her down.

She peeped her head out from under the covers. 'He was a big man with a long dark coat on and he wore a hat, but he had no face.'

'Wha' de yeh mean, he had no face?'

'Kathleen, it was just empty under the hat, and he was standin' there lookin' down at us.' She pointed to the end of the bed. She was starting to cry and getting really upset.

'It's okay, Clare. Don't be gettin' yerself in a state. Come on. Move in here beside me and I'll give yeh a hug.'

'Wha' about me, Kathleen?' Marion whispered. 'I'm afraid too. I don't want to stay down the end of the bed on me own.'

'Okay, get in and squeeze in beside Clare.'

The two of them wrapped their arms around one another. With that, Carmel and Jacinta jumped out of their bed. 'We're not stayin' over here on our own. Move over, Kathleen.'

'Ah, for Christ's sake. Yiz can't all fit in here beside me. Get down the end of the bed. Carmel, go with Jacinta.'

Carmel got her spoke in, which was unusual for her as she was always so quiet.

'Yeh want us to go down there, after Clare sayin' she saw a ghost standin' at the bed? Are yeh mad, Kathleen? There's no way, we're stayin' up here. Come on, move over.'

It didn't matter what I said; nobody was moving. We were like sardines in a tin. It seemed to take ages before they all finally dozed off. I lay there, unable to go back to sleep. Every now and then I'd have a little peep over the blankets and look down at the end of the bed. I could feel that shiver come over me again. I was lying there thinking to myself, *thank God it's the weekend and I've no work tomorrow. I can have a bit of a lie-in, seein' as how I'm awake most of the night.*

It was getting bright outside when I finally drifted off to sleep.

When I did eventually wake up, there wasn't a sound in the room. I looked around but everybody had gone. Normally there would be a couple of the kids running around messing and acting the eejit, as they always do. Just then, I got a quick flash of what Clare had said and how frightened she'd been. I wasn't long making my way down the stairs, taking the steps three at a time, looking over my shoulder as I went.

Ma was sitting by the fire feeding Paul. Da was in the kitchen with the rest of the gang making the porridge.

'Ma, it's after eleven. Why didn't yeh call me?'

'It's not very often yeh take a lie-in. I thought it best to leave yeh alone. If yeh stayed asleep, well yeh must have needed it.'

'I thought when I woke up I was in the wrong house. It was tha' quiet and peaceful.'

'Well, we all know the reason for tha', don't we? Last night, all tha' shoutin' and roarin' out of Clare.'

'She was just dreamin', tha's all it was, Ma.'

'Well, Kathleen, yeh must have really been dead to the world tha' yeh didn't hear the goin's-on around here this mornin'. Clare Doyle must have only opened her eyes when she started on about some man she saw standin' at the end of the bed with no face. Did yeh ever hear the likes of it? There's a ghost in the room. It's frightenin' the shit out of them all. I don't know how yeh didn't hear them. They nearly killed themselves tryin' to get out of the room and down the stairs. I'm sure Mrs Kennedy next door must think I reared a shower of lunatics. How tha' woman doesn't complain to me I'll never know. Kathleen, go in and talk to Clare. See if yeh can make some sense out of wha' she's rammagin' on about.'

As soon as I walked into the kitchen I got questions thrown at me from all sides. Of course, Phil and Noel had to get their spoke in straight away.

'Kathleen, did yeh hear wha' tha' tick Clare is sayin'? Tha' she saw a ghost last night. Bloody eejit.'

'I did too!' roared Clare. 'I'm not makin' it up!'

I sat down beside her, trying to calm her down. 'Shush, will yiz! Keep yer voices down.'

'And wha' was it doin'?' Noel sneered at Clare, with a smirk on his face. 'Was it flyin' around the room and goin' in and out of the walls?' he said, nudging Phil, the two of them having a right laugh at her.

'I told yiz wha' happened. Now fuck off and stop laughin' at me.'

'Come on, Clare. Don't take any notice of them.'

'They're just fuckin' ticks, tha's wha' they are, Kathleen.'

'Will yeh keep yer voice down and don't let Ma hear yeh.'

'Well, if the ghost comes back tonight, I hope it stands over them. I bet yeh they'll piss on themselves with the fright and we'll see who has the last laugh then.'

I sat there for ages trying to convince Clare that there were no such things as ghosts, but no matter what I said there was no way she was backing down on her story.

'I don't care if nobody believes me. I know wha' I saw and I'm tellin' yeh, it wasn't a dream.'

That night it took me all my time to get Clare up the stairs. Ma coaxed her by letting her sleep at the end of her bed. There was no way she would go back into our bedroom. After a good bit of an effort, and with a little bribe, she convinced Jacinta to sleep in the bed with her, promising her that she would give her tuppence as soon as she got paid from her turf round.

* * *

224

A few weeks went by and all was quiet for a while – until I woke up to the sound of Ma roaring, fucking and blinding out of her again. The whole house was in an uproar, with not only Clare, but Jacinta also screaming that she'd seen the ghost. 'It was standin' over Ma and Da.'

That was it. From that night on, Clare never slept upstairs again. She was so nervous after that night, and she had all the kids the same way listening to her go on and on about the ghost.

'Kathleen, wha' am I to do? I can't get Clare up them stairs for love or money. She's really convinced tha' she saw a man up in the bedroom.'

'I wonder *did* Clare see somethin', Ma? Wha' de yeh think? Do yeh believe in ghosts yerself?'

'I do believe tha' there could be spirits floatin' around out there tha's not ready to go over to the other side, for wha'ever reason. Only *they'd* know tha'.'

'But, Ma, wha' would a spirit be doin' here with us?'

'Well now, if Clare really saw somethin' – and she's adamant tha' she did – the only thing tha' I can come up with is this. Remember a few years back, tha' young man in the big lorry tha' crashed into the gates of the turf depot?'

'Tha's right, Ma. I remember now. Da and Mr Kearney carried him in here. They put him lyin' there on the kitchen floor. Wha's tha' got to do with all the commotion goin' on now?'

'Well, he died of a heart attack, there on the very spot where yeh're standin'.'

I jumped and moved away.

'Ma, yeh told us he was just a bit sick and he had to go to the hospital.'

'Of course I said tha'. Yeh hardly think I'd tell yeh the truth? Yeh were all too young at the time. Isn't tha' why I told yeh to get all the kids out of the way and up the stairs when he was being carried out of the house? Sure, the poor craythur was already dead when yer Da carried him in.'

'Jaysus, Ma, yeh don't think tha' could be him wanderin' around the house?'

'Could be, Kathleen, could be.'

'Oh, I wish yeh hadn't told me tha' now! I'm goin' to be shittin' on meself.'

'Sure wha' are yeh talkin' about, Kathleen? The dead won't harm yeh. It's the livin' yeh have to keep yer eyes on. Anyway, don't go tellin' any of the others about wha' I just told yeh. They're all nervous wrecks as it is without addin' fuel to the fire.'

* * *

My brother Phil was a swine. Every chance he got, with the help of Noel, he would be jumping out from behind doors, frightening the life out of us girls, until one time, in the early hours of the morning, it all backfired on Phil and Noel . . . well, you would want to have heard the roars and screams out of them.

'I saw it, I saw it! It's standin' there, just like Clare said,' Phil roared. 'Will yiz wake up, Ma, Da?'

Noel was screaming with terror. 'I saw it too, Ma. Are yeh awake?'

'Shut the fuck up, the pair of yiz! Yeh're screamin' like banshees,' said Ma. 'Yeh hardly think I'd be asleep with the noise outta yiz, yeh bloody gobshites. The whole house is awake now. Tha's it. I'm goin' downstairs to make a cup of tea and get meself a Woodbine before I go crazy mad and kill the lot of yiz. I'm sick to death listenin' to stuff about this bloody ghost.'

Ma was only down the stairs when all hell broke out. The roars of her again! I thought she had seen something as well.

'Holy Mother of Divine God! Wha' the fuck is after happenin' here? Phil Doyle, come down here. Kathleen, get yer arse down them stairs now!'

I fell down the stairs, with Da right behind me. When I walked into the kitchen, I couldn't believe what I was looking at.

The table and four chairs had been painted silver. All the jam jars that we drank our tea from, the plates and the only two cups that we had to our name, were all painted gold. Da looked at me; I looked at Ma, who was looking over at Clare, her two eyes nearly popping out of her head. Da quickly stood in front of Ma.

'Now, Lil, let's not get too worked up about this.' He gave me the eye and the nod to get over to Clare, who was standing at the side of the fire with the armchair pulled right up in front of her, hoping that Ma couldn't get at her. Ma was screaming, fucking and blinding out of her like I never saw before. It took Da all his strength to hold Ma back and, with a lot of effort, he got her to sit down on one of the silver chairs and smoke a Woodbine. Then he went through the presses, hoping to find a jam jar that Clare hadn't got her hands on so that he could make Ma a cup of tea to calm her down.

'Kathleen, she's goin' to kill me,' said Clare.

'Will yeh keep yer voice down? I'm goin' to have to get yeh out of here before Ma loses it altogether. Jaysus, Clare, yeh really did it this time. Wha' were yeh thinkin'? Yeh even painted the jam jars.'

'I don't know, Kathleen. I didn't mean to paint everythin'. I got carried away tryin' to keep meself awake.'

'Clare, yeh're goin' to have stop all this ghost business. There's no ghost. De yeh hear me?'

'There is, Kathleen, there is. I know wha' I saw. So did Phil and Noel, and I'm really glad about tha'.'

At this stage Ma was eating the Woodbines in the kitchen. I had Clare in the parlour, out of her way.

'Da, wha' are we goin' to do? Ma's really losin' the plot. She'll kill Clare if she gets her hands on her.'

Da shook his head. 'Kathleen can yeh blame her? I mean,

227

look at the state of the place.' He turned to Clare. 'Clare, yeh have me heart broke. Wha' am I goin' to do with yeh?'

'There *is* a ghost, Da. I saw it. I swear.'

'Be quiet, Clare, I'm not listenin' to any more of this nonsense. Kathleen, take her with yeh and ask Mrs Kearney can she stay with her for a couple of hours until I clean this mess up and try to calm yer mother down, if tha's at all possible. Oh, when yeh're up there, ask her if she has any empty jam jars lyin' around in her press. There's nothin' left to put a cup of tea in.'

It was starting to get bright out as I knocked on Mrs Kearney's door. She listened to me as I filled her in on the goings-on of the night.

'I don't know how your poor mother is still sane, Kathleen. You're a wild bunch. That's all I can say. Tell your father that's no problem. Clare can stay with me, but I think this will take more than a few hours to blow over. Come on in and sit down, the two of you. Kathleen, help me get these jam jars for your father. He knows I always save them up for your mother.'

Mrs Kearney had a soft spot for Clare and held on to her for a couple of days until Ma calmed down. There was no way the table and chairs could be cleaned, so they were chopped up for firewood. Da had got to know a couple of the shopkeepers beside Portobello Bridge from dropping in and out, selling bits of scrap to them over the years. He picked up a second-hand table and chairs, with the promise that he would take extra rubbish each week until the debt was paid. That way no money ever changed hands.

Ma was happy enough when she heard that. Things slowly got back to normal, if you could ever call it that in our house! Da got the priest down to bless the house, hoping it would settle Clare. It never did. She never, ever slept upstairs again, God love her! It cost her a lot of money, as all of the kids would charge her a couple of pennies to go upstairs with her whenever she had to use the bathroom.

* * *

On and off over the years there would be other sightings of the ghost, causing chaos every time. Everyone had the same story to tell – 'a man standing at the end of the bed, a man with no face'. I never did see the ghost myself, but was Clare's dream so real in her own head that she had convinced herself and everybody else that it was true? Could it have been the young man who died in the kitchen that day, his spirit unable to get to the other side, as Ma would put it? All I know is that the seed was planted that night, and the story still goes on to this very day among my family.

Is there really a ghost? I wonder.

24

The Engagement

It was Sunday morning and the sun was splitting the trees. I slipped out of the bedroom and made my way down to the kitchen. Ma was sitting there feeding Paul.

'It's really warm out, Ma. Will I open the back door and let a bit of fresh air in?'

'If yeh want, Kathleen.'

'Yeh must have been up very early. I see the porridge and all is made.'

'I didn't sleep very well last night.'

'Is Paul keepin' yeh awake then?'

'No, the child's fine. I've just a bit of a headache.'

'A nice cup of tea will sort tha' out, Ma. I got up early so's I could get all me work done around the house. Alan said he'd be down early. Maybe I'll go out to Portmarnock, seein's it's so nice out today. The beach is lovely there. We should try and bring the kids someday; they'd love it. Wha' de yeh think, Ma?'

'Wha'ever yeh say, Kathleen.'

I looked a bit more closely at her. 'Yeh're not even mindin' anythin' I'm sayin', Ma.'

'I've things on me mind, Kathleen. Now leave me be,' she snapped.

That was it – Ma was in bad form, so I knew to shut up. I kept out of her way for most of the morning, with a few of the kids helping me. We weren't long getting the cleaning done and the younger ones washed, while Da was out the back tidying around. He was doing everything and anything to try to please Ma, but she wasn't having any of it; even with him taking the pledge, it made no difference. I made my way out to him.

'Da, is there somethin' wrong with Ma? She's terrible snappy. She bit the head off me earlier. Did she say anythin' to yeh?'

'Best leave her be, Kathleen, she'll come around; she always does.'

'Okay, Da.'

Just then I heard Alan arriving. I ran back into the house. 'Ma, the place is sorted, and the young ones is washed and fed. I'll be off now – is tha' okay? I won't be late.'

'Right, Kathleen.' She didn't even lift her head as she spoke.

* * *

We finally got to Portmarnock and were walking along the beach holding hands. I loved the open space and the freedom was great.

'Come on over here, Kathleen, and we'll sit down. I want to talk to yeh about somethin'.'

'Yeh look real serious, Alan. Wha's wrong?'

'De yeh love me, Kathleen?'

'Don't yeh know I do.'

'It's just, yeh never say it.'

'Well, I get shy when it comes to all tha' stuff, Alan. I know I'm the happiest when I'm with yeh, and when yeh're not there, all I do is think about yeh. So I think tha' means . . . I love yeh. There, I said it.'

'Tha's all I wanted to hear, Kathleen.' He put his arms around me and gave me a big hug. 'I have somethin' for yeh.'

Alan always spoiled me rotten, buying me little presents, and I loved every minute of it. He handed me a little box and as I opened it he said the words . . .

'Will yeh marry me, Kathleen?'

I didn't have to think twice. 'I'd love to marry yeh, Alan!'

We kissed, not caring who saw us.

'Do yeh like the ring then?'

'I love it, Alan! Are yeh serious though – us gettin' married?'

'Yeah, of course I am.'

'Will I be able to have a long white dress and veil? Can everybody come? Oh, and the kids, I can't leave them out. They've to come before anybody else.'

I was so excited, he was laughing his head off at me. I ran around the sand dunes, jumping from one to the other like a child. When I think back now, that's all we were – two kids, so young.

Then I got a flash of Ma. I stopped in my tracks and screamed, 'Ma'll go crazy mad.'

'No, she won't. I get on real well with yer Ma and Da.'

'Da'll be okay, Alan, but Ma'll have a stroke. Yeh know she depends on me for everythin'. She won't let me, I know she won't.'

'Jaysus, Kathleen, I was alright until yeh said tha'. Now I'll be shitin' meself askin' them.'

'Leave it to me, Alan, I'll talk to them first.'

'No, I'm not havin' tha'. We'll do it together.'

'Okay, but not tonight. Ma is in the height of it. I don't know wha's wrong. She's snappin' at everybody the past few days.'

* * *

Alan dropped me off at the door and went on home. I went into the kitchen, Da was sitting at the fire reading the paper and Ma was making the lunches for the next day. A couple of the kids were looking at the telly.

'Yeh look tired, Ma. Will I take Paul in with me tonight? Give yeh a break. Let yeh get a good night's sleep.'

'Yeh've to get yerself up early for work tomorrow. He'll have yeh awake durin' the night lookin' for the diddy.'

'Why don't yeh squeeze some milk into the bottle? I'll look after him; I don't mind, Ma, honest.'

'Go about yer business, Kathleen, leave me be.'

Da gave me the eye and the nod to leave her alone. I said good night and went upstairs, not knowing what to think or what could be wrong.

I was standing in front of the bathroom mirror, squeezing a few blackheads out of my chin, when Phil tipped me on the shoulder.

'Jaysus, yeh're after frightenin' the life out of me.'

'Have yeh got a minute, Kathleen?' He sat on the side of the bath. 'I'm goin' away.'

'Stop messin', Phil, will yeh.'

'I'm serious. I'm off to Canada. I have me papers and all.'

'But yeh have no money. Yeh're not goin' away. Will yeh stop actin' the eejit.'

'The Canadian embassy pay yer fare and get yeh a job. Yeh don't have to start payin' them back until yeh're sorted. I'll get sixty pound for me Honda 50. Tha'll do me 'til I get meself goin'.'

'Does Ma know?'

'No, not yet, but Da does. He thinks it's great for me to get out there and see a bit of the world.

'I don't believe this – yeh're really goin' to leave us.'

'I got the word today. I'll be gone in about two weeks. There's no goin' back now; me mind's made up.'

My eyes started to fill up.

'Kathleen, I never thought I'd see the day tha' yeh'd be cryin' over me.'

'No, I'm not, yeh eejit, there's just somethin' in me eye.'

'Get away, yeh're only an oul' softie after all.' He put his arms around me. 'I thought yeh'd be glad to see the back of me.'

'Yeh drive me nuts most of the time, Phil, but I never wanted yeh to go away. Not tha' far anyway.' I pulled back and looked at him. 'I have a bit of news meself; Alan asked me to marry him tonight. Wha' de yeh think?'

'So wha' did yeh say, Kathleen?'

'I said yes. Look, he gave me the ring and all.'

'Alan's a skinny little fucker, but I like him. Yeh're doin' all right there. When's all this happenin'?'

'Not for about a year. It depends on how quick he gets the money together.'

'Good, I should've plenty of money made by then. The wages is great in Canada. So I'll be able to give yeh a few bob, help yeh get a few things.'

'Will yeh really, Phil?' I put my arm around and gave him a big hug. 'I'll miss yeh, so I will. Promise me one thing – yeh'll come home for me weddin'. I'll go mad if yeh're not there.'

'There's no way I'll be missin' tha'. Yeh don't have to worry there. But do me one big favour first; let me tell Ma me bit of news first, then yeh can drop yer bombshell.'

'Jaysus, Phil, wha'll Ma say when she hears the two of us is movin' out? I'm goin' to be shittin' meself tellin' her. She's goin' to lose the head altogether.'

'It'll be only for a day or two, and then she'll come around. Some of us has to start movin' out, for fuck's sake; we're like flies on shite – we're all on top of one another, and now there's Paul, another baby cryin', fartin' and shitin' through the night. You're alrigh', yeh have just one or two of them younger ones pissin' on yeh, but I'm in the same room with Ma and Da. He's gruntin' and snorin' like a pig when he has a sup on him, which is most of the time. Then yeh have Ma fuckin' and blindin' out of her about one thing or another. *And on top of all tha'*, I have Jap-eyes Noel sleepin' in the same bunk bed with me, his smelly feet stuck in me face all night. I wake up every mornin', gaspin'

235

for breath thinkin', *Oh my God, one of them is after shitin' on me face* – the smell's tha' bad. No, I'm on me way, I don't care; there's no changin' me mind. So yeh'll say nothin', Kathleen?'

'Okay, I suppose I'll have to wait with me bit of news.'

* * *

Phil told Ma the next evening. We were all sitting around the table having our tea when he just came out with it.

'Ma, I'm goin' to work in Canada.'

Ma nearly fainted. Da had to run and get her a cup of water.

'Where in God's name is tha', Phil?'

'It's beside America.'

'*Wha*'? Tha's the other side of the world! I'll never see yeh again.'

'Yes yeh will, Ma, sure won't I be able to send yeh loads of money?'

Da wasn't saying a word; Ma looked over at him.

'Did yeh know about this, Phil Doyle?'

'I did, Lil.'

'And yeh never told me about it, yeh connivin' bastard.'

'Young Phil wanted to tell yeh himself.'

Ma broke down crying. Da put his arm around her.

'Now, Lil, don't be gettin' yerself upset. It'll do him good to see a bit of the world before he settles down.'

She just gave him one of her looks and pushed him away.

'Fuck yeh and fuck the world! I don't care, I don't want me son goin' away. I'll never see him again. Leave me be, now, leave me be.'

She was crying really hard, and the kids were getting upset, so I got them all to come upstairs with me.

'I want yiz all to stay up here and be quiet.'

'Kathleen, it's too early for us to go to bed.'

'I know, I know – play a game or somethin', just don't come down. Ma's in the height of it.'

Phil and Da were on their way out when I got to the end of the stairs.

'Where are yiz goin'? Da, don't leave me with Ma in this state.'

'There's no talkin' to her, Kathleen. Best tha' I keep out of the way. Phil's goin' up to the boxin' club to do a bit of trainin'. I'll tag along with him.' Phil was a great boxer; he had become All-Ireland Middleweight Champion and had represented Ireland at international level.

And off they went, leaving me to try to sort things out. I made my way into the kitchen.

'Will yeh have a cup of tea, Ma? Are yeh alright? Are yeh sick? Will yeh talk to me?'

She just rocked backwards and forward in the chair. She had her face covered with one of the baby's towel nappies. I had only seen Ma this upset before when her mother and Maisie died.

'Yeh're not just cryin' over Phil leavin', are yeh, Ma? Will yeh tell me, please?'

She took the nappy away from her face; her eyes were red from crying.

'I'm tha' way again, Kathleen.'

'Wha' de yeh mean, Ma, wha' way?'

'Jaysus, Kathleen, yeh know wha' I mean.'

'I *don't* know. Wha' are yeh talkin' about, Ma?'

'De yeh not understand wha' I'm tryin' to say? *I'm havin' another child.*'

I couldn't get my head around what she had just said. Then the penny finally dropped. 'But yeh just had a baby! Paul's only four months old. Jaysus Christ, Ma, I don't believe this! Yeh're nearly forty-five. This is madness; yeh can't keep havin' babies like this.'

'De yeh not think I know tha', Kathleen? I'm goin' out of me mind with the worry of everythin'.'

Paul started crying. I picked him up and walked him up and

237

down, frantic, screaming inside my head. *Christ, wha' am I goin' to do. I'm never goin' to be able to leave! It's not fair, it's just not fair. I'm leavin', I don't care – I'm not mindin' any more babies. It's not my fault.* Paul was screaming at this stage.

'Kathleen, give me the child. He's lookin' for the diddy.'

I didn't hear her. I was still walking up and down, trying to take it all in.

'Kathleen!' Ma shouted. 'Give 'im to me, before he takes a fit with the hunger.'

'Sorry, Ma, here, here.'

I sat down while Ma settled Paul for his feed. *This is it, I'm sayin' it. I don't care, it's now or never.*

'Ma . . . I want to say somethin' . . . eh . . . eh . . .'

'Hold on a minute there, Kathleen, 'til I fix Paul.' She stuck the diddy in the baby's mouth. 'Now, wha' is it?'

'I . . . I . . . eh . . . Alan asked me to marry him today, and I said yes.' *Tha's it – I've said it.*

Ma went into shock and went silent for a few seconds. I didn't know what would come next.

Then all hell broke loose.

'*Holy Mother of Divine Jaysus!* Are yiz all tryin' to kill me around here with worry? Just when I'm startin' to make ends meet, yeh're all lookin' to leave me. I'm not havin' it! Anyway, yeh're too young, Kathleen. Yeh're only a child. De yeh want to end up like me, Kathleen, never a shillin' in yer pocket? Maybe young Phil is right. Get out there and enjoy himself before he settles down, and you do the same yerself when the time is right.'

'But when will tha' be, Ma? I'm not bein' cheeky, but if I stay here tha' won't happen. As far back as I can remember, all I do is mind kids and clean the house for yeh. I was never a child, *never*. I want to start doin' things for meself for a change.'

By this time I was balling my eyes out. It was my first time ever to speak out and say a little of how I was feeling. I would

238

say plenty inside my head, but never out loud. Ma sat there looking at me, tapping her foot up and down. I didn't know if it was temper or nerves. Either way, I was easing myself up off the chair, and taking a step back, getting ready to run, just in case.

'Sit yerself back down there, I'm not goin' to kill yeh. And wipe the snots off yer face. Yeh had a lot bottled up there in tha' head of yers, so yeh had.'

God, if she only knew! Tha' was only the tip of the iceberg.

'I know. I'm sorry, Ma.'

'Yeh should have said how yeh were feelin'.'

'But Ma, yeh had nobody else to help yeh, and I was too afraid to say anythin'.'

'Am I tha' hard, Kathleen?'

'Yes, yeh are, Ma.'

'Well, I don't mean to be, but if I don't keep things right around here, yer father certainly won't. Anyway, when yeh've things on yer mind, it's best to get them out in the open; otherwise they only seed inside, eat away at yeh, so they do. Tha's wha' I've been doin' the past couple of weeks. I've nobody to turn to, since Mrs Kearney moved to her posh new house out there in Dun Laoghaire; visited me only once, after all them years of us bein' neighbours. People don't be long forgettin' yeh, Kathleen. If only Maisie was here; she got me through so many bad patches in me life, always saw the funny side of everythin'. She's probably up there in heaven laughin' down at me, callin' me all the gobshites under the sun for gettin' meself into this state.'

'*I'm* here, Ma; yeh can always talk to me, and then there's Da.'

'Don't mention tha' man to me. I want to fuckin' kill him, so I do. The things I wanted to say and give out about yer father over the years weren't for yer ears, Kathleen. Anyway, there's just some things yeh don't say to yer child, no matter how old yeh are. Now, tha's enough said on tha' matter, but

I'm glad yeh know wha's been wrong with me and it's out in the open. But how will I ever manage without yeh? Yeh're the only one tha' looks after the place and keeps them young ones in hand when I'm not here.'

'Yeh'll be here yerself all the time now, Ma. Yeh won't be goin' back to work, not with another baby comin' along. It's time yeh stopped anyway. I don't know how yeh lasted this long.'

'Yeh're right there, Kathleen. I'm very tired and not able for them late nights anymore.'

'There's a couple of the others kids comin' up soon for work. Tha'll bring a few shillin's in for yeh and I promise I'll hand me pay packet up until the day I get married. It's not as if I'm goin' far away, like Phil.'

'Don't mention tha' to me or yeh'll start me off cryin' again.'

'I'll be callin' into the house all the time. Yeh'll see, Ma.'

'Does yer father know about this?'

'No, no, we were goin' to tell the two of yiz together.'

'Are yeh sure he wasn't keepin' this to himself as well? Bastard of a man.'

'I swear, Ma, it's just the way everythin' went tonight. Alan will go mad, he wanted to ask yiz himself.'

'Hmm, I see . . . He seems to be a good young fella, not afraid to put his hand in his pocket if he sees yeh're stuck for a smoke, and looks yeh straight in the eye when yeh talk to him. Are yeh sure about this, Kathleen? Is it wha' yeh really want?'

'It is, Ma, I really love Alan.'

'Right then, once yeh're sure, yeh have me blessin'.'

The words were only out of her mouth when there was a big cheer from all the kids. They'd been listening all the time. I didn't care; I wrapped my arms around Ma, hugging and kissing her.

'Jaysus, Kathleen, yeh're after knockin' the diddy out of Paul's mouth. The milk's after goin' into his eye. Will yeh calm yerself down and hand me tha' dry nappy there? For God's sake, wha' the hell's got into yeh?'

'I'm sorry, Ma, it's just yeh've made me so happy.'

'Right, right. I'll talk to yer father.'

'No, Ma, let Alan ask the two of yiz together, please.'

'Okay then, we'll say nothin'.'

* * *

We got all the kids ready and up to bed. I tidied the place and we sat there, just Ma and I, talking and working things out. Da was late coming home with Phil. I suppose he was half hoping everything was okay. It was, but Ma didn't let him know that, not for a while anyway. She gave him one of her looks and that was enough for him.

'I'll say goodnight then, Lil. I'm off to bed.'

She grunted under her breath.

As Da went upstairs, I followed him, telling him I knew why Ma was so upset.

'Thank God, she told yeh, Kathleen.'

'Just go along with her, Da. She'll come around, yeh'll see.'

'Good, good. Thanks for lookin' after things for me. I don't know wha' we'd do without yeh.'

I went back downstairs. Phil was in the kitchen.

'Yeh knew all along wha' was wrong with Ma, didn't yeh, yeh swine?'

He swore on everything that was holy that he knew nothing.

'I don't believe yeh! Yeh're a sly fucker, Phil Doyle.'

He was laughing his head off. 'Will yeh stop gettin' yerself all worked up, for Jaysus' sake; Da only told me on the way up to the club. Wha' beats me is, how are they managin' to do it with all of us sleepin' in the same fuckin' room?'

'Oh my God, Phil, will yeh keep yer voice down? Imagine even thinkin' about Ma and Da doin' things like tha'.'

'Yeh know somethin', in between all tha' snorin', the sly bastard must've been doin' it all the time and I never copped on. He has to be one fast man. I can tell yeh tha' for nothin'. In and out like a light.'

'Yeh know wha' you are, Phil? Just a filth, I mean it, yeh are.'

'Would yeh get away with yeh, Kathleen, actin' all high and mighty! Don't tell me tha' Alan never felt more than the top of yer leg or yer arse for tha' matter. He's not bringin' yeh out to Portmarnock every chance he gets for nothin'.'

'Will yeh stop, Alan's not like tha'.'

'Would yeh give it over. He'd have yer knickers off like a flash of lightnin' the first chance he got, which he probably already has.'

'Yeh can get tha' dirty grin off yer face, Phil, because he hasn't. I don't do things like tha'.'

'Yeh mean yeh're still a virgin after all this time with Alan?'

'Wha' are yeh talkin' about? I'm not a virgin, right – I missed Mass twice last month and I only said me rosary once this week, because I was tired. Now, wha' de yeh say to tha', smart arse?!'

At this stage Phil was rolling around the floor screaming, he was laughing so much.

'Stop, Kathleen, stop. I'm gettin' pains in me chest here. Are yeh for fuckin' real or wha'?'

'I don't know wha' yeh think is so funny, Phil.'

'I don't believe this – yeh're still so innocent, Kathleen. Ma!' he shouted. 'Ma, come out here and talk to this wan, will yeh? Before she's the laughin' stock of Crumlin.'

That's when Ma came in.

'Wha's goin' on with the pair of yiz, shoutin' at this hour of the night? Yeh'll have the whole house awake.'

'Don't mind him, Ma, it's nothin'. He's messin' as usual.'

'For Jaysus' sake, Ma, will yeh ever sit her down and tell her a few things. Yeh know, about men and women stuff – yeh know wha' I'm talkin' about, Ma. She knows fuck-all.'

'Mind yer lip there, Phil. Yeh're not too big to get the back of me hand.'

'Ah, I'm sorry, Ma, I can't help it.' He shook his head, still laughing as he went upstairs.

'Kathleen, wha' has Phil been sayin'?'

'He said tha' I'm still a virgin – the cheek of him. Well, I put him straight and told him I wasn't.'

She nearly choked on her cup of tea. *'Yeh wha'?!'*

'Phil thinks I'm a real Holy Mary because I go to Mass and say me prayers every night. He's always makin' a laugh of me.'

'Didn't I tell yeh, Kathleen, I don't know how many times, not to be lettin' Phil wind yeh up? Now, wha's this – are yeh tellin' me straight to me face tha' yeh've done the other with Alan?'

'Wha' are yeh talkin' about, Ma, wha' other? Wha' de yeh mean?'

'You know . . . yeh're not tha' fuckin' stupid, Kathleen. Men and women, together – doin' the other!'

The penny finally dropped with me. 'Yeh mean tha'? Oh my God! No, I haven't! Who said tha'?'

'*You* did. Yeh just said yeh weren't a virgin. Tha's wha' tha' means.'

'Good fuck! I didn't know tha', nobody told me. Ma, why didn't yeh say somethin'? I thought bein' a virgin meant bein' like the Virgin Mary herself.' I was off again, tears and snots everywhere. 'I'm such a gobshite, Ma, I know nothin'. No wonder Phil was laughin' at me.'

'Sshh now, Kathleen, yeh're no different than the rest of us women. These are things tha' nobody talks about. Yeh're just supposed to pick them up as yeh go along. It's my fault, I should've talked to yeh – not tha' I know tha' much meself, yeh know wha' I mean.' She got herself a bit flustered. 'But there's one thing I know for sure, and tha's how to have babies.'

'Yeh can say tha' again, Ma.'

I got a half-grin off her. I wasn't sure if I should laugh or stay serious, so I said nothing more.

'Just make sure yeh keep yerself to yerself, Kathleen, and don't be lettin' anybody interfere with yeh down below. A heart attack yeh nearly gave me, sayin' yeh're not a virgin and all! It's bad enough me bringin' too many babies into this God-forsaken world, without you startin'.'

I went to bed that night still mixed up, but a little bit wiser.

The next morning I had a hundred and one questions for Phil. 'Seein's yeh know so much, yeh better fill me in on a few things.'

'So the penny has finally dropped, huh, Kathleen?'

Phil wasn't long putting me straight on the facts of life.

'How de yeh know all this, Phil?'

'There was a few oul' fellas on the site when I started work. They don't be long tellin' yeh wha's for wha', and where it goes. Then I just picked meself up a mot here and there and, Bob's yer uncle, I was away in a hack.'

* * *

Every night for about a week, Alan tried to get Ma and Da on their own to ask them about us getting married, but with one thing or another – the kids fighting, Ma in the height of it, Da having a sup on him – no time was the right time.

Saturday night came and Alan was down early.

'This is it, Kathleen. I'm sayin' it tonight. I don't give a damn wha's goin' on or who's here. They can all listen. I don't care.'

'Right, then. We'll say it together.'

Ma and Da were sitting each side of the fireplace. Phil and Noel were lying head to toe on the old couch; the rest of the kids were sitting on the floor looking at the telly.

I nudged Alan and whispered, 'John Wayne's on, so none of the kids will move. They all love the cowboy films.'

'I don't care, let them.' Alan gave a little cough, trying to get Da's attention. 'Excuse me, Phil, can I have a word with yerself and Lil?'

'Ah, there yeh are, come in, come in. Move up there, Noel, and let Alan sit down.'

'Yeh're all right, Noel. I'll stand.'

We stood there, side by side, hand in hand. Alan stood tall, looking directly at Ma and Da and came right out with it. 'We'd like to get married, if it's okay with yiz.'

I squeezed his hand and thought, *he's so grown-up compared to me*. Ma just sat there and didn't bat an eyelid. I thought that she might have softened the blow a bit and helped him out; but no, she made him run the gauntlet all the way. The questions came left, right and centre, but Alan was well able for them. He had all the answers. I was so proud of him.

'Hmm . . .' said Ma, 'Yeh seem to have it all worked out then, Alan.'

Just then, Phil jumped up off the chair and switched the telly off. The kids all started giving out. 'Wha' did yeh do tha' for Phil? Put the telly back on.'

'Shut the fuck up, this is better than any John Wayne film.'

Alan gave a little cough again and answered.

'Yes, I think so, Lil.'

'Well now, Phil Doyle, wha' have you got to say about all this?'

There wasn't a sound. You could hear a pin drop. Da was surprised, but not shocked like Ma had been.

'It's comin' a bit earlier than I expected, but yeh're a good young fella, Alan, and I know yeh'll do well by Kathleen. Isn't tha' all any father wants for his daughter? Yeh're sure now it's wha' yiz want?'

Both of us answered at the one time. 'We do, we do.'

'Okay, but there's just one thing wrong, Alan.'

That soon took the smile off both our faces. 'Wha's tha', Phil?'

'We haven't got a shillin' to our name to help yeh out. Yeh'll have to carry the load yerselves, if it's a big weddin' yeh want and all.'

'Tha's fine, Phil. I'll look after everythin', yeh can be sure of tha'.'

'Right then, yeh seem to have yer minds made up. I'm happy for yiz. Wha' de yeh say, Lil?'

Ma had made her way over to the kitchen table. She was standing there with a large sliced pan in her hand, getting the supper ready. She buttered every slice without a word.

'For God's sake, Lil, will yeh answer Alan? Say somethin'!' Da roared.

'I will when I'm ready.'

She walked over and stood right in front of the two of us.

'Have yeh any smokes on yeh, Alan?'

'I have, Lil. I got yerself and Phil a packet each on the way down.'

She looked him straight in the face.

'Yeh're a smart young fella, Alan, so yeh are.' Then she looked at me. 'I won't say tha' I'm happy about yeh leavin', Kathleen. Ah go on then, yeh have me blessin'.'

Da jumped up and shook Alan's hand.

'It's about bloody time, Lil. I never saw anythin' to be dragged on so much.'

The words were only out of Ma's mouth when I had the ring out of the box, and on my finger. The girls were over in seconds, trying it on and asking if the diamonds were real and how many there were. Phil put his arm around the two of us.

'Yeh know somethin', Alan?'

'Wha's tha', Phil?'

'Yeh're one cute whore, so yeh are. Tha' was like lookin' at a boxin' match in the stadium. Yeh went every round, and didn't get knocked down once, but when yeh took them smokes out, I knew yeh had it won. Fair play to yeh, tha's all I can say.'

246

Alan gave Noel and Clare a few pound and sent them down for fish and chips and a few bottles of lemonade for everybody. We sat there for hours, the whole family, the younger ones sitting on the floor back looking at the telly, the rest laughing, joking and planning what they were going to wear and who would be doing what at the wedding. I looked over at Ma. She was smiling and talking to Da.

I thought to myself, *Good, she's comin' around at last.*

The table was full of food for a change; there was a full packet of smokes in Ma's pocket, thanks to Alan; Da was sober – and all in one night. *This is good; this is the way it should always be.*

It was a happy house that night.

25

Departures and Arrivals

The next two weeks went by so fast. It was the night before
Phil was due to go to Canada. We were all in bed; most of the
younger ones were asleep. Ma and Da were downstairs and
Phil and I were in our beds, talking to one another across the
landing. The rest of the kids were messing and acting the eejit.
Then Phil went really quiet. I thought he had gone asleep. All
of a sudden I heard this voice.

It was Phil singing.

'Shush, stay quiet, will yiz?'

I had no idea he could sing like that. I said nothing, just
listened. It was one of Roy Orbison's greatest hits:

'I hear the sound of distant drums
Far away, far away . . .'

He sang every word of that song, right down to the last
verse. There was complete silence when he finished. Nobody
said a word. They all let on they were asleep, but you could
hear the sobs under the blankets, including mine.

* * *

Phil was up bright and early the next morning. He filled a small haversack with his painter's overalls, a couple of scrapers, a few paintbrushes, and a few bits of clothes, heading off to make his fortune.

'Tha's me packed and ready to go, Ma.'

She sat there in silence.

His flight was early, so there wasn't much time to sit around. He knew full well how upset the whole family was; I think he planned it that way – and there was no way he would let any of us go to the airport with him.

'How will I know yeh're safe and well, Phil?' Ma asked.

'Don't worry, Ma, I won't be long gettin' friendly with somebody. I'll get them to scribble a few lines to let yeh know how I'm gettin' on.'

I stood back and watched him. One by one, he hugged and kissed every one of the kids. You could see he was choking, trying to keep the tears in. He tried to make a bit of a joke with Noel and Thomas, giving them each a clatter on the back of the head.

'You two keep yerselves in yer place. I'll be back.' He put his arms around both of them.

'Well now, Kathleen, it's yer turn. Come over here and give yer big brother an oul' squeeze and don't be puttin' any tears and snots on me good shirt. It's the only one I have.'

I hugged him as hard as I could. 'You come back now, Phil, de yeh hear me?'

'Didn't I swear I would?' I couldn't breathe, he was holding onto me so tight. He whispered in my ear. 'Cock yer ear up there, Kathleen. I want to ask yeh somethin' without the others listenin'.'

'Wha's tha', Phil?'

'Kathleen, are yeh still a virgin?'

He laughed his head off; all I could see were those pearly white teeth of his. Right to the very last minute, he was still trying to wind me up; but I wouldn't be wound up that day. I just gave him back a smile as big as his.

He went over and shook Da's hand; they looked into one another's eyes. There were no words. There didn't have to be; that special look was enough.

As he made his way over to Ma, there wasn't a murmur. Phil had been doing well up to that, putting on a big front. Now, his lip started to tremble. He gave her such a big hug. Ma held onto him and wouldn't let go. Her legs were nearly going from under her as she cried out.

'Don't go, Phil, please don't go.'

He was choking as the tears fell from his cheeks. Da made his way over.

'Come on now, Lil, I know it's hard.'

He eased Ma from the clutches of Phil's arms. She fell to her knees as Da tried to console her.

Phil picked his haversack up, stood back and looked at us all for a second, not saying a word. Then off he went, running down the road without looking back.

I cried my eyes out, watching him fade away in the distance, with little more than the clothes on his back and the sixty pounds that he got for his Honda 50, heading off to Canada to make his millions. *He'll do well,* I thought, *I know he will. With tha' big smile, how could he not?*

There was doom and gloom over the next few days. The house was very quiet for a change. Phil was such a messer. You'd always be looking over your shoulder, waiting on him to pounce out on you. If he wasn't doing that, he'd be sticking chewing gum inside your bra or putting balls of muck in the only pair of clean knickers that you had to your name. *I'll miss him, so I will.*

* * *

Over the next few weeks, every chance we got, Alan and myself were out pricing anything to do with the wedding. Alan sat down one evening for hours doing his sums.

251

'Right, Kathleen, if it's the Victor Hotel yeh want, with the prices they're lookin' for – and I can tell yeh, it's not cheap – the most tha' can come to the weddin' is fifty, no more.'

'Is tha' countin' all the kids, Alan?'

'It is; and if I put me mind down to it and save every penny, we can get married for Christmas.'

'I don't believe yeh! Jaysus, tha's very quick, Alan. But where will we live?'

'I have it all worked out, Kathleen. Me Granda said we could stay with him for as long as we want.'

'Oh Alan, I don't know about tha'. I don't want to live with anybody. Ma said it's best to have our own place.'

'Well then, we could forget about the big weddin' and wait until I have enough money for a deposit on our own house and just get married on the quiet – but tha'll take me about two years.'

'I don't want to wait tha' long, de you?'

'Yeh know I don't, Kathleen. I'll tell yeh wha' – I'll bring yeh down to see me Granda's house, see wha' yeh think. It's not far from yer Ma's house, just ten minutes' walk. It's still early; come on, we'll go down now.'

'Hold on, Alan, 'til I get me coat. Ma, de yeh need anythin' in the shops? I'm goin' out for an hour.'

'Tha's grand, Kathleen, yeh can pick me up five Woodbines and a couple of loaves of bread on yer way home. Have yeh got half a crown to spare, Alan? I'll pay yeh back on Friday as soon as Phil gives me the wages. There should be a couple of pennies left – see if yeh can get me one or two ice pops. Yeh know, the orange ones. Me mouth's waterin' here just thinkin' of them; I have a longin' yeh'd never believe.'

'Right, Lil, we'll pick them up for yeh and we won't be long.'

We were standing outside Alan's Granda's house before I knew it.

'Wha' did I tell yeh, Kathleen? Only minutes away.'

I took one look and wanted to run.

'It's in bits, Alan. Could we not get a flat or somethin'?'

'De yeh not realise how much a flat would cost, Kathleen? The rent's only five shillin's a week to stay with me Granda. We could kill two birds with one stone: yeh could have the weddin' yeh always dreamed about and save for a house while we stay here on the cheap. It would be just for a while; with the two of us workin', we'd have the money together in no time. Wha' de yeh say?' He put his arm around me and gave me a big squeeze. 'A drop of fresh paint and a bit of elbow grease, and I'll have this place spick and span by the time we move in. Come on, Kathleen. Me Granda is a quiet man; yeh'd hardly know he was around.'

'Okay then, once it's only for a short time – promise me, Alan.'

It was late when we got back so Alan went on home. The kids were all in bed.

'Here's the ice pops, Ma; sorry, they're nearly melted.'

I started to tell them all about the wedding.

'Hold on there for a second, Kathleen. Hand me one of them jam jars. These ice pops are breakin' up in me hand. I'll have to eat them with a spoon. Go on, wha' were yeh sayin' there?'

I launched into the ins and outs of what was going to happen and where we were going to live.

As soon as Ma heard I was going to live with Alan's Granda, she went mad. The jam jar was smashed down so hard on the table, it nearly broke in half. Lumps of ice pop splashed all over her dress. 'Kathleen! Look wha' yeh made me do!'

'Ma, will yeh just listen?'

'No, you listen to me and take good heed of wha' I'm sayin'. Don't move onto anybody else's floor; it never works out. Mark my words, I know wha' I'm talkin' about. Even if it's only one room with just floorboards and an orange box to sit on, yeh have to answer to nobody only yerself – isn't tha' right, Phil Doyle?' She gave Da the look.

He just rolled his eyes in the air and shook his head. 'I'll leave yiz to it. I'm off to bed. Goodnight.'

'I'll see yeh in the mornin', Da.'

Ma was still rammaging on; she was on a roll.

'People get set in their ways and don't like change, Kathleen, and tha's when the trouble starts. Yeh don't have to splash all tha' money on a weddin', not for us. Wait a bit and get yer own place. Listen to me, I know wha' I'm talkin' about.'

But no, I wasn't having any of it. I wanted to be a princess for a day.

'It'll only be for a while, Ma. I'll still get me house.'

'I can see yeh're takin' no heed to wha' I'm sayin', so I'll say no more on the matter, and tha's tha'.'

'Ma, don't get all annoyed with me. I just want to have me big day.'

'Big day me arse, Kathleen. It's the hard way yeh'll be learnin', mark my word.'

Everything went quiet for a minute.

'Ma, will I make yeh a cup of tea?' I said, trying to soften the subject. 'Oh, by the way, when is the baby due?'

'And why would yeh be askin' me tha'?'

'It's just yeh have to give the hotel and church plenty of notice. The weddin' is goin' to be around Christmas time, Ma.'

'Hmm, tha' quick now, is it? Well, the child is expected around the end of November, all goin' well, with the Holy Mother of God watchin' over me.' She blessed herself three times.

I put my arms around her. 'Yeh'll be grand, Ma. Don't worry. I'll make sure we wait until the baby is born and Christmas is over.'

'And tha's supposed to make me feel better, is it, Kathleen?'

'Come on now, Ma. Yeh gave me yer blessin' and all.'

'It's just tha' it's bad enough bein' down two wages and on top of all tha' yeh won't be here to give me a hand. How will I ever manage?'

'Ma, didn't I tell yeh, I'd look after everythin', and I will, I promise.'

* * *

We booked the wedding for the 27th of December 1967. I got my way: St Agnes' Church, Crumlin, and Hotel Victor, Dun Laoghaire. Not a week went by that I wasn't in town or up in Meath Street looking for bargains, trying to dress all the kids for the big day. The months went by so fast.

There were a couple of letters from Phil in the meantime; always a few lines scribbled down on one page, just to say that he was safe and working away, with a few dollars tucked inside the page. 'It's not much, Ma. I hope it helps.' He always signed the end: 'Love, young Phil.' That made Ma happy. She knew he wrote that bit himself.

In one of his letters, Phil told Alan to go ahead and ask Noel to be best man, as he wouldn't be getting home until the last minute and there would be no time to get measured for a suit. Noel was only fourteen, but he had grown so much in the past few months, he looked more like a man than a boy. All his puppy fat was gone. He wasn't far off six foot in height, with his black curly hair and tiny moustache.

'Tha's my Errol Flynn,' Ma would say. 'He should be in the films, so he should. He's tha' good lookin'.'

Carmel was to be my bridesmaid. That kept her happy.

* * *

Before I knew it, it was November. Ma was so big she could hardly walk.

'Yeh don't look the best, Ma; are yeh alright?'

'I don't feel well at all, Kathleen.'

'Have yeh started? Are yeh in labour?'

'No, but there's somethin' wrong. The child's after movin'

255

crossways in me. I can feel it. I better get meself down to the hospital. There's a brown bag under me bed with a few bits in it. Go up and tell yer father I want him; he's not to make a fuss. Just leave the bag at the end of the stairs. I'll get it on the way out.'

'Jesus, Lil, is it tha' time already? Will I get the ambulance?'

'De yeh want to put the heart crossways in them younger ones, lookin' at me goin' off in an ambulance? For fuck's sake, Phil, would yeh ever use yer head for once, and not be leavin' everythin' to me?'

I looked over at Da and gave him the nod to say nothing. Thank God Alan had just arrived; a few weeks earlier he had traded his bike in for a black Austin Eight Forty – not a big car by any means but it got us around and that was all that mattered.

'You look after the kids, Da. We'll take Ma down to the hospital.'

It must have taken us the guts of ten minutes to try and get Ma into the car. As we were pulling away I looked back and there were little Jacinta and Patricia balling their eyes out.

'Are the kids okay, Kathleen?'

'There's not a bother on them, Ma, they're fine – none the wiser.'

Ma was right. We were only in the door of the hospital when she was rushed off in a wheelchair. I couldn't get anybody to tell me what was happening. Every time I asked, they just kept saying, 'There will be somebody with you shortly.' We seemed to be sitting there for ever. Then, finally I saw a nurse walking over to me. I jumped up off the seat, not knowing what to expect.

'Can I see me Ma? Is she okay?'

'Mother and baby are fine. We had to do an emergency section. Everything went well.'

That night my brother Mano was born, Ma's twelfth and last baby.

* * *

It was late by the time Alan dropped me home. Da was walking the floor with Paul. When he saw me, he stopped in his tracks, white in the face with worry.

'Ma is fine, Da. A big baby boy, eight and a half pound!'

'Is yer mother okay, then?'

'I didn't see her, Da; she had to be sectioned.' I explained everything the nurse had told me. 'Here, Da, give me Paul, I'll try an' settle him'. Paul was a little over a year old and all he wanted was his Ma.

'He's cryin' since yeh left, Kathleen. I can't get any good of him at all.'

'He's frettin' for Ma, Da. Ah, look, his little eyes are all swollen. I'll put him in the bed between me and Patricia.'

'Sure she's as bad; herself and Jacinta are after cryin' themselves asleep, waitin' on yer mother to come home. I didn't know wha' to be tellin' them. Yer mother always looks after these things.'

Patricia and Jacinta were wrapped in Ma's coat, asleep on the chair. The rest of the kids were asleep on the floor in front of the fire.

I shook Jacinta and Patricia. 'Wake up, girls.'

'Kathleen, where's me Ma?' Patricia asked, her little voice trembling. I put her on my lap, my arm around Jacinta, the rest of them waiting to hear what I had to say.

'Ma's fine, she's just very tired and needs a rest for a few days.'

Paul was still screaming.

'Now, if yeh're all good and there's no more cryin', I'll bring home a big bag of chocolate sweets on Friday. Come on, give us a smile – let me see them dimples, Jacinta.'

A little grin, that's all I got. I was too tired to make up a story about the new baby. *I'll leave tha' one for Ma. See wha' she comes up with.*

257

'Right, up to bed with yiz.'

I finally got them settled and myself into the bed. Paul was still crying. There was no way I could settle him, even after a bottle. I was falling out of my standing for the want of sleep. He kept pushing his little head under my arm and into my chest.

'Kathleen, can yeh not keep him quiet?' Da shouted in. 'He's at it since this mornin'. The neighbours will think we're killin' him.'

'I'm tryin', Da. It's Ma he wants, not me.'

A voice came from under the blankets. 'It's her diddy, yeh mean.' said Clare, sticking her head out. 'Why don't yeh give him *yers*?'

'Clare, I'll give yeh such a kick up the hole if yeh say another word – I'm warnin' yeh!'

'Go on, Kathleen,' the rest of them said. 'He's drivin' us mad with all tha' cryin'.'

'I can't do tha'; anyway, I'm as flat as a pancake. I haven't got any.'

'Yeh can say tha' again,' Noel shouts in, laughing his head off.

'Don't you speak to yer sister like tha'. I've had a bad enough day without listenin' to the likes of tha' talk.' Da was really annoyed and tha' soon shut Noel up.

That's when I came up with what Da afterwards called a masterplan.

'Right, Clare, since you started all this, run downstairs and get me one of them tits tha's in the bowl of water in the kitchen.'

'De yeh want a bottle as well, Kathleen?'

'No, just the tit – and make sure it's one of the old ones. Marion, get me a bit of brown paper.'

'For wha', Kathleen? I'm tired.'

'To wipe her arse with, yeh gobshite, Marion,' Thomas shouts in.

'Tha's it,' Da said. I could hear him jumping out of the bed. 'It's the belt the two of yeh will be gettin', if there's one more word. Don't think just because yer mother's not here tha' yeh'll be carryin' on like bowsies.'

He was banging his belt off the end of the bed, trying to put the fear of God in them. Everything went quiet for a few seconds – except for Paul, who was still screaming. Then the giggling started. We all knew Da inside out; he never put a finger on any of us. He was just a big softy.

I stuffed the teat with the brown paper to make sure Paul wouldn't suck any wind in.

'Right, Carmel, hold him for a second till I take me jumper off. Turn around, the rest of yiz, and don't be lookin' at me.'

I put an old t-shirt on, leaving one arm out.

'Now, give me Paul.'

I got the rubber teat between my two fingers and placed it over the front of my own nipple (if you could call it that; it was more like a jelly tot). I stuck the teat in Paul's mouth. It took him a couple of minutes to get settled, and that was it. The crying stopped; he was asleep in no time.

'Not a word out of any of yiz outside the house about this, de yeh hear me?'

'We all swear, don't we?' said Clare.

I got the nod off all of them; they were just glad the crying had stopped and they could go to sleep. It took me a couple of nights, but I slowly got Paul off the teat and onto his own soother before Ma came home from the hospital. Thank God! The thoughts of her sitting there with two babies, one sucking off each diddy, didn't bear thinking about.

* * *

Ma was in hospital for over two weeks; with only a week to go to the wedding, my nerves were gone. I was running around like a lunatic, flying down to the hospital to see Ma for a few minutes each night, then on over to the dressmaker's, up to the church, out to the hotel, back to the kids. Alan was great and so was Da.

Da promised me the day Mano was born, 'I'll have a sup tonight, Kathleen, to wet the baby's head. I'll give yeh me word tha' not a drop of Guinness will pass me lips 'til the day of yer weddin'.'

And he was true to his word. He was there day and night with me, even when Ma came home.

I'll never forget the look on Jacinta's and Patricia's faces. Their eyes nearly popped out of their head when Ma walked in with Mano.

'Who's tha'?' Jacinta asked.

'Tha's yer new baby brother, love.'

'Where did yeh get him from, Ma?' little Patricia asked. The older ones started giggling and tipping one another.

'Hold on there till I get meself settled. Carmel, hold the baby for me. Kathleen, give Paul over here 'til I give him a cuddle.' He was only in her arms two seconds and he was asleep. 'It's grand to be back on me own floor again. Right, gather around and sit down beside me. Now, have yiz heard of Michael the Archangel?' One or two said 'Yeah'; the rest of them stood there with their mouths open, not having a clue what Ma was on about. 'For Jaysus' sake, are they teachin' yiz nothin' up there in tha' bloody school? Yeh should be gettin' told all about the angels in yer acadiacism class.' She stopped to light a Woodbine. 'Now, wha' was I sayin' before I interrupted meself? Oh yeah. Isn't Michael only one of the top guardian angels up there in heaven? Wha' does he only go and do?'

I thought to myself, *this should be a good one.*

'Wha', Ma, tell us, wha'?'

'He landed on me bed in the middle of the night in the hospital. Such a fright I got. He said he was lookin' for a home for a little baby. "Wha' baby?" says I. Tha's when his wings opened and there little Mano was. Sure, how could I say no?'

The older ones started to drift to the back yard one by one, knowing full well it was one of Ma's yarns. The rest wanted to know how big his wings were.

'The width of the room, so they were.'

I went into the kitchen to help Da with the dinner. Ma sat there chatting away about the Holy Mother, heaven and the angels.

'Kathleen, where does she get the stories from?' Da said. 'Would yeh have a look at them young ones' faces. They're gobsmacked. I tell yeh somethin' for nothin', tha' woman could nearly be a poet, if she put her mind down to it.'

I just looked at him. 'Are yeh for real, Da?'

He just laughed. 'Had yeh goin' there for a minute all the same, Kathleen.'

'I don't think so Da. Will yeh do me a favour?'

'And wha' would tha' be, Kathleen? If it's in me power, don't yeh know, I will.'

'I've to pick me weddin' dresses up on Thursday. I need yeh to stick a few nails in the wall up in the bedroom, so's I'll have somewhere to hang them. And yeh better put a few in yer own room for the fellas' suits.'

He was peeling the potatoes. I was going on about all the things I had to do before the week was out, and didn't notice how quiet Da had gone. I tipped him on the shoulder.

'Da, are yeh listenin' to me?'

When he turned around, I could see the tears were ready to drop.

'Jaysus, Da, wha's wrong with yeh? Are yeh alright?'

'Yeh know, it's only hittin' me now, Kathleen, tha' yeh're not goin' to be here all the time. I'm goin' to miss yeh. It's always been the two of us lookin' after things when yer mother's not here.'

I thought, *When Da? When was tha'? When were you here and not in the pub?* Even so, I got such a lump in my throat when he said that to me.

'I'll still be here, Da. I won't let a day go by tha' I won't drop in.'

'I know yeh'll be here, but yeh won't, if yeh know wha' I mean. Who's goin' to stop yer mother from bashin' me brains in when I have a sup on me? Yeh know tha' temper of hers.'

I put my arm around him.

'Come on now, Da. Don't get upset. Just make sure when yeh go for a pint tha' yeh don't forget to come home. My wages won't be there anymore, so yeh'll have to give an extra few bob. Ma's not gettin' any younger, and with two more babies to feed it's not goin' to be easy for her. Yeh can't blame her gettin' all fired up. Just look how hard the last few weeks were with her not bein' here. Just think about it, Da.'

He stood there thinking his own thoughts for a minute.

'Kathleen, yiz were always ahead of yer years, yerself and Phil. I suppose yeh had to be with the likes of me not facin' up to me responsibilities, shuttin' everythin' out with the drink. The coward's way out, tha's wha' it is.'

I wanted to agree with him but I hadn't got the heart to. 'Don't be too hard on yerself, Da. It's never too late to change.'

'And tha's wha' I'll be doin'. I really mean it this time, Kathleen. I'll take a sup at yer weddin' and then it's the pledge for me once and for all. Now, will yeh carry on with the rest of the dinner, so's I can sort them nails out for yeh?'

'Tha's grand, Da, thanks.'

Off he went believing to the very depths of his soul that he meant what he said, but I knew he didn't.

26

The Wedding

The next few days went by so fast. It was Thursday, two days before the wedding, and Phil was on his way home from Canada. You could see Ma's heart starting to lift. Her blue-eyed boy was coming home.

The look on Ma's and Da's faces was priceless when he walked in. The whole room lit up with that smile of his. You could have handed them the world, and it wouldn't have meant as much.

Between the kids and Da, he had a hundred and one questions thrown at him. Ma just sat by the fire with the two babies in her arms, as happy as anything. I slipped out of the room with Alan. We sat on the end of the stairs, chatting and going over the last few things that had to be done.

'Yeh've been so good over the past few weeks, Alan. Yeh've the patience of a saint. I've barely had time to talk to yeh, I mean, I know we talked and all, about the weddin' and stuff.' I was rammaging on and on. He sat there looking at me, not saying a word. 'Wha's wrong, Alan?'

I started to have one of my super blushes.

'Will yeh stay quiet for one minute and give us a kiss, Kathleen.'

263

I just about got a kiss when Phil jumped on top of the two of us.

'Caught yiz! I see yeh're still tryin' to get into her knickers, Alan.'

'The big city hasn't changed yeh anyway, Phil,' Alan answered. 'Nice to have yeh back.'

'Come over here, sis, and plant one right there,' said Phil, pointing to the side of his face.

I bent over to kiss him on the cheek. What does he only go and do: picks me up in the air, throws me over his shoulders, runs all over the house, lashing the arse off me. The kids thought this was great. I even caught Ma laughing.

'Put me down, yeh bloody eejit!' I screamed. And he did – right on top of Alan. 'Yeh didn't grow up at all, Phil Doyle. I thought yeh might have come back with some brains in tha' head of yers, but yeh're as mad as ever.'

'Fuck the grown-up stuff. I'll be doin' tha' for long enough. Come 'ere and give me a big hug, the pair of yiz.'

We were like two little kids underneath his big broad shoulders. It felt good. He had kept his promise, like I knew he would. I was so happy he was home.

We sat there for a while talking, Phil telling us all sorts of yarns; he was probably making up half of them, if the truth be known. I went in to Ma and left the two of them chatting away on the stairs. Half of the kids were asleep on the floor as usual. Da started carrying them upstairs one by one. Phil and Alan came in.

'Kathleen, I'll drop in tomorrow for an hour; we've to go out to the hotel. I'm off now so I'll say goodnight to yiz all.'

'See yeh tomorrow so.' I gave him a little smile as he left.

Phil looked around at all the kids. 'I see nothin's changed, Ma.'

'Would yeh give yer father a hand there, Phil?'

Phil bent down, put one on each shoulder, and had them all up in minutes where poor Da would have been huffing and puffing for the best part of half an hour. Some nights the kids would slip back down so that they would get a second jockey-back, as they called it. Da always knew but pretended he didn't, until Ma would let a roar. Then they'd nearly shit on themselves with the fright and wouldn't be long running back up to bed.

When everybody was gone to bed I sat there talking to Phil.

'I won't be stayin', Kathleen.'

'I know, Phil; I can see it in yer face.'

'I'll be gone as soon as I get a few bob behind me. I used up every penny to get meself home for the weddin'.'

I put my arm around him and rested my head against his. 'I knew yeh wouldn't let me down, Phil.'

'Kathleen, it was so hard out there in Canada, and I'm not talkin' about the work. I can do tha' standin' on me head. I was so lonely and missed everybody so much. I could have filled Niagara Falls up with the tears I shed.'

'Niagara Falls? Wha' the hell is tha', Phil?'

'Yeh never saw the likes of it, Kathleen, the most amazin' sight yeh ever saw. Mountains and mountains of water, never stops. Unbelievable, I swear. I know I'll make meself a good life out there. Would yeh not think about goin'? Yerself and Alan would do well with the two of yiz workin'. Yeh'd have a mansion in no time. Yeh'd want to see the size of the houses. First, they have half a house under the ground. Don't ask me why. They call tha' the basement. Then, wha' do they only go and do – build a full house on top of it again. There's tha' many rooms, sure yeh wouldn't know where to be sittin'. Wha's wrong with yeh, Kathleen? Why are yeh lookin' at me like tha'?'

'Alan already asked me to go to Canada. He got the forms and all, Phil.'

'Did he send them away?'

'Yeah, but I told him I don't think I'd go. He sent them, anyway. He's hopin' I'll change me mind.'

'For fuck's sake, Kathleen, there's half the battle won, him wantin' to go and all.'

'I wouldn't last a month, Phil. I'd die if I didn't see the kids. And wha' about Ma? I promised I'd always be here for her. And then there's Da. Wha' about when he hits the bottle? Who'd be here to help sort things out with Ma?'

'There's plenty of the other kids to do tha'.'

'They're all too young, Phil. Anyway, the thing is, you really want to go back to Canada, tha's yer dream. Alan would like to go, but I don't, and tha's the difference.'

We sat there until the early hours of the morning talking, Phil doing everything in his power to try to convince me to go back to Canada with him. Eventually we fell asleep there on the couch, my head on Phil's shoulder.

* * *

The next morning I was woken up by Patricia and Jacinta diving on top of us, hugging and kissing Phil, knocking me to the floor. That was the start of a hectic day.

'I see yeh're awake then, Kathleen,' said Ma.

'I am now, Ma. Wha' time is it?'

'After nine. There's some porridge in the end of the pot. Add a drop of milk and water, tha'll do yerself and Phil. When yeh're finished eatin', Kathleen, grab a couple of them older ones to give yeh a hand. The house needs a good goin' over. Yeh'll have a couple of the neighbours droppin' in in the mornin' to have a look at yeh, and don't yeh know they'll be glancin' around the place. I mightn't have much, but wha's here I want spick and span.'

'Right then – Carmel, Clare, Noel, we'll start upstairs. Marion, stay here and give Ma a hand.'

Once we were out of Ma's sight, the messing started. I had to do more shouting to get them to help me. My head was pounding. I was so tired and I could feel a sore throat coming on. I sat down on the side of the bed. Out of the blue, there were tears and snots everywhere. I couldn't help myself.

'Jaysus, Kathleen, wha' are yeh gettin' all whingey for?' Noel asked. 'We're only havin' a bit of laugh.'

'Leave her alone,' Clare chimed in. 'Can't yeh see tha' her nerves is at 'er and all? Yeh big eejit.'

'Don't call me an eejit. Yeh little fuck.'

Before I could open my mouth, the two of them were on the floor killing one another, each trying to outdo the other with the name calling: 'No brains!' 'Fat arse!' 'Gobshite!' 'Smelly knickers!' 'Rotten feet!'

'Will yeh stop, the pair of yiz. I don't feel well.'

They jumped up. 'Jaysus, Kathleen, wha's wrong with yeh? Yeh're real cranky.'

'I'm crippled here with a pain in me side, me throat feels like sandpaper, and yeh're not helpin' with the carry-on of yiz.'

'Kathleen, I can fix tha' pain in yer side,' Clare said. 'I know wha' it is. Tell 'er, Carmel, don't I know loads?'

I looked over at Carmel, who didn't see or hear what was going on. She was on another planet, as usual; too busy looking at herself in the mirror, trying on the hairpiece she'd got for the wedding. Carmel never gave two shites what was going on around her.

Clare carried on. 'Will I tell yeh, Kathleen?'

'Go on then. I'm listenin'.'

'It's a big fart tha's caught in yer belly, tha's wha' it is. Yeh have to get it out real quick or it goes all over yer stomach. De yeh want me to show yeh how to get it out?'

Before I could say anything, she was on the floor.

'Are yeh watchin'? Turn yer head, Noel Doyle. You don't look.'

'I'm not lookin' at yeh, righ'?'

'For God's sake. Don't start again, the pair of yiz.'

'Yeh just get yer two legs together and pull them right back over yer head, like this; rock back and forward for a minute or two.'

It took me all my strength not to laugh. There was muck all over her knickers, and they were all caught to one side.

'When yeh have tha' done, give a big grunt, and there'll be farts flyin' everywhere.' She sat up. 'Wha' de yeh think?

I burst out laughing. *How on earth could I leave them?*

'Yeh're laughin' at me, Kathleen.'

'No, I'm not, Clare. It's just . . .'

I didn't get time to finish. Noel was off again. 'Skid marks, skid marks! Clare has skid marks!'

She was on top of him like a light. 'Yeh fuckin' bastard. Wha' about yer rotten feet, huh, *Jap-eyes*?'

They were off again, punching and kicking one another. I just didn't have the energy, so I left them to it and went back downstairs to Ma.

'Wha's wrong with yeh, Kathleen? Yeh're like death warmed up, the colour of yeh.'

'I don't feel the best, Ma.'

'Would yeh listen to yerself? Yeh'd think there was a frog caught in yer throat, Yeh're tha' hoarse. I'll soon fix tha'.'

'Oh no, Ma, please, not the salt! It goes everywhere; I'll have a rash walkin' up the aisle. It does be in me skin for days.'

'And wha' does tha' matter, once it makes yeh better?'

'But it doesn't, Ma!'

'Don't talk nonsense, Kathleen. Haven't I been curin' yiz all for years with me remedies?'

There was no talking to her and at this stage I was just too tired to argue.

'Come 'ere, Marion, there's an oul' pair of tights in tha' bottom drawer, bring them here to me and tha' drum of salt from the press. Hurry yerself up there – and bring a knife in with yeh as well.'

Poor Marion, she'd get all flustered when Ma would shout at her. She was so quiet.

Ma cut one of the legs off the tights, poured the salt in, tied a knot at each end, rolled it until it looked like a long sausage and then put it against the fire until it got hot. She then wrapped it around my neck.

'There yeh are now, Kathleen! Doesn't tha' feel better already? Tha'll take all the badness away. Yeh'll be bran' new tomorrow.'

It never worked.

I looked over at Phil, who was still lying on the couch. He had one of Da's ties wrapped around his neck with his tongue sticking out to one side, pretending to be hanging himself. Sick or not, I still had to get on with tidying the house and that's all I did for the next few hours.

Alan arrived around tea time.

'Jaysus, Kathleen, yeh look terrible.'

'Me throat's just a bit sore.'

'Yer Ma's not still doin' tha' salt thing? Yeh know it doesn't work. Yeh'll have to go to the doctor.'

'Sssh, Alan, Ma will hear yeh. Anyway, I haven't got time for all tha'. Just pick me up a packet of Disprin. I'll gargle me throat a few times. Tha'll fix it.'

'Kathleen, we need to head over to the hotel. I have the cake out in the car. Are yeh right?'

'I can't. I still have a hundred and one things to do. Phil, will yeh go with him?'

'Thanks be to Jaysus, I thought yeh'd never ask! Get me out of this madhouse for an hour or two.'

You could see Phil had got used to living on his own and wasn't able for all the noise.

'See yeh then in the mornin'. Are yeh sure yeh're okay, Kathleen?'

'I'm grand, Alan. Don't forget the tablets. Give them to Phil when yeh're droppin' him off.'

I walked him out to the hall. He put his arms around me and gave me a big squeeze. 'Love yeh; can't wait for tomorrow.'

'Me too, Alan.'

Phil was out in the car, beeping the horn.

'Hurry up, Alan, for Jaysus' sake, will yeh? I'm freezin' to death out here.'

'I'd better go before the neigbours start givin' out. Don't keep me waitin' at tha' altar!' I got another little kiss.

It was non-stop from then. Between more cleaning, the shouting and the crying, trying to get the young ones washed and the older ones to wash themselves, it was bedlam all the way. It was well past two o'clock in the morning before silence fell over the house. There was just Ma and myself in the kitchen, and Phil asleep on the couch beside the fire.

'There's a drop of tea for yeh, Kathleen. By God, yeh got some work done here today. I haven't seen the place look this tidy in years.'

'For a while anyway, Ma. Once it's okay for tomorrow. Isn't tha' wha' matters at the minute, anyway?'

'Each day at a time, Kathleen, each day at a time. Hand Mano over here to me till I give him a few sucks of the diddy. Tha'll keep him goin' 'til the mornin'. Now, you get yerself up to bed. Yeh have a long day ahead of yeh.'

'I can't keep me eyes open, Ma. De yeh mind?'

I bent down to give her a kiss. As usual, there was no response, nothing back. She didn't lift her head.

'I'll go on up then, Ma.'

'I'll be awake with this fella before six, so I'll give yeh a shout, Kathleen.'

Just as I got to the hall, I turned and looked back at Ma, and thought, *I could do with a hug right now. I want yeh to tell me things, tell me everything's goin' to be fine.* But as usual, it was all inside my head, never out loud.

When I got to the top of the stairs, I peeped in on Da, half hoping he would be awake. He was dead to the world, along with Noel and Thomas. I went on into the girls' room. I stood and looked around. There wasn't much; just the two double beds, the press in the wall and about half a dozen black plastic bags that held everybody's clothes, in place of a wardrobe.

Clare and Marion were at the bottom of my bed, little Paul at the top. Carmel, Jacinta and Patricia were across in the other bed. I went around each of them, brushing the hair out of their eyes, fixing the blankets, sobbing as I bent down to give them a kiss, knowing that this would be my last night to ever share a bed with them again.

Jaysus, wha's wrong with me, gettin' meself into a state like this? I'm only goin' to be livin' ten minutes down the road. I stripped and slipped in beside Paul. He put his little arms around me, cuddling himself into me. I put my two feet up between the girls. They were better than any water bottle, especially on a cold winter's night.

I'll miss them all so much. Then I thought, *Sure all I have to do is bring a couple of them home at night with me. Alan won't mind. I know he won't. Just 'til I get meself settled.*

I finally managed to doze off a little bit happier with that thought in my mind.

* * *

I felt like I'd only closed my eyes for a few seconds when the alarm went off. There wasn't a stir out of any of them. Paul was lying across my chest. I checked his nappy – not too wet, thank God! He opened his eyes and gave me a little smile. 'Aren't yeh a great little fella?' Before I moved, I checked the sheets; they were dry. *Good, nobody pissed on me last night; tha's a good start, anyway.* I got up, put Paul over my shoulder and went around pulling the blankets off the others.

'Come on, wake up! Up, up, the lot of yiz!'

They were all giving out. 'Jaysus, Kathleen, it's still the middle of the night. Wha's wrong with yeh?'

Just then Da woke. 'Wha's goin' on? Who's cryin'? Where's yer mother?'

'It's nothin', Da. Come on, yeh'll have to get up, start helpin' me. Ma must be downstairs with Mano. Make them get up, will yeh?

271

'Right, Kathleen, I'm up.'

I went down to the kitchen; my brother Phil was sitting there with Ma.

'Ma, did yeh get to bed at all?'

'I dozed off for an hour or two on the chair, Kathleen. It wasn't worth me while goin' up. I knew yeh'd be up at the crack of dawn. Anyway, never mind all tha'; where's yer father?'

'He's gettin' them all up.'

'Right then. We better get movin'.'

They all started to dribble in one by one, as Ma dished out the orders.

'Carmel, fill tha' big kettle up to the brim. Clare, hand me the pan, I've a couple o' pound of sausages here and a few eggs; tha'll do yiz, with a bit of bread. Marion, get yerself over here and start butterin' the bread.'

I was sitting there giving Paul his bottle when Ma chimed in.

'All the same, Kathleen, I won't know meself, me sittin' there, bein' waited on hand and foot, gettin' tha' fancy dinner of yours handed up to me. Sure me body's nearly goin' into shock just thinkin' about it.'

'Yeh're in great form, Lil,' Da said as he walked in.

'Hmm . . . is tha' right?'

'Holy Mother of God, Lil, just for one day, and the day bein' in it, could yeh not be a bit civil? Not for me, of course, tha' would be too much to ask, but for Kathleen. She's put a lot into the weddin', so let's not spoil it on her.'

He stood there, right in front of Ma. You could hear a pin drop. Nobody said a word.

Da would usually just take his cup of tea and walk out of the room or go upstairs, but not today. He stood firm. 'Well, Lil?' He was starting to raise his voice.

Holy Jaysus, I thought, *there's goin' to be blue murder here. Of all days Da has to pick to stand up to Ma. I don't believe this.*

'Ah, sit yerself down and stop actin' the big fella, would yeh? With yer fancy words. Move over there and make room for yer father. Start dishin' them sausages out; these eggs are nearly ready. Marion, did I not tell yeh to do tha' bread?'

And on she went without blinking an eyelid. All the kids dived on the food; that's all they cared about at the minute. Da looked over at Phil and me. He had his two fists clenched. He never hit Ma – she did enough of that for the two of them – but that morning I really thought he was going to give her one.

'Sit down here, Da, and calm yerself down,' said Phil.

'Tha' woman, I swear, she'd bring the devil out of any man.'

'Wha's tha' yeh said, Phil Doyle?'

'Nothin', Ma, he said nothin',' I answered. I lowered my voice then. 'Please, Da, don't say anythin', will yeh. She'll only get all fired up and we all know wha' tha' means.'

'I'll stay quiet, seein's the day tha's in it, Kathleen, just for you.'

That was the start of my fairytale wedding.

'Noel, are yeh finished yer breakfast?'

'Yeah, Kathleen.'

'Well, will yeh get yerself dressed and up to Alan as quick as yeh can. He'll be waitin' on yeh. Mick said he'd be up there from early. Hurry!'

'I'm goin', Kathleen, stop shoutin' at me.'

Mick was Carmel's boyfriend. Alan and he became friends over the months and he asked him if he would like to do best man with Noel. That way he could keep an eye on Noel, who was only fourteen. I was like a sergeant out of the army, giving orders all over the place. I told Ma just to look after herself and Mano, and to leave the rest to me.

When all the kids were finally ready, I lined them up in the kitchen, making sure everyone was gleaming. Just then there was a knock on the door. It was one of the neighbours, coming to collect Mano, as she was going to mind him for the day.

'Ah, it's yerself Mrs Swan. Come in, come in, Lil's in the

kitchen, go on through,' Da said as he went upstairs to get himself ready.

Mrs Swan smiled over at the kids. 'Well, all I can say, Lil, is they're a credit to yiz.'

Ma was fixing Mano in his pram. She lifted her head up and looked across at us. 'They are, aren't they?' She didn't say anything else, but you could see she was well pleased, and so was I.

Ma carried on talking to Mrs Swan, telling her how she had squeezed enough milk into a couple of bottles to see the baby through the day, and rammaging on and on about I don't know what.

By this stage I was pacing the kitchen floor waiting on them to stop talking. Eventually I had to butt in, 'Ma, yeh know it's quarter past nine and I've still to do yer hair yet. The car's outside. Phil's takin' a couple of the kids with him on the first run. Then he'll be straight back for you and the rest of them.'

'Is it tha' time already? I'd better make a move, Mrs Swan.'

'Go on then, Lil, don't worry about the baby. I'll take care of him. Enjoy yerself.' Off she went with Mano in the pram.

I was so worked up I had my fist in my mouth, trying to stop myself from screaming. Just as well I had myself ready and only had to slip into my dress.

'Da, are yeh ready?'

'I'm dressed and practisin' me speech, Kathleen.'

'Tha' should be good,' Ma said, as she came into the bedroom. 'I see yeh have yerself all worked up as usual, Kathleen.'

'De yeh blame me, Ma? The mornin' tha's in it.'

'I'll have meself ready in two minutes. I had a good wash last night when yiz were all sleepin'. All I need now is a bit of lipstick and you just run the comb through me hair and help me clip me hat on. Carmel, me coat and dress is hangin' on the back of the door. Go get it for me.' That was it; Ma was ready. She stood there, puffing her Woodbine. 'Wha' did I tell yeh,

Kathleen? Two minutes. Look at yeh, gettin' yerself all excited for nothin'.'

Just then the driver started beeping. 'Yiz have to go, Ma.'

'Kathleen, slip into yer dress and let me have a look at yeh there.'

'There's no time, Ma, yeh have to go now.'

'I'm not movin' until I see yeh in yer dress.'

'Right! Carmel, help me, quick!'

I got the dress on. Ma stood there and looked at me for a few seconds. 'Well, Ma, wha' de yeh think?'

'Yeh did well, Kathleen.'

Not a hug, not a kiss; off she went to the church with not another word spoken.

Da called up to me, 'Are yeh right, Kathleen? They're all gone up to the church. The cameraman is here. He wants to take a few pictures before yeh leave the house. It's five to ten – hurry yerself up, will yeh?'

When I walked into the kitchen, the smile on Da's face said everything. 'Tha's a grand frock yeh got yerself, Kathleen. Yeh look smashin'.'

'Ah, thanks, Da.' It felt good to hear him say that.

There were a few pictures taken in the parlour alongside Ma's new china cabinet. Before I knew it, I was making my way out to the front garden, bursting with excitement, dying to show off, thinking all the neighbours would be outside to wish me good luck. To my surprise and disappointment, not a neighbour was to be seen, not even on my special day.

I was outside the church in no time. Carmel was fixing my veil when Phil came over to me.

'Kathleen, Kathleen, there's no music in the church for yeh.'

'Wha' de yeh mean? Course there is – I booked it ages ago. Now don't start yer messin' today, I mean it, Phil.'

'Jaysus, will yeh just listen to wha' I'm sayin, Kathleen? Alan's in there gettin' blood pressure and on top of all tha' the clerk hasn't turned up either. He can't be found anywhere.'

'*Wha'*! I'm not goin' in unless I have music, I don't care, Phil. I'll look stupid walkin' up the aisle with not a sound.'

'Yeh'll have to. Yer woman tha' plays the organ sent over word; her stomach's in a right oul' mess, and there's nobody else. Too short notice, the priest said.'

Da said in a low voice, 'More like the drink from the night before.'

He didn't think I heard him.

'I swear, Da, if tha' oul fuck is sick from the drink, I hope she gets the shites for a month. Lettin' me down like this on me big day.'

'Jaysus, Kathleen, will yeh watch yer mouth? Outside the house of God – if anybody heard yeh!' I wasn't moving. The tears flowed down my face and I couldn't stop them.

'Kathleen, yeh'd want to make up yer mind,' said Da. 'I'm freezin' to death standin' here, and if yeh don't make a move soon, I'll bring meself over to Mooney's pub. If I get settled with a pint in me hand and a bit of heat, yeh won't move me for love nor money, weddin' or no weddin'.'

'Would yeh really do tha to me, Da?'

'I'm tellin' yeh, if yeh don't move now, I'm goin'.'

Phil stepped in, trying to calm the situation.

'Come on, Kathleen, the kids are all gettin' fidgety. There's nothin' yeh can do now.' He put his arm around me. 'Come on, it's only a bit of music. I'll whistle a tune if yeh want.' He gave me a big smile, showing off his pearly whites. Phil would always try to see the funny side of things, but I wasn't laughing.

'Go away, yeh big eejit.'

I peeped inside the church. I could see Alan; he looked lost on his own. I made my mind up; nobody was going to ruin my big day.

'Right, Da, I'm ready.'

I could hardly breathe with the lump in my throat as I walked up the aisle, smiling and nodding, feeling like a fool, in complete silence. When I got to the altar, Alan took my hand

and gave it a tight squeeze. That helped, but only a bit.

When I looked and saw the priest, I nearly fainted. *Tha's not the priest tha' we spoke to. They gave me Blinkey! I don't believe this.* He was as blind as a bat; his glasses were like milk bottles. He needed the clerk big time to help him. I just stood there and thought: *This is goin' to be a right shambles.* As sure as hell I was right. Everybody stood when they should have been sitting, kneeling when they should have been standing and praying.

In the middle of the ceremony, a shower of water hit me in the face. I stood there for a second with my mouth open, turned and looked at Alan; the water was dripping down his face. He didn't blink an eyelid. The mascara started to roll down my face. Alan slipped a hanky in my hand. *I don't believe this! The blind fucker is after drownin' us with the holy water.* I could hear the giggling going on behind me. I didn't blame them one bit; it was like a funny farm up there.

We finally got through the Mass, then it was outside for a few quick flashes of the camera. The heavens were open, the rain was belting down, so off we headed for the hotel.

Alan always said the right things at the right time and knew how to calm me down, for a little while anyway. *God,* I thought, *wha' more could go wrong?* Little did I know what was ahead of me.

* * *

Everybody was there when we arrived. The Victor Hotel didn't know what had hit them. The kids were running around like lunatics, sliding down the stairs, swinging out of the curtains and screaming. You'd want to have seen the look on Alan's aunties' faces. *Stuck up bitches,* I thought. *Who do they think they are?* Anyway, I had promised I wouldn't fight with the kids that day. 'They are just excited,' I found myself saying as I walked by everybody smiling.

277

I went around and gathered the kids up.

'Right, are yiz listenin' to me? I want yiz to calm down. They're all watchin' yiz. Give them nothin' to talk about, right?'

'Okay, Kathleen,' they all mumbled.

'The dinner will be ready in a few minutes. Don't let me catch any of yiz eatin' with yer hands. Use the knife and fork like I told yeh.'

'De we have to use the two of them at the same time?' they asked.

'I went through this I don't know how many times over the past week. Just cut the food up and then use the fork the way I showed yeh, right?'

Clare was just about to butt in as usual, but she shut up. It was probably the grinding of my teeth that stopped her.

'Jaysus, wha's tha' smell?' I whispered.

'It's Paul, Kathleen,' Jacinta answered. 'He done a dirty big shite when yeh were in the church.'

My breathing nearly stopped as I looked over my shoulder to see if anyone was listening. 'Did yeh have to say it like tha', did yeh? Could yeh not just say his nappy was dirty? Makin' a holy show of me!'

'Sorry, Kathleen, I forgot.'

'Marion, take Paul over to Ma. She has a couple of nappies in her bag. She'll look after him. When yeh have tha' done, follow the rest of them over to Alan. He'll get yiz all some lemonade. Off yiz go. Don't let me down, now.'

'We won't Kathleen,' said Clare. 'We swear, don't we?' She laughed, with a dirty big grin on her face.

'Laugh, will yeh, Clare? Now, for bein' such a smart arse, yeh're goin' to get the job of watchin' Thomas for the day. Make sure he doesn't pick his nose at the dinner or any time through the day; and if I catch him even once, *you'll* get the box off me, not him. Now run along.' They all gave me the nod as they made their way over to Alan.

I made my way around, trying to mingle with everybody. It took every bit of energy I had. I could barely swallow the spit in my mouth, and the pain in my side was getting worse.

After a while Alan made his way over to me. 'Jaysus, Kathleen, the colour of yeh! Yeh're waxy in the face!'

'I'll be grand, Alan. Help me gather everybody up; the dinner's ready.'

'Will yeh go in and sit yerself down before yeh faint. Phil, come over here and give us a hand.' Sure enough, they had everybody sitting in their seats in minutes.

Da didn't spend too long on his speech, just a few quick words. Little did he know he was supposed to wait until everybody had finished their dinner. He was so nervous and just wanted to get it out of the way. We all let him get on with it and said nothing.

He cleared his throat. 'Thanks to yeh all for turnin' up. Alan, yeh're a good young fella and I know yeh'll do Kathleen well.' And down he sat.

I was mortified as the place erupted with the laughter. Da didn't realise the meaning everyone was taking – 'to do well' meant doing the other.

The kids did me proud. I couldn't help but laugh every time the waitress asked, 'Would you like more?' They all put their plates up, not only once, but two or three times. I caught a couple of them out of the corner of my eye, when they thought I wasn't minding, lifting the plate up and giving it a good lick. I looked over quickly to see if Alan's aunties were looking, and then I thought, *Fuck them, snobs, the kids are enjoyin' themselves and tha's all tha' matters.*

I couldn't eat a thing myself and was glad when the dinner was over. All the men made their way over to the bar and the women settled themselves around the room as the waitress cleared the tables. I was on my way over to Ma when I copped Noel, standing with a pint of Guinness in his hand, and him only fourteen.

'Jaysus Christ, Noel Doyle, wha' de yeh think yeh're doin'?'

'There yeh are, Kathleen.' He put his arm on my shoulder.

'Yeh're drunk. Who bought tha' for yeh?'

'Now, now, sis, don't be worryin'.' He picked me up in the air and threw me over his shoulder, twirling me all over the place.

'Put me down, yeh gobshite.' I was trying to whisper. 'If Ma finds out tha' yeh've drink on yeh, there'll be blue murder, never mind Da.'

'And who de yeh think bought me the last couple of pints? Only the oul' fella himself.'

I thought, *Good God! Da must be really plastered himself.*

He finally put me down. I was left sitting on my arse in the middle of the floor in the bar, the headdress lop-sided on my head. All the men were laughing as I struggled to get up. Noel was bent over from laughing. Finally, one of Da's friends came over and gave me a hand.

'Don't be gettin' yerself all annoyed, Kathleen. The lad's only havin' a bit of fun.'

I gave him a polite little smile as I tried to fix myself, when all I really wanted to do was scream from the top of my voice – what was left of it – *'Fuck off, everybody!'*

Alan came over and took me by the hand.

'Kathleen, before yeh say anythin', I tried to stop Noel, but every time I turned me back he had a pint in his hand, him bein' the best man and all. Tha's wha' happened. They all think he's older with the size of him.'

'Where's me Da?'

'There's no point sayin' anythin' to him, Kathleen. He's well on his way.'

'Alan, just tell me where he is.' My temper was starting to rise like a volcano.

'He's in the hall with Mr Daly. They're tryin' to get a sing-song goin'.'

'Don't let them start all tha', Alan. Get the music goin'.

Tha'll put a stop to it.'

'Tha's wha' I wanted to talk to yeh about, Kathleen. The band never showed up.'

'Oh my God, oh my God. I don't believe all this is happenin'. Wha' are we goin' to do?'

'Me uncle Joe is over there with the manager, they're tryin' to see if they can get some sort of music for us.'

I sat on the end of the stairs and cried. The whole day had been a big joke from start to finish. I just wanted to run out of there.

'Come on, Kathleen, please don't get upset. It's taken me all me time to keep on top of things. Wha' de yeh say, love?' He lifted my chin and gave me a tender kiss. 'Yeh know, I'd take on the world if I thought it would make yeh happy. I'll get up and do a jig meself to get things goin'. So come on and dry them eyes. Let's go talk to this manager fella, see if he's sorted somethin' out.'

And sure enough he did. It wasn't a band or anything like one – just one man on his own. Paddy was his name; he played the mouth organ and the accordion. I was so happy to get somebody at such a late hour. I wouldn't have cared if he'd just sat there banging two spoons together. By the time he got to the hotel everybody was well full of drink. While he was setting up, I asked if he knew any rock and roll. I knew that would get everybody going.

'You just name it, love, I can play it.'

He nearly had the mouth organ talking. Bill Haley's 'Rock Around the Clock', you name it; he had all the songs of to a T. The place was hopping. Even Ma and Da got up to dance. I couldn't believe it.

'Alan, would yeh have a look at this? Ma and Da!'

'Say nothin', Kathleen. I slipped her a few brandies through the day.'

'Good, help her forget all her troubles, for a few hours anyway.'

As myself and Alan danced around the floor, everybody was saying, 'Kathleen, it's a right oul' hooley yiz put on there.' I was well pleased when I heard that.

* * *

Everything turned out right in the end. The next few hours went by so quickly – talking to everybody, checking on the kids, trying to be so grown-up. I was so tired.

Phil came over to us. 'Why don't yeh take yerselves off, the pair of yiz. Meself and Carmel will look after things. Sure, the night's nearly over, anyway.'

'Phil, where's Noel?'

'Look at yeh worryin' again, Kathleen. Forget about him.'

'I said, where is he?'

'He's out cold in the bar on one of the sofas; he's green in the face. Don't worry, I'll sort him out. A couple of fingers rammed down his throat won't be long gettin' half of the drink out of him. I tell yeh, he won't do it again in a hurry by the time I'm finished.'

'Don't mind all tha',' Carmel said. 'Go and get changed. I'll tell them all yeh're leavin' soon.'

Alan took me by the hand and we made our way up to the room. I could feel myself getting all nervous inside.

'Are yeh alright, Kathleen? Yeh're all shaky.'

'No I'm not.'

As soon as we got into the room I started to take my clothes out of the case.

'Would yeh look at yeh, all fidgety. Come over here and sit down beside me. Come on!'

I sat down on the side of the bed. Alan had me lying down before I knew it. I was all right having a wear, but as soon as Alan's hands started to roam, that was it. I was up like a light.

'We better hurry, they're all waitin' downstairs.'

I had the wedding dress and veil off and I had changed in seconds.

'Jaysus, Kathleen, tha' was quick.'

'I know, I know. I can hear them all; they're waitin' on us, we have to go.' I was out the door before he could say another word. Poor Alan; the look on his face.

I stood outside the door, shaking; my heart was thumping. I felt so stupid. *Jaysus Christ, wha's after happenin' to me in there? I thought when this time came I'd be okay. Wha' am I goin' to do? I have to take me knickers off tonight and I don't want to.*

All those years saying, 'No, Alan, it's a sin, it's a sin.' Da had it drilled into my head: the church, the church. That's all you got, day or night, sober or drunk: 'If yeh bring a child into this world outside marriage, yeh'll be looked down on by everybody. No priest would let yeh set foot inside the holy grounds, ever. Not a man on this earth – I don't care who he is or where he comes from – would have any time for an easy woman. Mark my word, Kathleen, tha's the God's honest truth.'

Then there was Ma on the other side: 'Men, they're all bastards. They only care about one thing – satisfyin' their own selfish needs, nothin' else matters. Pigs, so they are.'

Then there were the girls in work – not that I mixed much with any of them; I was always a loner. But I'd always pick up bits here and there in the cloakroom or toilet. I overheard two of them talking one day, one telling the other how she would never forget as long as she lived the first time she'd had sex with her fella.

'Yeh want to see the size of his mickey – an elephant's trunk hadn't got a patch on it. I couldn't walk right for a month afterwards.'

I nearly fell down the toilet with the fright.

Is it any wonder my head was a mess with all that I was listening to? If all that wasn't enough to put me off sex and men for life, I don't know what would.

I could hear Alan moving around, so I made my way downstairs. Everybody started cheering and throwing confetti. Alan came down behind me with the suitcase in one hand and my coat in the other. I turned away so that I wouldn't have to look him in the eye.

I looked around the room. All the little ones were asleep on chairs. Noel was standing, leaning on Phil's shoulder, still green in the face. There were hugs and kisses from everybody. Da had one arm around Alan, while he held on tight to his pint of Guinness with the other.

'It's a man yeh are now, Alan, and I'll be keepin' an eye on yeh, makin' sure tha' yeh take care of my Kathleen.' Alan just smiled.

Ma waited until the last minute, until I was about to get into the car. She didn't kiss or hug me, but I thought she might have, given the day that was in it. She looked at me, held my hand for a split second, then turned and walked away. I wanted so much to talk to her, to say how I was feeling, how nervous and frightened I was. But it wasn't to be; she'd let herself get so hard over the years, she just wasn't able to show her feelings, ever.

Phil must have been watching. I swear, sometimes I think he could read my mind. He would always say or do some little thing that would be just right at the time, when I needed it most. He stuck his head in the window, gave me a kiss on the cheek and Alan a pat on the back.

'Away with yiz and have the time of yer life, de yeh hear me, Kathleen?' he said, banging the top of the car as we drove away. I turned and watched Phil waving and smiling as he faded into the distance.

I didn't have a clue where we were going. I had left all that to Alan. He broke the silence after a while.

'I got us a lovely place, Kathleen, just as yeh pull into Brittas Bay – Rochford House it's called. Uncle Joe phoned ahead. I booked us a table. We'll have a nice meal; yeh haven't eaten a thing all day. Wha' de yeh say, love?'

'Tha'll be nice, Alan.'

'I know yeh're not feelin' the best, with yer throat and all.

But is there's somethin' else wrong?'

'The day was hectic, Alan; I'm just a bit tired. I'll be fine.'

'Yeh're sure then, Kathleen?'

'Keep yer eyes on the road, Alan. The rain is gettin' very heavy.'

I sat in silence for the rest of the journey, watching the rain pelt against the windscreen, sick with worry, not knowing how I was going to cope with what was ahead for me.

27

The Honeymoon

It wasn't too long before we saw the sign for Rochford House. The plan was to stay there one night and then to head off and see a bit of Ireland.

'This is it, in to the left. Tha' took just over an hour. Looks good. Wha' de yeh think, Kathleen?'

'I can't see out Alan, the rain is so heavy.'

'I'll drive straight up to the door, you just jump out there while I park the car.'

'I'm not goin' in on me own.'

'Don't be silly, Kathleen, yeh'll be drowned walkin' from the car. Just stand inside the door. I'll be back in two minutes with the cases.'

'Right then, don't be long.'

I made my way inside. There was a woman standing beside a big blazing fire. She had the back of her skirt pulled up, giving her arse a good roasting. I just about had time to give the place a quick look over. I'd never seen the likes of it before. The walls were painted snow white and the lighting was dim. I could feel my feet sink down into the thick red carpet. Two large brown sofas sat beside the fire.

The woman got herself a bit flustered, fixing her skirt as she made her way over to me. 'You have to excuse me, love. I was out getting a few logs for the fire; I wanted to have the place nice and cozy for when you arrived. The cold must have gone straight through me. I just can't get the heat into me.'

'It's okay, sure me Ma does tha' all the time when she's cold.'

'You must be the young couple down from Dublin, Mr and Mrs McGrath. I'm Sheila, I'm pleased to meet you.' She put her hand out to shake mine.

Alan walked in just then. 'This is Alan,' I mumbled, 'my . . . oh, em . . . my husband.' Alan was well pleased when he heard that.

'Look at you, Mr McGrath, you're soaked! Let me get you a towel from the kitchen; I'll be back in a jiffy.'

'It looks very posh, Alan,' I whispered.

'It's supposed to be – we're on our honeymoon.' He put his arm around me and gave me a kiss.

The woman came in and caught us. I didn't half blush. She smiled as she handed Alan a towel.

'Would you like me to show you to your room now?'

When she said that I took the shakes inside. *Oh God, wha' am I goin' to do? This is it now; I'm so scared.*

So I jumped in quickly: 'No, no, tha's fine, we'll stay here for a while, if tha's okay with yeh.'

'Here's a menu, then, you can have a look while your sittin' there.'

'Before yeh go, Miss, could I have a cup of tea, please?'

'I'll get it right now. You just relax there.'

'Yeh're gas, Kathleen. Yeh should be orderin' Babycham or somethin' like tha', not tea. We're supposed to be celebratin'.'

'We are, we will, it's just, it's just . . .'

'Wha' is it, Kathleen? *Wha's wrong with yeh?*'

Before I could answer him the woman was back with the tea.

'There you are. Now, have you decided what you would like to eat?'

'I don't mind, Alan; just get me wha'ever yeh're havin'.'

'Right then, two nice juicy steaks and wha'ever goes with it – all the trimmin's. Oh, em . . . can I have a beer and a Babycham with the meal as well, please?'

'That will take me a little while to prepare; is that okay?'

'Tha's grand,' Alan answered, 'we're not rushin' anywhere.'

'I don't know why yeh got tha' drink for me, Alan; yeh know I hate the stuff. I won't touch it.'

'I know, I know, I suppose I'm just showin' off. Just let on yeh're drinkin' it, in case anybody's lookin'.'

'I don't think yeh have to worry there. It looks like we're the only ones here; there's not a sinner in the place.'

'Suppose it bein' Christmas time, they wouldn't be gettin' many visitors. Anyway, never mind all tha'. Yeh're not yerself at all today. I usually can't get a word in edgeways. Why are yeh so quiet? Oh, and another thing – wha' was all tha' about back there at the hotel? Yeh were out of tha' room before I could say a word, never mind get a wear.'

'Sorry Alan, I'm not feelin' great and now yeh're gettin' all worked up, givin' out to me.' The tears started rolling down my face.

'Don't cry, Kathleen. I'm not givin' out to yeh. I'm worried, tha's all. Come on, if tha' woman comes in and sees yeh like this she'll think I'm a right bowsie.'

'No she won't, Alan, nobody would think tha' about yeh.'

I just about got myself calmed down enough to get through the meal – not that I was able to eat much of it. I didn't know if I was feeling so sick from my throat, the pains in my side, or the pain in my head with the worry about going to bed. I never saw Alan talk so much – not that I minded; it was good for a change. I sat there, half-listening. Maybe he was just as nervous as me, and he wasn't saying anything either.

We finally made our way to our room; I couldn't stall any longer. It was lovely – really fancy, with a huge bathroom. You could have fit me and half of the kids in at the one time. My mind start drifting: *They'd love this. One of these days, when I've the money, I'm goin' to bring the lot of them to a nice place like this and spoil them rotten. There I go again; I'll have to stop thinkin' about the kids. Jaysus, I miss them already.*

'Kathleen,' I could hear Alan saying, 'yeh're miles away there.'

'Sorry, I was thinkin' . . . All the same, Alan, it must be great to have loads of money. Just look at this place.'

'We'll have all this some day, Kathleen, just you wait and see. I'll work every hour tha's goin' to give yeh all the nice things yeh ever wanted.'

'And I'll be right beside yeh, Alan'.

'Ah, come on, enough of all the serious talk, Kathleen. I'll hang the clothes in the wardrobe; you go get tha' famous bubble bath ready. Yeh know, the one tha' yeh're always talkin' about for years.'

'Shite! I forgot to get the bubbles.'

'Well, I didn't.' And out came a bottle of bubble bath from his case.

'I don't believe yeh remembered, with all the goin's-on!' I gave him a big hug.

'Go on, then, run the water. I'll be there in a minute. Make sure yeh don't fill it up too much. Yeh don't want the water flowin' all over the place with the two of us in it.'

The panic set in once more.

'Wha' de yeh mean the two of us? Yeh can't get in the bath with me.'

'Why not, Kathleen?'

'Because yeh can't, yeh just can't, Alan. I'm not lettin' yeh!'

'It's okay. We're married now; yeh're not doin' any harm.'

'I don't care, I don't care.'

He could see how nervous I was getting.

'It's okay, Kathleen, calm yerself down. You just go and have yer bath; soak yerself for a while. Anyway, I've to go lock the car up for the night. It went out of me head, rushin' in with the cases earlier. I'll be back in a while.'

The look on his face as he left the room; he was in shock.

I had myself so worked up, I shook the whole bottle of bubble bath in the water. The bubbles were halfway up the wall, flowing over onto the floor. I didn't care at this stage; I just wanted to slip into the warm water, relax and try get my head together.

I lay there thinking: *It'd be nice if Alan was in here with me. But then if I call him in, he wouldn't just sit there; he'd be thinkin' of me under all them bubbles with no knickers on. He's rarin' to go. Jaysus, can I blame him after five years holdin' him back? I better not. I'd probably drown meself in the panic tryin' to get out if he starts.*

I drifted off to sleep. It must have been quite some time before I woke; the water was cold and I could hear Alan knocking on the door, asking me if I was okay.

'I fell asleep.'

'I know yeh did. I kept checkin' to make sure yeh wouldn't go under and drown yerself.'

'Sorry I took so long. I'll just dry meself off.'

I stalled and stalled, sitting on the side of the bath, nightdress and dressing gown on, buttoned right up to my neck, with not a sight of flesh showing anywhere. I was only short of putting a veil over my head.

Alan called again. I said nothing.

'Kathleen, did yeh hear me?'

'I'm not comin' out, Alan.'

'Wha' de yeh mean yeh're not comin' out? Wha' the hell is wrong with yeh? Don't be silly; yeh can't stay in there.'

My voice trembled. 'I don't care, Alan. I don't want to do tha' – I don't want to do the other.' *There: I said it; it's outside my head at last.*

Alan went quiet for a minute or two. I sat there crying, not knowing what to do next. Alan, being the gentleman he is, called out: 'Come on, love, just come out and get in beside me; yeh don't have to do anythin' yeh're not ready for.'

I slowly opened the door and peeped out. Alan was stripped and under the covers.

'Yeh promise, Alan?'

'I promise. Now, will yeh come out and let me in the bathroom before I piss on meself?'

As I walked out, Alan jumped out of the bed. I stole a glance at him, checking to see if he had anything on. He had, thank God! I jumped under the covers, housecoat and all. It wasn't long before Alan was back in beside me.

'Now, Kathleen, wha's this all about? Gettin' yerself in such a state like tha'. Yeh know yeh can talk to me about anythin'.'

'I know. I didn't think I was goin' to be like this tonight. It was supposed to be special. I'm a gobshite, tha's wha' I am. I've ruined everythin'.'

'No, yeh haven't. Wha' have I told yeh before, Kathleen? Sex is not the be all and end all of a relationship. It's nice to have and yeh know I'm only goin' mad to get into yer knickers – me mouth's waterin' just at the thought of it – but I'll wait 'til yeh're ready. Wha's special here tonight is you bein' here beside me. It'll happen in time.' Then, with a big smile on his face, he added: 'But will yeh make sure yeh don't take too long?'

I finally got around to taking the dressing gown off. We kissed and cuddled and that was all. I lay there in Alan's arms as he slept, and thought: *How did he get so wise and grown-up for someone so young?*

* * *

I woke to the sound of banging on the door. It frightened the life out of me. I didn't know where I was for a second.

'Alan, get up, get up, quick!' He was in noddy land. I couldn't wake him for love nor money.

I jumped out of the bed, barely opening the door. Standing in the narrow corridor was the woman of the house with a big smile on her face and a tray in her hands.

I could feel myself blush.

'Himself said that you would be having breakfast in bed. I hope I'm not too early.'

'No, no, it's okay. I woke up ages ago. I was asleep all night – the whole night, I really was.' I was getting more embarrassed by the minute. I don't know what I was shiting out of me, but she just smiled again.

'If I could step inside there, love, and put this tray down; it's a heavy old thing.'

'Yes, yes. Come in, come in, sorry.'

'It's a nice Irish breakfast and homemade bread. Get it into you while it's nice and hot.'

I didn't know what to say. I'd never had a big breakfast like this in my life, never mind in bed as well. I just about got 'thank you' out of my mouth as she left the room.

I sat at the edge of the bed. Alan was starting to come around.

'Would yeh have a look at this, Alan. I never saw so much food for two people. This would feed us and all the kids.'

'I knew yeh'd be surprised, Kathleen. Come on, let's get tucked into it. I'm starvin'.'

Alan ate his and the best part of mine.

'Are yeh goin' to eat nothin', Kathleen?'

'It's me throat, Alan. I can't swallow.'

'Bend yer head back there and open yer mouth, let me have a look. Good Jaysus, Kathleen, yeh've blisters the size of grapes hangin' out of yer tonsils. I'll have to get yeh to a doctor quick.'

'It's okay, I have a few Disprin here in me bag. I'll gargle me throat a couple of times. It'll go away; tha's wha' I always do. Now, will yeh stop fussin'. We'll find a chemist in the town and I'll get a few more.'

'Right, then. I'll give it one more day and if yeh're still not better, yeh either go to a doctor down here or I'm drivin' back to Dublin. Yeh've hardly eaten a scrap in three days. There'll be nothin' left of yeh if yeh keep this up.'

'Okay, I promise yeh, Alan. Now, help me pack these few things. We'll get ready and go pay the bill. All the same that woman was real nice to us – de yeh think we should give her somethin' for herself? Yeh know, sixpence or somethin'?'

'If we're goin' to give her somethin', it'll have to be at least two shillin's.'

'Right then; I'll leave it to yeh, Alan.'

You could see he was as proud as punch paying the bill.

'There's a little somethin' for yerself. Have a drink on us.'

She smiled and wished us all the happiness in the world.

* * *

It wasn't long before we were pulling into White's Hotel in Wexford, right in the heart of the town. I took a shine to the place straight away.

'This looks like a nice town, Alan.'

We made our way around and found the chemist.

'Alan, will we come back out later and see wha's happenin'?'

'Okay but now let's go back and get ourselves a room.'

At the hotel, Alan wasn't long telling them we were just married. They made a right fuss over us and, as usual, I made an arse of myself. Alan was talking to the woman behind the desk when a fella came over and took our two bags and walked away with them.

'Hey you! Come 'ere, where de yeh think yeh're goin'? Put them bags back!' I shouted at him.

He looked over at the woman, who looked at Alan, who turned around to find me struggling, trying to get the bags off your man.

'Kathleen, wha' are yeh doin'? The man works here. He's the porter.'

'And wha's tha', Alan?'

'His job is to carry the bags up to the rooms for people stayin' in the hotel. I got us a room. He was bringin' them up there.'

Alan gave me the eye and the nod to let go of the bags, then he took me by the hand back to the desk. I felt such a fool.

'I'm sorry,' I told the woman. 'It's just it looked like . . .'

Alan tipped me on the arm to let me know to stop talking and not to make the situation any worse. She smiled and handed the key to Alan, who at this stage was red with embarrassment.

The two of us walked behind the porter, with not a word spoken.

'Here we are now, sir, the best suite in the place.'

'Sorry about tha' bit of hassle,' Alan said, handing the porter the price of a pint.

'Not at all, sir.' He gave me a wink on the way out, which made me feel a bit better.

'I'm such a gobshite, Alan, lettin' us down like tha'. I really thought he was robbin' the bags.'

'Would yeh stop worryin'? I wouldn't have known meself, only the woman on the desk had just told me. Come on, leave the bags there and let's go for a walk, see wha's happenin' in the town. There might be some music goin' on later on. We'll have an oul' dance, maybe a bit of a jive – of course, tha's if yeh're up to it.'

'Let me gargle me throat a couple of times before we go out. I should be feelin' okay by tonight.'

'Wha' did yeh say there, Kathleen?' He winked at me.

I knew what he meant and I should, right there and then, have dived on him and kissed the face off him – what any young newly-weds would be doing. But no, I just stood there with the glass in my hand, looking straight into his face, not moving, saying nothing. He put his arm around me. 'Yeh know how much I love yeh, Kathleen.'

'I know, me too, Alan.'

'Will yeh hurry yerself up there. The day will be over before we know it.' Once again he glossed things over.

We walked around the shops for a while, in and out of a

couple of pubs, me drinking a cup of tea, Alan having a shandy. As we walked back to the hotel, I could feel the pain in my side getting worse. Alan was going on about dancing the night away and having the craic. 'Yeh might even have a Babycham, Kathleen. Wha' de yeh say?'

'Maybe I will then, Alan.'

'Tha's the spirit; tha's my girl.'

When we got back to the room, I went straight to the bathroom to gargle my throat, trying to get rid of the 'grapes', as Alan mildly put it. How romantic I must have looked; my head hanging back, making all sorts of noises. How Alan didn't run a mile from me, I'll never know. He had the patience of a saint.

Suddenly, I felt a really sharp pain in my side. My head started spinning and I could feel my legs go from under me. I don't remember much after that; when I came around, I was lying on the bed with a wet towel across my head. Alan was talking to someone and I could hear the panic in his voice as I tried to sit up.

'Alan, wha' happened?' I asked.

'Jaysus, yeh've come around, Kathleen! Yeh put the heart crossways in me.'

Then I heard a woman's voice calling my name.

'Mrs McGrath, my name is Mary. I'm one of the staff from the hotel. The doctor's on his way. A right fright you just gave that husband of yours. The roars of him on the phone! I was half afraid to come into the room. I thought you were after dropping dead.'

Just then there was a knock on the door. 'That will be the local doctor.' She opened the door and this small man came in, with a head of snow-white hair and a high-pitched voice. 'So you're the patient?' He sat down beside me and picked my hand up, feeling for a pulse. 'What's this I hear – honeymooners?'

I lay there, too sick to answer.

Alan went on to explain what had happened and how I'd been feeling over the past few days. The doctor gave me a right going over, checking all my bits, from top to bottom.

'Now, young lady,' he said, taking the scope out of his ears. 'I'm afraid it's the hospital for you. Your temperature is sky high, your throat is in a right state, and on top of that, your appendix is grumbling like mad; sure, is it any wonder you fainted?'

I was struggling to get the words out. 'But doctor, I can't go into hospital. I'm on me honeymoon and all.'

'There's no buts about it. I'm phoning for an ambulance straight away.'

I looked at Alan. The shock on his face! He didn't know if he was coming or going. The doctor pulled him to one side. They stood talking for a minute and in no time at all I was being carried to the ambulance.

'Alan, I don't believe this.' I was off crying again.

'Yeh have to go, Kathleen. The doctor said yeh're real sick and tha' he wouldn't be responsible. They'll fix yeh up, yeh'll be as right as rain in a day or two. We'll be able to go off and have a great time. Wha' de say, love? Come on, don't cry.'

'Tha's all I seem to be doin' the past two days. Everythin's goin' wrong. It's not fair, it's just not fair.'

The hospital was just outside the town, so we were there in no time. The ambulance man left me in the hands of a lovely friendly little nurse, who relaxed me straight away. She chatted away to Alan as she read over the letter from the doctor.

'We'll have to get you seen to straight away to get that temperature down – that's first on the list. I'll put you into this cubicle and get this fan going to cool you down while the doctor checks you out. I'm afraid you'll have to leave, sir.'

'Please don't put him out, Nurse.'

'Can't I stay for a little while?' Alan asked. 'Just 'til she gets herself settled?'

'I'm sorry, sir, it's not me; Sister makes the rules and no one dare break them. Visiting time is over and no one is allowed in

297

the hospital after that. Here's comes the doctor; I'm sorry, you'll have to leave, sir.'

I got a quick kiss on the cheek and a whisper in the ear: 'I'll be here when yeh wake up in the mornin'.' And that was it. He was gone. I couldn't believe it was all happening so quickly.

The doctor gave me the once-over and handed me a few tablets to take. He told me the head man himself would see me first thing in the morning. The nurse brought me to a ward and tried hard to make me see it was all for the best. I wanted to be grown-up and not let them see me cry. I was so frightened. It was the first time in my life that I'd ever been on my own, without Alan or the family. I didn't get much sleep that night. The nurses were in and out all night sponging me down, with a fan going to keep my temperature down.

Bright and early the next morning, in walked the head sister herself. I could see why the nurse wasn't taking any chances letting Alan stay. You'd want to see the serious puss on her face as she stood at the end of the bed.

'Hmm . . .' she said, looking over the top of her glasses and checking the folder in her hand, 'they tell me you're married.' I turned my head and said nothing. *Bitch,* I thought to myself, *Alan could've stayed only for you.*

'Mrs McGrath, the doctors will be around soon, so any jewellery you have on, I want it taken off now. We have to have you ready in case they decide to operate.'

I nearly fainted when she said that. Reluctantly I handed her my engagement ring and the chain on my neck.

'And the wedding ring also, if you please.' She stood there with her hand stretched out into my face. I looked down at my hand, holding on tight to my wedding ring.

'Come on, child, I haven't got all day.'

'No! Yeh're not gettin' it.'

'What did you say?'

You could see she wasn't used to anybody back-answering her.

'I said, *No!* I'm not takin' it off. I only got it yesterday and it's stayin' on me finger always.'

'Now, stop this nonsense, child!' She bent over, trying to get the ring off me. I pushed her back, shouting, 'I'm all grown-up, I'm not a child.' I could feel the temper rising in me. I was sick and tired of being told I was a child when it suits everyone.

'I want to see Alan. Where is he?' I was getting more frightened by the minute.

'And who might that be, Mrs McGrath?' she said, a smart tone in her voice.

'He's me husband. He was to be here real early this mornin'. He promised me.'

'Oh, that's right. There was a Mr McGrath here at the crack of dawn this morning. I sent him on his way. Nobody gets into my hospital unless it's visiting hour, which is not until seven o'clock tonight.' She had a big sly grin on her face.

Now I was really mad. Just then, Ma popped into my head. She always taught us to have respect for our elders and never to be cheeky – but on the other hand she'd say, 'Sometimes there's special occasions when you have to fend for yerself and not be walked on.' This was definitely a special occasion.

'Yeh could have let Alan in for a few minutes. Yeh were just bein' bad – yeh're only a bitch.'

She put her hand out once more, 'I said, the ring.'

The blood rushed through me; my temper exploded. I don't know where the words or the nerve came from; it just flowed out of me.

I screamed, 'Yeh know wha' yeh can do with yerself? Yeh can go and . . .' Then, I stopped and thought: *No! I won't let meself down in front of this wan.* 'I want me clothes. I'm not stayin' here. Who de yeh think yeh are? There's no need for yeh to treat me like this.'

She glared at me once more, saying nothing, turning as red in the face as I was. She probably would have bashed me on the head with the folder if she'd had her way. She scribbled a few things down on the folder, got herself together and stormed out.

The nurse was biting her lip, trying to be really serious. I was shaking inside. I couldn't believe I'd said all that. I didn't want to be cheeky, but there was no need for her to carry on like that; she could have been a bit nicer. The nurse bent over me, pretending to be fixing the pillows.

'My, my, my, am I glad my shift's finished in a few minutes! Sister will be on the rampage for the day.'

'Will yeh get me clothes, nurse? Please, I wanna go. I'm leavin'.'

'Just wait until the doctor checks you out. Come on now, love, don't be too hasty; you're not well.'

I had no choice but to stay, since I had nothing to wear. I lay there watching the clock on the wall, every second ticking by, wondering what Alan was doing and if he was okay. Then Ma popped into my head again. I wasn't sure if she would have been proud of me for standing up for myself, or boxed the head off me for answering back. Not that I was feeling proud or anything like it myself. I was just scared and upset.

The doctors finally came around after about an hour – a big tall man and a small Chinese fella. They examined me from head to toe. Between the Chinese doctor's broken English and the strong country accent, I couldn't make out a word they were saying. It would have been all double Dutch to me, anyway.

After a while the Chinese doctor stood beside me. 'Appendix must come out,' he said in a low voice. I understood that bit alright.

'No!' I said. 'I'm goin' home, doctor, I'm not stayin' here.'

'What she mean?' he asked, trying to understand the thick Dublin accent. The other doctor came over and stood in front of me.

'Sister tells me she was in with you.' He didn't lift his head from reading the chart. I was sure she'd been giving him a right mouthful about me. Doctor Wang was still rammaging on but at this stage it was all going over my head anyway; all I wanted to do was get the hell out of there.

'You know, young lady, my colleague is right. Your appendix is very inflamed and has to come out.'

The tears started flowing again; I wasn't listening to anybody.

'I wanna go home, Doctor, I just wanna go home.'

'Young lady, you have yourself very stressed out and that's not good.'

I'd never heard that word before and didn't know what he was talking about. Not that I gave a shite; this wasn't the time or the place to be brushing up on my education.

He walked away and stood to one side as he spoke to the Chinese doctor. When they eventually came back over to me, the country doctor spoke.

'We have decided to send you back to Dublin. Your temperature is down now. It was very high last night and we don't want it going up again, but if you keep getting yourself stressed and upset like this, it's going to go back up and we won't be able to operate, anyway.'

In the middle of all this mayhem, my brain clicked in to what the new word, 'stress', meant. It was just a fancy word for being upset and worried. *They could've said tha' in the first place, with their fancy words confusin' me altogether.*

'I'm going to give you an injection for the pain. That should keep you going until you get to your doctor. Pick these tablets up in the chemist for your throat.' He handed me a piece of paper. 'I'll leave a letter at reception for you to pick up on your way out. And I mean this, young lady, you must go straight to your doctor. He will make arrangements with the hospital to get you in straight away.' He raised his voice a little and was getting worked up himself – not that I could blame him with my carry-on.

'Thanks, doctor. I will, I promise.' I would have said anything to be on my way.

The two of them walked off, mumbling to one another, the Chinese doctor with his hands up in the air, still insisting that I should get the knife there and then. It wasn't long before the nurse was in to give me the injection.

'I see your name is Kathleen,' she said as she gave me a jab in the arse.

'Nurse, if I give yeh the name of the hotel I was staying in, would yeh give them a ring and ask would they tell Alan McGrath – tha's me husband – to collect me?'

'A bride of only two days, I hear. Is it any wonder you're upset?'

'Yeh don't think I'm bein' stupid carryin' on like a kid, cryin'?'

'Not at all. Anyone would have themselves in a state, if they were as sick as you've been and on their honeymoon as well, you poor thing.'

'Thanks, nurse. Tha' makes me feel a bit better.'

'It will be at least two hours before you can leave – doctor's orders – so you just lie there and get yourself nice and calm, keep that temperature down. He won't let you leave unless it's right.'

'Okay, I will. Before yeh go, nurse, could yeh get me ring and chain when yeh're pickin' me clothes up? I don't want to see tha' sister.'

She smiled. 'I think that might be best. I'll go and make that phone call for you. Now, remember what I said, Kathleen.'

The two hours went by quickly. The nurse was in and out checking me and chatting, asking all about the wedding. She couldn't believe how many brothers and sisters I had, and how young they all were. That was it – once I started talking about the kids, I was happy.

'My, that father of yours was a busy man,' she giggled.

I didn't know how to answer that one, so I said nothing.

'And your mother, she must be some woman. How on earth does she cope?'

Without batting an eyelid I found myself saying, 'Because she's great, nurse, tha's how.'

'Now, isn't that a nice thing to say? I'm sure she'd be very pleased to hear that.'

I thought to myself, *Yeh never know with Ma, she'd probably tell me to stop being so sloppy, carryin' on like an eejit. Then again, maybe tha's wha's wrong with her a lot of the time; she thinks none of us care about her. I'll talk to Phil when I get home, see wha' he thinks.*

'Kathleen, would this be himself walking down the corridor?'

My heart skipped a beat when she said that. I jumped down to the end of the bed. 'Tha's him, nurse.'

'Look at you. You're glowing all over. That's one handsome lad you have there, I'd be keeping a tight rope on him, if he was mine.'

'I know, nurse, I will.' Then I blushed from head to toe. 'Ah, yeh know wha' I mean, nurse.'

Alan and I were hugging and kissing before I knew it. We forgot the nurse was standing there. She gave a little cough. 'Everything seems to be fine now, Kathleen. You can go ahead and get dressed. Your clothes are in the locker beside you.'

'Yeh mean they were there all the time?'

'Yes, but we weren't going to tell you that, now, were we?' She handed my ring and chain to me.

'I'll go and make sure the doctor left that letter out for you.'

The nurse met us on the way out and handed me the letter. She winked and said, 'Herself is in the office, so we'll say no more.'

Alan looked puzzled. 'She means the Sister. I'll tell yeh when we get in the car.'

'Make sure you do what the doctor said and the best of luck to you both.' She held an umbrella over me while I got in the car.

As soon as we on our way, I told Alan all about the Sister

pulling off my ring. 'And then there was this Chinese doctor – he wanted to give me the knife there and then, and yeh wanna see the height of the other doctor, he was real posh but nice.'

'Yeh're feelin' better then, Kathleen?'

'Now tha' yeh're here, Alan, I am.'

'Yeh haven't stopped talkin' for the past couple of minutes, so I know yeh're on the mend.'

'Will yeh stop yer messin'. Yeh're always teasin' me.'

I cuddled into him.

* * *

In no time at all Alan had us back at the hotel and checked out. We got plenty of waves and goodbyes as we pulled away. It wasn't long before we came to the main road: Dublin one way, Cork the other. The thought struck me: *I don't want to go back yet. I want to try and fix things; I have to make it right between us.*

'Stop the car, Alan.'

'Wha' de yeh mean? Wha's wrong?'

'Just stop – come on, let's go to Cork.'

'But, Kathleen, the doctor said . . .'

'I know, I know. I feel a bit better. Come on, Alan, I'll be okay. We didn't get a chance to talk or enjoy ourselves – yeh know wha' I mean.'

That was it; you could see the gleam in his eyes straight away. I didn't have to say another word. He revved the car so much there was smoke coming out of the wheels as he took the road to Cork.

It was a long drive. We talked and talked, planning out our future, the great adventures we were going to have. Two kids, with not a worry in the world at that moment in time, anyway, but for one thing – I only hoped I could get it into my head that loving was not dirty or bad. I was lost in my thoughts again.

'Kathleen, are yeh asleep or wha'? I'm talkin' away here and

I don't know if yeh're listenin' to me.'

'I was just restin' me eyes for a couple of minutes, Alan. Go on, wha' were yeh sayin'?'

'We haven't got far to go now. I was thinkin' we could get ourselves a room in the city. Tha' way we can have a mosey around, maybe find somewhere with a bit of music, have tha' oul' dance we were supposed to have the other night. I don't mean jivin' or anythin' like tha'; yeh know: a nice lurch. Or would yeh prefer just to go for somethin' to eat?'

'I don't mind, Alan. You can pick.'

'Right then, tha's settled; we'll have music and fish 'n' chips walkin' back to the hotel.'

This was no problem, as it turned out we were right next door to a pub that was blasting out some rock and roll. It was great to hear after being stuck in the hospital. We booked into the hotel, dropped the bags and headed for the pub. The place was hopping, everybody was singing along with the band and there were a few dancing over in the corner.

This is more like it, I thought. *The way it's supposed to be.*

But that was all soon to change. As the night went on, the pain came back with a bang. The injection was starting to wear off. I just about managed to get through the night without fainting. Alan knew that I wasn't feeling great when I didn't want to get up to dance. I was usually the first on the floor.

'Let's head back, Kathleen. Try an' get a few hours' sleep. Yeh look tired. We'll make our way back to Dublin tomorrow.'

I didn't argue. He was right.

* * *

We got up at the crack of dawn. By this time I was bent over with the pain. Alan was starting to panic once again.

'I shouldn't have listened to yeh, Kathleen. We should have made our way back to Dublin yesterday. Wha' was I thinkin'?'

'Will yeh stop gettin' yerself in a state, Alan. I'll lie down in the back of the car. It's not as bad when I do tha'. We'll be home in no time. Come on, I'll be okay.' I was trying not to let him know how bad I was really feeling.

He calmed himself down, paid the bill and we were on the road in no time.

Some honeymoon!

28

Marital Bliss . . .

Alan talked all the way up to Dublin. I don't know what he was going on about half of the time. I agreed with everything he said. He was going so fast he was taking lumps out of the road.

'If we keep goin' at this rate, Kathleen, I'll have yeh back in time for Dr Johnson's surgery. If anyone can get yeh into hospital quick, he will.'

And he did. I was only in the door when he saw to me immediately. I handed him the letter the other doctor had given me. He glanced at it and looked at me with a frown.

'Kathleen, you should have been here yesterday.'

'I know, doctor, but I was startin' to feel a bit better.'

'There's no "buts" about it. Alan, you should have had more sense. I'm not even going to examine you, Kathleen. I only have to look at your colour . . .' He scribbled out a few lines on a bit of paper. 'Take this and go down to the Adelaide Hospital straight away. I'll phone and let them know you're on your way. They'll see to you right away.'

And sure enough, as soon as we got to the hospital I was taken to see a doctor. He didn't pull any punches either. He nearly pressed my stomach up into my mouth; the whole

307

hospital must have heard the roars of me. 'Right, young lady, it's the theatre for you; the appendix has to come out now, and I mean *now*!'

'But, Doctor, me Ma doesn't even know I'm here.'

'And how old are you?'

'I'm nearly nineteen.'

'You're too young. Nurse,' he called out, 'we have to get a consent form signed.'

'Alan's outside. Will he do? He's me husband, doctor.'

'Send him in to me on your way out. Nurse, take this young lady and prepare her for theatre. There's no time to delay.'

As I brushed past Alan, I just about had time to tell him to sign the form for me. At this stage my legs were starting to go from under me with the pain. The nurse quickly got me into a wheelchair and stuck a bowl in my hand: 'Just in case, love.' And she was so right; I was only halfway down the corridor when there were noises coming from both ends, between the farting and spluttering at one end and the throwing up at the other. I was all over the place. Not that I cared; I wanted the pain to go away. They could have done anything to me at that stage.

The nurse wasn't long getting me ready and before I knew it, I was on a trolley getting wheeled down to get the knife. Just as we got to the door of the operating room – the theatre, as the doctor called it – the nurse let out a gasp: 'Christ, your nail polish is still on! It slipped me mind rushing about getting you ready.' She called to one of the other nurses, 'Quick! Help me get this off before doctor gets here. He'll have a blue fit if you're not ready when he comes in.'

He was having a fit anyway. Alan was too young to sign the form; you had to be twenty-one and he was only twenty.

The doctor came over to me as he glanced at the chart: 'Now, Kathleen, has your family got a phone?'

'No, Doctor.'

'Has anyone near your home got one?'

'The corner shop down the road from me Ma's has one.'

'And the name of that is . . .?' I could see he was getting himself all worked up; he was red in the face and grinding his teeth together.

'It's called the Windmill, Doctor.'

My bottom lip was starting to tremble. He knew he was making me nervous.

'Everything's going to be fine, Kathleen.' It was like he was trying to calm himself down as well as me. 'I have to operate very soon or you're going to be in serious trouble. Do you understand me? There's no time to waste.' Out he went, his hands flying in the air, mumbling and giving out to himself, frustrated as hell.

What did he only go and do? He got onto Crumlin garda station straight away and informed them of the situation. A garda was sent down to the house in no time. They brought Da down to the phone, and his consent was given. The doctor was back before I knew it.

I got a jab in the arse. 'Right, Kathleen, I want you to count to ten for me.'

'One, two . . .' wasn't even out of my mouth and I was gone.

* * *

When I came around I was so sick! Alan had to hold my head with one hand and a bowl under my chin with the other. Every time I tried to tell him I was sorry, up it kept coming. I looked a right mess, I'm sure.

That's when the nurse came in: 'I think it's best if you go, sir. She'll be like this for a couple of hours. If you leave it until tomorrow evening, there will be a big difference in her, I promise.'

And the nurse was so right. I was sitting up – still green in the face, mind you – but a lot better, when Alan walked in with Ma and Phil. Ma settled herself down on one side of the bed, Alan on the other.

'Kathleen Doyle!' Ma got her spoke in straight away. 'Yeh put the heart crossways in me and yer Da. De yeh know tha'? The police comin' to me door! Wha'll the neighbours think?'

'Sorry, Ma, I didn't send them – it was the doctor.'

'I thought it was one of them kids after gettin' into trouble, but when they said yer name and the hospital, I thought yeh were dead. I mean, who sends the police to yer door when somebody's only sick? Did yeh ever hear the likes of it?'

I looked across at Phil, who was standing behind Ma. He had a grin on his face from ear to ear. He was making all sorts of faces at me. Alan wouldn't look at him. I kept trying to move myself around, letting on to cough so that I didn't laugh. Sick or not, if Ma thought you were making fun of her, she wouldn't care; she'd still give you a right box.

After all that giving out and rammaging on and on about neighbours and what have you, she finally turned around and asked me: 'Anyway, Kathleen, how are yeh? Yeh're like death warmed up with the colour of yeh, with yer waxy face. How long are yeh goin' to be in this place for? I miss yeh terrible helpin' with the kids and the bit of cleanin'.' *Jaysus, Ma, I thought, put yer arms around me, tell me how happy yeh are tha' I'm okay.* But no.

'I have to stay in for ten days, Ma.'

'For God's sake, Kathleen. I'd be after havin' two babies and home in less time than tha'.'

'The doctor said it was very serious, Ma. Only Alan got me here when he did, I could have been a goner.'

'Hmm . . . is tha' so? Are yeh sure yeh took him up right, Kathleen? Yeh could have died, like. Was it tha' serious then?'

'Yeah, Ma!' I was pushing it a bit, hoping that she might soften. 'All this poison stuff leaks all around yer insides; the nurse told me all about it. If they don't get to yeh quick, yeh're finished. I mean, dead. Tha's why the police went to the house to get Da to give the go-ahead, because me and Alan were under-age.'

'Well then, when yeh put it like tha', I suppose it makes sense yeh not droppin' off at the house to let me know wha' was happenin'. Yeh were wise, Alan, to bring her straight here. I want to thank yeh for tha'.' I was well pleased when she said that, and so was Alan. 'Now tha' I see yeh're alright, I'll be on me way.'

'Wait, Lil. Just give me a few minutes with Kathleen. I'll drop yerself and Phil off.'

'Yeh're okay, Alan. I'm in this far now; I might as well make me way up to Meath Street. Come on, Phil. Yeh needn't think I'm leavin' yeh here with yer messin'. De yeh think I don't know wha' yeh do be doin' behind me back. I didn't come up on the last load, yeh know!'

'Ah, go on, Ma, don't be givin' out.' With that Phil grabbed her and lifted her up, squeezing her to bits – and he was able to. A fine big fella he turned out to be. The muscles on him! And by God, you'd need them to lift Ma; she was small but had plenty of meat on her. *Jaysus*, I thought, *she'll kill him when they get outside.*

'Put me down, yeh bloody gobshite.' She swung her bag and hit him on the head. But at the same time, she was trying to keep a straight face; I could see a little grin on the corner of her mouth. She was enjoying it, I could tell. 'This eejit's gone mad, Kathleen. Will yeh talk to him? I don't know wha's got into him since he came back from tha' Canada place.

'Ah, would yeh get away with yerself; yeh love havin' me home, Ma, don't yeh?' He kept tipping her on the arm, laughing his head off, watching her getting all riled up.

'See wha' I mean, Kathleen? I'll go before he gets us thrown outta the hospital. Yer father will be up tonight. I'll get him to bring a couple of the older kids. They're all dyin' to see yeh. I'll do me best to get up in a day or two and maybe bring a few of the little ones; I'll check if they'll let them in. Come on, Phil. Let them have a bit of time together. Yeh're okay then, Kathleen?'

'Thanks, Ma, I'm fine.'

On the way out Phil turned back towards us, laughing and making all sorts of signs with his hands.

'Wha's he doin', Alan?'

'Don't mind him, Kathleen. He's messin' as usual. I mean, yeh saw him with yer Ma; anythin' for a laugh. Anyway, never mind Phil. The visitin' time is nearly over. How are yeh feelin' now?'

'I'm just a bit sore, tha's all. I'm sorry, Alan. Nothin' seems to be goin' right for us.'

'It's just a bit of a blip, tha's all, Kathleen. Yeh'll be back on yer feet in no time. We'll put this all behind us. Just yeh wait and see.'

The nurse came in ringing the bell.

'I better go, Kathleen.' He gave me a hug and a kiss. 'I'll try and get up during the day on me own. Look! There she goes ringin' the bell again. It's really loud this time. I better run.'

* * *

Alan's Da had no problem letting him off work for an hour to come up and visit me. Phil made his way up one of the days and got there a bit early, before Alan.

'I see yeh're startin' to look a bit normal again, Kathleen. Yeh looked a bit ropey there for a while.'

'I'm okay now, Phil. Listen, I want to ask yeh somethin' before Alan comes up. Wha' were yeh on about the other evenin'? Yeh know, when yeh came into the hospital first. Yeh were makin' these signs with yer hands. Wha' did it mean?'

'Ah, tha'! I was just havin' a bit of craic with Alan. Yeh know him, yeh can say anythin', he never gets annoyed.'

'Well, yeh thought it was very funny and I could do with a good laugh. So go on, tell me.'

'No. Yeh'll only go and get all hyper on me.'

'I won't, Phil,' I promised.

'Okay. Yeh asked. I told Alan tha' he must have a right whopper in his trousers, tha' he ended up puttin' yeh in hospital.'

'Jaysus Christ, Phil, yeh didn't!'

'See wha' I mean? I told yeh, yeh're gettin' yerself all worked up. Blokes talk like tha' all the time to one another. It means nothin'. It's just a bit of craic.'

'Yeh don't understand, Phil. Yeh don't realise wha's goin' on with me and Alan.' And before I knew it, I was pouring my heart out, telling him everything. He sat and listened. And there was no messing.

'Wha' am I goin' to do, Phil?'

'Holy Jaysus, I don't know, Kathleen. Poor Alan. He must feel like shite; not sayin' tha' you don't, but this kind of thing, it's real big with blokes. When yeh get yer first score, tha's it. Yeh're up there in the clouds. Yeh're a man and all tha' stuff. This is real serious. Yeh're goin' to have to get yer head around this.'

'De yeh not think I know tha', Phil?'

'Kathleen, yeh're married and grown-up now. Yeh shouldn't be thinkin' about wha' Ma and Da used to preach. They were just afraid of yeh gettin' yerself up the stick. And don't get me started on about the church and priests – them fuckers, messin' with people's heads: this is a sin, tha's a sin, yeh can't do this, and yeh can't do tha'.'

'Jaysus, Phil, would yeh stop talkin' like tha'? If anybody hears yeh!'

'I don't give two shites who hears me. I've learned a few things in the nine months bein' away, and it makes me blood boil when I think of the way they try and rule people with their ways. They wouldn't tell me wha' to do. I can tell yeh tha' for nothin'.'

'Wha'ever yeh do, Phil, don't let Ma or Da hear yeh talk like tha'. There'll be killin's in the house, I'm tellin' yeh.'

'Just listen to yerself, Kathleen. We're not kids anymore.

We're grown-ups and should be able to say wha' we think.'

'Phil, de yeh always say wha's inside yer head?'

'If it's worth sayin', I do. Why?'

'Ah, it's nothin', I was just wonderin', tha's all.'

'Come on, Kathleen, seein's yeh're on a roll, spit it out.'

'Right then; there is one more thing but yeh're not to laugh.'

'Go on, I'm listenin'.'

'De yeh ever tell Ma tha' yeh love her, Phil? I want to know; it's important to me.'

'For Jaysus' sake, wha' are yeh on about, Kathleen? She knows we all love her.'

'Maybe she doesn't, Phil. Tha's probably wha' does be wrong with her half the time. She thinks we don't care and tha's why she's so serious all the time.'

'Will yeh stop, for fuck's sake, Kathleen. Imagine standin' there and sayin' to Ma, "Yeh know I love yeh, Ma." I know wha' she'd say: "Fuck off and give over yer messin'." I'm tellin' yeh, she would. Anyway, I think yeh have more to be worryin' about at the minute than to be thinkin' about wha's goin' on inside Ma's head. Yeh'll have to sort this out yerself. Nobody else can do it for yeh.'

'Promise me, Phil, yeh won't tell anybody about this.'

'Yeh won't have to worry there. I'm not a gobshite altogether. Look! I can see Alan walkin' up the corridor. I'll head off now. Give yeh a bit of time to yerselves.'

'Thanks for listenin', Phil. I feel a little better now tha' I told yeh. Say nothin', de yeh hear me?'

'Didn't I say I wouldn't?'

Alan walked in just then. 'Say nothin' about wha'? You two look very serious. Wha's up?'

I looked at Phil, not knowing what to say.

'I was just sayin' to Kathleen I might stay on for a while, if I get meself some work. I don't want her sayin' anythin' to Ma. Just in case it doesn't go accordin' to plan.'

I cocked my ears up straight away and couldn't keep my mouth shut. 'Tha' means yeh won't be goin' back to Canada, Phil.' I was so happy to hear he might be staying.

'It all depends on this fella I'm goin' to meet in the next half an hour. If he can get me in on the site he's workin' on, I'll be away in a hack. He was tellin' me yeh get paid by the house. Oh, another thing, Alan, it's all rollers now. I'd be able to get through a couple of houses a week. I'm a flyer when I get goin'. Jaysus! When I think about it. I'd be on savage money, if this all goes well.' He stood up to go. 'Anyway, Kathleen, yeh'll be out in a day or two, so I'll see yeh when yeh come home. Let yeh know wha's happenin'.' He gave me a wink on his way out.

'Alan, I'm gettin' me stitches out in the mornin'. Nurse said if all is well the doctor could let me home by dinner-time.'

'Tha's great news, Kathleen.'

'Jaysus! I was nearly forgettin' to tell yeh, we were talkin' tha' much to Phil. The doctor wants to see yeh before I leave.'

'I wonder wha' tha's all about?'

We sat talking and laughing. But the laugh was soon to be put on the other side of Alan's face when the doctor walked in the following day. He had a very serious face on him as he stood at the end of the bed, and looked at the two of us for a few seconds.

'Kathleen, I will be letting you home today. Everything seems to be fine.' Both of us had a smile on our faces the length of the ward. Then he went on: 'I understand you're newly-weds?'

'Tha's righ', Doctor,' Alan answered, as proud as punch.

'Well . . .' he said, putting his hand to his mouth and giving a little cough. 'I'm afraid you will have to put your sex life on hold for at least three months.'

Alan looked straight at me; as soon as I heard the word 'sex' I held my head down and wouldn't look at either of them. The doctor went on to explain the 'dos' and the 'don'ts', the 'whys' and 'why-nots'. I was only half-listening. I was too busy

315

thinking to myself: *Jaysus, this is great! I have a good excuse now – for a couple of months, anyway.*

Then I looked over at Alan. That soon stopped me in my stride. He was trying to take everything in. When the doctor left the room, all he said was: 'Tha' was a right mouthful, Kathleen.'

I didn't know what to say, so I said nothing. As Ma always said, 'Unless yeh know and understand wha's comin' out of yer mouth, keep it shut.'

* * *

We made our way up to Ma and Da as soon as I left the hospital. I was dying to see the little ones. They hadn't been allowed in to see me as they were too young.

When we walked in, Ma was sitting there feeding Mano, who was about five weeks old at that stage. Paul was asleep in the pram beside her. Da was in the kitchen, as usual cleaning up the mess after everyone. He was great when he wasn't on the drink, always helping Ma with one thing or another.

'Hi, Ma.'

'Ah! There yeh are, Kathleen. Come in. Sit down. Alan, pull over a chair. Phil, look who's here.'

'Yeh're lookin' grand, Kathleen.'

'Thanks, Da! Here, I have a few things – cakes, sweets and some biscuits. I wasn't goin' to leave them in the hospital, when I knew yiz could do with them.'

'Yeh never said a truer word. Phil, put the teapot on and hide them few bits – put them up on the top shelf, so's the kids won't see them. I'll share them out later tonight for a surprise.'

Alan sat in the kitchen with Da. They always had something to talk about. If it wasn't the boxing, it was football. They always got on very well together.

'Where's all the kids, Ma?'

'I got Clare and Marion to take them up to the park for a

while. Get them from under me feet, so's I might get a few things done around here. Kathleen, yer father took the pledge the other day. Let's hope it lasts a bit longer this time. He's a different man altogether when he's not in them pubs, as yeh well know more than anybody.'

'Tha's great news, Ma.' Just then little Paul woke up.

'He's been frettin' terrible after yeh. I've trouble every night tryin' to settle him.'

I went over and picked him up.

'How's my little fella?' He looked at me for a minute before he realised who I was. Then there was no end to the smiles I got.

'See wha' I mean, Kathleen? All I've got is cryin' since yeh left. I don't know wha' I'm goin' to do with him.'

'He'll be grand, Ma! I'll make sure I drop in every day. Won't I, little fella?' I gave him a big hug. He was as happy as anything.

It wasn't long before the rest of the gang started dribbling in. The house was full in no time. Phil made his way over to tell me that he'd got the job and wouldn't be going back to Canada. I was so happy with his news. I gave him a big hug.

'Does Ma and Da know?'

'I only got the word yesterday, so I told them straight away.'

I looked over at Ma. 'Isn't this great news about Phil stayin'?'

She held onto Mano with one hand and blessed herself with the other a half dozen times. 'Wha' have I always told yiz – Our Lady never forgets me; she always answers me prayers.'

I sat there for hours, Paul still in my arms, Jacinta and Patricia either side of my feet. Da made the dinner and Ma shared out the few goodies. Everybody got a taste.

'Ma, I'll bring Paul up to bed. Who's he sleepin' with now?'

'Stick him in between Marion and Clare. Not tha' it will make a difference. He's only down when the cryin' starts again. I had him in with Jacinta and Patricia the last few nights, but

Jacinta's pissin' rings around herself every night. I'll have to get tha' wan down to the clinic and get her checked. There's not enough hours in the day, I've tha' much to do. I don't know if I'm comin' or goin' half the time.'

'I told yeh, Ma, I'd be up real early in the mornin'. I'll bring Jacinta to the clinic while yeh're gettin' the little ones ready. Then we'll get stuck into the house.'

'Right yeh are, then.' And out came the diddy to give Mano a few sucks before putting him down for a couple of hours. 'Tha's it for me, Kathleen. Me diddies is all dryin' up now after all these years. I think it's time to retire them. It's a bottle for Mano from now on.'

'Tha' mightn't be any harm, Ma. Yeh've well done yer bit.'

I made my way upstairs to settle Paul. I was tiptoeing around in the dark so as not to wake any of them, but I should have known they wouldn't be asleep.

I slipped Paul in between the girls.

'Are yeh stayin' here tonight with us, Kathleen?' asked Marion.

'I'll stay for a little while. Then I have to go home with Alan.'

'But this is where yeh live,' went on poor Marion, being so innocent. 'Sure Alan can stay too. We'll move over and make room for him, won't we, Clare?'

'I can't, Marion, sure didn't I get married?'

None of them understood what I was trying to say.

'Don't be such a gobshite, Marion,' Noel butted in. 'Kathleen's left and she won't be stayin' here anymore, so yeh better get used to it.'

Marion started crying. Noel laughed at her. 'Na-na-nana-na! Look at the cry-baby.'

'Give it over, Noel, yeh don't have to tease her like tha'. It's as hard for me as it is for them.'

The kids settled after I told them I'd be up every day, and the only time I wouldn't be there was when they were asleep.

They seemed happy enough with that for the moment anyway and slowly, one by one, they dozed off.

When I got back downstairs, Alan had his jacket on.

'Are yeh right, Kathleen?' He handed me my coat.

'Yeh're off, then?' Da whispered. 'Don't take any notice of yer mother about helpin' out here. I'll look after all tha'. Just come up and see the kids and sit with yer mother for a while.'

'Okay, Da. It's gettin' late, so I best be goin'. I'll talk to yeh tomorrow.'

I could feel a lump in my throat. It was hitting me like a ton of bricks. I thought I felt bad the night before the wedding, but this was ten times worse. I really was never going to sleep there anymore. I wondered if everybody felt the same when leaving home for the first time, or was it me being childish?

Ma must have seen the panic in my face. She made her way over to me: 'I have to lock up now, so yeh better muffle yerself up there.' She wrapped an old scarf around my neck. 'I've to try and get meself a few hours' sleep before I start all over again tomorrow; now off with the two of yiz.'

That was it. I was outside the door before I knew it.

* * *

Alan's grandfather's house was just down the road so we were there in a couple of minutes. I felt strange walking in the door for the first time.

'Pop must be in bed,' said Alan. 'I asked him to make sure and keep the fire goin'. I wanted to have the place nice and cosy for when yeh came home.'

I was glad to hear this. It gave us a chance to be on our own, for a little while anyway. We stayed up talking for ages, Alan going on about one thing and another. 'Yeh'll end up back in the hospital if yeh don't listen to me.' But I was only half-listening, thinking to myself, *I don't want to be here. I want to go home.*

I'd have promised him the sun, moon and stars that night,

and said anything to make him happy for being so patient with me. We finally made our way upstairs. I could feel the cold hitting me in the face as soon as we opened the bedroom door. It was like walking into a fridge. There was a small fire in the corner, which must not have been lit in years. Alan was stripped and in the bed in seconds. I knelt down beside the bed as I always did. Alan peeped out over the eiderdown quilt.

'Wha' are yeh doin', Kathleen?'

'I'm sayin' me few prayers.'

He quickly pulled the quilt over his head.

'Are you laughin' at me, Alan McGrath?'

'I'm not, I swear, Kathleen.'

'I can hear yeh!'

He popped his head out with the pillow stuck in his mouth, laughing.

'Okay, I am – sorry, love.'

'Is it because I'm sayin' me prayers yeh're laughin'? Yeh must think I'm a right tick, Alan.'

'No, yeh're not – it's just, religion is very strong in yer family and tha's the way yeh are, but yeh don't have to kneel out there in the cold. Yeh can just as well say yer prayers beside me. Now get in before yeh freeze to death.'

I jumped into the bed, shaking with the cold, but I couldn't get the heat into me.

'Oh my God, Alan, this bed is so cold.'

'Tha's easily sorted out. I'll pick up a couple of water bottles on me way home from work tomorrow evenin', and an hour or two before we go to bed I'll light tha' small fire in the room. Tha'll take the nip outta the air. Then when yeh slip in beside me yeh'll be nice and cosy. Wha' de say? It'll be like yeh never left home, Kathleen.'

I don't know about tha', I thought to myself. *It's goin' to take a lot more than two hot water bottles to help me settle in this house.* 'Alan, it wasn't tha' Ma had blazin' fires lightin' in the bedrooms, or anythin' like tha'. It was just, by the time I used to get to bed the kids would have the sheets nice and warm and I would slip in between them, tha's all.'

'Yeh won't know yerself tomorrow night by the time I'm finished here. Now try and get a few hours' sleep. Yeh know yeh'll be up at the crack of dawn, wantin' to go up to yer Ma's.'

When we came down the next morning, Alan's granddad was already up and about. It felt strange sitting there, looking across the table at this little old man. He was blowing on a spoonful of porridge.

'Will yeh have some?' he asked. I looked at his hands; you could have made mud pies with the dirt under his nails; and looking at the rest of him, a good wash wouldn't have gone astray either. 'I said, *will yeh have some?*' He didn't even call me by my name.

'No, thanks very much . . . em . . . em . . .' I didn't know what to call him.

Alan was on the ball straight away. 'Kathleen, yeh can call him "Pop".'

'Is tha' ok?' I asked.

'Tha's the name I go by. Now are yeh havin' a drop of this or wha'?' He was getting crankier by the minute.

'I'll just do meself a bit of toast, if yeh don't mind. I'm not one for eatin' much in the mornin's.'

'Suit yerself, then. De yeh want some, Alan?'

'I'm okay, Pop. A cup of tea and a smoke does me until lunchtime. Just look after yerself.'

'I won't be goin' to this trouble again, yeh can be sure,' he mumbled.

I thought, *Thank God for tha'*.

While Alan cleaned out the fire, I gave the place a quick tidy around and then I was out of there. Alan dropped me off at Ma's on his way to work.

'I'll pick yeh up when I'm finished. And remember wha' I said about overdoin' it.'

'Will yeh stop worryin'?' I gave him a big kiss.

* * *

The weeks went by so fast, with me going up to Ma's every day, helping her with one thing or another. Before I knew it the three months were coming to an end and I was well over my operation. I would have been happy enough to leave things with a kiss and cuddle, but I could see Alan was raring to go. Every night I got into bed, I would say to myself: *This is it; I'm really goin' to do it tonight*. But it didn't happen. I'd freeze each time.

I started bringing little Paul home a couple of nights a week, pretending he was still fretting and to give Ma a break. I'd stick him in the bed between us. Alan knew full well what I was up to, but said nothing.

A few more months went by and I could see that his patience was starting to run out with me. He started getting very quiet and when he did have something to say he was snappy. I didn't blame him: any other fella would have lost it long before that.

I wasn't sleeping very well with the worry of all this. I was lying there one night, Alan asleep with his arms wrapped around me so tight. I looked at him and thought: *I love you so much, Alan, and I'm not goin' to lose you, but if I don't do somethin' about this problem, I will.*

That's when I made up my mind, there and then: I would go and see Dr Johnson the next day.

I was outside the doctor's surgery long before he arrived, making sure that no one got in front of me, so I'd be his first patient. I didn't want to have to sit in a waiting room, thinking, getting more nervous by the minute. At least when he arrived I could walk straight in and just say it. That was the plan, anyway.

He arrived after ten minutes. In that time I must have walked in and out of the garden fifty times: going, staying, going, staying, in and out; my head was all over the place.

I finally sat in the chair.

'Well now, Kathleen. How have you been since your stay in hospital? That was a right scare for you, but from the report they sent me all went well. What has you up here today?' He got his notepad ready.

I looked at him, trying to get the words in my head to come out of my mouth. I just couldn't.

'Kathleen, what is it?'

'I . . . em . . . em . . . I've, I'm . . . I can't sleep, I can't eat and me stomach is sick, Doctor.'

'Well then, we know what might be wrong here, don't we, Kathleen?'

'We do, Doctor?'

'You have all the signs. I'll just have to send off a sample to confirm it. Lie down there on the couch 'til I check and make sure everything is alright.'

'Confirm wha', Doctor?'

'You could be pregnant, Kathleen.'

When he said that, the tears started flowing out of me like a river. 'I'm not pregnant, Dr Johnson. I can't be. Yeh don't understand.' And then I said it at last: *'I've never had sex – never, ever, ever.'*

He sat looking at me for a few seconds with his mouth open. Then he moved his chair over beside me and held my hand.

'Calm down, Kathleen. Have you spoken to anybody else about this?'

'Only me brother Phil, but it didn't make any difference.'

'What about Alan? Has he?'

'I don't think so. We don't even talk to one another about this, never mind other people.'

'I have never had a patient myself with this problem, but I know a few doctors who have. You're not the only couple, Kathleen.'

That didn't make me feel any better.

He sat there with me for a long time. Usually I'd be in and out in five minutes, a piece of paper in my hand, trying to remember if I'd told him everything I went for in the first place; but not this time, even though I could hear the doorbell ringing every couple of minutes. The queue must have been out the door and halfway down the street. He still didn't rush. He went into everything with me, wanting to know every little detail. He examined me down below to make sure everything was where it was supposed to be, and that there were no lumps or bumps that shouldn't be there. When he was finished, he sat back down in his chair.

'Everything seems in order there. Now, the way I see it, Kathleen, there's nothing medically wrong with you. For whatever reason, you have put this blockage in your head; be it your mother, father, religion – they probably all did play a part in your mind, but I think fear of the unknown is what is wrong here. You have put it in your head that it's going to hurt you. That's why you won't let it happen. So what I want you to do for me is . . .' As he was talking to me, he was bending over to the press in front of him. He took out a jar and put it into my hand. I looked down at it and looked back up at him as quick.

'It's a jar of Vaseline, Doctor.'

'That's right, Kathleen. Plain old Vaseline, and this is what's going to sort a lot of this problem out for you. Before I go any further, would you like me to talk to Alan?'

I thought for a few seconds. 'No, I'll do it. If I'm goin' to try and get past this, we're going to have to talk to one another about it, together.'

'Good, Kathleen! That's the way to be thinking. Now, what I want you to do is not let tonight go by, no matter what. You are to make love tonight. It's the only way. Put plenty of Vaseline on where I just examined you and tell Alan he's to do the same. Oh, yes, another thing – he's to take it slow and easy, not to go charging in like a racehorse. He'll know what I mean.' I cringed when he said that. He stood up then and put his arm around me. 'In time, as you learn to relax, you will start to enjoy lovemaking. That's all I can say. It's up to you now, Kathleen. Drop up in a week or two and let me know how things are.'

'I will, Doctor, and thanks for listenin' to me.'

When I left his office I felt a lot better in myself and determined to do everything he'd said.

* * *

I thought the day would never end, waiting for Alan to pick me up from Ma's. Usually I would be stalling with the time, dragging my heels, dreading the thoughts of going down to Pop's. But not tonight; I just about gave Alan time to finish his cup of tea in Ma's when I started to put my coat on.

'Yeh're headin' off early,' said Ma. 'Are yeh goin' somewhere, Kathleen?'

I made up some lame excuse about my washing piling up and Alan having to sort the back garden out. Alan frowned over at me; he didn't say a word until we got into the car.

'Wha' was all tha' about, Kathleen?'

'Just let me wave to Ma and the kids. Paul was cryin' to come with me so I promised him I would blow lots of kisses to him and he was to catch each one and hold onto them until I come up tomorrow, and then he can blow them all back to me.' Paul was happy enough with that and was smiling as we pulled away.

'Well, wha's up, Kathleen?

'I'm sayin' nothin' not until I'm sittin' down and lookin' at yeh straight in the eye.'

'This sounds serious, Kathleen. Is somethin' bad after happenin'?'

'It's good, Alan. I mean, I think, I hope. Look, here we are; I'll tell yeh in two minutes.'

I never saw Alan get out of the car so quick. Usually, he'd

have a look in the mirror, take his comb out and fix his quiff and then light up a smoke, but not tonight. He was out of the car and in the door like a light.

Pop wasn't there, which was great.

'I'll make us a cup of tea.'

'Jaysus, Kathleen. Will yeh stop stallin'?'

'Right then. I've somethin' to tell yeh. I was up with Doctor Johnson today. I went to talk about us.' Alan was about to say something, but I held up my hand. 'No, Alan, I don't want yeh to say anythin' until I'm finished. I told him all about wha's happenin' between us. Yeh know, about . . .' I hesitated for a second. I was going to say 'the other', but I didn't. I just came right out and said '. . . our sex problem'.

I could see Alan's eyebrows rising and that little grin showing on the corner of his mouth when he heard me say the word 'sex'. That's when I took out the jar of Vaseline. 'Alan, this is wha's goin' to sort me out.' He looked at the jar and then at me, with a look of astonishment on his face. 'Before yeh open yer mouth, Alan, let me finish.'

'Right then. I'm listenin'.'

'We're doin' it tonight, no matter wha'. You've to put some Vaseline on you know where, and I've to do the same. Tha' way it'll make things a bit easier. Oh yeah, another thing – yeh're to take yer time and make sure yeh don't go chargin' in like a racehorse. The doctor said yeh'd know wha' he meant by tha'.' The grin on Alan's face was getting wider by the minute. 'Then maybe I won't be so tense and will learn how to relax. The rest will just come natural. Well, wha' de yeh think, Alan?'

I could see that he was stunned but very happy at the same time. He put his arms around me.

'Kathleen, I can't believe yeh went and did this on yer own.'

'Either can I, Alan.'

'Well, wha' I think is . . .' He gave me a big kiss. 'Pop's not here; Paul's not here; so there's no time like the present.'

He took me by the hand and we headed for the stairs. We

just about got to the bedroom door when I suddenly stopped in my tracks.

'Alan, stop, stop!' I ran back down the stairs.

'Ah Jaysus, Kathleen, not again, not again.'

I made my way back up. 'It's okay, Alan, I just forgot the Vaseline.' The relief on his face as we walked into the bedroom!

I can't say that I was floating on air or heard violins or anything like it that night. Between the slipping and the sliding, the hitting and the missing, there was a bit of laughing going on, which helped me relax and not be so tense or afraid. The main thing for me that night was that I faced up to the traumatic fears that I had built up inside my head, which could have destroyed us. We weren't long making up for lost time. There wasn't a night went by that one of us wasn't giving the nod and the eye over at the other to make our way upstairs.

And in time, I learned how to enjoy something that is so easy and natural.

From such an early age, I always had to be so grown-up for Ma's world, but now and only now was I ready to be grown up for me and ready to go out into the real world for Kathleen.

Epilogue

I kept my promise to Ma, dropping in every day, still cleaning, helping and slipping her a few shillings when I could. As soon as each of the kids hit fourteen years, they were out in the world, fending for themselves and earning their keep.

Slowly but surely, life started to get easier for Ma. There were still blips and rows along the way, but nothing that she couldn't master, building a lovely home around the family, which she well deserved. Each and every one of the kids did very well for themselves – how could they not with the full force of Ma behind them!

Da lived to be seventy years old, falling on and off the wagon over the years, but it never stopped any of us loving him. Ma lived to be eighty-four years old. She had twelve children, twenty-seven grandchildren, nineteen great-grandchildren and one great-great grandchild. She remained a strong influence in all her children's lives up until her death, surrounded by all those who loved her dearly.

Alan and I were delighted with the arrival of our first child, Martina, followed by Alan Junior and then Amanda to complete our family. I finally had a chance to follow a lifelong dream to train as a hairdresser, and went on to open three very successful salons of my own . . . but of course I couldn't have done it without the total support of Alan.

In 2008 we celebrated our fortieth wedding anniversary, surrounded by our three kids, three granddaughters and one-great-grandson.

* * *

I wasn't long coming back from the past with the roars of Ma in my face.

'Kathleen, will yeh answer me! I have been talkin' to meself here for I don't know how long. Every time I look at yeh, yeh're miles away in tha' head of yours. Even as a child yeh were always gettin' lost in yer thoughts. Wha'ever yeh do be thinkin', I'll never know.'

'Thoughts from a child, Ma, tha's all, just thoughts from a child. But I'll tell yeh one thing I was thinkin' about – and this has been goin' around in me head for ages. I think I'll write a book about yeh.'

'About me? Sure wha' have I done in me life tha's worth writin' about, only nothin'?'

'Ah now, Ma, yeh'd be surprised, yeh'd be very surprised.'

'Well then, get the kettle on and we'll have a nice cup of tea out of them fancy china cups of yers, and as soon as yeh have tha' done, sit yerself down there and I'll tell yeh a few yarns. But before I do start about the goings-on of me life, I'll tell yeh one more thing for nothin'.'

She sat there in the kitchen, looking around, giving it the once-over.

'Yeh've done well for yerself, Kathleen, so yeh have. It's a far cry from jam jars to china yeh've come.'

The End.

In Ma's Footsteps

Book 2

Prologue

I've been enjoying every minute of my retirement. Our family are all grown up, each of them doing well for themselves. Both Alan and I have our health. What more could I ask for?

We were lucky enough to be able to buy a little apartment in Portugal about five years ago and I have to say it was one of the best things we ever did. We always loved Portugal and the people there. Our apartment has become a home from home.

As I lay back in the heat of the Portuguese sun, I thought about all the hard work that Alan and myself had done over the years. Looking around me now at what we have today, it was worth every hour we put in. We've been married now for over forty years and love each other as much as we did when we first met.

Not that things came easy for us – far from it. We had some very tough times, but between us we always came through it in the end. I've always been good at counting the pennies – I got that from Ma – and would make sure that I would save every which way I could. No matter how small it was, there was always some money put by.

'All the same,' I said to Alan, who was lying beside me on the beach, 'did yeh ever think tha' yeh'd see us havin' our own little place in the sun, bein' able to come away on holidays like this? I mean, when yeh think back to when we lived with yer Grandad Pop, we didn't even have a bath to wash ourselves in. If we were lucky, we'd just about enough money to get by from week to week.'

'We've come a long way since then, Kathleen, but tha' was sheer determination and hard grafting from the pair of us. So tha's wha' has us sittin' here today – enjoyin' ourselves like this.'

'Yeh're so righ', Alan. I get tired just thinkin' about all the hours we put in between us. I must ask yeh, Alan, if yeh had yer time over again, would yeh have done anythin' different with yer life?'

'Yeh mean as regards you and me, is tha' wha' yeh're tryin' to say, Kathleen?'

'Well, actually, tha's not wha' I mean. I was thinkin' more about yeh givin' up yer job in Gallaghers and buyin' the ice-cream van. But seein' tha' yeh brought up you and me, wha' would yeh change?'

'Well now, let me see Kathleen . . . If I'd known yeh were goin' to be the biggest chatterbox tha' stood on this earth, I'd have traded yeh in years ago, and tha's for sure.'

I looked at him with half a smile. 'Jaysus, Alan, are yeh serious?'

He was laughing his head off as he spoke. 'Would yeh stop it, Kathleen! Yeh know I wouldn't change a hair on yer head for anythin' or anyone.'

'Tha's alrigh', Alan, 'cause I wouldn't change you either, so now.'

'As far as the ice-cream van is concerned, I think I would've thought it through a bit more, Kathleen, instead of jumpin' straight in the way I did. I mean, look at the way yeh had to start doin' the markets on Sundays after doin' a week's work because I wasn't bringin' in enough money in the winter. And when the van would break down and I'd be off work – it was times like tha' I was sorry.'

'Ah, would yeh get away with yerself, Alan. Yeh love bein' yer own boss and I never minded any of the extra work. Anyway, I used to enjoy headin' off for the day to spend a bit of time with me sisters. I had some craic with them over the years.'

'Wha' about yerself, Kathleen? Would you have done anythin' different?'

'There is one thing tha' I definitely wouldn't do again, and tha's live with Pop. Ma tried to warn me about livin' on somebody else's floor, as yer Da did with you, but I suppose yeh can't put an old head on young shoulders. We had to make our own mistakes. Now, havin' said tha', I was very happy livin' there and it did break me heart when we had to leave tha' little house. You know tha' more than anybody.'

'We never should've moved there in the first place, Kathleen. Tha' was all my fault.'

'It was meant to be, Alan, because so many doors opened up for us after we moved. I went out and started mixin' with people a lot more, somethin' I never did, which helped me become more outgoin', and tha's how I was able to go on and follow me dream to become a hairdresser. I really do believe everythin' happens for a reason.'

'Ah, maybe yeh're righ', Kathleen. Who knows? All I know is tha' we're at a very happy place at this time in our lives and tha's all tha' matters at the minute. Now, are yeh comin' down for a swim or are yeh goin' to keep rammagin' on all day?'

'You go ahead, Alan. I think I'll stay here for a while and get a bit of heat into me bones.'

3

As I lay back on the chair and closed my eyes, I listened to the sound of the waves on the beach – it was so relaxing. I thought of Ma and how tough her life had been. Between having us twelve kids, it took her all her time to keep her head above water. I'd love nothing better than to have her here with me now. I would spoil her so much. I know it's a bit of a cliché to say that we were poor but in our way we were happy, but that's the truth for my family. Anyway, I've told that story already.[1] This one's for us – for Alan and me.

1 See *What Would Ma Say?*

1

The Geyser

I was ready to settle down to married life at last. I was so happy being married and living with Alan; he was everything I had ever wished for and more. We were still lodging with Alan's granddad, 'Pop', in Kimmage, but hopefully that wouldn't be for too long. Alan was working really hard to get enough money together for a deposit for our own house, just as he'd promised.

'Alan,' I said as we sat there drinking a cup of tea one morning, 'I'm goin' to see if I can get meself a job at the hairdressin'. It's wha' I always wanted to do and then I'll be able to help with the savin's. It's not fair on you havin' to look after everythin'.'

'Kathleen, didn't I tell yeh I'd take care of all tha'? Now, don't be worryin' yer pretty little head, will yeh? Anyway, I was just lookin' at yer Ma the other evenin' and by the looks of her she needs yeh more.'

'I have to agree with yeh, Alan, she looks so tired and worn out. Maybe I will leave it for another while. She's not able for the last two babies.' These were my little brothers, Paul, who was only two years old, and Mano, barely twelve months. Mano was the last of Ma's kids – number twelve. I was the second, after young Phil.

'Come on, Kathleen, get yerself ready and I'll drop yeh off before I head off to work,' he said, giving me a nice big kiss.

'De yeh know somethin', Alan? Yeh're so good. Tha's why I love yeh so much.'

* * *

And that was it. Every morning, as soon as I had the place tidied and my washing done, I'd make my way up to Ma's house in Crumlin every day, helping her clean up and look after the kids. Phil and Carmel were working away and Noel hadn't been too long out there in the workforce, starting to fend for himself. Da had got a couple of rises in his pay packet and Ma made sure each time that he handed them over to her. Life was starting to get a little bit easier at last.

We were heading down towards Old County Road one day, making our way to the clinic to get Mano one of his needles, when Ma turned around to me and said, 'Kathleen, I have a bit of news for yeh.'

I stopped dead in my tracks, stood and looked her straight in the face 'Jaysus, Ma, don't tell me yeh're havin' a baby – please don't say yeh're havin' another baby!'

'Ah, for fuck sake, Kathleen, will yeh give it over. Didn't I tell yeh tha' door was long closed after little Mano was born? Didn't I say tha' to yeh?'

'I know, Ma. I know yeh did, but –'

'There's no buts about it, Kathleen. Now yeh're after gettin' me all annoyed and ruinin' me bit of news.'

'Sorry, Ma. Go on, tell us wha' it is.'

'Well. Well . . .' She pushed the pram through the doors of the clinic, still holding on to the words, but you could see she was bursting to tell me. 'Kathleen, I have enough money to buy the geyser for the hot water. Everybody will be able to have a proper bath from now on.'

'Jaysus, Ma, tha's great news. How did yeh manage to put the few bob by?'

'Well, Kathleen, when Noel started work I said to meself, "I don't care, I'm puttin' some of his wages by. No matter wha', come rain or shine, I'm not touchin' it." And I didn't. So will yeh come in to the gas company with me and help me pick one out?'

That's exactly what we did the very next day.

* * *

So the day finally came when there was hot water in Crumlin. No more running up and down the stairs for any of the kids the way us older ones had to, with your pot of water, getting ready to wash all your bits.

There was great excitement among the younger kids the day the geyser was installed. Even Da made his way home early that day. Ma was as proud as Punch, standing there waiting on the men to finish. They were only out the door when she was over to the taps to test the water. When that hot water came pouring out of the tap, the look on her face was priceless. She had waited so long for that day to come.

All the kids were pushing, shoving, screaming and shouting to see who'd be the first to have a splash in the bath. Ma wasn't long quietening them all down with one of her famous looks. She then turned around to me.

'Kathleen,' she said, 'I know yeh don't live here anymore, but yeh waited so long to have tha' bubble bath of yers in this house, I think you should be the first.' She handed me a bottle of bubbles. I couldn't believe Ma had remembered the way I had always gone on about that.

I got such a lump in my throat it took me all my time to hold back the tears.

'Oh, and another thing, Kathleen – when yeh're finished don't let the water out. Tha'll do a few of the younger ones to have a good wash and keep the bill down at the one time. Just because I have a few of them older ones workin' now doesn't mean I still don't have to watch me few pennies around here.'

She was still rammaging on as she gathered all the kids and made her way downstairs.

'Yer mother is righ',' Da said. 'You should be the first to hansel the bath.' He gave me a little wink as he closed the door behind him.

I thought to myself as I slipped into the water, *Things are really startin' to look up around here and it feels good.*

* * *

The months seemed to go by very quickly. I was so happy and in love that I didn't realise at first how quiet Alan had become – probably because I never stopped talking and he didn't get much of a chance to get a word in anyway. But he was extra quiet and seemed to be a million miles away, thinking to himself all the time.

'Wha's wrong with yeh, Alan?' I asked as we drove away from Ma's one evening. 'Yeh're not yerself. Is it me? Are yeh fed up? Wha' is it? Tell me.'

'Jaysus, it's nothin' like tha', Kathleen. It's me job. Me Da has to let me go. He barely has enough work for himself.'

'Oh my God, Alan, why didn't yeh tell me?'

'I was tryin' to hang out as long as I could, hopin' things might pick up.'

'How did this happen? Yer Da is always busy.'

'Ah, there's this fella after settin' himself up in business. He's goin' around the doors collectin' and deliverin' the shoes for repair. Sure, we're only gettin' half the work now. I've been sittin' on me arse for the past couple of weeks, doin' nothin'. I can't expect me Da to keep payin' me wages, so I said I'd finish up this week. I'll go around the factories, see if I can get some work. But I'll tell yeh one thing for nothin', Kathleen, I won't be gettin' anythin' like the money me Da was payin' me.'

'Tha's it, Alan, I'm definitely gettin' meself some work, I don't care wha' yeh say.'

* * *

Sure enough, a few days later, Alan had a job working in a handbag factory called Freedex, and into the bargain he got me a job there as well. Although it was only part-time, it paid more than I would have got from hairdressing, which suited me down to the ground at the time. I was bringing in a few shillings to help out with the bills and I was still able to go up to Ma when I was finished. But the money we were making between us was nothing like what Alan used to make and we were finding it a bit hard to manage. That's when Alan hit me with the bombshell.

'Kathleen, I want to talk to yeh about maybe us stayin' on here – livin' with Pop. There's no way I'm able to save any more money and we're just about gettin' by at the moment. So wha' I was thinkin', yeh know, the money tha' we have saved, we could put it into this house, and by the time I'm finished doin' it up, I promise yeh, yeh'll be well pleased with the results. It's either tha' or we try and get a flat. And believe me, they're not cheap.'

'Does tha' mean we'll never ever get our own house, Alan?'

'Who knows wha' lies ahead, love? All I know is, I'm tryin' to do the best for us for now. And stayin' here to me would be the best option.'

'Okay, if yeh think it's the righ' thing to do. But wha' if he says no?'

'By the time I'm finished suckin' up to him, tha' won't be a problem.'

* * *

Now on top of all that I had just found out I was pregnant, which wasn't supposed to be in the plans. Not at that moment in time anyway. Everything went arse about face. To top it off, Ma went crazy mad when I told her my bit of news.

'In the name of Jaysus, Kathleen,' she roared – I think half the road must have heard her that day – 'Have yeh learnt nothin' over the years, lookin' at me and rearin' most of them kids for me. Was tha' not enough to put yeh off, at least for a few years anyway? And now yeh say yeh're not goin' to have yer own house. Yeh'll be stuck down there with tha' oul' fella.'

'Ah, he's not tha' bad, Ma. Sure yeh wouldn't even know he was there half the time. Anyway I'm hardly ever there meself. If I'm not in work I do be up here with you.'

'Tha'll all change when yeh have yer own child. Mark my words, Kathleen.' Her voice was getting louder and louder.

Jaysus, I thought, *she's sayin' 'child' not 'baby'. She's really pissed off with me. I'd better try and change the subject before she has a fit altogether'*.

'Ma, Phil tells me he's goin' steady; did yeh ask him when we're goin' to meet her?'

She looked over at me, giving me one of her dagger looks, knowing full well what I was up to. 'Hmm! So I believe. He calls her Joan. She's a nurse.'

'Tha's right, Ma, he said she's real nice.'

That was it; I knew once I got her talking about Phil she'd be on a roll and that would take the suss off me, for a little while anyway.

* * *

Alan spoke to Pop about us staying on and everything was okay there.

'Yiz can stay for as long as yiz want,' he said. 'Sure I'm only too glad of the bit of company.'

'Tha's great, Pop. So is it okay if I paint and wallpaper the house? Maybe stick a bit of new furniture in. Would yeh mind us doin' tha'?'

'The place hasn't been touched in years, Alan, and I know it could do with a good overhaul, so yeh have me permission to do wha'ever yeh want. Just don't ask me to help!' I was so happy when I heard him say that.

'Yeh're all righ' there, Pop. Once I get meself goin' I'll have the place done up in no time at all.'

So we went and put every penny that we had saved into doing the house up. We already had our furniture for the bedroom, so we started there first, working our way down, painting all the woodwork white, with matching blinds for all the windows and fresh new wallpaper throughout the house. The carpet in both rooms and on the stairs was to match, a lovely chocolate brown and cream, with a wood-type lino, which was only coming into fashion at the time, in the sitting room and running on into the kitchen.

The kitchen was so small it was more like a little scullery and – can you believe this? – the bath was actually behind the kitchen door along with the sink! Not that Pop used it for washing himself in, no way; he had it filled up with turf. So that was the first thing to go, making room for a small table and chairs.

The toilet was outside the house, just off the kitchen, and it needed a right going-over, which I left for Alan to do. By the time he was finished it was spick and span. The last thing to buy was our black leather suite. (It was plastic really, but I didn't care.) I thought it was massive; with a few orange cushions here and there it really looked the part.

It took us a good few months to do but it was worth the wait and looked very well by the time we were finished. With everything so bright and fresh-looking, and with the new furniture and our bits and bobs, I was happy enough to stay living there. It felt like a proper little home now, ready to welcome our baby – which, by the way, was due any day now.

2

Dick the Cock

I'll never forget the day I went into labour. I'd finished up working two weeks earlier and as usual was heading up to Ma. I was just going into the kitchen when half the kids came charging at me, screaming their heads off. 'Quick, Kathleen, run!' they roared. 'It's Dick – he's on the table and gettin' ready to charge. Run!'

Before I go any further, I have to tell the story about Dick. Ma came home one day with a wooden box. I thought there was food in it. I suppose it was food, but in a different way – fresh eggs every day.

'Gather around, everybody,' she said as she slowly lifted the lid off the box. 'Look wha' I bought.'

There they were, twelve tiny little chickens. One of them turned out to be a cock, which we named Dick, who was mad from day one. Every time you looked at him he'd be up on the hens, tearing the backs off them. He was a randy little bastard. We were always throwing stones at him so he would leave them alone.

He never forgot that – us disturbing him in his hour of passion. Because of that, he hated every one of us. Except for Clare, of course – she wouldn't hurt a fly. He'd sit there and let her rub him. As for the rest of us, whenever he got the chance, you would see him getting himself ready. First the wings would spread; then he'd tilt his head, screaming out his chorus of 'cock-a-doodle-do'. The two legs would start pushing out the soil beneath him. Then the charge would come.

If you weren't quick enough, the ankles would be pecked off you, and if he was really wound up and got a good run at you, he'd latch on to your back and start pecking away.

Now you know why the kids were all running past me, and I was right behind them, holding onto my bump and struggling to get up the stairs after them. We just about made it into the bathroom, locking the door behind us. I sat down on the toilet seat, gasping for breath. You could hear Dick scratching away like mad at the door.

'Where the hell is Ma?' I asked. 'And how did he get into the kitchen?'

'We were sittin' there eatin' our breakfast while Ma went down to the shops for her Woodbines,' Jacinta answered, with the lip trembling, 'when he came flyin' through the window on top of us. It wasn't our fault, Kathleen.'

'I know, I know. Don't be gettin' upset. We'll have to wait here until Ma comes back.'

I only had the words out of my mouth when a big gush of water came pouring out of me. My waters had broken. *Holy Jaysus*, I thought to myself, *I don't believe this is happenin'*.

'Kathleen, why are yeh pissin' on yerself?' asked Jacinta.

'Will yeh stay quiet and let me think for a minute. Throw a few of them towels on the floor to soak up the water, and then give the door a good kick. Patricia, don't just stand there

– help her.' At this stage little Paul was crying and frightened out of his wits. 'Come over here to me, love. Don't mind the bold birdie. Ma will be back in a minute and she'll sort him out. Where the hell are Clare and Marion?' I was starting to scream myself at this stage.

'They're up gettin' the milk,' said Patricia. Back then, if you had a big family you could get free milk from the local clinic.

'It's always the bloody same; when you need one of them, they're never around.' I could feel the pains starting to come and panic was setting in.

There was no moving Dick; he was still scratching away and it felt like forever before we heard Ma opening the front door. She didn't know what hit her with the screams from all of us.

'Ma, Ma, is tha' you? It's Kathleen. I'm up here in the toilet with the kids. Dick's up here. He's gone mad trying to get in at us.'

'In the name of Jaysus, who let tha' bloody cock into the house? Can I not move for five minutes without all hell breaking loose around me?' Ma being Ma and afraid of nothing gave Dick such a kick up the hole, beat him down the stairs and out into the back garden that he didn't 'cock-a-doodle-do' for a few days after. 'I'm tellin' yiz, one of these days I'll ring his fuckin' neck, so I will.'

'Ma, will yeh calm down. It wasn't the kids' fault; he jumped in the window.'

'Is tha' wha' happened, Kathleen? Quick, Jacinta, Patricia, get down them stairs. Make sure the back door is closed and lock the kitchen window or he'll be back in again.'

It was only when all the shouting was over that Ma realised I was in labour.

'For Jaysus' sake, Kathleen, I thought yeh said yeh had another week or two to go?'

'So did I, Ma, but I think the fright I got trying to get away from Dick must have started me off.'

'Come on now, give Paul to me, and let's get yeh downstairs and make a nice cup of tea. We'll keep an eye on them pains. Yeh might as well be sittin' here with me for a while as be on yer own in the hospital. I've helped deliver a good few babies around here over the years, so yeh've nothin' to worry about. I'll know when to make a move.'

She sat there rammaging on about everything and anything that came into her head, all the while keeping her eye on the clock as my pains grew stronger. I wanted to hang on until Alan arrived to collect me, but Ma wasn't having any of it and, once she was sure I was ready, didn't waste any time in getting me into the hospital, with help from one of the neighbours.

Ma kicked up such a racket when I was being brought down to the labour ward. Back then there was no way anyone outside the doctors and nurses were allowed past those labour room doors. At this stage I was doing somersaults in the bed with the pain as Ma held on tight to my hand.

'We'll take over now, Mrs Doyle,' said the nurse.

'I'm not leavin'. I'm goin' in with her.'

'You know that's not allowed. Rules are rules.'

'I don't care wha' yeh say. Me child needs me.'

'Come on now, Mrs Doyle. Don't be makin' a fuss. We have to get Kathleen ready and I promise we will take good care of her.'

'I don't doubt tha' for one minute, nurse, it's just tha' I'm worried. I hate the thought of her goin' in there on her own.'

'I know that, and I'll make sure to keep you informed. Now, we really must go.'

I was scared as hell and wished Ma could come in with me, but I couldn't let her know that, or she would have kicked up more ructions.

'I'll be okay, Ma, don't be worryin'.'

'Our Lady will mind yeh, Kathleen, and I'll be here, standin' in this very spot, when they bring yeh back out.' She gave my hand a little squeeze.

* * *

First I was taken into a small cubicle.

'Right, Kathleen, get yourself up there on the couch. I have to take a look and see how many centimetres you are.'

'Nurse, de yeh have to look when yeh're doin' it?'

'Don't be shy, Kathleen, I'm doing this every day of the week. All you should be worrying about is baby. Now relax there while I give you a quick check. Yes, everything seems fine. Now, roll over on your side for me.' She stood there beside me with a plastic hose, a funnel and a bucket.

'Wha's tha' for?'

'Your enema, of course.'

'Ah, yeh're all righ', nurse, I don't need tha'. I went this mornin'.'

'Come, come now, Kathleen, this has to be done before baby is delivered. I'll have it done in no time at all.'

Talk about holding onto any bit of dignity I had – that went out the door as soon as she stuck that tube up my arse. Between the moans and groans out of me with the labour pains, if that wasn't bad enough, now on top of it I was farting and shitting to beat the band. I didn't know which end of me was up. Then I was finally brought into a small ward. There were two other girls there.

'Nurse, is this where it happens?'

'No, not at all, Kathleen. You have a fair bit to go yet, so we'll be keeping an eye on you for the next couple of hours in here. Then, at the next stage, just before baby comes into the world, we'll bring you down to the delivery room, which is

17

down there at the end of the corridor. Now, try and have a little doze in between, and when the pains come, remember now, big deep breaths.'

One of the girls was asleep. The other girl started talking over to me. 'Howyeh, I'm Frances. Is this yer first?'

'Yeah, tha's right. I'm Kathleen.'

'Don't be nervous, yeh'll be grand! Sure look at me, this is me sixth time to be in here.'

We chatted for a good while and then suddenly she let out such a roar that I nearly shit a brick – not that there was anything left in me to do that!

'Holy Jaysus, these pains are gettin' really strong. Nurse, nurse! I need a bit of gas.'

Then the other girl sat up in the bed and started rocking up and down, up and down. 'Oh please, oh please, nurse. Oh please.' They were the only words she spoke the whole time I was there. You could see it in their faces; they were cringing with the pain. The nurse was in straight away.

'That's right, Lulu, big deep breaths. In and out, in and out. Frances, you're coming along fine, it shouldn't be too long before we're bringing you down. Kathleen, how are you doing over there? Will you have some gas now?'

'Oh, I don't know, nurse. I hate anythin' gettin' put over me face. Maybe I'll leave it.'

'Yeh won't be sayin' tha' in a little while,' said Frances. 'Yeh'll be screamin' for the fuckin' stuff.'

And she was so right. When it came to it, I was eating the mask. I held onto it so tight that I had the imprint of it on my face for hours after. It wasn't too long after that when both girls were brought down to deliver their babies. I seemed to be on my own forever. All the while I kept thinking of Ma and how strong she was to have done this so many times.

'Right, Kathleen,' I could hear the nurse saying as I came back from my thoughts. 'Baby is ready.' I was so happy to hear those words at last.

I was only in the delivery room when I had to push like mad. The nurse was standing beside me, holding my hand. She knew how nervous I was.

'Come on, Kathleen, you're doing great.'

The midwife was at the other end and, believe me, at this stage I didn't care who was looking at what.

'Right, I can see the head. One more hard push and we're there.' I squeezed the nurse's hand so tight I don't know how I didn't break her fingers. I thought my brains were going to burst, never mind down below.

'That's it, Kathleen. The head's out. Now, take it easy. Hold on. Hold on, easy now.'

Then I heard a little cry.

'It's a girl, Kathleen. You have a beautiful baby girl.' The midwife put her across my chest for a few seconds. All I could see were these big blue eyes looking straight at me. It was the most wonderful, magical feeling ever. The tears rolled down my face as I held her close to me.

'We have to check her over, Kathleen, so the nurse will finish here with you and then we'll bring her straight back over. And well done again.'

As I was wheeled out through the doors with my baby, Ma was there with Alan, just as she'd promised. The first thing she did before Alan could even get near me was to bless me and the baby with I don't know how many medals and relics she had in her purse.

'Kathleen, didn't I tell yeh the Holy Mother herself would look after yeh? And she did, thank God.' She blessed herself a half-dozen times.

I was soon settled on the ward and I could see Ma was dying to get her hands on the baby. 'There yeh are, Ma,' I said. 'Hold her for me while I talk to Alan for a minute.'

'I thought yeh'd never ask me, Kathleen.'

Alan sat on the side of the bed with his two arms around me, like he was never going to let me go.

'Kathleen, are yeh okay?'

'I'm a bit tired, Alan, tha's all. Isn't she gorgeous?'

'I can't believe it, a little girl; she's lovely.'

'I like the name Martina. Wha' de yeh think?'

'Wha'ever makes yeh happy, love. I'm just so proud of yeh.'

I was so overwhelmed with happiness that day I thought I would burst. Alan had just become a Da, and what a great one he was going to be. Ma was sitting there with her first grandchild in her arms and by the look on her face she was well pleased. As for myself, well, I felt I was ready now to be a real Ma at last.

3

Knickers

Alan wasn't too long gone to work and I was pottering about getting Martina ready and doing my bit of housework when I remembered that I had left my washing out on the line the night before. It was lashing rain out, so I just grabbed everything quickly off the line and made my way back inside.

I was hanging everything on the clothes-horse when I picked up a pair of my knickers. I thought I was seeing things. The whole middle was cut out of them. I thought to myself, *Wha' the fuck is after happenin' to these?* I checked the other three pairs and they were all the same – big holes in all of them. I stood there trying to get my head around it. Just as well Pop wasn't there because at that stage I was talking out loud to myself: 'Now why the fuck would somebody cut me knickers up?'

Then I started getting really annoyed. Martina was only a few weeks old and I'd just got out of my big white cotton tea-strainers, which I'd been wearing over the months when I was pregnant. I had bought a few fancy pairs of knickers – which took me a couple of weeks to save for – and some gobshite goes and does this!

I got ready and made my way up to Ma, taking the knickers with me. I showed them to her as soon as I walked in the door.

'So wha' de yeh think, Ma?'

'Wha' do I think, Kathleen?! I'll tell yeh wha' I think: tha's some dirty bastard tha' can't get himself a woman and is gettin' his bit of enjoyment outta doin' the likes of this, and God only knows wha' else. I'm tellin' yeh, there's some disturbed fuckers out there, Kathleen. Yeh want to make sure tha' when yeh're on yer own down there in tha' house, yeh keep the back door locked.'

'Jaysus, Ma, will yeh not be sayin' the likes of tha' to me? Yeh'll have me a nervous wreck.'

'Well, tha's wha' I think!' She made her way out to the door. 'I'm headin' up to ten o'clock mass. Make yerself a cup of tea. I won't be too long.'

My brother Phil was sitting over beside the fire, laughing his head off, having taken in all of what Ma was saying.

'I don't know wha' yeh think is so funny, Phil. I'm goin' to be shittin' meself down in tha' house after wha' Ma just said.'

'For Jaysus' sake, Kathleen, will yeh ever give it over. Yeh know the way she gets carried away at times, especially if she thinks it's anythin' to do with a man. Anyway, never mind Ma. Yeh know wha's after happenin' here? There was probably one or two young fellas got a glimpse of yer bits of knickers and thought tha' it would be very funny to do the likes of tha'.'

'De yeh really think tha's wha' happened, Phil?'

'I'm tellin' yeh, Kathleen, young fellas are gobshites at times. They dare one another to do all sorts of stupid things. Believe me, yeh want to see some of the things I used to get up to. Mental, so they were. So don't be gettin' yer knickers in a knot. De yeh get it? Knickers in a knot!'

He was nearly falling off the chair laughing. I suppose it was funny and I had to turn my head so he wouldn't see me smile – or I'd never hear the end of it.

Later that day, Alan was only in the door to collect me from Ma's when I launched into telling him the ins and outs of what had happened and what Ma and Phil had said. He wasn't able to keep his face straight as he broke his heart laughing along with Phil. I stood there all serious, with a face on me like I don't know what.

'I'm sorry, Kathleen, but he's makin' me laugh.' He pointed over at Phil, who had a pair of my knickers on his head with his nose sticking out through the hole. The tears were rolling down Alan's face at this stage and, I have to admit, I was laughing along with them. That's when Ma got her spoke in again.

'Yeh're worse, Kathleen, encouraging the pair of them. The smile won't be long gettin' put on the other side of yer face if tha' maniac comes back.'

'Christ, Ma! Will yeh not be sayin' tha'? Yeh'll have me tha' I won't want to go home.'

'Come on now,' said Alan. 'Let's not get all serious about this. It's just like wha' Phil said. Young fellas messin' and actin' the eejit. There yeh are, Lil, yer few smokes as always, and where's tha' famous cup of tea yeh always have ready for me?' He was trying to whisper but I could hear every word they were saying.

'Yeh're a cute hoor, yeh know tha', Alan McGrath?' said Ma. 'Gettin' in there and changin' the subject on me.'

'It's best tha' way, Lil. Yeh know wha' Kathleen's like for worryin'. She'll have me and herself awake all night, thinkin' and talkin' about this.'

'Well, Alan, I suppose when yeh put it like tha' . . .' She took the smokes and put them in her pocket. 'I'll say no more.'

So that was me, having to get back into my white cotton tea-strainers or, as they were sometimes called, 'passion-killers'. I was only glad that I didn't throw them out or I would have had to go bare-arsed until I got a few bob to buy my little fancy ones again.

* * *

A couple of weeks went by and there wasn't a problem with the washing. That was until I hung my new knickers on the line – and the same thing happened again. Big holes in all the middles. But this time it happened during the day and that really scared me, thinking that there was someone in the back garden when I was there.

'Tha's it!' said Ma when I showed them to her. 'We're goin' to the guards.'

'I'm not going down to the police station, Ma, no way.'

'Yeh either walk down with me, Kathleen, or I'll drag yeh down – yer choice, because if yeh think I'm goin' to wait around until somethin' happens to you, yeh have another thing comin'. Now, get yer coat on and hand them knickers over here to me.' Once Ma got like this, there was no going against her and she never said anything that she wouldn't back up, so it was easier to go along.

I was mortified sitting there as we waited to be seen. As soon as the guard came out to speak to us, Ma was up like a light.

'Good afternoon, ladies,' he said. 'How can I help you?'

'I want to report a crime,' said Ma. 'There's a maniac goin' around. Look, he attacked me daughter's knickers.' She slapped them down on the counter.

He looked at them and then at me. You could see he was trying very hard not to laugh. He gave a little cough, clearing his throat.

'Now, what I would need to know is, where exactly were these garments when this happened?' And that was it, he started grinning and I didn't blame him one bit. I was blushing so much I couldn't answer. Ma stepped in again.

'Well, they weren't on her, if tha's wha' yeh mean! And yeh can wipe tha' grin off yer face and take wha' I'm sayin' serious.' You could see he was taken aback when Ma came out with that. She went on, 'Well, if yeh really want to know, guard, they were on the clothes-line, and this is the second time it's after happenin'. And in broad daylight too! Which means tha' dirty bastard is watchin' my Kathleen goin' in and out. She'll end up being a nervous wreck if this keeps up. So now, wha' are yeh goin' to do about it?'

After Ma lashing him out of it, he kept a straight face this time while he spoke. 'I'll take your name and address first. We'll then send out a garda car to check around the area and if it is somebody nearby, when they see the guards that will probably frighten them off and that will be the end of it. Other than that, unless you catch somebody in the act or you have a name for me, I can do no more.'

We gave him all the details. 'Will I take the knickers with me,' asked Ma as we were going, 'or de yeh need them as evidence?'

'Hmm . . . no, that will be fine. You can take them on home with you.' I'd say by this stage the guard had his legs crossed trying to stop wetting himself.

'Ma, are yeh right'? Come on, will yeh.' I just wanted the ground to open up and swallow me, I was so embarrassed. I didn't say anything to Ma; she was just worried and was doing what she thought was best for me.

The guards knocked on the door that evening and spent a bit of time in the back garden, letting their presence be known, which I was happy enough about. I hoped it would put an end to all this carry-on.

But no, it didn't. It happened again and again. So I stopped hanging the washing out.

* * *

'This is terrible, Alan,' I said one morning. 'I know it's a bit cold out but the weather is lovely and crisp and I can't hang me clothes out.'

'Leave it to me, Kathleen. I'll sort this out once and for all.'

So Alan had a talk with Phil and they decided they were going to catch whoever was doing it in the act, and sort it out themselves.

It was the middle of November so the nights were starting to get very cold. A couple of nights in, Alan got himself good and ready for the big watch. 'Righ', tha's me sorted,' he said as he put the lid on his flask. 'In the name of Jaysus, Phil, wha's keepin' yeh? They'll be here and gone yeh're takin' tha' long.'

'I'm comin', I'm comin',' roared Phil as he came out of the toilet. 'I hope the fuckers turn up tonight, Kathleen.'

'Jaysus, Phil, yeh're in a righ' mood.'

'So would you be. I was on a promise last night and tonight and, believe me, tha' probably won't come around again for God knows how long.'

'Would yeh ever give it over, Phil; de yeh ever have anythin' else on yer mind?'

Alan stood there with his woolly cap and his flask in his hand. You would think Phil was going to the North Pole with his big winter coat, gloves, scarf and, of course, the all-essential torch. The two of them were ready and rearing to pounce on whoever came over the back wall.

'Righ', Kathleen, now remember, turn off the lights here in the kitchen and go into the sitting-room and watch the telly. With a bit of luck, we'll catch whoever is doin' this tonight,' said Alan.

'I certainly hope so,' I said, 'or else you won't be on a promise for a very long time, 'cause I'll be back in me oul' tea-strainers again if the last few pairs of me fancy knickers get destroyed like the others.'

Off they went with a bit of a giggle. I turned the lights off just as I'd done the night before and went in to watch the telly. I wasn't five minutes sitting down when I heard all hell breaking loose in the back garden. I ran out and there were Phil and Alan, dragging two young fellas into the kitchen.

'Get in there, yeh little fucker,' said Phil. He gave one of them a right clatter in the head. 'Well, Kathleen, here's the "Knicker Rippers". Now, wha' have yeh got to say to her?'

'Sorry, Missus, we were just havin' a bit of craic. I promise we won't do it again.'

'And you!' said Alan, as he pushed the younger fella in front of me, who was starting to cry at this stage.

'Sorry, Missus. We thought it was funny. Sorry. Sorry.'

'Righ',' said Alan, 'Now get the fuck outta here, the pair of yiz, before I call the guards, and if I catch yiz around here again yeh'll get worse the next time.' He gave one of them a good kick up the arse.

I never saw anybody run and jump a fence as quick as they did, never to be seen again. I was happy enough the way things went and that it wasn't a dirty maniac, like Ma thought. Not only was I able to get a good night's sleep again, but it was also great to see my knickers blowing in the wind once more.

4

The Diggin' Match

There was no way I could go back to work after I had Martina. Ma had enough of her own kids without me asking her to mind mine, so the pressure was on Alan once more to take on the full load of being the breadwinner.

Alan's Da tried to give him a bit of work one or two evenings a week, finishing off some of the repairs on the shoes. We knew he wasn't all that busy and didn't really need him, but he was always so good to us, helping out every way he could.

Alan wasn't happy just living from week to week. Nor was I, barely getting by, never having money over to buy the little extras, maybe even having a holiday some day, which we both dreamed of. There was no way that was going to happen with the wages he was bringing in. So off he went back out into the workforce looking for a job with better money, which he got with the help of his uncle Joe, who knew somebody that knew somebody that put a good word in for him. He was so excited the day he found out he'd got the job.

'Kathleen, I can't believe it. A job in Gallagher's on the port docks; it's so hard to get in there. De yeh realise how great this is? Wha' this means for us? Me wages will more than double, and they tell me jobs come up every now and then in the main cigarette factory in Tallaght. If I can get meself in there, we'll be laughing all the way to the bank.'

I sat there listening to him going on and on. I really didn't want to burst his bubble but thought to myself, *Now's as good a time as any.*

'I have a bit of news meself, Alan, and I hope yeh'll be pleased with wha' I have to say.'

'Go on, Kathleen. Spit it out.'

Well, me being me, who never shuts up and launches into the ins and outs of everything, instead of just coming out with what I wanted to say, went on a bit that day. Alan had to stop me in my tracks.

'Tha's it, Kathleen. Stop talkin'. Now, just tell me wha' it is yeh're tryin' to say.'

'I'm afraid yeh might be annoyed, Alan.'

'Kathleen –'

'Righ'. I'm pregnant.'

His jaw dropped and I could see he was taken aback a bit, just as I had been. We both thought we had been so careful. He was quiet for a second or two, then came out with the words I needed to hear.

'Well now, Kathleen, aren't we lucky I got meself this job, now tha' we're goin' to have another little mouth to feed.'

* * *

Ma wasn't too bad the second time around when I told her my news. She never said a word but still managed to give me one of her dagger looks, which I suppose wasn't too bad, knowing Ma.

Our son Alan was born six months later, when Martina was barely two years old. There was definitely no way I would be getting myself a job and my dream of becoming a hairdresser seemed to be gone forever.

Alan was as happy as anything working in his new job, getting in as much overtime as he could get his hands on, which was great for the extra money. There's no doubt that we needed it, but I did miss him terribly and would hate going home when he wasn't there. So I would stay on a bit later in the evenings with Ma and Da.

If the truth be known, I loved all the hustle and bustle that went on, with the older ones coming in from work, fighting over who was going to get their dinner first, checking out whose chop was the biggest and giving out if anyone got more chips than they did. Chip days were a classic. Ma would be cooking for hours by the time she got around the whole gang. She would start with the smallest ones and work her way up. The rest would be starving, waiting their turn, borrowing a chip off each other as they were fed, with the promise that they would give back two in return. There was no way anyone would let you off, so by the time the older ones got their dinners, there would be very little left on their plates. I would sit there laughing to myself, listening to the wheeling and dealing going on, with some of them trying to get off paying back what they owed, and Ma in the background shouting her head off.

'Wha' do I keep tellin' yiz? Wait yer turn! But de yiz listen? No. Now yeh have to pay the price, so hand over the chips and be done with it, or yeh'll have me to answer to.'

* * *

There was never a dull moment, with plenty of scraps and digging matches going on. One particular night saw one of the biggest fights ever, or at least the biggest that I was there for.

I was sitting with young Alan in my arms, and Martina was out in the back garden playing with the younger kids. I was talking away to Da, while Ma was cooking as usual. Phil and Noel were sitting at the table with a couple of the older kids when all hell broke loose. Phil, being the messer that he is, and always getting up everyone's back, started on Noel, who had just turned seventeen and wasn't too far off as big as himself. Noel had this terrible habit of tapping his fingers on the table and it really got Phil's back up.

'Noel, stop tha' tappin'. Yeh're annoyin' me,' said Phil.

Noel stopped and then started again. I could hear all this going on in the background as I tried to listen to Da tell me about his day.

'Did yeh hear me, Noel? I told yeh to stop!'

'Yeah, and yeh're goin' to make me stop, righ'? As if I'd let yeh.'

The tapping turned into a hard banging at that stage, and Phil gave Noel a right clatter in the back of the head. Noel was so fast, he was up on his feet in no time, giving Phil a dig, straight into the face. The blood pumped out of his nose and the kids all scattered, leaving just the two of them standing there, face to face. Phil rubbed some of the blood away with his hand, laughing as he spoke.

'So, yeh're puttin' it up to me, Noel, is tha' wha' yer doin'?'

'Tha's righ', Phil. If tha's wha' it takes, yeh won't be hittin' me again.'

'Well then, may the best man win.'

With that, he went in at Noel with a left hook, right into the stomach, knocking him on top of the kitchen table, smashing it to pieces. The kids were screaming and shouting, egging on whichever of them they wanted to win. Ma was fucking and blinding out of her about the house being broken up and who was going to pay for it. I was shouting my head off for them to stop, not realising I was frightening the life out of young Alan.

Because both of them were boxers, it was like looking at a boxing match in the National Stadium. Da made sure that all the boys joined the local boxing club as soon as they were old enough. He used to make his own boxing ring in the house, making sure they all got plenty of practice in on the side. He'd use Ma's old tights, tying them around four of the kitchen chairs. He always wanted them to be the best. I think it was something he would have loved to have done himself but never got around to. So he was living his dream through the boys and, believe me, they were well able to fight.

Between the clinches, the right and left hooks were flying. At one stage I looked over at Da. He was doing a bit of shadow-boxing himself, living the part with them. That's when Ma stepped in.

'Phil Doyle,' she roared in Da's face, 'enough's enough. Now get yerself over there and stop them pair. It's gone on long enough. Look at them – neither of them will give in. They're wreckin' the fuckin' house on me.'

Poor Da got caught up between the pair of them, getting one of their fists in the face which knocked him out cold. That soon brought the fight to a halt, calming the pair of them down. They weren't long getting Da up off the floor and onto a chair. Noel splashed water on Da's face to bring him around, while the other gobshite, Phil, was at the other end tickling his feet, breaking his heart laughing as he looked up at Noel.

'De yeh know somethin'? Tha' was the best scrap I've had in I don't know how long. We should do this more often, Noel. But I tell yeh one thing, I'll be ready the next time, now tha' I know yeh're a sly fucker. The way yeh came in at me with the left hook – caught me right off me guard, so yeh did.'

'I have to say, Phil, it was a beaut.'

And, as Da finally came to, on they went with their cut lips, bloody noses and raw knuckles, talking about who got more digs in at who. At the same time they were promising Ma that they would fix her up with a new table, which kept her happy.

There were many punch-ups and digging matches over the years, some maybe a little more serious than others, but never any that wasn't sorted out at the end with a handshake and a laugh.

* * *

Phil was the only one who kept the boxing up. The rest of the boys slowly gave it up as they got older. Not a week went by that Phil wasn't fighting in the National Stadium or travelling around the country to boxing tournaments. His name became well known, which led to him boxing for the national team. He travelled to many countries in Europe, representing Ireland.

Ma and Da were so proud of him; they never missed any of his fights. I even went along with Alan a few times and, I have to say, he was some boxer, afraid of no-one. It didn't matter if his eyes were cut to bits, blood pumping from his nose, he was like a bulldog, charging in. He would just keep going until he won the fight.

I even found myself jumping up and down one night, screaming, 'Knock him out, kill him!' God, when I think back, that was a terrible thing to say, but you really got so worked up, especially when it was your own brother and his fight was the last one on the night, the one that would decide if Ireland won the title. After the match was over, we waited for the judges' decision. We were all standing there, not a sound to be heard. You could hear a pin drop. I thought Da was going to have a heart attack.

Well, when the referee lifted Phil's fist up in the air, the whole place erupted. Phil lifted the referee up, swinging him around the ring. Everybody was shaking Ma's and Da's hands, saying how proud they should be – not that they needed anybody to say that to them. They were proud as Punch. I even saw Da wipe away a tear or two when he thought nobody was looking. There were write-ups in all the papers and television interviews. In all our eyes, Phil was a star.

* * *

I really thought Phil would have settled down here, but that wasn't meant to be. He had moved to Canada but had returned around the time I got married and was here for about three years afterwards. The two of us were having a chat one day, when I turned around and asked him, 'Well, wha's the story with yerself and Joan? Yeh seem to be hittin' it off really well.'

'Well, now tha' yer after bringin' it up, Kathleen, we're thinkin' of gettin' married. Nothin' fancy, just a small weddin'.'

'Yeh sly fucker, Phil Doyle, and when were yeh goin' to tell me this? Or were yeh even goin' to bother?'

'Don't be gettin' yer knickers in a knot, Kathleen. I was hangin' on for a while just to make sure before I said anythin'. Yeh know the way it is; sometimes yeh have a few scraps, and then I'd be thinkin' to meself, for fuck's sake – is this wha' I really want – to be tied down and all tha'? I mean, Kathleen, surely yeh must've felt a little bit iffy at times before yeh tied the knot with Alan?'

'I have to say, Phil, I never felt like tha'. So yeh'd want to be really clear in yer mind wha' yeh want; otherwise, don't go ahead.'

'I'll be grand. I suppose me feet's just gettin' a bit cold, now tha' I'm actually plannin' things. Anyway, say nothin'. I'll drop the bombshell meself when I'm ready.'

And that's what he did after a few months. He not only announced that he was getting married, but that he was also going back to Canada. He'd been dropping hints here and there for a good while, so it wasn't too much of a shock for any of us.

* * *

It was a small wedding. There was just Ma, Da and a couple of us older brothers and sisters, and the same on Joan's side of the family, along with a few friends from the boxing. Phil was a cute hoor and always had a back-up plan; he had the dinner booked out in the airport hotel and their flights a couple of hours after. That left very little time between for him or any of us to get too upset. We'd all been very upset the first time Phil left for Canada. It didn't seem to be as hard the second time around as we all said our goodbyes. Even Ma held herself together a bit better this time. It helped that Phil promised that as soon as he got settled and got money behind him, he would send for both of them for the holiday of a lifetime. He was still following his dream, and who could blame him for that? Emigration had got into his blood; there was no turning back.

He seemed to settle down really well this time, so much so that they decided to start a family over there. Ma was so excited one day when a letter arrived from Phil with a ticket in it, asking her if she would be able to come over to Canada, as Joan was about to have their first baby any day, and he would love nothing better than to have her there for the arrival. It would be Ma's first holiday.

'Kathleen,' said Ma, 'yer father says he'll take care of things here, tha' he has a few weeks' holidays due to him. Would yeh drop down in between just to make sure everythin's okay? And maybe Alan might slip down the odd evenin' for a smoke and a cup of tea, keep yer Da company for an hour or two? So wha' de yeh think about me goin'?'

'Jaysus, Ma, it's the best bit of news I've heard in I don't know how long. Of course yeh should go. Yeh're after waitin' all this time to go over to Phil. Don't be worryin', Da and the kids will be fine. I promise I'll keep an eye on things.'

'Phil said tha' I don't have to worry about money. I just have to bring meself. But yeh know me, Kathleen, I like to have me own few shillin's in me pocket, especially for me smokes.'

'Yeh'll be fine, Ma, yeh won't be short. We'll all throw yeh a few bob. Anyway, never mind all tha'. Imagine, yer first holiday and all the way to Canada! I wouldn't be able for yeh.'

'I have to say, Kathleen, I have meself a bit worked up and excited at the same time. And yer Father was just sayin' to me, wouldn't it be great if it's a boy? Yeh know, to carry on the Doyle name and all tha'. Once the baby is okay, tha's all should matter, but he takes all tha' stuff serious, with him being the only boy in his family.'

Ma headed off within the next couple of days, making it just in time for the arrival of her new grandson, Philip, which Da was delighted about. Ma stayed on for a few weeks, helping out every which way she could and enjoying every minute.

She talked and talked about it for months on end afterwards, so much so that Da thought he'd never get over to see Phil and Canada. So, the following year, he took out his first credit union loan and the two of them went out. I was so happy to see them take off together. They were starting to have a bit of a life at last.

Phil went on to have two more sons, J.J. and Andrew, and ended up making his life in Canada, bringing Ma and Da over many times down the years, just like he promised.

5

Messers and Pancakes

When Ma was away in Canada with my brother Phil I would drop down to the house to check on the kids, just like I promised. It was late one afternoon when I arrived. Carmel was hanging out the washing while Paul and Mano were playing around.

I tipped Carmel on the shoulder and she jumped. 'It's very quiet around here, Carmel,' I said. 'Where's everyone?'

'Jaysus, Kathleen, yeh're after givin' me an awful fright. Why didn't yeh knock on the front door?'

'Don't be such a wimp, Carmel. The side gate was open so I just came on in. Is Da in the house? Alan gave me a few smokes for him.'

'He slipped out there about ten minutes ago to back a horse. He shouldn't be too long. Come on and I'll make yeh a cup of tea. Did yeh not bring the kids with yeh, Kathleen?'

I followed her into the kitchen and put the teapot on. The two of us sat at the table talking away about one thing and another.

'Ah, they were playin' around in the garden with a couple of their friends. Alan said he'd keep an eye to them until I got

37

back. Anyway, I never leave them; they're always with me, everywhere I go. It'll do me good to get a break for a little while. How's Da doin' with Ma not around? Is he stayin' off the drink? And no lies, de yeh hear me?'

'I swear, Kathleen, he's home every day as soon as he's finished work, with not a drop on him.'

'Tha's good. Ma will be well pleased when we tell her. All the same, Carmel, isn't the house very quiet? It's not the same without Ma. Yeh get so used to her roarin' and shoutin', fuckin' and blindin' about one thing or another.'

I only had the words out of my mouth when I heard some weird sounds coming from upstairs.

'Did yeh hear tha', Carmel? Who's up there?'

'I'm not too sure. I think Thomas is with a couple of the kids.'

'There it is again – listen, Carmel.'

As we made our way into the hall, the sounds came out, louder and clearer: *hee-haw, hee-haw*, like a donkey; *moo, moo, moo*, like a herd of cows; and the noisiest of all was grunting like a pig. That one was so real, and it went on and on. Then we could hear Thomas's voice: 'Faster, faster; louder, louder, or I'll tickle yiz to death.' He was laughing his head off.

'Holy Jaysus, Carmel, wha's tha' Thomas fella up to? Come on upstairs and let's see wha' he's doin'.'

We didn't make a sound as we sneaked up the stairs and had the door open before he knew it. There was Thomas, standing on the bed with a fishing rod in his hand and a big feather attached to the end of it. He had Jacinta and Patricia tied to the bars at the head of the bed. He had taken off their socks and was running the feather across their feet and faces, tickling the life out of them.

'Kathleen, Carmel, save us!' both of them cried. 'He's been torturin' us here for ages.'

I was trying really hard not to laugh when I gave out to him. 'Thomas, yeh stupid thick, would yeh have a look at the pair of them? Can yeh not see how worked up they are? Yeh're drivin' them mad.'

'Ah, would yeh give it over Kathleen,' he laughed. 'I'm just havin' a bit of craic with them, tha's all.'

'We know tha', Thomas, but yeh keep the jokes up too long. Yeh never know when to stop. Now, help me get these knots open. Da will be back soon and there'll be blue murder if he finds out wha' yeh were up to. Yeh're just lucky tha' Ma is not here. She wouldn't be long kickin' the shite out of yeh.'

Jacinta was around thirteen at this time, with Patricia going on eleven. As soon as I had them untied, they were on top of Thomas before I knew it.

'Yeh fuckin' pig, Thomas Doyle,' Jacinta roared, as she tried to put the boot in, which of course was no good, since she had no shoes on. So the pair of them ended up trying to pull every blade of hair out of his head, until myself and Carmel dragged them off him. Of course, we gave them just enough time to get their own back, which he well deserved.

'Yiz are all a shower of mad bitches,' shouted Thomas as he struggled to get himself up off the floor. 'I'll get yiz back for this when yeh least expect. Are yeh listenin', Jacinta? I mean it. Patricia, just you wait and see.'

'Don't be such a spoil-sport, Thomas,' I said. 'If yeh're able to dish it out, then yeh have to be able to take it. Now, tha's the end of it, or I'll be tellin' Da on yeh.' He was still mumbling and giving out to himself as we left the room.

'Jacinta, take Patricia with yeh,' I said, 'and go down to the shops and get a couple of ice pops for yerselves. And bring back two for Mano and Paul. I suppose yeh'd better throw one in for Thomas or he'll only end up gettin' jealous.'

'Can we get a packet of crisps as well, Kathleen?' the pair of them chimed in.

'Go on then, seein' tha' yeh've been through the mill with the Thomas fella. But tha's all. Bring the rest of me change home. Tha'll do me for the bus fare. Carmel, make us a hot cup of tea, will yeh? This one's gone stone cold over the carry-on of them.'

'Yeh know Thomas won't let tha' go, Kathleen. First chance he gets, he'll pounce on them, and God only knows wha' antics he'll put them through the next time.'

'Well, he didn't exactly lick it off a stone, did he? Watchin' Phil over the years gettin' up to all sorts – I swear, he was one mad bastard. Carmel, de yeh remember the day when Thomas was around eight or nine and Phil tied him up?'

'No, I wasn't there tha' day, Kathleen. Meself and Ma headed in to Meath Street early tha' mornin'. I only got bits and pieces about wha' happened off the kids. Go on – fill us in then, seein' as you were there for the whole thing.'

'Well, Da had just gone out and I was upstairs cleanin' around as usual when I heard Thomas whingein'. I didn't take too much notice – yeh know the way he was always cryin' about one thing or the other. Tha's when I heard Phil let out such a roar tha' the whole road must've heard him.

'"Yeh're startin' to do me head in, Thomas! Shut the fuck up, I'm tellin' yeh or yeh'll be one sorry little bastard."

'But did he listen, Carmel? No. He kept goin' on and on. "I want pancakes, Phil! Ma said tha' I could have pancakes. She said yeh'd make them for me." He kept goin' on and on, whingin'. Tha's when Phil lost the plot altogether. I was out on the stairs peepin' in, breakin' me heart laughin' at the goin's-on of the pair of them. Phil jumps up off the chair, runs into the kitchen to the press and grabs a few pairs of Ma's old tights. Thomas saw wha' was comin' and tried to run. He didn't stand a chance in hell of gettin' away from Phil. He had Thomas tied to the chair in seconds and wrapped in the tights, from his ankles right up to his shoulders. He couldn't move.

'"Yeh want pancakes, Thomas, is tha' wha' yeh're sayin'? Well, I'll give yeh all yeh want, and by the time I'm finished yeh won't look for a pancake for a very long time."

'"I'm sorry, Phil. Please let me out. I swear I'll be good," cried Thomas.

'"It's too late, yeh little fuck; yeh're goin' to pay the price."'

'Ah Jaysus, Kathleen, yeh should've gone in and helped Thomas,' said Carmel. 'I'd say he was shittin' himself at tha' stage.'

'Are yeh for real or wha', Carmel? Me try and stop Phil when he gets into one of his crazy moods? There's no way I was gettin' meself involved. Anyway, shut up and let me tell yeh wha' happened. Phil takes out one of the bowls from the press, puts the flour and milk into it, as yeh do when yeh're makin' pancakes. I thought to meself, tha' looks okay. Tha' was until I saw wha' came next. He mixed white puddin', beans, dog food, cod liver oil and a lump of drippin', and to top it off, yeh know tha' white chalky medicine Ma drinks when her stomach is at her with the acid? Well, tha' went in last.'

'Oh my God, Kathleen, I feel like gettin' sick just thinkin' about it.'

'Tha's nothin', Carmel. Wait 'til I tell yeh wha' he done next. He whisked it like mad, makin' it into a thick gooey paste. I have to say, me own stomach was turnin', just lookin' at the colour of it. He poured it onto the sizzlin' pan, which by the way was floatin' in drippin'. He made about six or seven pancakes, leavin' each one to cool down as he went on cookin', all the while breakin' his heart laughin' as he looked over at Thomas, who was goin' into a frenzy at this stage. He knew full well wha' Phil was goin' to do next and so did the rest of the kids, who weren't long about scarperin' out of the house.

'"Righ', Thomas," said Phil. "Yer pancakes awaits yeh. Now, open up."

'"I'm sorry, I'm sorry, Phil. Please don't make me eat tha'."

'"But yeh wanted me to make them for yeh and tha's wha' I've done, Thomas. Now, open up and get it over with."

'Carmel, yeh want to see the dirty big grin on Phil's face as he forced those pancakes down Thomas's throat. He kept tryin' to spit them out but Phil wasn't havin' any of it so he held Thomas's mouth closed, makin' him swallow every bite. Thomas was startin' to turn a funny colour so I couldn't sit there any longer. I went into the kitchen when Phil tried to stuff the third pancake in Thomas's mouth.

'"Tha's enough, Phil," I said. "He's goin' to be sick. Yeh've made yer point, now leave him alone."

'"Ah, there yeh are, Kathleen. I was just tryin' to teach the little fucker a lesson. Maybe now he'll think twice about whingin' and cryin' in everybody's face when he doesn't get his own way."

'And tha' was it, Carmel. Ma and Da were none the wiser. Thomas didn't open his mouth or cry for ages after tha', which was great, and he definitely never ever cried in front of Phil again. He knew better not to. Jaysus, Carmel, surely yeh must have noticed how quiet Thomas was when Phil was around?'

'Ah, yeh know me, Kathleen, I was always busy playin' with me dolls. I never took much notice of anythin' tha' was goin' on around me. Except for the time tha' you and Phil had tha' big fight. Tha' always stuck out in me head. Yiz were always so close. I couldn't believe tha' yeh wouldn't talk to him for ages.'

'I know, Carmel, I was a stubborn bitch back then. It was stupid of me to keep it up for so long, but then again, I was only sixteen and thought I knew it all. I'll never forget tha' day meself, Carmel. Alan had bought me this little record player only the day before from Phil's friend Patsy, for nine pounds, which was a huge amount of money back then, as yeh well know. Anyway, there I was gettin' meself ready for goin' out tha' night with Alan. I was happy as anythin' with life while I blasted out Elvis's latest record. I was dancin' away, doin' a few twirls with one of the kids, when Phil walks into the kitchen.

'"Jaysus, Kathleen, there's a great sound comin' out of tha'. De yeh want to have a jive?"

'"Would yeh stop, Phil, there's no room in here."

'"I'll soon fix tha'," he said, pushing the table against the wall. "Come on, Kathleen, and I'll show yeh a few moves I'm after learnin'." There the two of us were, dancin' away while a couple of the kids clapped to the music. Then, all of a sudden, the song stopped.

'"Jaysus, Phil, wha's after happenin' there? Did any of yiz touch tha'?" I asked the kids.

'"We never went near it, Kathleen," they all chimed in together.

'"Hold on, I'll have a look," said Phil.

'"No, I don't want yeh to touch it. Alan will check it over when he comes down."

'"Would yeh give it over, Kathleen – it's probably a bit of dirt caught in the needle. I'll have it fixed in two seconds and then we can carry on dancin'."

'"I said yeh're not to go near it, Phil. Just in case yeh can't put it back together. And if it's not workin' righ' Alan can

bring it back to Patsy and get his money back. Now leave it."
Before I could do anything, he slowly started to take the
record player apart in front of me.

'I was startin' to grind my teeth at this stage. I don't know
wha' came over me. I got meself worked up into a righ'
frenzy. When I look back now, I suppose it was childish of me
the way I carried on, but then again maybe not. I felt that it
was my present, bought for me and nobody else, and I didn't
want Phil messin' with it. That's when all hell broke out
between us.

'It was our first time ever to have a serious fight. He kept
laughin' at me, gettin' all worked up, ignorin' everythin' I was
sayin'.

'"I'm tellin' yeh, Phil, if yeh don't leave the record player
alone, I'll go upstairs and rip yer one and only shirt in half."

'"Would yeh get away, yeh mad thing, Kathleen. I know
tha' yeh wouldn't do tha' on me."

'"Yes, I would," I said as I made a charge up the stairs. His
black suit and snow-white shirt tha' Ma had got out of the
pawn shop earlier on tha' day were hangin' on a nail in our
bedroom, all ready for Phil's date tha' night. I know, I know –
wha' I did next was terrible, but I couldn't help meself. This mad
rage came over me. I not only ripped his shirt down the middle,
I then got his suit and rubbed it under his bed in all the dust and
God knows how many cups of tea tha' was spilt there.

'Phil was callin' up to me as he was makin' his way up the
stairs. "Yeh were righ', Kathleen, I should've left it alone. I
have all the bits in a bag downstairs. Maybe Alan can put it
back together when he comes down." Then he stopped dead
in his tracks. I was standin' there with half of his shirt in my
hand.

'"I told yeh, Phil. Yeh should've listened to me. Yeh
pushed me temper too far this time."

'He stood there with his mouth wide open in shock, not sayin' a word. Phil was built like a lion and as strong as an ox, so there was no problem for him to lift up my seven stone. Before I knew it, he had me up in the air, shakin' the livin' daylights out of me.

'"Yeh stupid fuckin' bitch," he kept roarin'. "There was no need for tha'. I've no clothes now." In the middle of all this mayhem I was still tryin' to get a dig in at him. I don't know what happened after tha'; all I know is I woke up on the bed with Phil at the end of it, laughin', ticklin' me feet.

'"Oh, me head. Wha' did yeh do to me, Phil Doyle?"

'"Yeh're a lunatic, Kathleen. I didn't do nothin' – you tried to head-butt me because I wouldn't put yeh down, and yeh knocked yerself out. Yeh gave me a terrible fright when yeh passed out. I thought yeh were after droppin' dead on me. By Jaysus, yeh're every bit of Ma with tha' mad temper of yers. I'll tell yeh one thing for nothin', I'll think twice the next time before I cross yeh."

'"I don't believe yeh – and there won't be a next time, Phil Doyle," I said as I stormed off to the toilet. "Because I'll never ever be speakin' to yeh again."

'I couldn't believe it when I looked in the mirror. My nose was double its size, with my eyes turnin' black already. Phil wasn't long gettin' his spoke in with Ma and Da as soon as they came home from town. I was lyin' on the bed in the dark when Ma made her way up to me, switchin' the light on as she came into the room. I could see by her face tha' she'd got a fright when she looked at me.

'"Before yeh open yer mouth, Kathleen, Phil just told me his side of the story and I'll hear yeh out, but I have just one thing to say – I won't be sidin' with either one of yeh and I told yer father to do the same. Yeh're big and hairy enough to sort this out between the pair of yeh. Now, havin' said tha', could yeh not have smashed a few jam jars or plates when yeh got yerself all riled up? I mean, the suit and shirt – for fuck sake, Kathleen, yeh could have left them alone. Now I have nothin' to pawn on Monday when I need an extra shillin' to get me through the week."

'I lay there crying my eyes out. Then I launched into my side of what happened. Ma sat there listenin', not sayin' a word.

'"Come on now, let's get yeh into the toilet and bathe yer eyes. See if we can get some of tha' swellin' down before Alan gets here. He's goin' to have a blue fit when he sees the state of yeh, and I wouldn't blame him one bit for gettin' annoyed. But as I said, it's best tha' it's kept between yerself and Phil and I'll be tellin' Alan tha' meself. Tha' way there'll be some chance of yeh makin' up."

'"Tha' won't be happenin', Ma," I said. "Me and Phil are finished. I mean, would yeh look at me face? It's gettin' worse by the minute. I won't be able to go to work. There'll be no wages for yeh and all because Phil Doyle, Mr Know-It-All, wouldn't listen to me. No, I'm sorry, Ma, but this is all his fault." Back then there was no way anybody could tell me that I did any wrong, which of course I had and was too stubborn to admit it.

'"Righ' then, Kathleen, we'll say no more at the minute. Come on downstairs and have a bite to eat."

'I was makin' me way into the kitchen when Phil came over to me. "Holy Jaysus, Kathleen, I'm sorry over the record player and the fight, but I didn't do tha' to yeh. Tha' happened when yeh tried to head-butt me. I'd never do anythin' like tha' to any of yiz and you should know tha' more than anybody."

'"I've nothin' to say to yeh, Phil Doyle, now or ever again."

'Da just looked over at the pair of us and shook his head from side to side, not openin' his mouth. It wasn't too long after the dinner when Alan arrived. Ma got her spoke in straight away, pulling Alan to one side, letting him know the ins and outs of what happened. "Best keep out of it, Alan," she said. "They'll sort things out in time themselves." I knew by the way he was looking over at Phil that Alan wanted to dig the head off him, but he held back and did what Ma asked.

'I was up with the doctor the next day and was relieved when he told me that my nose wasn't broken. It took the guts of two weeks for my face to come back to normal. Phil did everything in his power to try and get me to laugh and talk to him, telling his funniest jokes as soon as I would walk into the room, or hiding upstairs, waiting to pounce on me in the dark, but I wasn't having any of it.

'I kept it up for months on end, until one day when I came in from work and found Ma crying in the kitchen.

'"Jaysus Christ, Ma, are yeh all righ'? Wha's after happenin'?"

'"Oh, thank God yeh're home, Kathleen. It's Phil, he's after takin' bad in the hospital."

'"Ma, he's only gettin' his tonsils out – it's no big deal."

'"I know tha', Kathleen, but he's after bleedin' real bad. I was givin' him a sup of water to wet his lips, them being all dry after the operation, when next the blood spat out of his mouth nearly into me face. I nearly had a heart attack on the spot with the fright I got. The blood was everywhere. Yeh'd want to hear the roars of me, screamin' for help. The whole hospital must've heard me. Not tha' I gave two shites wha' anybody thought. I just wanted somebody to help me son."

'"Oh Ma, is he okay? Please tell me he's all right, tha' nothin' bad is after happenin' to him."

'"I have to say, them doctors and nurses are angels from heaven. They were in like a light. Now, mind you, it took a while before the bleedin' stopped. And yes, he's fine again. Thanks to the holy Mother herself, who has her own way of helpin' me sort things out when I need a bit of help. De yeh know somethin', Kathleen? The worry tha' I'm after goin' through today was worth every second of it, just to hear yeh say those words about yer brother. Me heart was broke lookin' at the pair of yiz driftin' apart."

'"I know, Ma, and I'm sorry. It was stupid, but the whole thing just seemed to get out of hand and then I didn't really know how to fix it without lookin' as if I was givin' in to Phil. Yeh know him, I'd never hear the end of it."

'"Well, this is yer chance now, Kathleen. Go up to the hospital to see him and make things righ' between yiz. I know Phil wants tha' more than anythin'. He's told me so many times how he misses yeh."

'That was all I needed to hear. I had myself ready in a flash and was down in the Meath Hospital just in time for visiting hour. I felt nervous because we hadn't talked for so long, and at the same time excited about all I had to tell him. Phil copped me as soon as I walked into the ward, and the big smile that he gave me said it all. That was enough for me. We sat there laughing and joking about the fight and how crazy I got.

'"I'm sorry about wha' I did, Phil," I told him.

'"Me too, Kathleen. I mean, the record player ended up goin' in the bin over me messin' and pullin' it apart, losin' half the screws along the way, but about wha' happened after tha' – I'm innocent, and I think yeh know tha' now."

'"I know, Phil, so let's make a pact tha', no matter wha' happens or wha's goin' on in our lives, we'll never fall out again." And we never did. We were the best of friends – always.'

* * *

'Jaysus Christ, Carmel, would yeh have a look at the time? I got lost there for a while, goin' back down memory lane. I came down to give yeh a dig out with the bit of cleanin' and I've ended up doin' nothin'.'

'Yeh're all righ', Kathleen. I'll get the others to help me later on. Anyway, I enjoyed our little chat. It was nice for a change. We should do it more often.'

'We will, Carmel, I promise. Now, where in the hell are Jacinta and Patricia with me change? They seem to be gone forever.'

With that, the pair of them burst in the door, with Da right behind them.

'There yeh are, Kathleen,' said Da. 'Are yeh stayin' for a bit of dinner?'

'I better not, Da, the time is gettin' on a bit now. I'd best be on me way.'

'Well, at least stay and have a cup of tea with me.'

'All righ' then, go on, put the teapot on. I'll hang on for another half an hour.'

'All the same, Kathleen,' said Da, 'the house isn't the same without yer mother, with all her roarin' and shoutin' and givin' out about one thing and another. I have to say I do miss her around the place. She's the only one apart from yerself tha' keeps the kids in hand from gettin' up to all sorts of mischief. But havin' said tha', things have been very quiet around here. They're all behavin' themselves. Isn't tha' righ', Carmel?'

Carmel looked over at me with a big grin on her face. 'Yeh never said a truer word, Da – they're all so good.'

6

Big Changes

I was expecting my third baby and was in and out of hospital for the first three months. I was unwell through the whole pregnancy, with the threat of miscarriage hanging over me all the time. I had to rest so much, which meant I wasn't able to go up to Ma every day and had to stay at home with Martina and young Alan. Ma would drop down to me, checking to make sure I was okay, always bringing a few of the kids with her, which I thought wouldn't be a problem.

I felt this was my home now, especially after Alan's granddad Pop sat the two of us down one day. He told us he had forty years' tenancy with the Corporation and that it would be a pity to let it go to waste. He suggested that we should put in to buy the house, saying he wasn't too far off eighty years old and wasn't going to last forever. He'd put his name on the form with us; that way, we would get it for little or nothing.

Alan didn't waste any time in bringing Pop down to the Corporation, and was told that we could get the house for as little as eight hundred pounds. We couldn't believe it; we were over the moon. We worked out all the bills and it was well within our means.

Of course, I got carried away as usual, making all sorts of plans about building on a new bathroom, maybe a new kitchen and definitely another bedroom. Alan would sit there listening to me rammaging on and laughing, knowing full well that wouldn't happen for a long time. He would never burst my bubble, though.

Pop, on the other hand, was listening and taking it all in. I don't know what was going on in his head, but it wasn't good for us. He always had his meals with us and there was never a bother with the kids playing around. But that all changed when I was sick and Ma started dropping in every day to me.

Pop didn't say anything, but you know when things are not right. He stopped coming down for breakfast and then I would hear him slipping out the front door. I would cook his dinner every day and it would be left there. I asked him one day, because it was getting the better of me.

'Pop, are yeh okay? De yeh not feel well? Yeh're not eatin' a thing.'

He didn't answer or look at me, just went about his business and headed out the door. I was left speechless, and believe me that doesn't happen very often. I told Ma when she dropped in to see me, but I was immediately sorry I opened my mouth.

'Wha' did I tell yeh, Kathleen? Didn't I tell yeh it never works out livin' on somebody else's floor? But would yeh listen to me? No.'

'He's probably a bit sick or somethin', tha's wha' it is, Ma. I'll get Alan to talk to him. He'll sort everythin' out.'

'I'm tellin' yeh, Kathleen, tha' oul' fella is up to no good. Mark my words, it'll all come out in the wash. Just wait and see.'

Ma kept going on and on about how we should have got our own house from day one. And she was so right, but I couldn't see that at the time.

Shortly after she left Alan came home. I didn't waste any time in telling him what had happened. He listened to me, taking it all in, not saying a word and not looking too surprised at what was coming out of my mouth.

'Alan, de yeh know somethin' I don't?'

Then he came out with the words which were the furthest from my mind.

'Kathleen, he wants us out. Pop wants us to leave.'

I heard what Alan said, but it didn't seem to connect with my brain. Not for a couple of minutes anyway. He went on to tell me what was going on.

'I didn't say anythin', Kathleen, with you being sick and all. Yeh've enough to be worryin' about there. But with yer Ma droppin' in, tryin' to keep an eye on yeh, and all the kids runnin' around playin' and makin' noise. It didn't go down very well with Pop. Me Da was tellin' me tha' he's been goin' up to him, givin' out like shite, and to top it off, when I told him that we had to go in and sign the final forms about buyin' the house, "No way!" he said. "I want yiz out." I couldn't believe it Kathleen.'

I nearly fell through the floor when he said that to me.

'But I don't understand, Alan – he's the one tha' wanted us to buy the house in the first place. And as soon as I have the baby, Ma won't be comin' down here anymore. It was only because I was sick – did yeh tell him tha', Alan?'

'I know all tha', and yes, I told him. There wasn't a bother on him until some of these oul' fellas he drinks with start sayin' that we'd probably fuck him into a home the first chance we get once the forms are signed.'

'Oh my God! We'd never do anythin' like tha'. How could he ever think such a thing, Alan?'

'Kathleen, me and me Da are after spendin' the last two weeks tryin' to convince Pop tha' would never happen, but there's no gettin' through to him. He has this in his head now and there's no changin' it. There's no two ways about it, we have to leave.'

'And go where, Alan? Where are we supposed to go with two children and another little one on the way? I can't believe this is happenin'! I mean, we're after buildin' our home here. We've spent every penny over the past six years on this house. Wha' are we goin' to do? We've no money behind us.'

'We'll have to go into the Corporation, Kathleen, and see if they can offer us somethin'. All I can say is, thank God yeh went in tha' time with yer Ma just after we got married and put our names on the list.'

I cried so many tears that night I could have filled a river. We went over and over it again, talking and talking, trying to make sense of what was happening. I was too upset at the time to realise how Alan must have felt about his own granddad doing that to him. That was hard.

* * *

I was up at the crack of dawn the next morning getting the kids ready. I didn't care how sick I was or how much I was supposed to rest; there was no way I wanted to see Pop. I was too upset and annoyed with him. So Alan dropped us off to Ma's and I wasn't long filling her in on everything. Well, all hell broke loose, just like I knew it would.

'The dirty, conniving bastard of a man! And him with nearly one foot in the grave as it is. He'll fuckin' rot in hell for doin' this to yiz, the pig. Didn't I tell yeh he was up to no good?'

'I know.' The tears rolled down my face once more. 'Please Ma, it's hard enough.'

She calmed down and pulled her horns back in.

'Righ', Kathleen,' she said, 'finish tha' cup of tea and, if yeh're up to it, we'll head into the Corporation righ' now.'

'Well, I have to be up to it, don't I, Ma? I've no choice in the matter.'

As soon as we got there I filled the lady in at the hatch about what had happened. Because our names had been on the list a few years, they offered us a flat straight away. She was nice enough to tell me that if I waited until my baby was born, which was only about three months away, we would be entitled to a house. I didn't get a chance to answer. Ma did that for me.

'Tha's great,' she said, 'put her down for the house.'

As we made our way home, Ma came up with a plan. 'Fuck tha' oul' fella, Kathleen. Alan can tell him yeh're not goin' anywhere until the baby comes into the world and if he has anythin' to say about it, I'll come down and sort him out. He can stick his house up his hole, so he can. Now wha' yeh do is, get Alan to drop yeh off in the mornin's before he heads off to work. Tha' way yeh won't have tha' long walk. Yeh'll be able to rest here. I'll take care of the kids; they can play out in the back garden with the rest of them. Yiz can all have yer bit of dinner here. Then yeh'll only have to sleep there. Things always have a way of workin' themselves out, Kathleen. So don't be worryin'. The only thing tha' should be on yer mind right now is keepin' yerself well so this little baby can be brought into the world safe.'

She knew I wasn't able for any more ranting and raving, but those last few words were so full of wisdom it made me put everything into perspective. I realised my baby was the most important thing. Everything else was just material things that could be replaced in time.

* * *

The next couple of months seemed to take forever. Then my little baby girl Amanda came into the world. She was so tiny, not even weighing five pounds.

I only had her with me two days and she was not feeding very well for me. I noticed her colour changing; she was turning orange. I called the nurse over. She took one look at Amanda and ran to get a doctor. He was up straight away and she was rushed down to the special baby unit. The doctor explained to me that her liver wasn't functioning and she also had a kidney and ear infection.

I watched through the glass as her lovely blonde hair was shaved off so they could put a needle into her head. I was frantic with worry. I could feel the blood draining from my face and my legs starting to go from under me. One of the nurses was over straight away.

'Sit down there, Kathleen, before you fall and hurt yourself. I'm sorry, but we have to get fluids into your baby fast to get her liver working and this is the quickest way. Believe me, it's not as bad as it looks, and I promise she didn't feel a thing. As soon as you're okay, I'll bring you in to her.'

'I'm fine, nurse, please bring me in now.' And she did.

'Look, Kathleen,' she said as we both stood by the cot, 'what did I tell you? There she is sleeping away, not a bother on her. And that's what you should be doing – getting yourself a good night's sleep while you can.'

Of course, I didn't get any sleep that night from the worry.

* * *

Amanda was kept in hospital for the next three weeks. Ma was great, looking after Martina and young Alan along with her own, while I spent all the hours I could in the hospital, getting as many feeds as I could into Amanda, helping to build her up. They finally let me take her home.

In the meantime, Alan didn't waste any time in getting her birth cert into the Corporation to prove we had our third child, making us eligible for a house. I knew as soon as Alan walked in the door that there was something wrong. The news wasn't good.

'Wha' is it, Alan? Tell me!' I asked.

'We can have a house now, straight away. The only thing is, it's over the northside of the city. A new scheme called Darndale. It's not too far from Portmarnock.'

'Jaysus, Alan, tha's miles away. I'll be out there on me own. I won't know anybody. Wha' will I do if one of the kids gets sick? Who will I turn to? I won't have me Da or Ma.'

'I know, Kathleen, and I did me best tryin' to see if they had any houses on the southside. They've nothin' and they won't be buildin' over here for another three years. We've no choice. We have to take it. I'm not stayin' in tha' house a night longer than I have to. It's hard enough as it is, but knowin' it's me granddad, me own flesh and blood tha's doin' this to us . . . No, I'm sorry, Kathleen, there's no turnin' back.'

* * *

And there wasn't. Within the next couple of weeks, we were in and signed for our house and were handed the keys on the same day. We drove out straight away to have a look. Alan was so excited, but I wasn't. We made our way up to Crumlin to tell the family our news.

When I told Ma and Da where I was moving to, Da got a bit upset.

'Yeh'll be missed around here, Kathleen, I can tell yeh tha' – and I don't only mean for all the cleanin' yeh do and keepin' them kids in hand for us. It's for yerself.'

It took me a big effort to keep myself from falling to pieces when Da said that to me. 'Don't worry, Da, I'll still be over, I promise.'

Ma was a different kettle of fish altogether. She went ballistic. I had a right job stopping her from going down and battering Pop. The fucking and blinding went on for I don't know how long. But eventually she calmed down, as she always did.

'I'm goin' to miss yeh around here, Kathleen. It won't be the same, you not droppin' in every day.'

'I'll still make me way over, Ma. Even if it's only two or three times a week. Sure I won't be able to stay away. Yeh know me; I'm glued to yiz all.'

I could see Ma looked and felt a bit better in herself then, for a little while anyway.

* * *

I was so upset over the next few days as I started to pack all the bits and bobs we had gathered over the few years since we had first moved in with Pop. I had come to love the little house that I had made my home, still hoping, even up to the very last, that he would ask us to stay. But that wasn't to be.

Pop had himself up and gone out of the house from early that morning. Alan had everything planned out to a T. He knew the way I felt about leaving, so he organised a lift with his Uncle Joe for me and the kids and sent us ahead of him. It all happened so quickly that I didn't have time to think, and maybe that was just as well.

I sat in silence the whole way out, listening to Joe giving out like shite about Pop, while Martina and young Alan giggled and played with one another. They were too young to understand what was going on; all that was on their minds was how soon we were bringing them to the seaside.

As soon as we got to the house, Joe didn't waste any time in hanging about and headed back over to give Alan a hand. I settled Amanda in her pram while the other two ran about.

It was a lovely house; it had three fine-sized bedrooms, a bathroom and toilet, which we hadn't had in Pops'. I should have been over the moon with this. There was a lovely big kitchen with plenty of built-in presses, and a huge sitting-room. I looked around me and none of it meant anything. All I wanted to do was to go home.

Alan settled in really well, as did the kids. But me? At first you might as well have put me on the other side of the world. I felt so isolated and lonely. Although I didn't realise it at the time, this move was to be a big turning point in my life, which, I might add, was for the better. At that particular time, I didn't mix very well outside my family circle. I was very shy but in time I learned to overcome that. Slowly but surely, I started to mingle, between the school and the local shops, which did me the world of good.

* * *

Amanda was nearly three months old on the day I got the letter from the Coombe. I got such a fright, as they wanted to see me straight away. I was only starting to get back on my feet again, after being so sick during the pregnancy. There seemed to be no end to my health problems, and I really didn't need to hear this news.

I got my sister Patricia to mind the kids while I made my way in to the hospital. I had myself in a right tizzy as I waited to be seen by the doctor, who looked very serious when I sat down in front of him. He read over my chart before he spoke.

'Hello, Mrs McGrath,' he said. 'I'm Dr Roche and I see here from your records that you have been in and out with us a lot over the past year.'

'Tha's right, Doctor.'

'Well, Mrs McGrath, I'm afraid you will be seeing us on a regular basis, because we are going to have to keep a check on you from now on. Your last smear test was very nasty, very nasty indeed. You have cells there that are not healthy. In normal circumstances, we would carry out a hysterectomy straight away, but since you're only twenty-six, we have decided that you are far too young to be going through the menopause. So we are going to go down a different route for the moment. You will have to come to the hospital every six weeks to get this particular procedure done, and then we will take it from there.'

I still found it very hard to talk to doctors in white coats, so I went along with what they said and did. When I think back now, I was such a gobshite. I never asked a thing. I should have been asking, 'How serious is this? What will you be doing? How long will it go on for? Could I die?' The most important question of all: could I die? But I asked nothing and was told nothing.

The word 'cancer' was never used – only, 'it's very nasty'. Maybe they just didn't want to frighten me. I really don't know. I remember on my first visit I asked one of the nurses what it was I was getting done. Her very words were, 'They're trying to burn off the unhealthy cells, Kathleen.'

Oh my God, I was so sore for days afterwards. It felt like I'd had a hot blowtorch down below. That went on for a good few months, and the doctor finally brought me back in for another chat.

'Now, Mrs McGrath, your last smear test results are much better than previous,' he told me. 'But – and I must stress this – they are still not as clear as we would like. So you must continue with the regular check-ups. I will see you again in six months and if that result is as positive as this, we can move to an annual visit.'

I wanted to jump up and kiss the face off him, but I wouldn't dare. All I said was, 'Thank you so much, Doctor.' Then I was gone like a flash.

Even though the news wasn't one hundred per cent, I was still happy enough with what he had to say, for that moment in time anyway. I was so happy that I didn't have to go back into hospital and have surgery that I slowly found myself starting to settle down a bit better.

* * *

I got to know a few girls around the estate, all like myself, each of us with a couple of kids, which meant we had something in common to give out and talk about. I could feel myself getting confident and more outgoing as the weeks and months went by, and it felt good.

I asked Alan if he would bring me into town one of the evenings when he finished work. I wanted to check out a hairdressing salon called 'The Witch's Hut'. 'One of the girls up at the school told me she had her hair done there by hairdressin' students. She said tha' they teach people in the evenin's to cut hair. So wha' de yeh think, Alan? If we could manage, I would love to do it.'

He sat there with a smile on his face, pleased with the big change in me. 'It's wha' yeh always wanted to do, Kathleen, so go for it!'

That was all I needed to hear. In I went the following evening, while Alan waited outside with the three kids in the back of the car. I was so nervous as I made my entrance – but determined. When I came back out I had a smile on my face that lit up the whole of Grafton Street. I had just booked my first three lessons, unsure how or where the extra money was going to come from; but knowing Alan, he would work things out and make it happen.

Paul and Mano, the tough guys

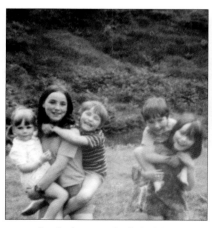

On the boats at Butlin's: Mano,
Paul, Patricia and Martina

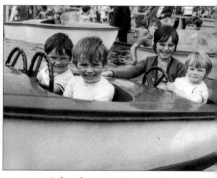

A fun day out: Martina, Jacinta,
Paul, Mano and Patricia

Ma and Da in Canada

Phil the Champ

Phil's boys, Philip, JJ and Andrew

Ma in Crumlin

Amanda on her first communion, with myself, Ma,
young Alan, Martina and baby Treasa

My three kids, Martina, Amanda and young Alan

Growing up: myself with Amanda, Martina and King the dog

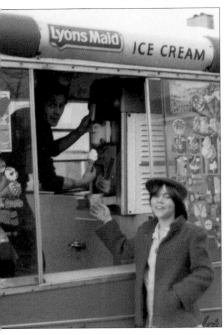

Martina with Alan and the ice-cream van

Martina with little Danielle

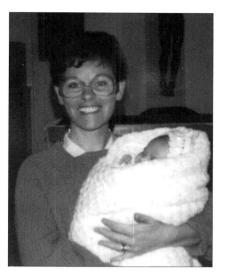

Kathleen and Danielle when
I first because a granny

Myself and my other
granddaughter, Jessica

Granddaughter, Robyn

The wild one: Clare's son Dominic on the "funny farm"

Clare's youngest, Romano

Hot wheels: Alan and I on holiday

Ma

Ma with her great-granddaughter, Danielle

The whole gang: Clare, Marion, Noel, Carmel, Mano, Jacinta,
Paul, Patricia, me and Thomas. Only poor Phil is missing

Baby Conor with his great-grandmother and
great-great-grandmother

Myself and Alan, still in love

And that he did. By working two late nights and all day Saturday as overtime, he brought in enough to pay for my training.

* * *

I think when Ma brought me into this world I was given enough energy for a dozen people. I let nothing faze me. I would be up from the crack of dawn, always getting ahead of myself.

I was so excited that first evening I was to start my classes. Alan's dinner was in the oven. I had the three kids fed and ready in their pyjamas. Martina was five years old, Alan three and Amanda barely six months. I was ready to run with them as soon as Alan pulled up outside the house. I had to be there by seven o'clock, so there was no time to waste.

I sat in the back of the car; Amanda was on my lap, with Martina and Alan either side.

'Now, Martina,' I said, 'yeh're to be a good girl for me. Mammy has to work, so I want yeh to hold Amanda in yer arms real tight for Daddy when he's driving yiz home. And wha'ever yeh do, don't let go of her.'

'Okay, Ma,' she smiled, delighted with the bit of responsibility.

As we pulled up outside the salon, I sat there for a minute, getting myself together. I was nervous as hell, but, as always, Alan said the right words just when I needed them most.

'Yeh can do this, Kathleen; all yeh have to do is believe in yerself, because I know I do. Now run along; yeh don't want to be late for yer first class. And don't worry about the kids, I'll take care of all tha'.'

So in I went with those words in my head, ready to take on the world.

* * *

I took to hairdressing like a duck takes to water. I had a great teacher called James, who I got on very well with. He only had to show me something once and I could do it. He would tell me all the while that I was a born hairdresser, which helped build my confidence more and more.

The days that I didn't have classes I would make my way over to Ma, just as I promised, practising what I had learned the night before on all the kids, which helped me move forward faster. The more models I got, the better I became. There was no stopping me. Every chance I got, I had my scissors in my hand, cutting everyone and anyone's hair that I could get my hands on.

In less than two years, with the help of a few courses in between, I had perfected the art of hairdressing. I followed my dream and it came true for me at last.

I now felt I was ready to start making some money and reap the rewards for all my hard work. That's when I put my first plan into action, telling Alan what was going on in my head.

'Alan, yeh know the way the sittin' room is really big? Well, de yeh think tha' yeh could put a wall along there, takin' part of it away? I'd just need enough room for one mirror and a chair. I could put a hooded hairdryer over there in the corner behind the door. Tha's all I need for doin' me perms and sets. So wha' de yeh think?'

I showed my pearly white smile from ear to ear, bursting with excitement at the thought of starting my own little business.

'I knew yeh were up to somethin', Kathleen. I've been watchin' yeh, sittin' there starin' into space, schemin' away to yerself, wonderin' wha' yeh were goin' to come out with, and I have to say it sounds good. I'll be able to do the work meself; tha' way, it won't cost too much. Yeh'll be up and runnin' in no time.'

* * *

Alan did a great job on dividing the sitting-room, giving me enough space to work in, but still leaving plenty of room for us to sit in as a family. Because the houses had their own back entrances, it made it very handy for me to keep the hairdressing separate from the house.

I didn't waste any time in telling all the girls at the school and the neighbours nearby, asking them to pass the word around, which they all did. I built myself a nice little business over the few years we lived in Darndale, working every hour that I could, doing as many haircuts as I could while the kids were in school. As soon as they were in bed, I'd start all over again. With Alan's overtime and the money I was making, we were starting to get a nice few pound behind us, enough for our first holiday abroad.

7

Spain

We decided on the sunny island of Majorca for our first holiday
– just Alan and myself. My sister Carmel came out to Darndale
with a few of my younger brothers and sisters to mind our three
kids for us. I wanted to make sure they had plenty of company
while we were away and wouldn't miss us too much. I did feel
a bit guilty about not bringing them with us, but I also felt Alan
and I needed some time for ourselves. We had been chasing our
tails over the past couple of years, between one thing and
another. There never seemed to be any time for us, and maybe
now we could have the honeymoon we'd never had.

There were loads of waves and kisses from all the kids as
we drove away from the house. I was so excited as we pulled
up to the airport. It was my first time there because I had
never been outside Ireland before. I couldn't believe the
numbers of people all heading off to different parts of the
world. There was such a buzz around the place and it felt
great because we were part of it. I have to say, I was a bit
nervous when the plane took off, but that soon passed. I
talked away like mad through the whole flight.

'Isn't this great, Alan? Did yeh ever think tha' we would be headin' off on our own for our first holiday?'

'To tell yeh the truth, Kathleen, I couldn't believe it when yeh came out and said no kids. Yeh know yeh're always worryin' about them – not tha' I ever mind, but it is nice just the two of us for a change. It'll be like old times. We'll hire a bike and go all over the island together. I promise yeh, we'll have a great week.'

'I know, I know, Alan. I can't wait. I just can't wait to get there.'

I was like a child heading off on a big adventure. Before I knew it, the pilot was announcing, 'Fasten your seat-belts, ladies and gentlemen. We'll be landing shortly.'

I couldn't believe the heat as I walked down the steps of the plane. It nearly took my breath away. It didn't take us too long to get through the airport and in no time at all we were on our way. My mind was blown as the coach drove us to the hotel. I'd never seen the likes of it before, except maybe on the telly, but this was real and I was here in the middle of it all. I soon let everybody on the bus know that too.

'Oh my God, Alan, would yeh have a look at the height of them buildin's? And did yeh ever see so many flowers in yer life? Look how tall all them palm trees are. They're massive. I'd love one of them in our garden. Christ, Alan I just saw a swimmin' pool. Did yeh see, Alan, did yeh see it? Oh, there's another one . . . and another one.'

Alan was laughing his head off at my excitement. 'I have to say, Kathleen, it's the business all right. Now, will yeh try and calm yerself down – the whole bus is listenin' to yeh.'

I hadn't realised I was jumping up and down, shouting and roaring all over the place. With that I slowly slipped back down into my seat, embarrassed as hell, blushing all over.

65

Then I felt someone tap me on the shoulder. It was the woman sitting across from me. She was wearing this big flowery hat, with the fuzziest blonde curls you ever saw underneath, bright pink sunglasses with lipstick to match, and a big friendly smile to top it all off.

'Yeh're all right there, love. I have to say I enjoyed every minute listenin' to yeh,' she said as she put her hand out to shake mine. 'By the way, I'm Maggie. Yer first holiday?'

'Tha's righ'. I'm Kathleen.'

'It brought back memories to me, so it did, of when I came on me first holiday. Yeh think you were bad, I was like a ravin' lunatic, runnin' up and down the aisle of the bus, askin' people did they see this and tha'. Marty said I made a holy show of meself, but fuck it, I didn't care. Marty is me husband, who's sittin' here next to me – he was mortified. Marty, tell the girl – weren't yeh mortified?'

Maggie's husband, who was reading his paper, looked over at me, not saying a word, shook his head from side to side, rolled his eyes in the air and turned away.

'He gets a bit shy at times. But don't mind him.' She went on talking about all the different places she'd been to. I listened, taking it all in, but still trying to have a peep out along the way. I didn't want to miss a single thing.

The bus finally pulled into our hotel, with Maggie shouting as we got off. 'Enjoy yerself, love, and remember wha' I said – once yeh get a taste of this kind of livin', there's no turnin' back. And believe me, I know wha' I am talkin' about. Isn't tha' righ' Marty?' I could hear her saying as the bus pulled away.

She was so right. It opened up a whole new world to us, which both of us agreed we wanted.

I had to keep myself from screaming when we walked in the hotel entrance. It was really big and plush. There were cream leather sofas throughout with matching stools on either side. The coffee tables were made of glass with thick chrome legs and the most beautiful spray of flowers on each one. The gleaming tiles on the floor were a champagne colour. I was half afraid to walk on them as we made our way over to the reception to book ourselves in.

Everybody was so nice and friendly. We were shown to our room straight away. I couldn't believe it when I looked around – a big king-size bed, more sofas, shower room, bathroom. Everything was perfect and seemed too good to be true.

'Alan, would yeh have a look at this? I don't remember the rooms lookin' anythin' like this in the brochure. I think they're after makin' a mistake and bringin' us to the wrong hotel.' Alan started laughing. 'No, I'm serious, Alan. Look around at this place, it's really posh. We'll end up gettin' a big bill at the end of the week and we won't be able to pay for it. We'll have to say somethin'.'

'Kathleen, stop rammagin' on, will yeh, or yeh'll end up blowin' a fuse. I changed the hotel, just before we came away. I wanted it to be a surprise. I got a bonus in me wages tha' I wasn't expectin' and I knew if I gave it to you it would end up gettin' lost in with the bills along the way. So I decided, with this being our first holiday, tha' we were goin' to do it in style, and I have to admit it is class. Now, will yeh go and get yerself ready and we'll have a swim in one of these famous swimmin' pools tha' yeh were screamin' about all the way here.'

'I'm speechless, Alan.'

'Well, tha' doesn't happen very often, so yeh must be pleased.'

We had ourselves changed and down to the pool in no time at all. The place was packed, with not a sun-lounger to be got anywhere. Not that we minded; we spent the best part of the morning in the swimming pool, taking out only enough time for a bite to eat before we headed over to the beach, which happened to be across the road from the hotel.

'This just keeps gettin' better and better, Alan. Would yeh have a look at tha' water – it's as blue as the sky, and the beach is so clean. Yeh know wha', the kids would love this. We'll have to bring them on a holiday.'

'I was wonderin' how long it'd take before yeh mentioned the kids.'

'I know, sorry, Alan, I can't help it.'

'If the truth be known, I was thinkin' the same meself. Now, come on and let's see wha's happenin' around here tonight.'

There was plenty to do, between the bars, clubs and every type of restaurant you could think of. I thought I was in another world. You would have needed a month to get around them all. Having said that, we managed a fair few, enjoying every one of them along the way.

Alan hired a bike and, with me on the back, off we went day after day, making sure we saw every inch of the island, always getting back in time to have a swim, which for me was a great finish to the day.

* * *

One of the highlights of the week was the 'Spanish Night', which I'll never forget. You could drink and eat as much as you liked. It was Alan's first time to drink wine and he was knocking it back like it was water. He was pissed out of his brains before I knew it and had the whole place singing 'Is This the Way to Amarillo?' along with him. The atmosphere was brilliant.

It wasn't too long before the show started and the flamenco dancers were on. We were all standing up on the tables, clapping like mad, when Alan decided to get up on the stage. He grabbed one of the flowers off the table, stuck it between his teeth and danced away with them, and they didn't mind a bit. The place was hopping, with everybody cheering him on.

'Are yeh righ', Kathleen?' he roared over to me. 'Come on, help me out here.'

There was no way I was getting up there in front of all those people, me with not a drink on me – no way! But before I knew it, this gang of young fellas who were sitting at the table with us, who just happened to be Irish, all started banging the table and shouting, 'Kathleen! Kathleen! Kathleen!' They too were pissed and with that the whole place started calling my name. I kept laughing, but then I thought, *Wha' the heck – fuck it!* I stuck a flower between my teeth and danced all the way over to Alan, not realising that all the young fellas were dancing behind me, doing the same. With that, everybody was up on the floor.

'Yeh know somethin', Alan, yeh're a mad thing when yeh get goin'. Them flamenco dancers didn't get a look in once yeh started. Now, havin' said tha', the craic was ninety lookin' at yeh.'

'Tha's wha' it's all about, Kathleen – lettin' yer hair down and havin' a bit of fun. Now, come on, dance with me!'

We had one of the best nights of the week and such a laugh we had on the bus back to the hotel, a right sing-song got going. Between 'Molly Malone' and every rebel song you could think of, everybody had to be Irish.

While all this was going on, Alan downed another bottle of wine, which wasn't good and soon changed the course of the night.

Our hotel was the first stop.

'Are yeh righ', Alan?' I said. 'Here we are.'

He didn't see or hear me and was lost in noddy-land at this stage. With the help of two fellas, I managed to get him off the bus. There were loads of waves and goodbyes as I stood there trying to hold him up.

'Come on, Alan, let's get yeh up to bed before yeh fall down. It's after three o'clock in the mornin'.'

'Jaysus, Kathleen, is tha' yerself? I was wonderin' where yeh'd got to. Give us an oul' kiss.' He was slipping and wobbling all over the place.

'I will in a minute, Alan. Now, stand up straight against the wall while I look for the key before we go in.'

I only took my eyes off him for a few seconds, but when I looked up he was gone. I tried not to shout out too loud as I went around calling for him.

'Alan, stop yer messin', will yeh? I'm tired.'

I kept expecting him to jump out from one of the bushes. I was starting to get scared, walking around on my own. There wasn't a sinner to be seen anywhere. Then it dawned on me, 'Oh my God, the swimmin' pool! Wha' if he's after fallin' in there?' I was shaking as I walked around to look, and was relieved to see that the pool was empty.

I was in floods of tears as I made my way into the hotel, only to find out that the night porter couldn't speak a word of English. I was like a traffic warden, standing there doing hand signals. But no matter how hard I tried, there was no getting through to him.

I was too afraid to go up to the room in case Alan would wander in and go back out again, so I sat there, frantic with worry, thinking only the worst. It was starting to get bright outside and it was a big effort for me to stay awake. There was hustle and bustle as the hotel started to come alive as the workers arrived. With that the porter came over to me with a young girl who could speak some English.

'Hello, my name is Anna. My friend tells me you are upset. Can I help you?'

I was so happy to hear those words and told her what had happened, crying and sobbing as I tried to speak. She explained to the porter what I'd been trying to tell him. They spoke together for a couple of minutes before coming back to me.

'Señorita, we have decided, before going to the police, if you can come please with us and we will check the grounds of our hotel first. Then the surrounding area.'

'Thank you. Thank you. Thank you so much.' I nearly took the hand off her I shook it so much. She went around and gathered some of the staff to help us with the search.

It was now coming up to midday and there was still not a sign of Alan anywhere. I didn't know if I was coming or going and was starting to feel really ill at that stage. We were on our way back to phone the police when I heard my name being called.

'Kathleen, is tha' you?'

I looked down the road and there was Alan in the distance, walking towards me. I thought my heart was going to jump out of my body, I was so happy to see him.

'This is your husband?' said Anna.

'Yes, yes, tha's him.'

'Good!' She gave me a smile before heading back to the hotel with the rest of the workers.

I could feel a mad rage coming on me the closer I got to Alan. Instead of hugs and kisses, he got such a dig off me and a right kick in the ankles.

'Where the hell were yeh?' I screamed. 'I'm after bein' up the walls, sick with worry over yeh. I was just goin' back to the hotel to ring the police.'

'I don't know where the fuck I was, Kathleen. I'm after wakin' up in a ditch. Look at me! I'm eaten alive by them bloody mosquitoes. The last thing I remember was gettin' on the bus – after tha', everythin' else is a blank.'

No matter what, I could never stay annoyed at Alan for very long, so I calmed down and took a good look at him. He was in a right mess. There were lumps all over his face and arms. I couldn't help but laugh.

'Come on, Alan, some of them bites look very nasty. We'd better go find a chemist and get yeh sorted out or yeh'll end up in hospital.'

'I'm sorry, love, yeh know I'd never leave yeh on yer own like tha'. It was tha' bloody wine. Never again, Kathleen, I mean it. I'll just stick to me shandies. Tha' way I know wha's goin' on around me.'

'And believe me, Alan, I'll make sure yeh do.'

We bought a big bunch of flowers for Anna and some chocolates for the staff, to thank them for all their help.

* * *

Other than that little hiccup, we had a great holiday, the best time ever. We had meals out every night, dancing the night away until the early hours of the morning. Blue skies and sunshine every day. What more could you ask for?

The week went by so fast that we were back on the plane heading for Dublin before we knew it. I sat there, lost in my thoughts as Alan slept, and I made a promise to myself: no matter what, I would work my arse off for us and our family, to give us a piece of this life.

8

The Snip

Alan came in from work one evening, looking very serious in himself, which is not like him; he's usually so happy-go-lucky, but not that night. I waited until the kids were asleep in bed before I said a word.

'Yeh're very quiet, Alan. Wha's the matter? Did somethin' happen in work? Is yer Da okay?'

'No, it's nothin' like tha', Kathleen. I want us to have a chat about havin' more kids.'

'Jaysus, Alan, yeh want me to have another baby? Amanda's only a couple of months old. Are yeh mad!'

'No, no, tha' came out wrong. Wha' I mean is – and I've been thinkin' about it for a while, but I'm not too sure how yeh feel about this . . . all I know is, I don't want any more kids, and if we keep goin' the way we're goin', we'll end up havin' as many kids as yer Ma.'

'Well, Alan, if tha's wha' has yeh all serious in yerself, yeh've nothin' to worry about there. I'm happy with the family tha' we have and certainly don't want any more. But wha' are we to do? I seem to get caught very easy.'

'Tha's wha' I want to talk about, Kathleen. There's this fella in work, he was tellin' me he got this job done on himself. Yeh know, down there. It's called a vasectomy. Well, in other words, the snip.'

'Jaysus, Alan, wha' exactly gets snipped?' I was cringing just saying the word and imagining all sorts of bits being 'snipped' off.

Alan went into the ins and outs of what it all meant, finishing off by saying, 'It's permanent. There'll be no going back once I get it done.'

'Tha' won't be a problem, Alan, once it's safe for yeh.'

'Yer man said it was just a little nick. He was back in work the next day.'

'How and where does all this happen?'

'There's this doctor, he flies in from Holland every few weeks. He has a clinic in one of the houses down there in Wicklow. He does a couple of fellas over the weekend and then he's gone as quick as he came. I have a phone number here to ring, to get me name put down on the list. So wha' de yeh think, Kathleen?'

'It sounds great, Alan, and it means I won't have to worry any more, watchin' meself all the time, wonderin' every month am I pregnant or not.' Then I thought of something else. 'But how much is this all goin' to cost us?'

'Around a hundred pound.'

'Oh my God, Alan, where are we supposed to get tha' kind of money?'

'It's all right, Kathleen. I've it all worked out. I'll get a loan off me Da, tellin' him the car is givin' me trouble, and yeh know wha' he's like. There'll be no rush havin' to pay him back all in one go. I'll give him a few bob every now and then when we have it. He'll be none the wiser.'

'Jaysus, Alan. Yeh gave me a fright there for a minute. I thought yeh were goin' to say yer Da knew wha' yeh were up to. I'd never be able to look him straight in the face again. Yeh know wha' they're all like about religion.' I thought about my own side of the family then. 'Christ, Alan, I just got a flash of me Da there. Wha'ever yeh do, never tell him about this. I'd never hear the end of it, with him tellin' me I'm flyin' in the face of God. And then there's Ma. I don't think she'd bat an eyelid, and knowin' her she'll be happy enough tha' I'm not bringin' any more babies into the world. There'll be some lame excuse made by her, glossin' things over as usual when it suits, of course.'

'Right then, it's settled. Yeh're happy enough with everythin' I've told yeh, Kathleen?'

'Would yeh have a look at me face, Alan, I can't get the smile off it. Believe me, I'm more than happy yeh're gettin' this done.'

* * *

A few weeks went by before the appointment came through. Alan thought he'd never get there, to get it over and done with. Not really knowing what to expect and just in case he felt a bit ropey on the way home, he brought my younger brother Thomas with him for a bit of company, swearing him to secrecy.

The night seemed endless and they seemed to be gone forever. I paced the floor as I watched the clock every few minutes. Finally the car pulled up. I was so relieved when Alan walked in the door, looking very pale, I might add, but also very pleased with himself.

'Sit down there, Alan, and I'll make us a cup of tea. Then yeh can tell me all about it.'

He filled me in on what had gone on at the doctor's. 'Now yeh know all the gory details of what was said and done, Kathleen. I'll tell yeh the good part,' he started laughing his head off, not able to get the words out.

'Are yeh goin' to tell me or wha'?'

'Righ', are yeh ready? We've to have sex, sex, sex, and sex again, as often as we can, as much as possible.'

I started laughing. 'Will yeh stop yer messin', Alan.'

'I'm tellin' yeh, Kathleen. The doctor told me there's millions of them little swimmers down there tha' I have to get rid of, or it won't be safe for yeh. Yeh'll end up gettin' pregnant again, and we don't want tha', do we? So it's up to us how long it takes before we get the all-clear.'

Once I heard that, there was no stopping me. Alan would only be in the door and as soon as I got the kids out of the way and the coast was clear, I would be giving him the nod, the eye and the wink. There was no way I was having any more babies, so whatever it took, I was on for it. Having said that, we had the best fun along the way, and Alan had a permanent smile on his face.

After about two months we finally decided to have a test done, which meant Alan had to fill a little bottle. I won't go into the details!

'Righ', Kathleen, today's the day.' He handed me the bottle.

'Why are yeh givin' it to me, Alan? Yeh're bringin' it to the hospital, not me.'

'Jaysus, Kathleen, I don't want to go in there with all them nurses and all. Anyway, I can't be late for work. Yeh know I have me name down on the transfer list for Tallaght and I don't want them thinkin' I'm acting the mick. Yeh know tha' this will have to be done a couple of times, just to be on the safe side. So it's best tha' you go from day one. Go on, Kathleen . . . please.'

'Righ' then, Alan. Wha' do I have to do?'

'Well, it has to be kept at body temperature. So yeh'll have to put it on yeh somewhere until yeh get to the hospital. Yeh can't delay, Kathleen; yeh'll have to get in there as quick as yeh can. We don't want any of them little swimmers dying before yeh can get them tested.'

'Well, I'll tell yeh one thing for nothin', Alan, it won't be goin' down me knickers, and tha's for sure. I'll stick it in between me diddies. It'll be safe enough there.'

I got a quick kiss on the cheek and Alan was out the door like a light, in case I changed my mind. I dropped Martina off to school, and got myself into town in no time. So there I was, charging up O'Connell Street, heading for the Rotunda Hospital, pushing Amanda in the buggy and dragging young Alan along the way, all the while checking that the little bottle was still there. Only to be told, when I phoned up a few days later, that the results were still positive.

'I'm afraid, Mrs McGrath, that everything is still very much positive. Come back again in a month's time.'

* * *

And that's what I did, for the next couple of months, with the results the same each time – positive.

'Alan, I don't think tha' this is after workin'. One of the nurses was sayin' to me tha' yeh should be gettin' negative results by now. She said for us to go along to the family plannin' clinic and have a chat with them there.'

'Kathleen, the reason I didn't go there in the first place was because of our age. Yeh're only twenty-six, I'm twenty-seven. They won't do it, I'm tellin' yeh. One of the fellas was sayin' he knew somebody tha' was turned down because they were too young.'

'Come on, Alan. It's worth a try. Wha's the worst thing tha' can happen? Only that they say no.'

* * *

So in I went and made the appointment, which we weren't too long waiting on. I remember the morning we were heading in to see the doctor. Alan seemed to be nervous and never stopped talking, which is unusual for him.

'We have to get this righ', Kathleen. So I want to talk to yeh about a few things before we get there.'

'Wha' about, Alan? '

'Now don't get annoyed with me when I say this, but yeh know the way sometimes yeh can come out with things without thinkin'? Yeh just say wha's on the tip of yer tongue. Well, when the doctor asks yeh a few questions, will yeh try and not be so blunt? Just go along with wha'ever he's sayin'. I don't want anythin' to go against us here.'

'Yeh mean yeh want me to suck up to him. Is tha' wha' yeh're tryin' to say, Alan?'

'Yeah, if tha's wha' it takes, Kathleen. So, will yeh just be careful how yeh phrase things?'

'Yeh're worryin' yerself too much, Alan, but if it makes yeh happy, I'll try and not be too outspoken. Now, come on, let's go in and get this over with.'

It wasn't long before we were sitting in front of the doctor, who was very nice and didn't waste any time in launching into what he had to say.

'Well now, Alan, I see here from your form that you had a vasectomy carried out less than a year ago.'

'Tha's righ', doctor. But it doesn't seem to have worked. Tha's why we're here.'

'In you go there behind the curtain, Alan, so I can examine you.'

They were in there for a while, and I could hear Alan talking away, telling the doctor all about who did it and where he had it done. The doctor didn't say very much on the subject, only to confirm what we already knew – it hadn't worked.

'Now,' said the doctor as he sat back down in his chair, 'I have just one or two questions I would like to ask both of you. Why do you want to get such a permanent job done? I mean, you're very young to be thinking along those lines.'

'Well,' said Alan, 'we had a good talk about this, doctor, and both of us decided tha' we definitely don't want any more kids and tha's for sure.'

'I understand that, but there are contraception methods out there you could use. For instance, Alan, there's Durex; or Kathleen, you could take the pill.'

'Excuse me, doctor,' I said, 'if it's okay, can I say somethin' here?'

You could see Alan breaking into a sweat, not knowing what I was going to say.

'By all means, Kathleen, I would like very much to hear what you have to say.'

'Well, first of all, I can't take the pill – it makes me go crazy mad. I wanted to kill everybody around me when I was on it and tha's not good. And about them Johnny Overcoat things, it's all righ' usin' them now and again, but not forever. Anyway, they're not tha' easy to get.'

'I have to say, Kathleen, that's the first time I've ever heard them called that. Anyway, carry on.'

'No, tha's it, doctor. This is the route we want to take.'

'Hmm, I see. Now, I have just one more thing I would like to ask.' He was looking straight at me as he spoke. 'What if, in a few years' time, you get the longing for another baby? You might be sorry.'

I looked over at Alan while I thought for a second or two. I could see the panic on his face, not knowing what I was going to come out with. I didn't know myself; the words just seemed to flow out of me.

'I don't think tha' will happen, doctor. But if for some reason it does, well then, we'll adopt. Isn't tha' righ', Alan? We did talk about this, doctor, and most definitely tha's wha' we would do.'

'Both of you seem to have your minds made up about this, but because you are so young, I will have to consult with my colleagues and we will let you know in a day or two.'

We must have given the doctor all the answers he wanted to hear, because a few days later Alan had his appointment to get the job done once more, with the results being negative on the first go. Alan was so relieved when I told him, but not half as much as I was.

9

The Priest and the Pay Packet

I had made a good few friends and got to know so many people around Darndale through the hairdressing, and I had tried really hard to settle, especially since the holiday, knowing that I was able to make good money where we were living. But I still longed to live back over near Ma and Da in Crumlin. I missed my brothers and sisters so much; no money could put a price on that. I also knew that if I was able to set myself up once, well, why not again?

With that thought in my mind, I was more determined than ever to move. Alan was happy enough to go along with the plan, which was to save every penny we could and try to get a deposit to buy our own house. But in the meantime, he came in one evening, excited as hell.

'Kathleen, I've great news. Not only for meself, but for you as well. I got me transfer. I'm movin' up to the factory in Tallaght. This not only means tha' I'll be on better money, but we'll be eligible for a house – back over on the southside of the city. It'll be like killin' two birds with one stone.'

'How come, Alan? I don't understand. Why would the Corporation let us change houses just because yeh're movin' in yer job?'

'I found out tha' once yeh live so many miles away from where yeh work, yeh can put in to move. So wha' de yeh think of tha', Kathleen?'

'Oh my God, tha's great news, Alan. Tha' means with the money we have saved we'll be able to do the new house up really nice, and maybe have enough over to buy a shed for me to do the hairdressing in. It doesn't have to be big, just enough room for meself and one or two clients.'

'Jaysus, Kathleen, there's no flies on you. Yeh're always two steps ahead of yerself. Always plannin' away in tha' head of yers, which is no harm at the end of the day.'

'Will yeh mind movin'? I mean, after all the work yeh done in the house, Alan.'

'I knew yeh'd never settle, Kathleen, no matter how hard yeh tried. It's just too far for yeh. So I think it's best tha' we make the move while the chance is there and as yeh said, we have the few bob to do it up straight away. I'll go in first thing in the mornin' and get the forms.'

* * *

There was no way we could get a house in Crumlin or anywhere in or around there. They were like gold dust. The only place that was on offer to us was Tallaght – a place called Killinarden, which we took in the end.

Ma was a bit upset when I told her where we were going to move to.

'I've been prayin' to the Holy Mother herself, mornin', noon and night. I've been askin' her to try and get yiz a little house beside me.'

'I know, Ma, and I would have loved nothin' better, but at least this house is only one bus run for me. Sure I'll be down to yeh all the time. Just wait and see.'

'Every time I think of tha' oul' Pop fella and wha' he did on yiz – havin' to walk away from the lovely home yeh built around yerselves, and not even six months gone by when the fucker went and died, with the house goin' back to the Corporation. May he still be burnin' in hell for wha' he done.'

'Jaysus, Ma. Will yeh keep yer voice down! If Alan hears yeh, no matter wha', he was his grandda.'

'Ah, I can't help meself, Kathleen. When I think back to the way things were. The two of us always together, goin' up and down to the shops, pickin' up our few bargains. Alan droppin' in every other evenin' to pick yeh up. Me and him would sit there havin' a smoke and an oul' yap. De yeh not think I miss all tha'?'

'I tell yeh wha', Ma. We've to pick the keys up in the next couple of days. Why don't yeh come with us?'

That cheered her up a little. 'I suppose I could do tha'. It'll let me see how far it is for when I want to drop out to yeh.'

Just then, Clare came charging in. 'Ma, Ma, Ma – look wha' I have for yeh.' She handed over a little brown envelope. 'I found it up the road. It was lying there on the ground – it's full of money!'

Sure enough, when Ma opened it, it was full of pound notes.

'Phil!' she roared in to Da, who was sitting in the kitchen with Alan, the pair of them talking away, lost in conversation as usual. 'Phil, did yeh hear me?'

'I heard yeh the first time, Lil. Now, wha's all the racket about?'

'Have a look at tha'. There's a name on the front. De yeh know who it is?'

'I can't say I do, but whoever he is I'd say he's frantic by now, after losin' his wage packet.'

Ma sat there thinking for a minute or two as she held on to the money.

'Righ', Kathleen,' she said, 'de yeh want to come for a walk with me?'

'Okay, Ma, but where are we goin'?'

'We'll go up to the priest, see wha' he has to say. Maybe he'll say somethin' about it after mass in the mornin'. Clare, get me coat – yeh're comin' with us, yeh can tell him exactly where yeh found it.'

'Ma, why don't yeh just keep it for yerself? If yeh give it to the priest, tha's probably wha' he'll do,' said Clare.

'I wouldn't have an hour's luck if I did the likes of it, and if yer father hears wha's after comin' out of yer mouth, we'll never hear the end of it.'

'But I was only sayin', Ma.'

'I know, I know, and yeh were a good girl to bring the money in to me, but there's just some things tha' yeh don't do and this is one of them. Now, hand the coat over here to me. Are yeh righ', Kathleen? It'll be dark before we know it, best we make a move.'

So off the three of us headed to the priest's house, while Alan and Da kept an eye on the kids. I looked around as we went through the big iron gates. The grass was neatly cut and there were lots of fresh flowers planted throughout the garden. Not a pebble out of place. Snow-white lace curtains hung perfectly through the gleaming glass windows.

Ma stood there as proud as Punch as she knocked on the door, telling us, 'Wait 'til yeh see Father's face, how pleased he'll be when I hand him the pay packet. He won't be able to thank me enough for being so honest.'

She knocked and knocked again, giving the door a good hard bang on the third go. With that the lights went on and the door was opened. It was the priest, who stood there in all his black, looking as cranky as hell and not a glimmer of a smile on his face. He lashed out at us before Ma could get a chance to open her mouth.

'What is it? What are you looking for at this hour of the night? Can it not wait until tomorrow?' I looked over at Ma and I could see that she was really taken aback. It was far from what she expected and it took her a few seconds before she opened her mouth.

'Is it beggin' tha' yeh think I'm up here for, Father? Is tha' wha' yeh're thinkin'? Well, shame on yeh, tha's all I have to say. God help any poor craythur tha' would be needin' a bit of help, if this is wha' they have to listen to. Shame on yeh again, Father!' With that Ma took out the pay packet and placed it in his hand. 'If it's not puttin' yeh out too much, me child found this a little while ago and I'm sure the poor man is at his wits' end with worry as to how he and his family will get through the week, with not a penny in his pocket. I'd like for yeh to mention it after mass in the mornin' – of course, without sayin' whose name is on it. I don't want any Tom, Dick or Harry tryin' to put a claim on it. And I'll be there meself, of course, if tha's okay with yeh, Father.'

Well, he started to suck up to Ma then, but she wasn't having any of it.

'How kind of you for being so honest. You will get your rewards in heaven for this. What was it you said your name was?'

'I didn't – and yeh can forget yer fancy words and yer airs and graces, it's too late.'

She turned her back and beckoned for us to follow. He was left standing there with his mouth open, and rightly so. We were only out the gate when Clare got her spoke in.

'I told yeh. Yeh should've kept it.'

Ma took no heed of Clare. She walked along in silence, too upset to say anything. As soon as we got home, I told Da what had happened. But of course, he made all sorts of excuses for the priest. They could do no wrong in his eyes. Religion played a big part in Ma and Da's life; the church and priest were always up there on a pedestal, never to be questioned.

The priest wasn't long finding out where Ma lived and made it his business to drop in to see her, letting her know how thankful the man was for the return of his money. He knew how wrong he had been and glossed things over well.

'Well, seein' yeh put it like tha' . . .' said Ma. 'Would yeh like a cup of tea, Father?' All was forgiven.

* * *

A few days later, we picked up the keys from the Corporation and collected Ma on the way. We were up in Tallaght in no time. It was like driving onto a building site. There were no roads, no shops, no schools – nothing. Just a couple of rows of houses plonked in the middle of the mountains.

'This can't be it. Yeh must've taken a wrong turn, Alan.'

'No, I didn't, Kathleen. Killinarden was on the sign as we drove in. Come on, let's see where number seventy is.'

Ma was puffing away on her Woodbines as we struggled through the muck. 'De yeh know somethin', Kathleen?'

'Wha's tha', Ma?'

'This brings back memories to me, so it does, of when I saw me house in Crumlin for the first time. It wasn't too far off like this and I have to say it was the best feelin' ever.'

Just then Alan called out to us. 'Are yeh righ'? It's this one over here.'

There must have been a couple of pounds of muck on the soles of my shoes by the time I got to the house, but I didn't care. I was so happy with what I saw. It was a big corner house, with a fine-sized front garden and a driveway for the car. The inside was just as impressive, but what really got me going was the back garden. It was huge. My brain started ticking over like a race car. I was planning everything out by the second.

'Alan, would yeh have a look at this? We could put a shed along tha' wall for me hairdressin'. I could plant loads of flowers over there. Good Jaysus, there's a back entrance as well. The clients could come in tha' way. Tha' means they won't have to come near the front of the house. I can't believe it, Alan. This is great. It couldn't have turned out any better if we'd planned it!'

'Yeh're gas, Kathleen, most women would be goin' on about doin' the inside of the house up, but not you. Yer business brain always gets in there first. Anyway, I'll have tha' up and runnin' in no time for yeh. Now, we'd better get back inside to yer mother, before she lets out one of her famous screams. She'll frighten the shite out of the builders if she starts.'

Ma wasn't long getting her spoke in. 'I have to say, it's a fine house – there's no way yeh'd get the likes of it anywhere around Crumlin. Yeh have three fine bedrooms there, and would yeh have a look at this kitchen? It's twice the size of mine and then there's tha' big long window in the sittin' room – right down to the ground, with the sun beamin' through it. Yiz landed on yer feet all right. I'm more than happy for yeh.'

'Tha's great, Ma. Tha's after takin' such a load off me mind, just to hear yeh say tha'. Yeh were so upset the other night when I told yeh about the new house. I had meself up the walls with worry, thinkin' about yeh going up and down to the shops on yer own and missin' us and all.'

'I feel a lot better in meself, Kathleen, now tha' I see where yeh're goin' to be livin'. And it's not as far as I expected, so we can take turns droppin' up and down to one another. Tha's if it's okay with yerself, Alan, and knowin' me, half of the gang will tag along.'

'Tha'll never be a problem, Lil. Yeh'll always be more than welcome and I think yeh know tha'.'

'Good. Now we better get back before yer father tears the little bit of hair out tha' he has left on his head, mindin' all them kids.'

As Alan and Ma made their way back to the car, I stood in the garden for a minute or two, giving the house a final look-over. I knew straight away that it was going to be our home for many years to come.

'I know I will definitely settle here.'

10

The Shed

I felt a bit sad when we were moving from Darndale. Even after four and a half years, I still hadn't really settled in, but I knew in the long run that it was best all round for us.

It didn't take us too long to get everything organised. We had moved and were living in Tallaght within the week. Because we had a good few bob saved, we were able to do up the inside of the house straight away. Alan did most of the work himself, so we saved a fair bit of money there.

After about nine months, when most things in the house were done, I had just enough left over to set myself up with my hairdressing business – which, by the way, was to be in a six-by-ten-foot Barna shed. I know, I know; how could you work in something so small? Well, I did, and that's what got me started in my career.

I was so excited the day we went out to buy the shed. We were out for hours, looking everywhere we could think of, trying to get the best deal. I kept getting drawn over to the big fancy sheds. My mouth was watering, thinking of all I could do with the big windows and porch to the front. In my mind

I could see it all done up with snow-white blinds on the windows, a couple of hanging baskets here and there, and maybe a few terracotta pots stuck over in the corner on the porch, all bursting with flowers of every colour you could think of.

But Alan wasn't long bringing me back to reality. He tipped me on the shoulder.

'Come on, Kathleen, yeh're only annoying yerself lookin' at these. There's no way we could afford anythin' like this. Tha's more wha' I had in mind.' He pointed over to the six-by-ten-foot Barna shed.

I sighed. 'Yeh're righ', Alan, tha'll have to do me to get started. As they say, yeh have to creep before yeh walk. And I could always put one hangin' basket beside tha' little window, couldn't I?'

'Tha's my girl. We'll ask yer man how soon he can have it delivered.'

* * *

That happened to be bright and early the very next day.

'Righ', Kathleen,' said Alan, 'they have the shed put together and I've arranged for two fellas to come later on to put the water and electricity in. Now, show me where yeh want everythin'.'

'I have it all worked out in me head, Alan. Put the hooded hair dryer and chair there to the left as I open the door. In the middle I want me dressin' mirror and chair; tha's where I'll work on the clients. Put the sink over there to yer righ' in the corner and I want two shelves above it. They'll hold the shampoo bottles and me bit of stock. Oh, I nearly forgot, Alan – some lino for the floor. Will yeh try and get some of tha' heavy-duty stuff? It'll help keep the heat in and with tha' small heater we have it'll be nice and cosy. So wha' de yeh think?'

'Jaysus, Kathleen, it's goin' to be very tight. Yeh'll barely be able to move, but knowin' you tha' won't stop yeh. Anyway, it won't take me long, I'll have all this done in a couple of days.'

* * *

When it was finished it was tiny but looked really well. That was me ready and rearing to go. All I needed now were a few clients. That was going to be a bit harder this time around, since there was absolutely nothing in the area whatsoever. Only a shop van selling groceries, which just happened to be parked on the road we lived on, which turned out to be lucky for me in the end.

'Alan, you were up buyin' cigarettes off yer man in the van. Wha's he like?'

'He seems friendly enough. Why?'

'De yeh think he'd let me put up a sign about me hairdressin'?'

'Sure all yeh can do is ask him, Kathleen, but I don't imagine there'll be a problem.'

And there wasn't – he was so helpful. The following morning I dropped the kids off extra early to school and was over at the van as he opened the doors.

'Howyeh, mister. I'm Kathleen and I was wonderin' if yeh could put this sign up on the door of yer van for me? I'll throw a free hair cut in for yerself if yeh do.'

'Certainly, love, hand it in here to me. By the way, I'm Paddy. Is it on this road yeh live or the houses at the back of the estate? So's I can tell people when they ask.'

'Jaysus, tha' would be great if yeh could do tha' for me. It's the last corner house on the righ'-hand side at the end of the road – see, there.' I pointed down. 'And I'll tell yeh wha', Paddy, I'll trim yer beard for yeh as well. So don't forget to drop down.'

He did just that and seemed very pleased with the results, telling all who came to his van about me.

Martina and young Alan went to school over on the far side of the main road, through a settled estate called Springfield, which had been there for the past couple of years. It was a good distance from our house, so I made sure I got my spoke in as I walked along chatting to all the other mothers.

It took a while but the word started to spread around and in no time at all I had my first client.

* * *

I'll never forget the first morning I opened up. I was feeling a bit nervous as it was, but when I heard the back gate open, my insides did a somersault. A very tall woman walked in – and I mean tall. I thought to myself, *Good fuck, she'll never fit in me shed*. I didn't get a chance to open my mouth; she launched straight in.

'Righ',' she said, 'are you the wan tha's doin' the hairs? Yer man at the van said I was to come in the back gate – is tha' okay?'

'Yeah, yeah, tha's fine. I asked him to tell people for me.'

I was sweating as she sat in the chair, hoping and praying that she would be looking in the mirror and not at the roof of the shed. I could just about see her face in the mirror and got away with it.

I went to introduce myself but got stopped in my tracks again. 'Now,' she said, 'I just want to say a few things before I let yeh near me. I've had me hair done many times over the years and was never happy. So I started doin' it meself and, as yeh can see, I've made a righ' fuckin' mess of it. I couldn't give two shites about the rest of me, but when it comes to me hair, it's me pride and joy. So I hope yeh get it righ' on the first go.

Cause yeh see this mouth of mine? Well, it'll either do wonders for yeh or it won't. So am I clear in wha' I'm sayin'?'

I was starting to shit myself at that stage and I hadn't even touched a hair on her head, which was a canary yellow colour with about six inches of black roots – and she said she was fussy!

I cleared my throat, hoping that what I wanted to say would come out right. 'First of all, before we go any further, I'm Kathleen. Yeh're very welcome; and yer name is?'

'Me name is Rosalina, but everybody calls me Ro.'

'Well now, Ro, wha' we're goin' to do first is have a little chat. You tell me wha' yeh like and don't like and I'll throw a few suggestions in along the way and I'm sure we'll come up with a nice style between us.'

She had settled down by the time I was finished talking. I worked for the best part of the morning transforming her hair. I was very happy with the results; all I needed now was for Ro to feel the same.

I stood there anxiously waiting as she checked the colour out, played around with her fringe and fluffed the back of her hair out a few times, still not saying a word.

'Well, wha' de yeh think, Ro? De yeh like it?'

'It's massive, Kay. I fuckin' love it. Wait 'til all me sisters and friends see this. I'm tellin' yeh, yeh'll be out the door with work by the time I'm finished.'

Thank God, I thought. The relief – I was able to breathe again!

'Oh, by the way, Ro, as I said, me name's Kathleen.'

'Well, I hate long names, righ', so I'll be callin' yeh Kay.'

It didn't matter how many times I said it, she always called me Kay and that's what I became known as in the hairdressing business.

* * *

Ro went on to be one of my best clients and a good friend over the years, spreading the word about me to all she knew. After that first day I couldn't believe the number of people who were knocking on the front door or coming in the back gate.

I was so busy and, with the shed being so small, I had to start taking appointments, which was better for me in the long run. I would try to do as many haircuts as I could while the kids were at school. If I couldn't fit a client in at that time, I would work the odd evening when they were in bed.

There was one evening in particular that always sticks out in my mind. Josie, who became a regular client, asked me if I could do her perm after hours, which wasn't a problem – or so I thought. She arrived on the dot of eight as planned.

'There yeh are, Kay, thanks for fittin' me in at this late hour. I would have come durin' the day, but I just couldn't get anybody to mind the four kids for me and there's no way I'd go into hospital lookin' like this. So make sure tha' yeh give me a nice tight perm tha' will last me a while, because as soon as this baby comes into the world, God only knows how long it will be before I'll be around to see yeh again.'

'Josie, yeh seem to be goin' around forever with tha' bump. When exactly are yeh due?'

'I should have been gone two weeks ago, Kay. I don't know wha's wrong this time. I'm always bang on me dates. If this keeps up they'll have to put a bomb up me arse to shift me.'

'Two weeks, yeh say, Josie? Tha' means yeh could go any minute . . . No, I don't think I should give yeh a perm. Just get a cut and blowdry until afterwards.'

'Ah, for Jaysus' sake, Kay, don't say tha'. I've been lookin' forward to gettin' me hair done all day. Sure come on, don't be worryin', yeh'll have it done in no time at all. Yeh know you – yeh're like Flash Gordon when yeh start.'

So I went against my better judgement and started the perm. 'Righ' then, Josie, lie back there at the sink and I'll get yeh washed.' She had tons of hair, which meant I had a good few hours' work ahead of me.

I was halfway through the perm when I saw Josie bite her lip and make a few faces. I didn't want to keep going on about it, so I didn't say anything but kept working and chatting away, trying to get the perm done as quickly as I could. That was, until she let out such a roar and then went into the heavy breathing sound.

'Holy Jaysus, Josie, yeh're after frightenin' the life out of me. You didn't just start gettin' pains now – when did yeh go into labour?'

'Kay, I'm sorry for lyin', but I hate me hair straight and I really wanted me curls back in. I knew if I told yeh there was no way yeh'd do it for me.'

'Josie, tell me, when did yeh start?' I was actually grinding my teeth at this stage as I spoke.

'Me waters broke early this afternoon. Ah! Ah! Ah!' she roared, over and over again.

'Oh my God, oh my God! That means yeh're not far off havin' this baby. Wha' am I goin' to do? I'll have to get the ambulance.'

'I want me hair finished. Yeh can't let me go into the hospital with me hair straight on one side and curly on the other.'

'Fuck yer hair, Josie! Who de yeh think yeh are, the Holy Mother herself? De yeh want to deliver yer baby here in me little shed? Now please, come on, I'll have to get yeh to the hospital."

I screamed in for Alan to come out to me while I tried to calm myself and Josie down. He didn't waste any time in phoning for the ambulance.

Josie was rocking and roaring in the chair but I managed to take the rollers out and was spraying water like mad to rinse the lotion out.

'I promise yeh, Josie, when yeh come home I'll come round to yer house and do yer hair.' I was doing and saying anything I could think of to pacify her. At this stage she was bent over in pain and didn't give two shites what I was saying. 'Now, come on, yeh know wha' to do – big deep breaths. In and out, in and out, tha's it'

I was never so happy to hear an ambulance siren. The two men were so friendly and took charge straight away.

'There you go, madam, your chariot awaits.' One of them helped her into the wheelchair and took her out through the back gate to the ambulance.

'Don't worry, Josie,' I shouted after her. 'I'll slip around and tell Eddie tha' yeh're gone to the hospital.'

I made my way around to the house straight away. Eddie wasn't too happy when I told him what had happened.

'For fuck sake, Kay – I told her not to go around, but would she listen? No! Sorry about all this, I'd better make me way down to the Coombe. I'll let yeh know what happens. Thanks again.'

I couldn't believe it the next day when he told me the news – that their little baby was born in the back of the ambulance as they drove down the Greenhills Road, less than ten minutes' drive from my house. I got the shakes just thinking about what could have been.

I gave Josie a couple of days after she came home from the hospital before I made my way around to do her hair. She was well pleased when she saw me standing there. It was far from funny at the time, but we had a good laugh about how easily her baby boy could have been born in my little shed.

* * *

Over the next two years I saved every penny I could, cutting corners every which way I could, always with the help of Alan. I had a goal set in my mind, which was to expand my business. So I decided it was time for me to get a proper building out in my back garden. It looked like a real hairdressing salon by the time Alan was finished, with plenty of room this time, which helped me to go from strength to strength, building up a very good established business. But it was my little shed that got me off the ground, and that I will never forget.

11

The Runaway

I was very lucky to be able to work from home. That way I was there all the time for the kids, who were starting to get a bit older and needed a good eye kept on them, especially Martina. She was around eleven and a half at that stage, as cocky as they come, trying to be more grown up than her years, but I wouldn't be long putting her in her place.

Except for one occasion. It was Saturday afternoon. I was busy working on a client's hair when in she walked.

'Hi, Ma, can I go down to the roller rink in Crumlin? There's a whole load of girls goin'.'

'Yeh know yeh're not allowed, so the answer is no. Now, go back out to the front of the house and play around. And keep an eye to Amanda when yeh're there.'

'Ah, Ma! Please? Go on. Yeh never let me do anythin'.'

That's when I gave her the look, which should have been enough; but no, she kept it up, going on and on at me, hoping I would say yes in front of the client. There was no way that was going to happen.

'I'm sorry about this, Mary. I'll be back in two minutes.'

I took Martina by the hand, half-dragging her out the door, with the client shouting after me, 'Don't worry about me, Kay. I know wha' they're like. I have a few little fuckers at home meself. Do yer head in, they would.'

'Martina, wha' did I tell yeh about goin' on and on at me when I'm workin'?'

'But Ma, they're all goin'.'

'I don't give two shites who's goin' where – *you're* not. Now get yerself back out there and don't move off the road. De yeh hear me?'

As I made my way back to the client, little did I know the worry and upset that was ahead for me that night.

* * *

It was around half past five when I finished work and locked up for the night. My younger sister Patricia arrived just as I was about to call the kids in.

'Howyeh, Kathleen. Any chance of a haircut? I would've been up earlier than this only I missed the bloody bus.'

'Go on in, Patricia. I'll be with yeh in a minute.'

I turned to young Alan. 'De yeh know where Martina is?'

'She said tha' she was goin' up to the shops, Ma.'

'Did she now – well, I'll sort her out as soon as she comes in. It'll be straight up to bed for her for goin' against me. Now, come in, the pair of yeh. It's startin' to get dark out.'

'Wha's wrong with yeh, Kathleen?' said Patricia. 'Yeh're all fired up. Is it me comin' late?'

'Jaysus, no, Patricia. It's Martina; she's gone off the road and I told her not to move. She keeps wantin' to do things tha' she's too young for. I swear, when I get me hands on her . . .'

'Yeh know somethin', Kathleen, yeh sound exactly like Ma. Now, will yeh sit yerself down and I'll make yeh a nice cup of tea. Wait'll yeh see, she'll be knockin' on the door in the next half-hour, suckin' up to yeh. I used to do it with Ma all the time.'

'Ah, I suppose yeh're righ', Patricia. De yeh really think I'm like Ma?'

'Yeah!'

I had the dinner on in no time, while the other two watched the telly with Patricia. I was still uneasy, so I slipped up to the shop, checking to see if Martina had been in. The women said no. She wasn't to be found anywhere. I had myself in a right tizzy as I walked back to the house, thinking all the while, *If tha' little bitch is after makin' her way down to tha' roller rink, I swear to Jaysus I'll fuckin' kill her. No, she wouldn't do tha'. Sure where would she get the money from?*

Then it dawned on me; that's when my blood really started to boil. As soon as I got to the house, I went straight upstairs to where I kept my bill money and, sure enough, thirty pounds was missing. Talk about being worked up! I was doing somersaults in my head.

It was just as well Alan walked in then because I was getting ready to let out such a scream that I would have frightened the life out of the other two kids. I was ranting and raving so much, Alan couldn't make sense of what was coming out of my mouth.

'Good Jaysus, Kathleen, will yeh calm yerself down and tell me wha's after happenin'?'

So I went into the goings-on of the day. I was convinced in my mind that Martina was down in the roller rink. Alan checked straight away – not a sign of her there, or at any of her friends' houses. Up to this, I had been so angry at her for not doing what she was told and then, to top it off, robbing money!

There was no way Patricia was going to get her hair done that evening. Instead, she ended up looking after the younger kids for me.

My anger soon changed to fear as we walked the streets looking in every nook and cranny of the estate, with not a sighting of her anywhere to be found. I was frantic and sick to the pit of my stomach, as was Alan.

It was now ten o'clock and we were starting to think the worst. It was rare back then to hear of a child going missing and never to be found, but it did happen. With that thought in both of our minds, we decided to go to the police, only to be told that she had to be missing for twenty-four hours before they could do anything about it. But they asked us for a description of Martina and what clothing she was wearing, letting us know that the local cars would keep an eye out for her.

I don't know how Alan drove the car home that night. He was green in the face with worry, but still trying to keep a front up for me. I was falling to pieces, thinking only the worst.

'Come on, Kathleen, she's probably in somebody's house tha' we haven't checked. I'll go around again when we get home. Now, try and pull yerself together. Yeh'll only be upsettin' the other two kids.'

'Yeh're righ', Alan. Tha's wha' it is. She's hidin' out in somebody's house, too afraid to come home after wha' she's done.'

When Alan dropped me off to go and check once more, I tried really hard to keep that thought in my mind, at the same time hoping and praying that she would be there when I walked into the house. But there was only Patricia sitting there, with young Alan and Amanda asleep beside her.

Martina was nowhere to be found. Alan paced the floor, smoking his brains out while I drank cup of tea after cup of tea.

* * *

101

It was coming up to midnight when the phone rang. I had it in my hand before Alan could get to it.

'Hello? . . . Hello!' I said. There was silence at the other end. 'Martina, is tha' you? Please tell me where yeh are and we'll come and get yeh.'

A young girl's voice answered me – not Martina. 'Yeh're all righ', Mrs McGrath, we're okay.' And that was it – she hung up.

I stood there with the phone in my hand, my mouth open, unable to speak. Alan was frantic.

'Kathleen, will yeh say somethin', for Jaysus' sake! Was tha' Martina?'

'No, no, Alan, it wasn't her. It was some young wan, sayin' they're okay, and then she hung up. Wha' will we do? Should we phone the police and tell them?'

'Yeh heard wha' they said, Kathleen, we'll have to wait it out and hope tha' she's safe in somebody's house.'

'We can't just sit here, we have to do somethin'. I'm going back out again to look for her.'

Alan came over and put his arm around me. 'Come on, love, there's no point. I've been everywhere. Anyway, it's best tha' we're here, just in case she comes home.'

* * *

That was one of the longest nights of my life. I never closed my eyes for one second. I cried and cried so much, thinking the worst all the time. Eventually the light shone through the sitting-room windows. It was morning at last. I looked over at Alan, who looked tired and worn out with worry, but still trying to keep a front up for all of us.

Patricia looked after the kids while we both walked the streets once more, looking everywhere and anywhere we thought she might be. Still she was nowhere to be found. My legs were starting to go from under me as we made our way back to the house. I couldn't help myself. I was falling to pieces. Alan got me to lie down on the couch, trying to calm me down.

'Please, Kathleen, try and keep it together. Yeh're upsettin' the other two kids.'

'I know, I know, I'm sorry, Alan. Amanda, come over here, pet. Young Alan, sit down here beside me.'

I sat there with my arms around both of them for I don't know how long, as I watched the minutes on the clock tick by.

Then the phone rang. I nearly jumped out of myself, I got such a fright. Alan answered it this time. I was sitting there with my hands up to my mouth, not knowing what to expect as I listened to him speak.

'Yes, yes, tha's righ'. I'm Mr McGrath. Okay, could yeh hold onto them for me? It'll take me about fifteen minutes to get there.' He hung up. 'Come on, Kathleen, she's okay. Tha' was the receptionist up in the Downshire Hotel in Blessington. They booked in there last night.'

'Did I hear yeh righ', Alan? Martina's been in a hotel all night? Is tha' wha' yeh're sayin'?'

'Kathleen, let's just go and get her. We'll talk about this later.'

'Wait 'til I get me hands on her, Alan. I'm goin' to fuckin' kill her for wha' she's after puttin' us through.'

* * *

Alan drove so fast there was smoke coming out of the wheels. We were there in no time at all.

Just as we were walking in the front door of the hotel, Martina and another girl whom I recognised – she lived in a house on our estate – were walking down the stairs, with not a care in the world and looking none the worse for wear. They stopped dead in their tracks, not knowing where to look when they saw us and at the same time getting ready to run. Of course, they didn't get a chance to do that; Alan made sure of it.

Out of the corner of my eye, I happened to get a glance over at the reception area, where two wans were standing there, giggling to one another. I was fit to be tied and wasn't long letting them know how I felt.

'I'm glad yeh're amused. De yeh realise the night we're after havin'? Why didn't one of yeh get the police to check them out? Surely to God yeh knew they were too young? And by the way, where did yeh get our phone number from?'

'One of the young girls phoned down to reception for an outside line. The number was in the log,' one of them replied.

'Well then, why the hell didn't yeh ring us last night?'

Neither of them knew what to say or where to look.

'Leave it, Kathleen,' said Alan. 'Take the pair of them out to the car while I talk to the women.'

My first reaction was to hug Martina, as any mother would do. I was so happy that she was okay and safe. Then my blood started to boil as I sat there in the car thinking about the night we had just been put through. All I kept hearing was 'Sorry Ma', 'Sorry Mrs McGrath'. I would neither look at nor answer either one. I was afraid that if I opened my mouth, I wouldn't be able to hold back. I thought it best to wait until I got into my own house; then I'd explode.

There wasn't a word spoken all the way home. We dropped the young girl off outside her house, making sure she went in. As soon as we got inside our door, Alan sent Martina to her room, before I got a chance to lose the plot altogether. And he was so right; screaming and shouting wasn't the answer. So I calmed myself down and we both made our way upstairs to

Martina to talk and try to find out what brought all this about.

She sat on the end of her bed and told us, point-blank to our faces, 'Yiz never let me go anywhere! Every time I ask yeh, it's always, "no, no". I made up me mind that I wanted to be like the hippies and see wha' it's like without all yer rules.'

Just at that very second I wanted to give her such a clatter, but I stopped myself because I had promised Alan I wouldn't. So I bit my lip and listened until she was finished.

'Now,' said Alan, 'and how did yeh like it out there without us and our rules?'

'I didn't, Da. Because nearly all the money was gone. We bought fish and chips and loads of bars of chocolate and had a party in the room and then Tara bought a brush for her hair, 'cause it goes all fuzzy and I'd forgot mine, and then the women wanted money off us. And there was hardly any left, so she made us pick up all the leaves around the hotel, and I didn't know wha' to do next. I'm sorry, Ma. I'm sorry, Da. I'll never do anythin' like tha' again, I promise.'

'Well,' I said, 'I certainly hope not.'

I could feel the anger leave me as I moved over to put my arms around her. I was only glad to have her home safe and sound but, at the same time, if only to teach her a lesson, I made her pay us back every penny out of her weekly pocket money – which took her a very long time.

As I was walking out the bedroom door, I couldn't believe what she said next.

'Ma, it was lovely in tha' hotel. Any chance we could all go back up sometime?'

'No problem, pet – when *you're* payin'!'

12

The Party

Da was sixty-six now and coming up for retirement soon. He had worked all his life, taking very little time off work for himself, so we all decided that we were going to have a big night out. Nothing but the best for our Da, so we booked Clontarf Castle.

You could see he was well pleased when we told him, but he put up a front. 'Now wha' did yiz go and do tha' for?' he said. 'Spendin' all tha' money when there's no need for it.'

'Ah, would yeh listen to yerself, Phil Doyle,' said Ma. 'Puttin' on the act when I know, and so does everybody else, tha' yeh're only delighted with yerself.'

'Yeh always have somethin' to say to me, Lil, don't yeh? Will I ever see the day tha' somethin' nice will come out of tha' mouth of yers?'

'Go and ask me arse and don't be annoyin' me,' said Ma as she made her way into the kitchen.

'I swear, Kathleen, one of these days tha' mother of yers is goin' to push me too far. I mean it, too far.'

'Yeh're worse, Da, to be takin' any notice of her. Yeh should let it roll off yeh like wha' we all do. And if the truth be known, I think she does be windin' yeh up most of the time just to get yer back up'.

'Well then, if tha' be the case, Kathleen, there's no need for it, no need at all.'

'Come on now, Da, forget about all tha'. We have another little surprise for yeh before yer big night out. Noel is goin' to bring yeh into town on Saturday to kit yeh out with all the trimmin's – new suit, shoes, shirt and tie, and to top it off, a new trilby hat. So wha' de yeh think of tha'? And before yeh say anythin' about money, Da, we all chipped in, costin' each of us only a few pound.'

'Well, I suppose when yeh put it like tha', Kathleen, I'll be lookin' forward to me big night out. But wha' about yer mother – will she be gettin' a new frock?'

'Don't worry about Ma, tha's all sorted. Carmel and Jacinta are bringin' her in to Meath Street to pick up a few nice bits. Anyway, yeh're gas, Da, less than five minutes ago yeh wanted to kill her.'

'Hmm,' he said, 'well, tha' was different.'

'The pair of yiz will be like film stars when yiz make yer entrance.'

And so they were, with both of them looking really well on the night – and what a night it turned out to be.

* * *

I had to laugh at Alan that night as we were getting ready to go to Da's party. Every time I looked at him, he was stuck in front of the mirror admiring himself.

'Are yeh lookin' at yer pearly whites again, Alan?'

'I know, I can't help it, Kathleen. The difference these new teeth make, it's unbelievable, after all the problems I've had over the years.'

107

'And so they bloody well should with the price of them!' I laughed and gave him a nudge. 'Now, will yeh come on or we'll be late.'

The night started off well, with a nice big fancy meal. Ever so posh it was. There was a big show after, which Da was very impressed with, followed by a bit of dancing, with every one of us up on the floor, having the best craic ever. Even Ma and Da got up to dance together, which was great to see.

I was breathless from jumping around dancing with them all and had to sit down for a minute or two, when out of the corner of my eye I copped Alan, heavy into conversation with Paul, one of my younger brothers, who had just turned eighteen. I could see that Paul was getting himself into a right tizzy. As I watched, he turned on his heels and went outside. I made my way over to Alan who at this stage was swaying from side to side, just about keeping himself off the floor.

'Jaysus Christ, Alan, this is not like you. Yeh're langered. Come over here and sit down. Now, wha' did yeh say to Paul?'

'I was just tellin' him a bit of home truth. He was sayin' he's goin' to start bringin' yer Da for a pint now tha' he's old enough and I told him tha' will never happen – as soon as tonight's over he'll go about his business and won't bother his arse, just like the rest of them. So he got annoyed and stormed off.'

'Can yeh blame him gettin' annoyed? It's a wonder he didn't give yeh a dig. I can't believe yeh said all tha', Alan! You of all people tha' never has a bad word to say about anybody – and of all the nights yeh pick to speak yer mind!'

But I might as well have been talking to myself. He wasn't minding a thing I was saying. He was away with the fairies, which I wasn't used to looking at and didn't like one bit. I made my way out to Paul, who had a right sup on him as well and was giving out like mad.

'Paul, don't be mindin' Alan, tha's just a load of shite-talk comin' out of him. It's the drink, tha's all it is. He'll be sick tomorrow when I tell him wha' he said to yeh, and he'll be even sicker when I'm finished with him.'

I thought it was all going to be left at that, so I made my way back in to Ma and Da, who were just finishing off the last dance of the night. They both said that they'd had the best night ever. The place slowly started to empty. People were gathering their belongings and making their way home and in no time at all the crowds were gone, leaving only our family standing around outside the castle.

I looked over and there were Thomas, Paul, Mano and Patricia's husband Josh, with Carmel's boyfriend Shay. I could see that there was something brewing; their voices were getting louder and each of them was trying to talk over everybody else.

I called Noel over. 'Get Ma and Da into a taxi, quick. I think there's goin' to be trouble.'

'Where, Kathleen, where? With who?' said Noel.

'I'll fill yeh in in a minute; just get them off side.' Noel got it sorted and they were gone before I knew it, giving me enough time to tell him what Alan had said.

'He's a stupid little fuck, Kathleen. Of all nights, he decides to say his piece! I mean I don't know wha' he's scutterin' about. Paul and Mano were too young to go to the pub and meself and the Thomas fella have been out many a time with Da for a drink.'

'I know, Noel, yeh don't have to tell me. I want to fuckin' kill him meself.'

Just then I saw Alan making his way over to all the fellas. Josh and Shay walked away, with Carmel taking them and the other girls home in her van – leaving me with all these lunatics.

That's when the pushing and shoving started. Alan got knocked to the ground. I ran over as Noel tried to stop them. I got a fist in the face myself and landed on the ground beside him.

At that, Alan said, 'Now, wha's going on here, fellas, for yeh to be all fired up, hittin' me and threathenin' me like tha'?'

Can you believe it? And him after starting the whole thing! I wanted to punch the head off him myself. Well, one word borrowed another and soon they were all punching and killing each other. Alan got a dig in the face that knocked his false teeth out and sent them flying in the air, teeth we had just paid two hundred pounds for the previous week.

I let out such a scream: 'Stop, stop!' And they all did, for a split second. 'Don't move! It's Alan's teeth,' I said, 'don't walk on them, wha'ever yeh do.' When I looked, they were lying right beside Thomas's foot. I bent down, picked them up and stuck them in my pocket.

I thought that might have stopped them, but, no, the fight carried on. This time Noel was the one who got the full force of a punch in the nose, even though he was the one doing everything in his power to stop them. The blood poured down his face and you could see at this stage that he was really pissed off. Noel is quiet enough when left alone, but when pushed he has the temper of a lion.

I knew if he got involved, they should all look out, so I ran over to one of the bouncers and asked if they would please help me break the fight up. One of them turned around and said, 'Are you mad? Look what they're doing to one another, and they're family! No way!' Instead, they went in and locked the doors behind them.

When I turned around and looked over, Noel had Alan up in the air. He was like King Kong, twirling him around.

Before I could stop him, he threw Alan over the wall of the grounds and then made a run at the rest of them, with each one running to get away from him. I don't know how Alan didn't break his back because he fell across the stump of a tree and screamed in pain. Between the roars of him and the noise of the police sirens arriving, I don't know who was loudest, but it wasn't long bringing the fight to a stop.

We all stood there, me with my swollen eye; Noel with the blood still pumping from his nose; Thomas, Mano and Paul with their lips and eyes cut to bits, and all of their shirts hanging off them covered in blood; and last but not least, the upstart of the whole thing, Alan, bent over in pain, with not a tooth in his head, still mumbling away to himself, talking a load of shite.

'Right,' said one of the gardaí, 'my colleague here tells me that he has spoken to the manager and there is no damage done to the premises. So, do any of you want to press charges against the others?'

'Now, why would we do tha', guard?' said Thomas. 'We're all brothers.' Each of the others said the same.

'Okay then,' said the gardaí, 'none of you are in any fit state to drive, so all cars will be left here – and I mean this, if any of you attempt to drive, and we will be keeping an eye out, I'll throw the book at each and every one of you, so bear that in mind. Now, my advice is, get yourselves home and sleep it off.'

'I don't drink, guard,' I said. 'I'll make sure to get them all home.'

And off they went, leaving us standing there. We all scarpered over to my van as quickly as we could in case they came back and changed their minds. As I drove home, with Alan asleep in the front, all I could hear from the back was who got the better digs in at one another, and then the singing started.

Alan was in a right mess the next morning and couldn't remember a thing, but I filled him in about the goings-on of the night. I showed him the black eye that I got, all because of him.

'Yeh better go around them all and make yer peace, Alan McGrath. Because I'll never hear the end of it if yeh don't. And believe me, neither will you.'

'Kathleen, are yeh sure yeh're not addin' a bit more on here than wha' really happened? I mean, yeh know you and yer family – arms and legs are added on before things get around.'

'Yeh needn't start all tha', Alan. There's no way yeh're getting' outta this. So yeh may head off now and start doin' yer rounds, makin' Paul's yer first stop. And he won't be long tellin' yeh wha' happened.'

And off he went, with egg all over his face and his tail between his legs, having to suck up to each and every one of them.

They all made sure he never forgot it. With the slagging that they gave him, for such a long time afterwards, Alan made sure that he was on his best behaviour for future parties to come.

13

The Crasher

It was two weeks before Christmas. Martina and young Alan had gone to school. I was getting myself ready to go into town with Amanda, to get her Christmas clothes, when Alan's brother Paul knocked on the door.

'Howyeh, Paul. Come in. Wha' has yeh up here so early?'

'There yeh are, Kathleen. Is Alan around?'

'Yeah, yeah, he's out in the garage.'

'I was goin' to ask him would he give me a hand doin' a bit of paintin'. Yeh know the way he's good at the decoratin'. I'm hopeless when it comes to all tha'.'

'I'm sure he won't mind givin' yeh a dig-out, Paul. Here he is now, ask him yerself.'

The two of them sat in the kitchen yapping away while I tidied around the house before I headed off myself. They decided to take my small van, leaving Paul's brand new car parked in our driveway, and the keys in full view on the kitchen table, which shouldn't have been a problem.

That was until young Alan, who was thirteen at the time, came home on his lunch break from school and decided to take the car out for a drive – which, of course, he couldn't do.

* * *

I was in town the best part of the day and it was coming up for around five o'clock when I got off the bus. Amanda was skipping along in front of me, while I was lost in my thoughts, planning the dinner.

Just as I came around the corner onto our road, I was stopped dead in my tracks. I couldn't believe my eyes. There was Paul's brand new car, crashed through the front garden of a neighbour's house, only inches away from their front door, with walls knocked down all over the place. Never in my wildest dreams would I have suspected that young Alan would have anything to do with this, but as soon as I knocked on the door I found out the truth. Our neighbour lashed into me straight away, screaming and shouting at me, and I couldn't blame him one bit.

'Where the hell have you been? Look wha' yer son's done – look!' he said. 'De yeh realise he could have killed me or me wife if one of us had been standin' in the garden – or, for tha' matter, a child playin' around out there.'

I stood there with my mouth open, not knowing what to say. The only words that eventually came out of my mouth were, 'I'm sorry, I'm so sorry.'

'I've been waiting hours for one of yous to show your face. You will be sorry by the time I'm finished – because it's the guards I'm ringin' now!' He closed the door in my face.

I made my way over to the house in a complete daze. I ran around looking for young Alan but he was nowhere to be found. I was only in the door a couple of minutes when my sister Patricia, who lived nearby, knocked on the door. I broke down crying when I saw her standing there.

'Before yeh say anythin', Kathleen, young Alan is in my house. But don't worry, he's not hurt, and neither is anybody else.'

'Thank God for tha', Patricia. I didn't know wha' to be thinkin'. I can't believe he's after doin' this. Oh my God, wait 'til Paul sees his car. Alan is goin' to go mad when he hears about this. Christ, wha' am I goin' to do?'

'First of all, Kathleen, come up to my house and talk to young Alan. He has himself in an awful state; he's green in the face with worry.'

'And so he should be, Patricia, for bringin' all this trouble on us. And for wha' – a jaunt in a car? I'll fuckin' kill him when I get me hands on him'.

As soon as I got to Patricia's house I made a run to give Alan a dig, but he was like lightning and I couldn't catch him. All he kept saying was, 'Sorry, sorry Ma', as I chased him around. I was breathless and had to sit down.

'In the name of Jaysus, Alan de yeh realise how serious this is? Yer man is gettin' the police for yeh. Wha'ever possessed yeh to do such a thing?'

'I'm sorry, Ma, I just wanted to see wha' it was like to drive. I didn't mean to do any harm. Me foot slipped and I hit the accelerator instead of the brake. Sorry, sorry.'

'Listen to this, Kathleen, it might put a smile back on yer face,' said Patricia. 'De yeh know wha' he did after he crashed the car? Put the keys back in the house and went back to school – can yeh believe tha'? He was hopin' yiz might think somebody robbed it. And he would've got away with it, only yer man was up on the roof of his garage lookin' at him drive the car through his garden.'

'How de yeh know all this, Patricia?'

'Well, Alan told me everythin' when he came up and one of the neighbours stopped me when I was goin' in to yeh earlier on – sure yer man was tellin' everyone.'

I shook my head and looked over at young Alan, giving him 'the look'. 'I'd better go back down to the house, Patricia. Can he stay here with yeh for a while? There's goin' to be blue murder when Paul sees his car, never mind when Alan finds out how it happened.'

'You go ahead, Kathleen; I'll drop him down in a couple of hours. Things might have cooled down a bit by then.'

'I don't think so, Patricia, but we'll see. And listen here, Alan McGrath,' I roared, shaking my fist into his face, 'don't move outside this house, de yeh hear me?'

He just looked at me, not saying a word.

* * *

Just as I got to our house, Paul and Alan were driving around the corner. The look on both their faces said it all – they were in shock. Paul jumped out of the van first.

'Holy fuck! Look at me car – wha's after happenin' here, Kathleen?'

I didn't get a chance to open my mouth, because the neighbour was out straight away, screaming and shouting again. We tried to talk to him, saying that we would pay for the damage.

'Bloody sure yeh'll pay,' he said, 'and so will yer son because I'll be pressin' charges against him.'

I nearly fainted when I heard that. I made my way over to the house with Amanda, who was starting to get upset with all the carry-on, leaving Alan and Paul to see if they could change his mind about bringing the police into it. There was no way they could reason with him, so they followed me over.

Alan was in the height of it. I had never seen him so angry before. 'Kathleen, where is he?' he asked.

'Up in Patricia's house, Alan. He went there after school.' I told them the full story. I could see a grin coming on Paul's face, which I was so happy to see.

'Come on, Alan,' he said, 'at least nobody got hurt. The wall and the car can be fixed and maybe when yer man calms down he won't go ahead with the charges.' That helped, but only a bit. Alan sat there brooding in silence.

Then there was a knock on the door. I jumped up with the fright. I could see through the glass as I went to open the door that it was the police and I could feel myself shaking inside as I called to Alan.

'We would like to speak to you about the incident down the road, concerning the car in the garden.'

'Come on in, guards,' said Alan. 'This is me brother Paul here, who owns the car, and it was our son who tried to drive it.'

'I see,' said the guard, 'and where is your son now?'

'He's up the road in me sister's house. Will I go up and get him for yeh?' I asked.

'No, leave him there for the moment.' He asked us all about young Alan. Had he ever been in trouble before? What kind of a boy was he? Even though Alan was still very annoyed, I could see how proud he was telling the guards about our son being on the hurling team in the school, playing matches every weekend and also being into the soccer. I was taking everything on board, but at the same time praying like mad, asking all my guardian angels to please make all this go away, which of course they didn't.

The guards seemed to be happy enough with what we told them, but they made it clear how serious it was. 'Even if the gentleman decides not to press charges,' said one of the guards, 'more than likely we might have to. Your son did steal a vehicle and drove with no tax or insurance.' I could feel the blood drain from my face.

'Can I say somethin' here, guard?' said Paul, 'I won't be reportin' tha' me car was taken.'

'Is that so, sir? Now what you're telling me is you gave your car to a minor, to take out on the road to drive, and if that is the case, then we will be charging you.'

Holy Jaysus, I thought to myself, *this is gettin' worse by the minute*.

That's when Alan stepped in. 'Guard, me brother is just tryin' to help out here, tha's all. It happened like I said. Our son will have to pay the price for wha' he did and, believe me, he won't be gettin' off lightly with us. So if yeh can try and keep him out of the courts, I'd very much appreciate it.'

'Right then, Mr McGrath,' said the guard as he got up to leave, 'bring Alan down to the station tomorrow evening around seven o'clock and I'll have a talk with him and we'll take it from there. But in the meantime, go over and get the car out of the gentleman's garden and see if you can come to some sort of an arrangement about getting the walls fixed straight away, and any other damage that was done.'

'I'll do tha' now,' said Alan, 'and all I can say is I'm sorry about all this bother me son is after causin'.' Alan was sucking up like mad to the guards.

It wasn't too long after they left that Patricia walked in with young Alan, who was shitting himself. He got lashed out of it by both Alan and Paul, with the pair of them ranting and raving to beat the band. And that was the easy part. Then he had to run the gauntlet with me. I would usually scream, shout and maybe throw a few fucks in along the way, but this was too serious and had to be handled with great caution. So I was very calm, which surprised even me, never mind everyone else.

'Alan, go to yer room,' I said. 'I'll speak to you later. Martina, take Amanda upstairs with yeh. I'll call yiz down as soon as dinner is ready.' The pair of them thought they'd never get up the stairs fast enough to find out what their brother had been up to.

After Paul and Patricia left, I sat there with Alan trying to work out the best way to handle the situation.

'Kathleen, he's definitely grounded,' said Alan. 'At least for a week. No, I changed me mind – two weeks.'

'I agree with yeh, Alan, and tha' will happen, but tha's not enough for me. Wha' I'd really like to do now, at this very minute, is to run up them stairs and give him such a dig, but tha' would be over too quick. Anyway, I'd only end up hurtin' me hands with the size of him now. We'll have to make him realise how serious this all is and tha' he's goin' to pay for the damage – not us.'

'And how are we goin' to tha', Kathleen?'

'Well, first of all, yeh know the money tha' I have put by to dress him for Christmas? And, believe me, he needs new clothes badly, with the height he's after gettin'; nothin' fits him – well, tha' won't be happenin' now. So tha' money and the money tha' he would be gettin' for his Christmas present will get tha' wall fixed. I'm tellin' yeh, Alan, tha' won't go down well with him. Havin' to go out on Christmas Day in front of his friends with all his old clothes on and not a penny in his pocket. Tha' will hurt him more than anythin'.'

'Righ' then, Kathleen, yeh seem to have it all worked out in tha' head of yers as usual. But I do have to agree with yeh – he won't like this one bit.'

And he didn't. As soon as the dinner was over, we sat him down. You'd want to see the look on his face as we dished out his punishment. He sat there quietly, with the biggest mush on him you ever saw.

'Young Alan, are you listening to me?' I said. 'If this is all tha' happens, yeh can thank yer lucky stars, because if the guards go ahead and charge yeh, there'll be a black mark on yer record forever. And tha's not good for yer future.'

He finally spoke up. 'All I can say is tha' I'm sorry, righ', and I'll never do anythin' like tha' again. I don't know **wha'** else to say to yiz.'

I thought to myself, *Typical fuckin' teenager!* I was starting to get a bit worked up at this stage and wanted to clatter him. But I held back once more. What can you do? You can't keep going on and on, so I just hoped that he would take heed of what we were saying and prayed that there wouldn't be a next time.

I have to say, the guard was great when we went down to the police station the following evening. He was firm in everything he had to say, giving Alan a good caution, but also very fair. There was great relief on all our faces when he said the police would not be bringing any charges against him.

'I will talk to the gentleman,' he said, 'and I'm sure when he calms down he won't take things any further. Just remember everything I've said, Alan. Keep your nose clean and stay out of trouble or you won't get off so lightly the next time.'

'I will, guard. Thanks,' said young Alan, and then he was gone out of that police station like a light, as we were after thanking him ourselves, in case he changed his mind.

Our neighbour finally calmed down. We had the wall fixed in record time, which he seemed to be happy enough about in the end. All was forgiven and the charges were dropped.

* * *

By this stage young Alan had been grounded for the best part of a week and I could see that it was starting to get to him, even though he tried to pretend it wasn't. School had just finished for Christmas, so he was in the house all day, every day.

I was upstairs tidying around and he was in his room, lying stretched out on the bed with his hand behind his head.

'I have to say, Ma,' he said, 'this is the life. Wha' more could yeh ask for? I think I'll do this more often. I'm really enjoyin' the rest.'

'Is tha' righ', Alan?' I said. 'Well now, seein' as yeh're havin' such a good time with yerself there, I'm addin' another week onto yer punishment.' Well, you'd want to see his face! 'Now, wha' de yeh think of tha'?'

I strolled out of his room with a big smile on my face. After a while I called out for him to come for his dinner. There was no answer, so I called out again.

'Alan,' I said, 'get yer arse down here now, while the food is still hot.'

Still not a sound, so I raced up the stairs, taking them in twos, only to find him gone and the window wide open.

'Holy Jaysus, I don't believe this. He's after jumpin' out the top window. Tha's it, I'm going to fuckin' kill him when I get me hands on him!'

Then I copped a note on his locker. 'I'm sorry, Ma,' it read. 'Your rules are too strict. I won't be back. Goodbye.'

I didn't know whether to scream my brains out or laugh my head off. I charged down the stairs, only to fall over the Hoover in the hall. I fell flat on my face, and banged my head against the door. Well, if I hadn't been in a temper before, I certainly was now. We had this big Alsatian dog called King, who followed me everywhere I went. He jumped on top of me and had me pinned to the floor, licking the face off me. I pushed King off me, grabbed one of the tubes off the Hoover and stuck it up the sleeve of my coat as I went out the door to look for young Alan, with King hot on my heels.

It didn't take me long to find him and as soon as he saw me he ran straight over.

'Ma, don't say anythin' in front of me friends.'

'Is tha' right', Alan?' I pulled the tube out and made a run at him, giving him a right bang on the shoulders. While I was doing this, King was jumping on top of him, trying to bite the arse off him. You'd want to see the shock on his face as he tried to get away from me.

'Yeh'd better make yer way home, Alan.' I was screaming my head off at this stage as I chased him down the road and on into the house.

'Yeh didn't have to do tha', Ma,' he was roaring. 'I'll be the laughin' stock of the place tomorrow.'

'Yeh should have been happy enough to take the punishment tha' was dished out to yeh,' I said, 'and you were gettin' off light for wha' yeh did. But I'm tellin' yeh here and now, there'll be no more pussy-footin' around here, Alan McGrath. From now on, if yeh bring any more trouble to this door, tha's nothin' compared to wha' I'll do to yeh. So bear tha' in mind. Now, get back up to yer room.'

* * *

I won't say that young Alan didn't get up to more mischief along the way – far from it, but there was nothing too serious that Alan and myself couldn't handle.

14

Little Girl

Martina was driving me nuts. She wanted to leave school altogether. There was no way I was having any of it, as she was only fifteen. Because I had very little education myself, I wanted our children to get as much schooling as possible.

Martina worked with me on the weekends, washing hair and tidying around for her pocket money. Even though she was a great help to me, I felt it would do her good to get out there and work with girls her own age, not having her stuck out in the back garden working with me all the time. So I decided to see if I could get her a Saturday job in the hairdressers where I got my own hair done, which happened to be in the city. I got on very well with the girls there. I asked if there were any openings; luckily enough there were.

'Righ', Martina,' I said, 'sit down there. I have a bit of news for yeh and I think yeh'll be pleased. I'm after gettin' yeh some weekend work. It's the same as wha' yeh're doin' here for me, washin' hair and cleanin' around, so it shouldn't be any bother to yeh. Tha' way yeh can see if tha's wha' yeh'd like to do when yeh leave school – after yeh do yer exams, of course. It'll give yeh a little sample of wha' life is like out there in the real world.'

'Oh, Ma,' she screamed, 'tha's great, I can't believe it! When do I start? When do I start?' She was jumping up and down with the excitement, hugging and kissing me at the same time.

'This comin' Saturday. Now, I have just one or two things to say on the matter, Martina. The rest will be up to you. Keep yer head down and do the jobs yeh're given. Listen and take in everythin' tha's been said. And most of all, zip yer mouth up and have nothin' to say about anybody. And I mean anybody – there's people out there tha' get pleasure in carryin' stories, addin' their own little bits along the way, so take heed in wha' I'm saying – de yeh hear now?'

'I will, Ma, I promise, I promise. I swear!'

'Other than tha', love, enjoy yer adventure.'

There were more hugs and kisses. I watched her skip along out to her friends. She thought she'd never get out to tell them her news. With that I could feel myself starting to get a bit upset, looking at my little girl, who was now starting to grow up. I hoped that life would be good to her along the way.

* * *

She settled in really well and took to the hairdressing just as I did. She worked all her school holidays and loved every minute of it. So much so that, as soon as her Inter Cert exams were over the following year, she asked us if she could leave school. There was a full-time job going and it was offered to her.

I was dead set against it in the beginning. But then Alan said to me, 'If tha's wha' she really wants, Kathleen, remember you at her age – tha's all yeh wanted to do and yeh were stopped for different reasons. I know tha' couldn't be helped, so before yeh say a flat-out no, have a good think about it first.'

'Please, Ma, please!' Martina kept saying, over and over again. 'It's wha' I really want to do.'

'Are yeh sure? Yeh're not doin' this just to get out of goin' to school? Because if yeh are, Martina, I'm tellin' yeh' . . .'

That's when she stopped me dead in my tracks and looked me straight in the eye.

'Believe me, Ma, I know this is wha' I want.'

When she said those words to me, for a split second I got a flashback to nearly twenty years earlier when I said those very words to my own Ma and how upset and disappointed I felt when I was told no. So I made up my mind there and then, with the support of Alan, and said yes.

That was it; Martina was on her way to follow her dreams.

* * *

Martina loved her job and was as happy as anything, making lots of new friends along the way. She came home one evening with a grin on her from ear to ear.

'Yeh're lookin' very pleased with yerself, Martina. Wha's happenin'?' I asked.

'A fella asked me out on a date, Ma. Can I go?'

'And who is this young fella? Do I know him?'

'His name is Rob. He's not from around here, Ma. He lives in town. I met him at the roller rink the other night. We had a great laugh. He was chasin' me all over the rink. We had the best time ever. Please, Ma, can I go out with him?'

How could I say no? It was like looking at myself when I asked Ma the very same thing, and I was even younger. So that was it; we said yes and Martina had her first date.

I didn't force her to bring him home to meet us. Alan and myself decided that we would let her do that in her own time, when she was good and ready. And she did, after a few weeks. He seemed nice enough, so we didn't overdo it by asking too many questions. We left the pair of them sitting there chatting away to young Alan and Amanda.

Over the next couple of months, Rob was up at the house more and more, so much so that he was there nearly every night. I pulled Martina to one side one night after he had gone.

'Sit down there, love. I want to have a talk with yeh.'

'Wha's wrong, Ma? Yeh look all serious.'

'Everythin's fine, Martina. It's just . . . I don't really know how to say this to yeh.' I hummed and hawed for a few seconds. 'Ah, to hell with it, I'll just come righ' out and say wha's on me mind. Are yeh doin' anythin'? Yeh know, like sex and stuff. Because if yeh are, we'll go down to the doctor and I'll get yeh the pill.'

She was trying to be serious and not laugh in my face but at the same time couldn't keep her face straight.

'Jaysus, Ma, will yeh not be askin' me things like tha'. Of course I'm not doin' anythin'! How could yeh even think such a thing?'

'Well, yeh're goin' out with this young fella a good few months now and I'm worried about yeh, tha's all. Everythin's so different now, Martina, as to when I was yer age, and I'm not too sure wha' yiz get up to these days.'

'Yeh worry too much, Ma,' she said, as she gave me a kiss, and off she went to bed.

Was that a good sign or not? I wasn't sure. But that's the way things were left over the coming weeks. I went around with not a care in the world, thinking everything was okay.

* * *

Martina arrived home early from work one day.

'Wha' has yeh home at this hour, Martina? Have yeh not got classes tonight?'

She just sat there and looked at me, not saying a word, which was unusual for her, as she is nearly as bad as myself for talking.

'Are yeh in trouble at work? Don't tell me yeh're after gettin' sacked. Jaysus Christ, Martina, I hope yeh haven't lost tha' job.'

There still wasn't a word coming from her, only plenty of tears. Then the penny finally dropped with me.

'Well, then,' I said, 'there's only one other thing tha' would have yeh this upset. Yeh're pregnant, aren't yeh?'

She looked up at me with such a lost look in her eyes as she sobbed out the words, 'Yes, Ma.'

I thought I was going to faint, I got such a shock. I stood there for a few seconds, looking at my very young daughter, who had just turned sixteen not too long before, only a child herself, telling me she was going to have a baby. I wanted to scream the house down – but I didn't. I took a deep breath and sat down beside her, putting my two arms around her. We both sat there and cried together.

'I'm sorry, Ma,' she kept saying. 'I'm sorry.'

'We won't talk about it now. Just let me sit here and hold yeh for the minute while I try and get me head around all this.'

That wasn't easy to do. I sat there thinking, for I don't know how long. Part of me wanted to box the head off her for being so stupid and not looking after herself. The other part wanted to keep holding on to her and not let go, knowing the pain her tiny body was going to have to go through, the responsibility that lay ahead, taking all of her youth with it along the way. Was I angry? Yes, very.

I came back from my thoughts with Martina shaking me.

'Ma, I think I can hear Da comin'. I can't face him. Please, will yeh tell him for me? Please!'

'Go on then, up to yer bed. Yeh look as if yeh could do with a good night's sleep. I'll talk to yer Da.' I got a quick kiss on the cheek and she was gone like a light before I could say another word.

I waited until they were all asleep and we were alone before I said a word. Alan knew me so well. I'm a cleaning freak at any time but when I'm in a temper or feel nervous I go on the rampage altogether, taking the place apart. I had myself in such a state I was only short of scrubbing the ceilings.

'Righ' Kathleen,' he said, 'spit it out, wha's wrong?'

I kept humming and hawing for a few seconds. 'Hmm, hmm . . . I don't really know how to put this, Alan. I mean, I know how to say it, tha's not wha' is hard; it's how to put it in a way tha' it doesn't sound too bad. If I just say it . . .'

'Kathleen, wha' have I told yeh over and over again? When yeh want to say somethin' will yeh just come righ' out and say it, instead of pussy-footin' around for God knows how long.'

'Okay, Alan – Martina's pregnant.'

He was drinking a cup of tea and he nearly choked right there and then in front to me with the shock. I had to bang his back like mad until he got his breath back.

'Jaysus, are yeh all righ', Alan? Yer tea must have gone down the wrong way. This is why I was tryin' to build it up to yeh.'

'Fuck the tea, Kathleen,' he roared, 'fuck, fuck, fuck and fuck again.' It wasn't very often you would hear Alan swear. I usually did enough of that for both of us, but I suppose that night it was his way of letting his anger out.

We sat there the best part of the night, talking and crying, trying to work out in our minds what the future held, both for us and for Martina, and how it was going to change all our lives so much.

Alan could never stay angry at any of our children for very long, so as soon as Martina walked into the kitchen the next morning – and God love her, she was waxy in the face – he put his arms around her and said, 'Don't worry, love, we'll work things out.' There was such relief on her little face when she heard her Da say that.

* * *

And we did work things out. Not to say that it was easy, far from it. I remember the day she brought Rob up to see us, about two weeks after we found out. He stood there acting all shy, with the 'I'm sorry' bit. I wanted to give him such a fucking dig. I know it takes two to tango, but for a split second to me it was all his fault, which of course it wasn't. But that's how I felt.

Then there was the first visit to the Coombe. Oh my God, I didn't know where to be putting my face when the nurse told me to stand on the scales. I had a quick look around to see if anybody was listening as I whispered, 'It's not me, nurse; it's me daughter Martina.'

Martina looked about twelve. She was wearing these little black pump runners, three-quarter-length leggings and the brightest orange shirt you ever saw, which looked as if it was three times too big for her, and her crazy pink Mohawk hairstyle to finish it off. Talk about standing out in the crowd.

Anyway, when all was said and done, she was well on her way – three and a half months pregnant.

I made sure that I was on my own the day I told Ma and Da they were going to be great-grandparents. I thought Da was going to have a fit. Because he was so religious and worrying about what the neighbours thought, he had to blame somebody, which of course was me.

'This is all yer fault, Kathleen,' he said, 'lettin' Martina dress in all them mad-lookin' clothes. I don't know wha' she's like goin' around. As for tha' stupid-lookin' haircut . . . is it any wonder she got herself into trouble?'

I sat there and let him rammage on and on. I wasn't in any humour to get into an argument with him. At the end of the day he was just letting off a bit of steam and would calm down in time.

I had myself all ready to run the gauntlet with Ma, expecting her to lash me out of it too, but to my surprise she didn't.

'Yeh got her checked out then, Kathleen?' she said.

'I did, Ma, and everythin's fine.'

'Good, tha's all tha' matters. Once her and the baby are well, everythin' else will fall into place. Don't be mindin' wha' yer father or anybody else thinks, because it's nobody's business only yerself and Martina's. Now, tha's all I'll say on the matter.'

* * *

Martina worked right up to the last couple of weeks, not losing a day of work. I went in and spoke to her boss, who I have to say was so nice. He let me know her job would be there for her when she was ready to come back, which I was well pleased about. I wanted her to finish her apprenticeship, no matter what. I felt there would always be a future both for her and the baby.

The night finally arrived when Martina went into labour. I kept her with me for as long as I could, checking on her pains, just like Ma did with me all those years ago. But unlike Ma, I was a nervous wreck and was trying really hard not to let Martina see it.

As soon as she said, 'Ma, I think me waters are broke', I nearly fell out of the bed.

'Hold on, Martina, I'm comin' to yeh. Don't get out of bed.' I grabbed a big bath towel out of the press on my way into her room. 'Quick, stick tha' between yer legs and try not to let it get on the new carpet.' God love her, she wobbled into the toilet with me holding onto the towel before the big gush came.

'Quick, Alan,' I roared, 'Martina's in labour.'

He had himself dressed in a jiffy. Martina was bent over in pain as we helped her into the van. Alan had us at the doors of the Coombe in the blink of an eye. 'Alan, will yeh go down for Rob? He said he wants to be at the birth.'

Because he was living nearby they were back in no time at all. Alan went on home to the kids while I sat there. I'll never forget what I did and said next and I still don't know if I was right or wrong, but at the time I felt very strongly about it. One of the nurses came over to me and asked me to sign a form for Martina to get the epidural needle. I didn't even think twice about it; 'No' came out of my mouth. You could see that she was taken aback with my answer.

'First of all, nurse,' I said, 'I don't know enough about this needle tha' yeh want to give to me child. I hear tha' sometimes it can have side-effects. The other reason is, I don't think a bit of pain will do her any harm. She'll know now tha' makin' the baby is the easiest part, but it's a different kettle of fish when yeh're bringin' them into the world. So we'll leave it at tha'.'

I went in a couple of times to sit with Martina and fell to pieces as I looked at her in so much pain. Finally the nurse told me I was only upsetting her and it would be better if I waited outside. I had myself in a right state, worrying all through the night if I had done the right thing. Should I have made the birth easier for her?

It seemed to take forever for the morning to arrive and it wasn't too long after that the hustle and bustle of the hospital started. I jumped every time I saw a nurse come out of the labour ward. Each time I was told, 'She's nearly there.'

Finally, after the guts of another hour, Rob came bursting through the doors and told me that Martina had a baby girl. I couldn't hold back the tears any longer.

'Thank God, thank God, thank God,' that's all I could hear myself saying over and over again. 'Are Martina and the baby okay?'

'She's great. There's not a bother on her and the baby is gorgeous. Go on into her, Kathleen, I'll wait out here,' Rob said.

'Will yeh ring Alan and tell him? I'm sure he must be frantic by now.'

I got myself together and made my way in. I stood there and looked at my little girl as she held hers. I could see straight away, young as she was, that she was going to be a great mother. All the worry and anger that I had felt for months on end left me as soon as I held my two little girls.

I suppose some mothers would have gone mad at the thought of becoming a granny at the age of thirty-eight, but I have to say, I totally enjoyed every minute of it. I loved my little Danielle.

15

The Van

Alan always seemed to be happy enough in himself, working away in Gallagher's, but as the years went on I could see that he was getting tired of the long hours.

'Yeh know somethin', Kathleen?' he said one day. 'I'm sick and tired of bein' on the clock and havin' to answer to people all the time. I wish, I just wish tha' I could get meself somethin' to work at and be me own boss.'

'Yeh have a very good job there, Alan. De yeh really hate it tha' much, tha' yeh want to give it up?'

'Yeh don't understand, Kathleen. It's the system I want to get out of, not the work. I mean, there's you, for example; I know yeh work most days, but if yeh really want to take a day off from doin' hair, yeh can just go ahead and do it. There's nobody breathin' down yer neck if yeh're a few minutes late. Then there's the shite tha' I have to go through when the holidays are given out. It's when they say I have to take them, not when I want to.'

'Jaysus, Alan, I never knew yeh felt like tha'. Yeh should have said somethin' instead of lettin' it get on top of yeh like

133

this. Well then, wha' about openin' up yer own shoe repair shop, like wha' yer Da use to have?'

'It's a dyin' trade, Kathleen. I'd never make a decent wage out of it. No, forget about tha'. Ah, don't be mindin' me, Kathleen, it'll pass. I'm just lettin' off a bit of steam, tha's all.'

* * *

I kept my eyes and ears open, hoping that something would come my way that would help Alan get out of this rut that he felt he was caught up in. Then, out of the blue, to my surprise it did.

My sister Clare was over with me one day and I was filling her in on what Alan was saying and how he was feeling.

'Yeh know wha', Kathleen,' she said, 'I might have the very thing for him. There's this girl I know, and her sister is headin' off to Australia with the husband and two kids to start a new life there, sellin' every screed they have so's tha' they'll have as much money as possible for when they get there . . .'

'Clare,' I interrupted her, 'wha' are yeh tellin' me all this for, and about somebody I don't even know?'

'Will yeh wait and listen to me, Kathleen. I'm buildin' up to it. I know yeh're goin' to be over the moon when I tell yeh about this . . .'

'In the name of Jaysus, Clare, will yeh stop pussy-footin' about and just say it.'

'His ice-cream van – they're sellin' it. Alan could buy it! So wha' de yeh think?'

I stood there for a moment, my brain clicking in and out all over the place. This could be the very thing that Alan was looking for.

'Clare, are yeh sure about this? They're definitely goin' away?'

'I'm tellin' yeh, Kathleen, I was up in their house only the other night buyin' a few bits of furniture. Sure I got the stuff for half nothin', tha's how I know about the van.'

'Alan will be in soon, Clare. Will yeh hang on for a while and tell him about this?'

'Sure don't yeh know I will, Kathleen.'

While the two of us sat there yapping, I kept glancing over at the clock every few minutes, thinking about how Alan would feel when he heard the news. I was getting butterflies in my stomach just thinking about it.

Alan was only in the door and didn't even have time to take his coat off before I launched into everything. 'I have the best news ever, Alan! Wait 'til yeh hear wha' Clare just told me. Yeh'll be able to be yer own boss – tha's if yeh want it, of course! I mean, maybe yeh might not want to drive an ice-cream van? I never thought about tha'. But if yeh do, we know a fella tha's sellin' one and Clare said tha' yeh'll probably get it real cheap because yer man needs the money fast because they're all goin' to Australia and Clare was sayin' . . .'

'Kathleen!' said Alan. 'Stop talkin' for a minute and take a breath before yeh faint. Now, first of all, I haven't a clue wha' any of tha' meant, so yeh're goin' to have to slow down and fill me in on wha' yeh're talkin' about.'

'I'm just excited for yeh, Alan, tha's all.'

'I know tha', love, so will yeh come on and tell me, nice and slow, and I might get a bit worked up with yeh.'

I could see Alan's face light up when I went into the details of what Clare had told me. He listened, taking everything on board that I was saying. As soon as I finished talking, to my surprise, Alan didn't waste any time in asking Clare if she would bring him over to meet the fella.

'Come on, Alan,' said Clare, 'we'll go over now. There's no time like the present.'

'I'm comin' with yiz,' I said. 'Yeh're not leavin' me here. Hold on 'til I get me coat.' I went running out after them.

It didn't take us too long to get there. While I sat in the car, Clare went into the house with Alan. I was on tenterhooks. It seemed to take forever before they came back out. Alan stood talking to the fella for a few more minutes as Clare made her way out to me. She was giving me the nod and the wink and a huge smile to go with it.

'Jaysus, Clare, will yeh hurry up and tell me wha's happenin'. I'm burstin' here to know.'

'I'm saying nothin', Kathleen. It's not me place. I'll let Alan tell yeh himself.'

And he did, as soon as he got into the car. 'Well, tha' went very well, I have to say, Kathleen. Joe – tha's yer man's name – said he'll take me out in the van with him at the weekend and one or two nights next week to see wha' I think of it, and then we'll take it from there. Now, if it's a thing tha' I do like it, then you and me will have to sit down and have a good talk about me givin' up the good job tha' I have.'

'Well, the way I see it, Alan, I know yeh make good money and yer job is permanent, but it's no good to you or me for tha' matter if yeh're not happy. Wha'ever yeh decide, I'm behind yeh all the way. So there's no need for us to have any big talk.'

I could see by the big smile he gave me that he was well pleased with this.

Alan went out on his few test runs and was as happy as anything each time he came home. So he ended up buying the van and becoming the local ice-cream man of our area.

* * *

It took Alan a good few months to get the hang of things. He had to learn so much about the ice-cream machine and the running of the van – and that was before he faced the gangs of kids in the streets. But none of that was a problem to him. Once he made his mind up to do it, he'd make sure that he would master anything that would come his way; and he did. Nothing fazed him.

So life was good. Alan was happy and contented in himself. He was his own boss at last. He must have been nearly a year in the ice-cream business and was working away, day in and day out, with not a care in the world.

That was until one evening when he came in early from work. He looked very pale and was very quiet.

'I have yer bit of dinner ready, Alan. Will yeh have it now?'

'Ah, just leave it there for a minute, Kathleen. I think I'll go up and lie down for a while. I'm feelin' a bit off.'

'Jaysus, tha's not like you, Alan. Yeh're never sick.'

'It's probably a flu or somethin' comin' on me. I'll be grand once I get a couple of hours sleep.'

Of course, he wasn't all right, as I found out very early the next morning. I was up at the crack of dawn. Amanda was going to England for a few days' holiday with Clare. When I went back upstairs, Alan was sitting up in the bed holding his chest.

'Jaysus, wha's wrong with yeh, Alan? Oh my God, look at the colour of yeh!' He looked as if every drain of blood was gone out of his body. 'I'm phonin' for an ambulance. Oh my God, Alan . . .' I was frantic.

'Will yeh stay quiet, Kathleen. I don't want yeh upsettin' the kids. Look, there's Clare over to pick Amanda up. Say nothin' until she's gone.'

I flew back downstairs and had Amanda on her way in no time at all. As I stood there smiling and waving her off, I was telling young Alan to get his arse up to his Da. As soon as Clare's car was out of sight, I was back up to Alan in a flash. He had himself up and dressed.

'I don't care wha' yeh say, Alan, I'm gettin' an ambulance righ' now.'

'I can't wait, Kathleen; just get me to a hospital, quick.' By this stage he was bent over and nearly on his knees with the pain.

'Ma, I'll run down and start the van up. You help Da down the stairs,' said young Alan.

At the time I had a small Suzuki van I used as a run around. I got in the back of it with Alan while young Alan drove. The nearest hospital was St James's and in my mind it seemed to be a million miles away.

Young Alan drove so fast down the Greenhills Road. He had lights flashing and his hand on the horn all the way down. He was screaming out at all the cars to let him pass. Most of them moved over – they could see there was something wrong. For the few that wouldn't move, he drove up on the paths and around them. We had no seats in the back of the van so, as you can imagine, we were getting thrown all over the place. I was trying to get Alan to lie down but he kept pushing me away. He was boxing himself in the face.

'Holy Jaysus,' I screamed to young Alan, 'yer Da's goin' mad back here. He's punchin' the head off himself.'

'Leave him, Ma,' roared young Alan, 'he know's wha' he's doin'. He's tryin' to stop himself from goin' unconscious. Look, we're nearly there. I'm goin' to drive right up to the front door. You jump out and get the first doctor yeh see.'

I fell around the casualty department, roaring for a doctor, and grabbed the first person I saw in a white coat, who happened to be a woman. I couldn't speak, I was crying so much. I just pointed to the door and kept pulling her along with me. She knew straight away it was something serious, as she called over to one of the nurses to come with her.

Alan was unconscious when we got there. I thought he was dead. I was hysterical. The doctors and nurses were great. In seconds, he was taken into the emergency room and given oxygen straight away. I was told to stand outside the door.

I could hear the doctor saying, 'Stand back; one, two, three.' I knew when I heard this that they were trying to get Alan's heart going. I was never so frightened in my whole life. I couldn't move. Young Alan put his arm around me as we waited patiently on someone to come out to us.

'Don't worry, Ma,' he said, 'Da will be okay. Yeh know him – he's as tough as nails.'

'I hope so, love, I just hope so.'

We seemed to be standing there forever. When the doctor finally came out to talk to me, I was so afraid of what he was going to say.

'Your husband had a very severe heart attack, but don't worry, we have him stable now. Getting him here as fast as you did saved his life.'

'Oh my God,' I said, 'Alan's never sick. How did this happen, doctor?'

'We will be doing some tests over the next few days and I will let both of you know then. You can go in now but only for a few minutes. He is very tired and needs to rest.'

'You go on in, Ma,' said young Alan. 'I'll wait out here for yeh.'

As I made my way in and looked at Alan lying there, I got such a fright. He was like death warmed up. It took me all my time to keep myself from falling to pieces. Alan took my hand and held it so tight.

'Come on, love,' he said, 'keep it together.' He tried to give me a little smile. 'Anyway, yeh won't be gettin' rid of me tha' easy.'

'Don't you die on me, Alan McGrath. De yeh hear me? I swear, I'll kill yeh if yeh die on me.' I couldn't hold back the tears any longer.

The nurse came over to me just then. 'I'm afraid you will have to go. Your husband has to go up to intensive care now and I need to get some general information about him from you.'

I gave Alan the biggest hug ever before I had to walk away. I wasn't too long with the nurse, then we headed on home. I sat in the van while young Alan drove.

'De yeh know somethin', love?' I said. 'I'm so proud of yeh. The way yeh held yerself together, gettin' us to the hospital so fast. Now, mind you, I thought we were gonners a few times when yeh started goin' up on the paths and all, but no matter. Yeh got us there, tha's the main thing. I don't think yer Dad would have made it only for yeh.'

'As I said, Ma, he's tough as nails, so don't be worryin'.'

He was so like his Da in many ways. There he was, barely seventeen and he handled something so serious in such a grown-up way. What would I have done without him?

Poor Martina was up the walls with worry by the time we got home. With all the upset, I had forgotten to ring her. It was only when I walked into the house that it entered my head.

'Please, Ma,' she said, 'tell me tha' Da is okay!'

I told her the news and she was a lot happier by the time I had finished. I got on the phone to Amanda straight away, filling her in on everything and reassuring her.

* * *

I thought that the next day would never come so I could go to see Alan. By the time I got there, some of his tests had been done and he was sitting up in bed, looking a lot better.

'Well, Kathleen,' he said, 'as yeh can see I didn't die, so come over here and give us a kiss.'

'Yeh nearly killed me with the fright yeh gave me, Alan McGrath, never mind yerself.' We gave each other a big hug. 'Well, tell me wha's happenin', Alan. Have they found out wha's wrong with yeh?'

'The doctor was in with me just before yeh got here. The bottom line is, I have a couple of blocked arteries around me heart and maybe – now only maybe, so don't start getting' yerself all upset – I might need to have an operation.'

I took a deep breath and held myself together and started rammaging on about God only knows what, just to keep my mind off this. Then Alan started going into the details of a test they had done called an angiogram.

'Yeh want to see it, Kathleen. I was sittin' there lookin' at the doctor puttin' this tiny little wire through me veins, startin' at the top of me leg righ' up to me heart. It was connected to a tiny camera and I could see everythin'. I'm tellin' yeh, it was really somethin' else.'

Just at that very moment, without any warning whatsoever, I could see Alan turning a dreadful colour and going unconscious – right in front of my eyes. I was off screaming all over the place again, and two nurses came in straight away, putting me outside once more.

'Oh my God, oh my God . . .' was all that kept coming out of my mouth as I walked up and down outside the ward. I don't know how long it was before one of the nurses came out to me.

'Don't tell me anythin' bad, nurse, please, please don't!'

'It's okay, Mrs McGrath, try and calm down, everything's under control. This can happen sometimes after the angiogram. There was a clot, but we've managed to disperse it now and everything's fine. You can go back in now, and make sure Alan stays lying down flat. We have some sand bags on his legs to make sure it won't happen again.'

I made my way back inside and true enough, there he was flat on his back, looking the colour of a Granny Smith apple.

'Jaysus Christ, Alan, yeh'll have to stop doin' this or I'll be havin' a heart attack along with yeh.'

'Ah, don't be givin' out to me, Kathleen. Sit yerself down there and talk to me. Did yeh think of gettin' young Alan to wash the machine and clean the van out for me before he locked it for the night?'

'Are yeh for real or wha', Alan? Here yeh are, nearly at death's door, and yeh're askin' me was I thinkin' of yer van last night? No – I don't think so and neither was he. Anyway, tell me wha' else the doctor was sayin'.'

He told me all he was getting done over the next few days, which turned out to be very much in his favour, as he didn't need to have surgery. He was nearly a week in hospital by the time he got the good news.

'Well, Alan,' the doctor said, 'we have decided not to operate because you are so healthy in every other way, and very fit I must say for a forty-year-old man. You have all that going for you, but for one thing – and I think you know what you have to do there: stop smoking.'

I listened to Alan lie through his teeth, promising the doctor the sun, moon and stars about how he would never let a cigarette pass his lips again. Which, of course, he did, only the very next day. He had me watching out to make sure none of the nurses were around so he could have a quick puff out the window.

No matter how much I would give out, it didn't matter. Alan's outlook on life was, and still to this very day is, 'Wha's goin' to happen, will happen, no matter wha' yeh say or I do, Kathleen, so why worry about it?'

When Alan came home from hospital first, I was a nervous wreck, keeping an eye on him all the time, phoning for every little thing. He couldn't breathe without me watching him. I was so scared that he would take bad again and this time be taken from me for good. But in time I learned to take a step back, not worry so much and let him enjoy life. Which he did. Alan didn't look or ask for much for himself ever. Everything was always for me and the kids.

So I was very happy to watch him doddle out every day in his van, knowing that, for once, he had got what he wanted, which was to work for himself and be his own boss.

16

The Markets

When Alan decided to give up his job and buy his ice-cream van, it was great for him, he was so happy. But we didn't really think it through or realise, with the long winters we get, how bad things could get and that there would be times when his income would drop considerably.

I was down in Ma's one day and I was telling my sisters, Jacinta and Carmel, that things were very tight with us and that I was finding it hard to keep up with my bills. They were dressmakers and worked for themselves, making all their own clothes through the week and selling them in the markets over the weekends.

'Yeh know wha', Kathleen,' Jacinta said, 'why don't yeh do the markets with us on Sundays? Yeh could make yerself a grand few bob there.'

'But how? Wha' would I sell, Jacinta?'

'Clothes, of course! Yeh bloody gobshite, Kathleen. We'll bring yeh down to the wholesalers; I know one or two of them real well. I'll get yeh some stuff on tick to get yeh started. We'll pick out some nice trendy dresses and jeans, they sell quick, and then yeh can pay the bill off as yeh're goin' along.'

'I have a spare rig there and a cover,' said Carmel. 'Yeh can have tha'. And yeh know somethin' else, Kathleen? When yeh're doin' yer bit of hairdressin', yeh could have a rail of clothes out there with yeh, tha' yer customers could be rootin' through while they're waitin' to get their hair done.'

'Jaysus, tha's a great idea, Carmel. I can't believe I didn't think of tha' meself.'

* * *

True enough, between the pair of them they got me started in the markets. I would check out what was in fashion in the bigger shops and then, after taking my own few bob out for myself, I would go in every Monday and buy as much as I could, selling it on to my clients throughout the week. They were all well pleased, since I was a lot cheaper than the shops.

I would be up at the crack of dawn on Sundays, with Alan helping me load the van, before heading out to the Finglas market for eight o'clock, and then on out to the Stardust for the afternoon. Carmel and Jacinta were always ahead of me and would help me get set up as soon as I arrived. I never would have managed without them. They were great.

It didn't take me long to get the hang of things. I think it was something that was in all of us – the gift of the gab, which we got from Granny Kitty. Between the hairdressing and then the markets, by the time I was finished I could have sold sand to the Arabs. I actually used to look forward to Sunday and meeting up with my sisters. We would have great craic throughout the day.

I remember one day in particular, we were in the Stardust market and I had just finished hanging the last of the clothes on the rails, when the crowds all started to gather. It was a lovely sunny day, so there were plenty of people out and about and I thought to myself, *This is great, I'll make a grand few bob today*. And sure enough, everybody seemed to be buying that day.

'How are yeh doin' over there, Kathleen?' asked Jacinta.

'I'm doin' really well. See all them trench coats, they're gone bar one. And wha' about yous – have yeh made a few sales?'

'Would yeh have a look at the rails, Kathleen? We're nearly cleaned out and we have about twenty orders between the two markets for next week.'

On the chit-chat went between us and before I knew it the day was nearly over. I was starting to pack up the few bits I had left when these two wans came over to me.

'Can I help yiz?' I asked.

'Could you kindly tell us, how much is that blue trench coat, please?'

'It's twenty-five pounds, miss. But seein' as it's the last one, and the day is comin' to an end, yeh can have it for twenty. Now, is tha' a bargain or wha'?'

The younger one of the two tried the coat on.

'Mummy,' she said, in an ever-so-posh accent, 'I think it might be slightly too long for me. What do you think?'

I jumped in straight away, before the other wan could get a word in.

'Tha's the latest fashion,' I said. 'They're just in from France, love, and I mean, they know their stuff. If they say tha's the length, well then tha's gospel.'

'I'm not really sure, Mummy,' she said. 'There's no mirror for me to look in to judge.'

Now, this is when 'Mummy' put her plan into action. I couldn't believe afterwards that I fell for it, with me always being bang wide, but nevertheless . . .

'Would you mind awfully letting us go around to our house,' she said, 'which is right at the back of the market, so that my daughter could have a quick look before she pays you? It will take us all but five minutes.'

Now, talk about being a gobshite. Instead of saying, 'I'll hold onto the twenty pound until you come back,' which is what I should have done, I went and handed the coat over, and that was the last I saw of them. I think it was the posh accent that put me off guard, making me think they'd have money and that there was no way they were pulling a scam. But as they say, you live and learn. It wasn't even the money at the end of the day that got up my back. It was that they made a fool of me, and I didn't like or forget that.

Well, you'd want to hear Carmel and Jacinta rammaging on at me as soon as I told them.

'Are yeh a thick or wha', Kathleen? I can't believe yeh broke the golden rule,' said Jacinta. 'Always, money in the hand first, before anythin' is given over. Isn't tha' wha' Ma taught us all? Never, ever, trust no one when it comes to money, because tha's when people can change their tune.'

'I know, I know now! Don't keep goin' on at me about it, Jacinta.'

* * *

But, of course, she did, and into the bargain told everyone else in the family that I had been taken for a sucker. None of them let me forget it.

'Go to Kathleen's stall,' they kept saying. 'She gives clothes out for nothin'.'

They all made a right laugh of me.

Every single week after, I was on the look-out. I watched and watched. I knew there would come a time when they'd breeze back into the market. And they did, six months later, in the depths of winter. Everyone was wrapped up really well, with their hats, gloves and heavy coats on. I was standing there with a hot cup of soup in my hand when I copped the same two wans walking towards me. They had themselves well muffled up, but that didn't matter to me. Their two faces were stuck inside my head, which I never forgot. They must have seen me because they side-tracked really quickly in between a couple of the stalls, thinking that I hadn't seen them.

'Quick, Jacinta,' I roared, 'them wans tha' done me outta the money are in the market. Go over to the entrance and don't let them out. Carmel, watch me stall, will yeh?'

I ran after them and tipped 'Mummy' on the shoulder.

'Remember me?' I asked as I stood there face to face with them.

'I beg your pardon, do I know you?' I could see she was starting to get herself into a bit of a tizzy.

'I'm fuckin' sure yeh know me. Yeh robbed me a while back – remember, the trench coat? "It's too long, Mummy",' I mimicked, as I glared into the daughter's face. 'All tha' shite tha' yeh gave me.'

'Oh, tha's right. I think I vaguely remember now,' said Mummy. 'We came back down with the money and you were all gone. Isn't that right, pet?' She turned to her daughter, who at this stage was shitting herself. 'And we came in a few times over the months, checking to see if you were here, but you weren't to be found.'

'Yeh know wha', yeh're not only a robber, but yeh're a bare-faced fuckin' liar as well, because I hung around here for the guts of half an hour tha' day, waitin' on yiz to come back, and I haven't missed a week since then. Now, hand over me money.'

The two of them went to walk away; that's when I grabbed Mummy's arm.

'De yeh see her over there?' I pointed over to Jacinta who was standing at the entrance to the market with two men. 'Yeh'll have to go through them to get out, and believe me, tha' won't be happenin'. Now, as I said, me money. Thirty pounds, if yeh don't mind.' I stretched my hand up to her face.

'If I recall properly, it was only twenty pounds.'

'Is tha' right?' I said. 'Well, the other ten pounds is for six month's interest.'

As I stood in front of the pair of them, she looked over at Jacinta and then at me.

'Don't even think about makin' a run for it,' I said.

That's when the daughter stepped in. 'Mummy, will you just pay the money, please, and let's get out of here now. I'm absolutely mortified.'

Mummy bashed the thirty pounds into my hand and stormed off, and I have to say it felt great. I was jumping up and down, waving over to Jacinta, letting her see I'd got paid and to let them pass.

I made my way back over to Carmel with a smile on me the length and breadth of the market.

'Well done,' she said, as I got a big pat on the back. Word wasn't long getting around, and I got a big round of applause from the rest of the traders. I was well pleased with myself.

It's a hard enough job to have to do, especially during the long hard winters, standing out in the cold for hours on end. I often thought my fingers were going to fall off when I would be breaking my stall down at the end of the day. Sometimes the canopy and bars would be covered with thick frost, sleet or snow. Then, for the likes of those wans to come along and take your bit of profit! Worst of all, I felt like a bloody thick because I'd trusted them. Money wasn't the issue; it was more of a pride thing with me. I had broken the golden rule, which didn't happen very often, and never happened again.

I thought I'd never get up to Ma to let her know what had happened. I could see by her face that she liked what I told her.

'Hmm,' she said, 'and yeh tell me yeh made yerself an extra ten pounds, Kathleen?'

I started laughing, knowing full well what she meant.

'Tha's righ' Ma,' I said. 'Tha's for you.' I handed her a few pound. She nearly took the hand off me as she spat on it for luck.

'Tha'll get me a grand few messages tomorrow.'

We were all happy bunnies that day, thanks to those two wans. I stuck with the markets for a couple of years, making a good few bob along the way, which made life a lot easier for Alan and myself. It was only when I opened my first salon that I decided to give up the markets, but I never ever forgot how good they were to me through those years.

17

Da

I dropped down with Danielle one day to see Ma and Da. I told them about how well Martina was doing in her apprenticeship.

'De yeh know wha', Kathleen?' said Ma. 'Tha's the best bit of news yeh've told me in I don't know how long. It'll do her the world of good to get out there and not just be sittin' at home, playin' with the baby. Keep her busy, tha's wha' I say, and maybe she won' get up to any more mischief. Isn't tha' righ', Phil?'

Da just looked over at me, rolling his eyes when Ma wasn't looking.

'Kathleen, I'm after makin' a nice pot of stew,' he said. 'Will yeh have a bowl?'

'I could smell it as soon as I walked in the door and thought yeh'd never ask me, Da. No matter how hard I try, I don't seem to get it as good as yers. I'm just listenin' to yeh talkin' there, Da, yer voice sounds very dry and hoarse. Yeh want to go and get tha' checked out by the doctor.'

'I keep sayin' tha' to him,' said Ma. 'But does he listen? No!'

'It's only a bit of a cold, tha's all. Anyway, never mind all tha', Kathleen. How's young Alan? Is he behavin' himself?'

'Well, he seems to be keepin' his nose clean but yeh know yerself, Da, yeh can't watch them twenty-four hours a day. But I tell yeh one thing, I'm not too far off. I have all me clients keepin' an eye out for me and if he's carryin' on or actin' the mick, I get a phone call and I'm out like a light and don't be long sortin' him out. Yeh'd want to see him run when he sees me comin'.'

'Just give him a good fuckin' dig, if he gets out of hand,' said Ma, 'because if I bring meself up to Tallaght, I swear to Jaysus I'll run amok and kill him if he brings the police to yer house again.'

'Please, Lil, don't be interferin'. And another thing – there's no need for tha' language,' said Da. 'Will I ever see the day tha' yeh'll hold a conversation without cursin'?'

'Ah, me arse, Phil Doyle, would yeh ever give it over, with yer frog voice on yeh.'

* * *

I laughed that day, but it was far from funny, as we were to find out over the coming months. I kept at Da each time I came down to the house to get himself checked. His answer was always the same: no.

'Please, Da,' I said. 'I was tellin' Dr Johnson about yeh the other day and he said tha' there's probably a few little nodules at the back of yer throat. They'd be like small warts tha' can be treated no problem, but if they're left it can get very serious.'

He just sat there listening to me, taking it all in, not saying a word; not that he was able to say much at that stage, with his voice nearly gone.

'Come on, Da, wha' de yeh say? Everybody's worried about yeh. Even Ma said to try and get yeh to go to hospital. I mean, is tha' not sayin' a lot?'

With that I got a nod of the head and a big smile. He agreed at last to go to the doctor and get a few tests.

As soon as the results came back, there was no time wasted. Da was taken into hospital and operated on straight away. The hospital didn't know what hit them when the whole gang of us came in to see Da. I slipped out with my brother Noel to speak to the doctor, not expecting what I was about to hear.

'We have taken all the nodules off,' said the doctor. 'Now, having said that, there were traces of cancer present. Hopefully we got it all but I can't promise what the future holds. We will just have to wait and see.'

I was so upset I couldn't speak, so Noel stepped in.

'Doctor,' he said, 'would yeh mind not tellin' me Da wha' yeh told us? He's a terrible worrier. Tha's why it took us so long to get him here, he was afraid of being told the likes of this.'

'I won't say anything for the moment,' said the doctor, 'but you must bring him for regular check-ups so we can keep a close watch on him.'

'Tha' won't be a problem,' said Noel, 'You tell us the time and the place, doctor, and we'll have him there.'

After the doctor had gone, I sat there with Noel for a few minutes, talking.

'Well, wha' de yeh think?' I asked.

'The first thing we should do is keep this to ourselves, Kathleen. No point in worryin' Ma and the rest of them unless we have to, and with a bit of luck all will go well for Da and nobody will be the wiser. Now, let's get back to the ward before he starts smellin' a rat. And will yeh ever put a smile on yer face, for Jaysus' sake, or yeh'll have Ma askin' twenty questions, and before yeh know it one of us will trip up.'

You'd want to see the big smile on Da's face when Noel told him everything was clear, but letting him know that he had to be checked out every now and then. I thought he was going to jump out of the bed and do a jig, he was so happy. And that's the way we left things, with only Noel and myself unsure of what the future held for Da.

* * *

I kept myself busy all the time, trying not to think about what might happen to Da, but it was always there in the back of my mind. Little did I know all the things that were about to happen over the following couple of years.

I went back to the hospital for months on end with Da for his check-ups. Even though the results seemed to be good each time, I could see that he was pale and had got very thin. He was such a worrier that none of us passed remarks about how he looked, and neither did he.

I spoke to Noel and we decided that we would go and talk to the doctor ourselves. He suggested lots of tests, which Da wasn't happy about and refused to have. I sat up in the bedroom for hours one day, trying to convince him it was for his own good. That's when I said the words that I know he didn't want to hear, but I couldn't help myself as I broke down crying.

'Please, Da, I don't want yeh to die. The doctors can help yeh. Please come to the hospital with me.'

He sat there for a while before he spoke. 'Okay, Kathleen, I will, because, yeh know somethin'? I'm not ready to leave yiz all yet or for tha' matter this earth.'

I threw my arms around him and held on so tight, not wanting to let go.

* * *

They did so many tests, showing up clear each time.

'How can this be?' I asked the doctors. 'Me Da looks so sick, there has to be somethin' wrong.'

'We didn't want to say anything until we were absolutely certain, but your father has what we call a hiding/moving cancer. It showed up in his lungs once and then when we looked again there was nothing there.'

'Tha's good, doctor. No, I mean, tha's great,' I said. 'Tha' means it's probably gone now for good and it won't come back and me Da will get better and everythin' will be like always.' I was trembling as I spoke.

The doctor listened to me going on and on. I so wanted to believe the words that were coming out of my mouth and not his. 'I am very sorry,' he said, 'we have one more test to do and then we will know for certain what is wrong with your father.'

* * *

It seemed to take forever for the day to come to go back to the hospital for the results. I was very nervous but didn't let Da see it. He held onto my arm as we walked down the long corridor.

'De yeh know somethin', Kathleen?' he said in a very low voice. 'Wha'ever the doctor has to say to me today, it doesn't matter wha' it is, once I'm not told tha' I have cancer. Other than tha', I'll handle anythin'.'

'Of course yeh will, Da. Haven't we all got over so much through the years between the whole lot of us? This is just a little blip along the way. Now, come on, straighten them shoulders up and let's see wha' this fella has to say to us.'

I made it my business to speak to the doctor before I brought Da in.

'Doctor, I'm Mr Doyle's daughter, Kathleen. I need to speak to yeh first.' He listened as I spoke. 'If me Da has cancer, please don't tell him.'

'I am sorry, Kathleen, but I have to give the proper results if he asks me.'

'He won't ask yeh, doctor; he doesn't want to know. Please, he won't be able to take it.'

The doctor said no more except, 'Bring your father in.'

I was sick to the pit of my stomach as we sat facing him, not knowing what was about to be said.

'Mr Doyle, we now know what is wrong with you.' He looked over at me as he spoke, 'You have tuberculosis – more commonly know as TB.'

Da jumped off the chair before he heard another word and nearly took the hands off the Doctor, he shook them so much. 'Thank you, thank you, doctor. I had meself in an awful state, worryin' tha' yeh might tell me I had cancer.'

'You are still a very sick man, Mr Doyle, and will have to be on a lot of strong medication.'

'No matter wha' yeh say, doctor, with tha' bit of news yeh just gave me I could take on the world.'

'Right, Mr Doyle, I'll get you to sit outside while I talk to your daughter about your prescription.'

As soon as Da left the room, the doctor didn't waste any time in telling me the truth. 'I am afraid your father has lung cancer and he has only a matter of weeks left.'

I couldn't believe what I was hearing. Deep down, I suppose I knew, but I didn't want to know. I had been in complete denial, as had the rest of the family. I couldn't keep myself together; I fell to pieces right there and then.

'Will you just give me a minute, doctor? I can't let him see me cry.'

'Take all the time you need. I have this form filled in and ready for you to sign for him to go into the hospice.'

'Thanks, doctor, but no thanks. If we were to do tha', then he would surely know he had cancer. I think I can speak for all the family when I say this: we'll take care of our own Da. But, if need be, when it comes to the time tha' we need a bit of help, I'll let yeh know. And thanks for doin' tha' for me Da.'

I stood up, took a deep breath and went out with a smile to Da. He was like a different man walking out of the hospital compared to the weak frail man who had held onto me only a short time earlier. He had straightened up, his shoulders pulled back, walking a few steps ahead of me.

'Will yeh hurry yerself there, Kathleen,' he said as I got a big smile. 'I can't wait to get home to tell them all me bit of good news.'

* * *

To this very day, I don't remember driving my car home that day. I could hear Da talking away to me in the distance, but my mind was still trying to take in what I had just been told. *My Da is dying – he won't be around anymore. How can this be? There is no way I'm ready for this. No way at all.*

I barely had the car stopped outside the house when Da was out and heading for the front door. All I could hear was cheering as I walked in. I stood there and looked at everyone. So happy, hugging and kissing Da.

'Kathleen, isn't this the best news ever?' they all kept saying. 'Da is goin' to be okay!'

I got a glimpse of Noel standing in the background. I shook my head and gave him the nod. He knew what had to be done, before I could say anything to the rest of the family.

'Yeh look a bit tired, Da,' he said. 'Why don't yeh lie down for an hour before yer dinner?'

'Now tha' yeh say it, Noel, I think I could do with a bit of shut-eye. I'm after drainin' meself with all the excitement of the day.'

I waited for a few more minutes, making sure that he was settled and asleep before I came out with the words I didn't want to say.

'Stay quiet, everyone, I have somethin' to say.' I could feel myself shaking as the tears rolled down my face.

'Jaysus, Kathleen,' one of the girls said, 'wha' the hell is wrong with yeh? Yeh're cryin' when yeh should be happy and laughin'.'

'I'm sorry, there's just no other way to say this . . . Da has lung cancer. He's dyin'; he has only a few weeks left to live.'

'But Da said . . .' they all kept saying. 'Da said . . .'

There were tears and hysterics when I told them what had happened in the hospital. Ma sat there, not saying a word. She seemed to be lost in her own world. I wasn't sure if she had taken in what I had said and wanted to be left alone. I thought that she might have cried, even a little. But there was nothing; there didn't seem to be any response from her at all. Everybody was too upset, so I said nothing about Ma and let it go for the time being.

When everyone had calmed down we had a talk amongst ourselves.

'This is how I feel,' I said, 'and I think Noel agrees with me. Da doesn't want to know wha's wrong with him. He made that very clear to me today. So, if you all agree, and I know it's goin' to be very hard, we'll try and carry on as normal.'

And that's what we all did, as best we could. When Da came back down that evening for his dinner he was so happy and had such a big smile on his face that we all knew immediately we'd made the right decision.

* * *

Over the next couple of days, whenever I went down to Crumlin, Ma seemed to be asleep a lot of the time and when she was awake she wasn't her usual self. She was too quiet. So I made it my business to speak to my sister Carmel, who spent more time than any of us with Ma and Da, as she had never left the family home.

'Carmel, de yeh think Ma is goin' a bit strange? I'm not sure the news about Da has her like this or if there's somethin' else wrong.'

'Yeh know wha', Kathleen, I kept meanin' to have a talk with yeh about Ma, but with yeh runnin' to the hospital so much with Da, and then with one thing and another, I forgot. Yeh know wha' I caught her doin' one of the days? Now this is before yeh told us about Da. He was givin' out to her about somethin', I don't know wha' it was. Anyway, she was makin' him a sandwich and then I saw her crush a couple of her sleepin' tablets and put them on the bit of corn beef, smotherin' it with brown sauce. Only I caught her, God knows wha' could have happened.

'"Ma," I said, "wha' the hell are yeh doin'?"

'"Tha' fuckin' oul' fella is annoyin' me," she said. "He's givin' out all mornin' like I don't know wha', so this will shut him up for a while." It took me all me time to stop her givin' it to Da. And then the other mornin' I came down and she was sittin' there with about three sets of clothes on.'

'Ah, for Jaysus' sake, Carmel, how could yeh not tell me tha'?'

'Everybody thought it was real funny, Kathleen. I mean, she never done anythin' like tha' before. And then, as I said, it went out of me head.'

I didn't waste any time in getting Ma to the doctor and then on to the hospital to be checked out, only to be told they could find nothing wrong. She sat there chatting away to the doctor, with not a bother on her. The way he was looking at me, I think he thought I was the one who needed help. I was told to come back in six months and they would assess Ma again.

* * *

159

In the meantime, Da was getting weaker by the day, so we put one of the single beds down in the sitting room. That way there were always a couple of us with him at all times. It was now time to let the doctor know we needed some help, which we got straight away. The nurses from the hospice were so kind to Da. They made sure that he was in as little pain as possible.

My sister Marion, who had married and settled in Canada, came home with my brother Phil to spend the last few days with Da. Although it was such a sad and heartbreaking time for us, we were all together as a family and that's what got us through.

Phil and I were sitting at Da's bedside on the evening he passed away. Phil, as usual, was joking and telling a few yarns. Then, just out of the blue, he held Da's hand and said, 'Don't be afraid, Da. Yeh won't be on yer own for long. I'll be with yeh soon.'

'Jaysus Christ, Phil,' I whispered, 'will yeh not be sayin' such things.'

He gave me one of his big smiles and said no more.

We all stayed together that night, sitting on the floor in front of the fire, just like when we were kids, crying and laughing at the same time as we all went down memory lane, before we all eventually fell asleep.

* * *

I woke up to the sound of someone sobbing. It was still night. Phil was sitting beside Da's bed and crying so hard as he held Da's hand. I made my way over to him and put my arm around his shoulder.

'De yeh know somethin', Kathleen? All those years away – wha' was it all for? A bloody house and a fancy car tha' I would have got here anyway in time? Me Da is dead and Ma hardly knows who I am half the time. I should've been here to look after them. Half of me brothers and sisters I don't even know. They're like strangers to me, they were so young when I took off.'

'Come on, Phil, don't be beatin' yerself up like tha'. Yeh were just followin' yer dream, like all of us.'

'I know tha', Kathleen, but did mine have to be on the other side of the fuckin' world? I've missed out on so much because of it.'

'For Jaysus' sake, Phil, will yeh not be cursin' like tha', or yeh'll have Da jumpin' up there givin' out like shite to the pair of us.'

I got a tiny little grin when I said that.

'All the same, Kathleen, wouldn't tha' be somethin'? I'd give the world to have him back, even just for a little while.'

'Wouldn't we all, Phil? Now let's go into the kitchen and I'll make us a nice cup of tea.'

My own heart was bursting, but I was trying so hard to keep up a front, Phil was falling to pieces that much. We sat there through the night talking and laughing as we went over the past once more and then crying as we were brought back to the present.

Before we knew it the morning light was breaking through the curtains and the rest of the family were starting to wake up. It was going to be a long, hard day ahead for each and every one of us.

* * *

There was hustle and bustle over the next couple of days with Da being laid out in the house. There was no end to the people coming to pay their respects.

Ma sat in her chair staring out, not saying a word. I knew deep down in my heart there was something seriously wrong with her, especially when she turned around without the blink of an eye and said, 'I want me telly on. I want to look at the funnies.' 'The funnies' were the cartoons.

Everyone in the room went quiet for a few seconds, with a few of the neighbours giving the eye to one another. There was our Da, laid out in his coffin, ready to go and meet his maker, and all Ma wanted was to watch Mickey Mouse on the telly. I looked over at Phil and Noel, not knowing what to say or do. I could see that Noel was in shock like the rest of us. But Phil, being Phil, was laughing his head off. He got up and put the telly on, saying, 'Wha' harm is she doin'? If it makes her happy, wha' the heck.' And that was it; the funnies played as the wake went on.

The priest came down that evening to say mass. We had to move all the furniture around to make as much room as possible. We had a parrot called Rocky, who was supposed to be put upstairs out of the way, as he had a terrible mouth on him and never stopped cursing. But, of course, somebody just happened to put his cage behind the very chair that the priest was standing in front of. There we were, all upset, crying and sniffling, when suddenly we heard the words, 'Yeh're only a bollocks, yeh're only a bollocks!'

We all looked at each other, not knowing what to do, biting our lips, trying not to laugh. The priest didn't bat an eyelid; he just gave a little cough and carried on with the mass, while Clare took Rocky upstairs, apologising on the way out.

The funeral went off as well as any funeral does. We were all grieving in our own way, but all feeling the same loss inside, now that our Da was gone. After a few days, we said our goodbyes to Phil and Marion as they headed back to their lives so far away, and then we all settled back into our own lives. Little did any of us realise the trauma and pain that lay ahead for Ma.

18

Ma

After Da died, I used to dread going down to Crumlin, walking into the house, with him not being there. I loved and missed him so much.

I used to get into some debates with him over the years, mostly about religion, which I started to find many faults with as I got older. He would go mad when I pointed out different things that he had no answer for, about the priest or where all the money was going and so on. His response was always the same: 'Mark my words, Kathleen Doyle' – when he used my full name I knew that he was really pissed off with me – 'one of these days yeh'll be struck down dead for flyin' in the face of God.'

We would either hammer it out, hot and heavy, or if he saw that he wasn't getting the better of me, he would storm off up to his bedroom and sulk for an hour. If he didn't come back down, I always made it my business to go to him, making the peace with a smoke and a cup of tea.

'Yeh're an awful girl, Kathleen,' he would say, 'gettin' me all roiled up like tha'. Yeh really know how to get me goin'.'

Oh, how I miss those times.

I suppose if Ma had been her old self, going around ranting and raving, throwing the odd 'fuck' in here and there, the house wouldn't have been so quiet and maybe I wouldn't have felt the loss so much. But that wasn't to be. She just sat in her chair saying very little, like someone lost in another world. She never cried once for Da and when we would ask her where he was, she'd shake her head and turn away, not saying a word.

It had been a couple of months since I had last been at the hospital with Ma and in that time she had got a lot worse. I thought to myself as I waited to see the doctor, *Surely to God this time they will be able to see that there is something wrong?* I had asked over and over again if they would do a brain scan for me. The answer was always the same: 'I'm afraid your mother will have to go on the waiting list like everyone else.'

'But, doctor,' I would say, 'if it's the money, tha's not a problem. There's plenty of us in the family to pay for it.' But they didn't listen.

It was only on her last visit, after I insisted that they do a test for diabetes, that somebody finally listened to me. I knew by the doctor's face that Ma's results must have been serious. His words to me were, 'I'm afraid your mother's sugar levels are quite high. As soon as the first bed becomes available, she will have to come into hospital for further tests.'

'Yeh mean they're sky high, is tha' wha' yeh're tryin' to tell me, doctor? I've tried to tell yeh for I don't know how long tha' there was somethin' very seriously wrong with our Ma. And it's not only diabetes; there's somethin' else there, I know there is.'

'And you would know this how, Mrs McGrath?' he asked smartly.

'Well, I don't pretend to know the medical terms, doctor, but in my line of work I deal with people every day and I *listen* to my clients telling me about their mothers and families, and the different symptoms they would have. Tha's how I knew my Ma had diabetes and tha's why I'm fightin' to get a brain scan, because I think there's something wrong there. I know by the way she's goin' on.'

I could see that he was getting annoyed at me for speaking out to him like that, but at that stage I didn't care. I was sick and tired of them passing me around from Billy to Jack and not one of them coming up with any answers. Anyway, I got the usual little cough off the doctor, and I could tell he didn't know what to say. He kept his head down as he wrote on Ma's chart while he mumbled out a few words to me.

'The nurse will tell you about your mother's medication and she will also make arrangements about her coming in for the test as soon as a bed is ready.'

I didn't have anything else to say to him, so I took Ma by the hand and left.

Incredibly, I was only in the house ten or fifteen minutes when the phone rang. It was the hospital, asking if we could bring Ma straight back in, as they had a bed for her.

Good Jaysus, I thought to myself, *I should have got annoyed with them months ago*.

'Carmel,' I said, 'run upstairs and pack a bag with Ma's few bits in it and I'll get her back down to the hospital as quick as I can. We don't want them changin' their mind now, do we?'

'Thank God they're takin' her in, Kathleen. I don't know wha' she's goin' to do from day to day. I came down the other mornin' and the front door was wide open; Ma wasn't to be found anywhere. I was frantic. De yeh know where she was when I did eventually find her? Up the top of the road, not dressed, still in her nightdress. And tha's not all; she's gettin' up in the middle of the night to make herself a cup of tea, which is no harm I know, but she's puttin' the gas cooker on and not lightin' it. Only I woke to go into the toilet and smelled the gas, we'd all be dead today.'

'I know it's hard on yeh, Carmel. Yeh're with Ma more than the rest of us. But I promise we'll get to the bottom of it this time. Now, I'd better go. Will yeh ring around the rest of the family and tell them wha's happenin'? I'll stay with Ma until one or two of yeh come up and then I'll go on home and have a break.'

* * *

I was only in the door of the hospital when Ma was seen to straight away. They had her settled in a ward in no time at all. I was sitting there talking to her, trying to get her to understand that she was only going to be there for a couple of days.

'The doctors want to do a few tests,' I said, 'just to make sure you're okay, Ma. And then yeh'll be straight back home, I promise.'

Not a sound came from her. She was yellow in the face and had this glazed look in her eyes. You know, like when someone is looking at you but they're not seeing you. She looked as if she was lost in another place and couldn't find her way back.

My brother Noel arrived. The two of us were sitting there talking away when suddenly Ma started twitching and shaking. Then she went into a major fit. Noel jumped up with the fright.

'Good Jaysus,' he roared, 'quick, Kathleen, get a nurse, get a doctor!'

He was trying to put Ma on her side while I ran out screaming for help. Two nurses came straight away with the doctor following minutes after, putting Noel and myself out in the corridor while they looked after Ma. Then the rest of the family starting to dribble in one by one and there was no way any one of us would be allowed back in to Ma.

She continued having more fits through the night and into the early hours of the morning. Then and only then was the decision made to send her for a brain scan, over to Elm Park Hospital. The brain scan showed that she had a brain tumour the size of a large egg, pressing on her memory bank, which was causing her to be so confused. When we spoke to the brain surgeon we were told, 'Your mother has a fifty-fifty chance of pulling through the operation, and even then I can't promise anything. But if she does make it through, don't expect too much. She will never be the same woman again.'

'So wha' yeh're sayin', doctor, is Ma will be the same as she is now,' I said, 'and still not know any of us?'

'I'm afraid so. But without the operation she will surely die, and it will be sooner rather than later.'

We were all in shock, trying to take it all on board. Our Da was only two months dead, and now Ma . . . I was screaming inside my head, *Why is all this happenin' to us? It's not fair. It's just not fair!* Such a hard life Ma had had rearing us kids. Now, at the age of only sixty-three, when she should be starting to enjoy life, all this was happening to her. We didn't want our Ma to leave us, so each and every one of us gave the go-ahead to operate.

They operated straight away. Such a long day it was, taking nearly eight hours before they were finished. We all handled it in our own way. Some wanted to be on their own; some paired off together. Myself and Clare sat in the little church in the hospital. Both of us knew full well that if one of us was sick, that's where Ma would be. I couldn't help but let my mind wander back in time, thinking about all the mad things us kids used to do on her. How she put up with us I'll never know. I was laughing and crying at the same time as I spoke to Clare.

'Remember the day we made the swimmin' pool in the house, Clare? God, she nearly killed us all tha' day. I don't know how one of us didn't end up in the hospital, she was throwin' tha' many rocks at us.'

'She never caught me, Kathleen, ever, not even on the day tha' priest came down to the house – yeh know, the one tha' made Ma cry over the purse. I swore I'd get me own back on him for doin' tha'. He was a righ' pig, so he was. Well, he was down knockin' on the door one day, givin' out shite about me being cheeky. I wasn't long about sortin' him out. I fucked a load of potato skins, tea leaves and any rubbish I could get me hands on out the top window all over him and then scarpered over the back wall before Ma could catch me.'

'Jaysus, yeh were a mad bitch, Clare. I'll never forget tha' evenin'. I was only in the door from work when Ma launched into tellin' me wha' yeh did. Now, havin' said tha', yeh could see tha' she was tryin' to keep a straight face herself. If the truth be known, Clare, she was probably pleased with wha' yeh did after the way he treated her. But, of course, she couldn't let us know tha' at the time.'

Both of us sat there laughing about the past, but at the same time crying as we waited to see what the future held for Ma.

The doctor told us that the operation went well but the next twenty-four hours were crucial. We were to leave it until the following evening before coming in. We phoned all the family, letting them know that Ma had pulled through.

I was so tired and drained from all the running around that I had done with Da the previous few weeks, up until he died, back and forward to Crumlin, up and down to the hospital, trying to work and look after the kids. I really thought that I might have slept that night. Instead, I lay there thinking about Ma on her own. Was she all right? Would she pull through? Would she ever know any of us again? I cried so much just thinking about that.

I pottered about the next day, doing a few hours work to keep myself busy, wishing and hoping that the time would come when I could make my way up to Ma, leaving Alan to take care of the kids. I didn't hang about waiting for any of the others. We all said that we'd meet up in the hospital. I got there a bit early and made my way up to the ward.

I was not expecting the sight that awaited me. I thought Ma's head would be covered in bandages. I went into shock when I saw her. She was propped up in the bed. Her eyes were wide open and they were black and blue. Most of her hair had been shaved off and her head was badly swollen. But the part that I couldn't handle was that, from one ear right across to the other, big silver staples were holding her head together. It was like something out of a horror movie. I ran outside and couldn't breathe with the fright I got. I was standing there shaking, I was so upset. Shortly after that I saw Clare walking up the corridor.

'Wha's wrong with yeh, Kathleen? Yeh're green in the face. Don't tell me Ma's dead – Jaysus, don't tell me she's after dyin'!'

'No, no, it's not tha',' I said. 'Oh Clare, yeh'd want to see Ma. It's terrible. Wait until yeh see her. Oh my God, wait 'til yeh see her.'

'Will yeh give it over, Kathleen. It can't be tha' bad.'

The two of us made our way back in and I could see that Clare felt the same as me, but she held it together a bit better.

'Holy Mother of God, this is not righ'. Ma never deserved this.'

I couldn't even answer her, I was crying so much.

As each member of the family arrived, the shock on all their faces said it all. We all stood there, not knowing what to say or do. After a few minutes, Noel spoke up.

'Righ',' he said, 'Ma always did her best for us and now it's our turn to take care of her. We have to make sure there's two of us here at all times every day, keepin' an eye on her.' We all nodded in agreement.

* * *

After a couple of days, the doctor had a talk with us.

'As soon as we take the staples out of your mother's head,' he said, 'which will be after the weekend, we would like her to go home.'

We all started chiming in together, saying the same thing. 'But doctor, Ma's real sick. We can't take her home – not like this.'

'I am sorry, but your mother has to be in her own home, among familiar surroundings. She needs all of you to keep talking to her, over and over again, about the past and the present. That is the only way we will get her brain to start working again. I have done my part now; the rest is up to all of you.'

'We know yeh have, doctor,' said Noel, 'and we all thank yeh for savin' our Ma's life.'

The doctor was well pleased when Noel said that, smiling at each of us before he went about his business.

* * *

And that was it; Ma was back home less than eight days after her operation. It was so hard to watch the mother who was always so strong, who took care of us so well, but who was now like a baby and had to be taught everything all over again. It was very slow and needed so much patience.

Ma didn't come back to her old self the way she had been before, but a little part of her was still there. She still remembered to give you 'the look' if there was something going on around her.

I remember the day so well; I was talking away to her, saying my name, going over and over again.

'Ma, it's me, Kathleen. De yeh know who I am? Ma, it's Kathleen.'

I must have said it a dozen times. I was sick listening to myself, when suddenly she turned around, looked me straight in the eye and said, 'Feck off, Kathleen. I know yeh!' She didn't say 'fuck', but feck was good enough for me.

I couldn't believe it; I started screaming. 'Carmel, Carmel, come quick. She knows who I am.' Carmel rushed in and I turned back to Ma. 'Ma, tell me, who's tha' standin' there?' She looked and thought for a minute or two.

'It's Carmel.'

Carmel was delighted when Ma said her name. The two of us started screaming together, jumping up and down, hugging one another. We were over the moon. We knew it would still take time, but it was great to see Ma was on the mend.

19

The Funny Farm

As the weeks and months went by, Ma slowly remembered us all. She was as happy as anything, sitting in her chair every day, looking at the cartoons and all the old films, laughing her head off, with not a care in the world.

But she still needed constant care. I know we all dropped down to see Ma and give a dig out when we were there, but it still wasn't the same. Because Carmel was living there, she had so much more to do than the rest of us. She was worn out from looking after Ma and badly needed a break. So she headed off to Spain for a week's holidays.

We were all down in Crumlin – now, when I say all, I mean me and my sisters; there was no way the fellas could do much for Ma, other than to sit and talk to her, in the hope that she might say something back to them. We were trying to work out what would be the best arrangement for Ma for the week and who would have the most time during the day, with the rest helping out in the evenings.

'I'll take Ma up with me,' said Clare, 'once yiz don't let me down when I'm bringin' the chipper out at five o'clock. Other than tha', it won't be a problem.'

Clare had a mobile chipper van that she would get ready during the day and then tow over to her spot beside one of the local pubs. She had a couple of women working for her, so she had a bit more time on her hands than the rest of us.

I didn't live too far from Clare's house, which was a big bungalow on a half-acre of land. So I made it my business to be there every day. It was like going over to a funny farm. She had two sons, Dominic, who was around thirteen, and Romano, who was going on eight. They were so wild. No, I take that back – they were mad. I never knew what to expect when I went into that house.

I had just arrived one day and Clare was waving to me as she pulled out with the chipper. 'I won't be long, Kathleen,' she said. 'Go on in; the kids are there with Ma.'

I was knocking away on the door for ages, with not a sign of anyone letting me in. They were in there all right; I could hear them screaming and laughing their heads off. I went around to the side window, and I couldn't believe what I saw. They had all the furniture pushed up against the walls. Ma was sitting on a woollen blanket on the floor and there were Romano and Dominic pulling her along, flying up and down the room, twirling her all over the place. Well, you'd want to hear the laughs off Ma, never mind the other two! She looked as if she was having the time of her life.

I nearly lost my breath. All I could think of was Ma's head and what damage would be done if she banged it. The window was only short of shattering all over the place, I knocked on it so hard. Finally I got their attention and they opened the door.

'Ah, there yeh are, Kathleen,' said Dominic. 'We're having great craic here with me Nanny.'

'I know yiz are. Haven' I been watchin' yiz for the past ten minutes? Yeh ravin' lunatics, tha's wha' yiz are. Now, help me get yer Nanny off the floor.'

Ma was still curled over with the laughing. 'Are yeh okay, Ma?' I asked as I got her up and settled in the chair.

Still giggling, she said, 'Funny, great, funny.' Just to hear her say that was worth the fright I got.

'There, we told yeh, Kathleen,' the other two chimed in. 'Nanny does have the best fun ever when she's with us.'

'I can well imagine, after wha' I saw. Now get in there, the pair of yiz and make us a nice a cup of tea while I talk to yer Nanny.'

Clare was back before too long and I told her what had been going on. Now, before I go any further, I have to tell you that Clare is the most easy-going person on this planet. Nothing, and I mean nothing, gets her excited.

'Wha' are yeh gettin' yerself all worked up for, Kathleen?' Clare said. 'I told them before I went out tha' when they got down to the end of the room with Ma to make sure to slow down a bit when they're twirling her around. Just in case one of them would slip, like. But they were grand. She was laughin' her head off.'

'Are yeh for real or wha', Clare? I mean, say she had banged her head . . . wha' would yeh have done then?'

'But she didn't, did she, Kathleen? Now, don't be gettin' yer knickers in a knot there. She's fine.'

'I know, Clare. I'm just afraid somethin' will happen to her, tha's all.'

'Well, the way I see it, Kathleen, we can wrap Ma up in her blanket and have her all nice and cosy and safe there lookin' at the telly. And if the truth be known, she's probably just starin' into space half the time. Believe me, I know them two little fuckers of mine are as mad as hatters, but if they can make Ma laugh the way I just saw, well, tha's good enough for me.'

'I have to say, Clare, even though I nearly had a stroke when I looked in the window, part of me was laughin' along with them. It was great to see her havin' a bit of fun instead of just sittin' in the chair.'

'I know them doctors were real good, Kathleen, with everythin' they did for Ma and, God only knows, she wouldn't be here only for them. But yeh know when they told us not to expect too much? Tha' she'd never come back to anythin' like she was before and tha' we were lucky just to have her alive? Well, I stood there and listened while yeh all asked yer different questions about one thing or the other, and I said to meself, *Yeh're so wrong, doctor, because yeh don't know our Ma and how strong she can be.* She didn't pull through all this just to sit in a chair and be molly-coddled like a baby. It might take a bit of time, but we'll get her back.'

'De yeh know somethin', Clare? Yeh're so righ'. Ma wouldn't want this, and de yeh know wha' else? She's probably fuckin' like mad inside her head, wantin' to give us all a good dig at the same time. Tha's it now, Clare – when I have her on the weekends I'm goin' to back off and start lettin' her do things for herself.'

'Righ' then, tha's enough of all tha' serious talk, Kathleen. Would yeh have a look in at her now.'

There Romano was, breaking his heart laughing, lying on the floor with a feather at Ma's feet, tickling the life out of her; and there she was, fist in the air, trying to swing a dig at him. It was great to see.

* * *

The week was nearly over and Carmel was on her way back from her holiday, so I made my way over early to Clare's to help pack Ma's few bits before bringing her home to Crumlin. When I walked into the kitchen, I thought I was seeing things.

As I said, Clare had a good bit of land around her bungalow and what went with that were a load of chickens and about fourteen dogs at any given time; one cat that looked more like a small lion, mainly because he ate dog food and all the scraps that went with it; 'Goldy' the horse, who was absolutely gorgeous; and a pony called 'One-Eye Jack'. Clare took in every stray from around the area.

When I walked into the kitchen, Ma was sitting there drinking a cup of tea. Dominic and Romano were with her, having their breakfast. But guess who else was there? One-Eye Jack, the pony! And he wasn't a little pony, he was a good size. He was standing beside Ma as she fed him slices of bread and butter.

'Holy Jaysus, Dominic, are yiz gone fuckin' mad altogether? Wha' are yiz doin' bringin' the horse into the house? Where the hell is Clare?'

'She's still in bed,' the two of them chimed in together. 'Nanny was laughin' and wavin' out to Jack to come over to her and it was lashin' rain out. We didn't want to bring her out, in case she'd get wringin' wet, so we brought him in to her! Look, she's havin' great fun with him, Kathleen.'

True enough, when I looked at Ma, she was as happy as Larry, sitting there with nearly half a loaf of bread in front of her as she fed Jack his breakfast.

'Clare will have a blue fit when she sees the state of this kitchen. I'm tellin' yiz, she'll kill the pair of yiz. Yiz better get off side by the time she gets up. Look, there's muck everywhere!'

With that, Jack gave himself a right shaking, drowning the whole lot of us and into the bargain lashing me out of it with his tail. Ma and the other two thought this was so funny. I ran to Clare's room to get away from him.

'Clare,' I roared, 'yeh better get up, it's like a lunatic asylum out there. They have the horse in the house!' Not a blink or a sound came from her. 'Clare, did yeh hear wha' I said – the horse is in the fuckin' house! Will yeh wake up, for Jaysus' sake. I have to get Ma ready for goin' home.'

Still not a sound. I was really getting pissed off at this stage. I had splashes of muck all over me and Dominic and Romano were standing in the hall, laughing their heads off.

'We'll get her up for yeh, Kathleen, but it'll cost yeh!'

'Wha' de yeh mean, it'll cost me? Cost me wha'?'

'Money, of course!' said Dominic. 'Give us a few shillin's and we'll have our Ma out of the bed before yeh know it.'

I stood there and thought for a minute. *The crafty little fuckers.* At the same time, it was like looking at myself and Phil, the way we used to get up to all sorts to make a few shillings.

'Righ' then, anythin' to get out of this madhouse!' I handed over the money.

I thought that they might jump on the bed and maybe shake Clare hard, like most normal kids would do, but I should have known when I looked at the pair of them. You could see the devilment in their eyes.

'Righ',' said Dominic to Romano as they stood at the doorway of Clare's bedroom, 'go down and get Jack and bring him up here to me. I'll get the rope when yeh're doin' tha'.'

While all this was going on, Clare still didn't blink an eye; she was dead to the world. I couldn't believe that she was still asleep with all this commotion going on around her.

'Wha' de yeh mean, Dominic?' I said. 'Why are yeh bringin' the horse down here?'

'Yeh want me Ma to wake up, don't yeh, Kathleen? Now, just stand over there at the window and let us get on with it.'

I stood there with my mouth open as I watched them. I couldn't believe what they were about to do. I have to admit,

I was laughing to myself at the same time. While Romano was fixing the rope around the horse's neck, Dominic was tying Clare's two legs together with the other end of the rope. As soon as they were finished, Jack got a right wallop on the arse and he made a charge down the hall, dragging Clare out of the bed along with him! Well, you'd want to have heard the screams of her as she bounced all over the place throughout the house! I swear to God, I wet in my knickers, I was laughing so much. I watched the other two lunatics roll around the floor with laughter.

'In the name of Jaysus,' Clare kept roaring, 'when I get me hands on yiz, yeh're dead – fuckin' dead – de yeh hear me? Dead! Now, get these ropes offa me. Yeh bastards!'

Dominic was trying to keep a straight face as he held Jack and fed him a sweet. In the meantime, Romano was untying Clare's feet. They didn't waste any time in scarpering out the back door, leaving me to face Clare and help her up off the floor.

'Kathleen Doyle, I can't believe yeh helped them two little fucks of mine to do this to me! You of all people! Look at me. I'm in bits. I won't be able to walk righ' for a month.'

'I swear to God, Clare, when I was givin' them the money to wake yeh, I didn't know this is wha' they had in mind.'

'Yeh mean yeh paid them to do this to me? Yeh're fuckin' as bad as they are!'

With all this going on I had completely forgotten about Ma, who was still sitting in the same spot, laughing her head off. She soon stopped us in our tracks when we heard her say, 'Clare, so funny . . . mad . . . Clare.' The two of us screamed together when we heard her speak. She would be quiet for so long and then out of the blue she'd say a few words here and there.

'Oh my God, Clare! Did yeh hear tha'? Ma has said more this week than she has in I don't know how long.'

'Isn't tha' wha' I was only sayin' the other day, Kathleen? I mean, I haven't got time to be pussy-footin' about with Ma every minute of the day. I just have to let her get on with it. When yeh're all asleep in yer beds at night, I'm out until three and four o'clock, towin' tha' chipper home. Then when I have tha' done I start cuttin' me fish up for the next day. And I'm doin' tha' until the early hours of the mornin'. So is it any wonder I'm dead to the world and can't get outta the bed?'

'I'm sorry, Clare. I do forget about tha'. I wasn't thinkin'.'

At that moment the two head-bangers made their way back in to us.

'Are yeh okay, Ma?' asked the pair of them as they stood there with dirty big grins on their faces.

'Yiz are bastards, tha's wha' yiz are!' said Clare.

Romano lay his head on Clare's shoulder and wrapped his two arms around her as he said, 'Ma, tha' was the best fun ever.'

And that was it. Clare melted as usual and they got away with murder once more.

'Anyway, Clare,' I said, 'now tha' all the madness is out of the way, the reason I'm over early is to get Ma ready and bring her back home to Crumlin. Carmel is flyin' in later today. I tell yeh wha', you sit there and I'll pack her few bits. Dominic, make yer Ma a cup of tea and some toast. It's the least yeh can do after wha' yeh just put her through.'

He was up like a light, sucking up to Clare like I don't know what, while I packed up for Ma.

'Are yeh righ', Ma?' I said as soon as I was finished. 'I'll help yeh get dressed now. It's time to bring yeh home.'

She would neither budge nor look at me.

'Come on, Ma, wha's wrong with yeh?'

She looked up at me and then straight at Clare. 'Stayin' here!' she said.

179

'I'm sorry, Ma, but yeh have to go back home.'

She sat there and didn't say another word, but kept looking into Clare's face.

'She doesn't have to go at the minute, Kathleen. There's no problem if Ma wants to stay on for another week or two with me.'

Well, you'd want to see Ma's face brighten up when she heard Clare say that.

* * *

Those couple of weeks ended up turning into six years for Clare and Ma. There was always hustle and bustle going on in Clare's house. Between the fish man, the chip man and all the other deliveries that went with running her chipper, there was always somebody dropping in or something going on. And that's without mentioning the two head-bangers, Dominic and Romano, who got up to all sorts of mischief along the way.

But between them, they looked after Ma so well. I think in Ma's mind it reminded her so much of all that went on when we were growing up, the bedlam and mayhem that surrounded her throughout her life. Crumlin had gone so quiet, especially since Da's death, with each and every one of us going our own way. Maybe inside her head, she couldn't handle that. We all thought that we were doing the right thing by wrapping her in cotton wool, not realising that we were probably smothering her all the time. So the best thing that could have happened was Ma going to live up in Clare's funny farm. I think that at the end of the day, that's what really helped her come on so well.

Ma still wasn't able to do very much and needed so much care, but as time went on she got a lot better. We signed her up to one of the local clubs, so that she would be mixing with people in and around her age. That helped so much to bring her out of herself. She loved going there. They would have their nights outs and plenty of weekends away. She ended up being the life and soul of the party everywhere she went. Always the first up on the floor and the last one to leave, Ma became more outgoing, in a way that she never was before

The doctors couldn't get over the change. I remember sitting in the hospital on one of the visits with Ma. She was chattering away like I don't know what to the doctor. There was no stopping her. I was well pleased with what he had to say, and very happy with Ma's reply.

'Do you know, Mrs Doyle, you have a great family. The support and hard work you got from them is what has you sitting here today.'

She stopped dead in her tracks and looked me straight in the eye, just like she did so many years ago.

'De yeh think I don't know tha', doctor?'

That's when I knew our Ma was slowly coming back to us.

20

Hospital

I had been attending the Coombe hospital for the past twelve years because of my gynaecological problems, and I have to say the doctors were very good. They kept a close eye on me in that time. I was due back for my yearly visit, which I didn't give much thought to, mainly because I had been told for so long, 'Your smear tests have settled down, Mrs McGrath, but they're still not clear, so we will see you next year.' As usual, I would go off about my business and didn't give it another thought until I was due to go back again.

Now, I was sitting in front of the doctor and I suppose I should have known there was something wrong, because it was the head man himself this time, whom I hadn't seen for years. The difference a few years can make. I had grown up so much and was more confident in myself than I had been the first time I had sat down in front of this doctor in his white coat. I was no longer afraid of him.

There was no beating about the bush; he just came right out and said what he had to say. 'Mrs McGrath, I'm afraid it's time for you to come in and have a hysterectomy. It can't be left any longer.'

I came right out and asked it. 'Doctor, have I got cancer?'

He looked me straight in the eye for a second or two before he spoke. 'Yes, you have, so we can't waste any time. You have to come in straight away or we won't be responsible after that.' Confidence or no confidence, when that word is spoken, no matter how much you think you are prepared, it doesn't half knock you for six. I was really shook up inside and was trying not to let the doctor see it. I could feel myself shaking and my voice trembling as I spoke.

'Can I have a bit of time to sort a few things out at home, doctor?'

'Yes, you can, but I want you back down to the hospital in the next two days. I will schedule your operation straight away.'

I thanked the doctor and left. My head was all over the place as I made my way out of the hospital. *Jaysus Christ*, I thought to myself, *how am I goin' to work around things?* Martina was working away, finishing her apprenticeship, and there was no way she could take time off. Myself and Alan had taken on the role of helping her rear Danielle, who was only around nine months old, and the news I had just been given was not in my plans.

I'm sure anyone who was looking at me while I walked along must have thought I was mad. I was talking way out loud to myself. 'I'll keep Amanda out of school. I know she's only twelve but with the help of Alan they should manage okay. But then again, I swore that, no matter what, I'd never keep any of my kids out of school for anything. But I suppose this is a bit serious and hopefully it'll only be for a few days.'

I was still having a conversation with myself as I got into my car. I sat there for God knows how long, staring out the window before, finally, I broke down and cried. It was only then, when the silence came over me, that I realised what I had been told. Just then I got a flash of Ma. I would have loved nothing better than for her to put her arms around me and say, 'Don't worry, Kathleen, everythin's goin' to be fine.' But that wasn't to be; she was lost in another world and knew very little of what was going on around her.

As soon as I got myself together I decided that I wouldn't tell anyone what the doctor had said, not until it was all over, in the hope that the outcome would be good. I thought there was no point in worrying everybody unless I had to.

I waited until Alan and myself were on our own before I said anything.

'Alan, I was back at the hospital today for me yearly visit.'

'Jaysus, Kathleen, tha' was a quick year all the same. I forgot all about it. Anyway, how did yeh get on? Everythin' okay with yeh?'

'Well, I had a good chat with the doctor and he was sayin' tha', with all the problems I've had over the years with one thing and another, and I'm thirty-eight now, so he said it might not be a bad idea for me to come in and have me few bits out. Well, he said it different, with fancy words and all, but yeh know wha' I mean, Alan. So what de yeh think?'

'Well, Kathleen, I think tha' yeh should listen to wha' the man is sayin', because at the end of the day he's the one tha' knows wha' he's talkin' about.'

'The only thing is, Martina has to go to work. Wha' about Danielle? Will yeh be able to take time off to look after her?'

'Tha' won't be a problem. I'll park the van until Martina comes in from work. And don't be worryin'. I'll still get me night run in. I just had a thought there, Kathleen – wha' about the nappies? I'm no good at changin' them.'

'I'm goin' to keep Amanda off school to help with tha', so yeh don't have to worry there, Alan.'

'Thanks be to Jaysus for tha'! The last time I changed a nappy was when Martina was a baby and I can still remember; the shit was everywhere. And yeh know I never did another nappy change after tha'.'

He just about got a little smile out of me when he said that. I was trying to keep a front up and not fall to pieces, but it was so hard. Alan would usually know straight away when there was something wrong with me. But with Da not too long dead and so much going on with Ma, I wasn't myself anyway. So the fact that I was a bit quiet at that moment wasn't out of the ordinary.

'Anyway, Kathleen,' said Alan, 'when's all this happenin'?'

'I've to be back in the hospital over the next two days. The doctor said tha' he could fit me in straight away, tha' he had an openin', or he could put me on a list. So I thought, best to get it over and done with now.'

I'm not one for telling lies – well, maybe a little white one now and again – but they just seemed to flow out of me that day. I felt that this time it was allowed. I gave the same yarn to the rest of the family, with no-one being the wiser.

* * *

The next two days seemed to go by so slowly. Every time I looked at Alan or the kids, I could feel myself starting to fill up inside, with the tears ready to burst out of me. I would make some lame excuse and head upstairs. I'd sit on the side of the bath thinking, *Wha' if I don't make it? Who'll take care of Alan and the kids? Oh my God, I can't die. I have to be here always to look after my family. Anyway, I've too much to do with me life. I'm only gettin' started. There's no way this is goin' to drag me down – no way!* With that thought in my mind, I'd pull myself together and carry on as best I could.

Alan dropped me down to the hospital and stayed for a while. He knew that I was nervous.

'Don't be worryin', Kathleen,' he said. 'This time tomorrow it'll all be over and yeh'll be grand, so try and get a good night's sleep. Will yeh do tha' for me?' He gave me a big hug and kiss before he left.

There were three other girls in the ward with me, each of them having the same operation as myself. As the nurses moved busily around, getting us all ready for the following morning, we sat there talking away, mostly about our families and life itself. When I think about it now, we all knew why we were there but none of us spoke of it. Maybe they too had been told the same news as myself and none of us wanted to hear the word 'cancer' mentioned. That way, we could pretend it wasn't there, for that moment anyway.

I didn't sleep much at all that night. I lay there thinking about what the future held for me. That's when I decided to have a little chat with the Holy Mother herself.

'Righ',' I said, 'there's no way I'm ready to go anywhere, so please watch over me tomorrow and make this all go away. Please.'

I must have dozed off for a while, because the next thing I remember is someone tapping me and calling out my name.

'Wake up, Kathleen,' said the nurse. 'It's nearly time for us to bring you down to the theatre. I want you to take this tablet to keep you relaxed and I'll leave this gown and hat for you to put on. We'll be back in about ten minutes.'

It all happened so fast that before I knew it, I was on the trolley and on my way. The two nurses were talking away as they wheeled me along, telling me not to worry, that I was in good hands. I smiled and said nothing. I was too busy thinking of Alan and the kids. With that, Da popped into my head. I could see his face as plain as anything and felt that he was really there with me. Maybe the tablet had me feeling like that. I really don't know, but it made me feel a lot better and I wasn't scared anymore. In my mind Da was there watching over me.

As I lay there waiting for the anaesthetic to take effect, counting backwards, the last thing on my mind was Alan and the kids. I just about got a tiny prayer said before I drifted off.

* * *

It took a day or two for me to get back on my feet and I was so sore afterwards, but that didn't bother me. All I cared about were my results, which seemed to be taking forever to come back. I pestered the nurses every time they came into the ward. I'd keep asking, 'Nurse, have yeh heard anythin'? Is there any word back yet?'

'Don't be worrying, Kathleen. As soon as the doctor has your test results back he'll be straight in to see you.'

And so he was, the following day. I remember it so well, as if it was only yesterday. The girl in the bed next to me got her results early that morning, and it wasn't good news. As soon as the nurse pulled the curtain around her bed, I cocked my ears and had a listen as the doctor spoke.

'We're so sorry,' he said, 'but the cancer has spread. It's gone too far, I'm afraid; there is no more we can do.'

I got such a lump in my throat as I lay there listening to her cry. At the same time, I wanted to get sick with the thought of what I might be told myself.

It was well into the day before the doctor arrived to see me. There was a nurse and a lady doctor with him. They both gave me a smile and I thought, *Tha' looks good. They're not all serious, so tha' must mean somethin'.* Either way, I was shitting myself as I waited for the head doctor to speak.

'I have very good news for you, Kathleen,' he said. I couldn't believe it; he was calling me by my first name after all these years. 'The cancer was only in the womb, which we removed, and did not spread to any of your other organs. So you are a very lucky young woman that we have been keeping a check on you over the years.'

The relief I felt when I heard those words! It was like the weight of the world had been lifted off my shoulders.

'Thank you, thank you, thank you so much, doctor. I'm after bein' up the walls with worry, not knowin' wha' yeh were goin' to tell me.'

'You still have to come in to see us for the next two years,' he said, 'because if the cancer was to come back, which I doubt very much, it would be in that timeframe. I will leave instructions with the nurse and your appointment card. You can pick them up when you're leaving. And remember, take it easy for a while. So, best of luck, Kathleen.' He shook my hand and on he moved to the next ward.

I couldn't help but cry, only my tears were out of joy and happiness, unlike the girl who was next to me. She was still sobbing her heart out, trying to come to terms with what she had been told. I thought, *That could so easily have been me.* I couldn't stop thanking the Holy Mother and every angel that I asked to watch over me, but most of all my Da. I really do believe that he was there looking after me.

* * *

I thought Alan would never get up to me so I could tell him my news. Well, he turned green in the face when I told him the truth.

'Holy Jaysus, Kathleen, yeh should've said somethin'. I thought yeh had to get this done because of all the women's problems yeh were havin' over the years. I had no idea it was tha' serious. I can't believe yeh didn't tell me. I mean, keepin' the likes of tha' bottled up inside yeh . . . Don't ever do anythin' like tha' again, no matter wha' it is – de yeh hear me?'

He put his two arms around me and hugged me ever so tight for such a long time afterwards. The kids were none the wiser, but I did tell the family. I especially wanted my sisters to know so that they would go and have regular check-ups. There were loads of snots and tears, with each of them giving out to me for not letting them know. And as for my brothers – well, you know fellas – I got a nod of the head and 'Tha's a grand bit of news yeh got there, Kathleen.'

It wasn't too long before I was home. I was told to stay off work for at least three months and I nearly went mad into the bargain. I had never been out of work before, except to have my babies, and even at that I didn't stay off for long, so I wasn't used to all the sitting around, which was giving me loads of time to think about the fact that I wasn't bringing any money in. I was looking at the few pound that we had stashed away vanishing before my very eyes, having to dip into it for one thing and another.

Even though I made a good living from doing the hairdressing for the locals in my shed, I still had this drive in me and always seemed to want more from life. So that's when I decided to have a chat with Alan about opening my own hairdressing salon. That way I'd have people working for me and I'd always have wages coming into the house. To me that was definitely the way to go forward.

But before I could take that step towards my dream, one more thing was to happen in that horrible year, after Da's death, Ma's operation and then my own scare. We thought the worst was behind us, but how could anyone have foreseen the awful tragedy that lay ahead, which would tear all our hearts apart?

21

Heartache and Joy

So much had happened over the previous few months that I felt my brain couldn't take in much more. I was only starting to get back on my feet after my operation and I was nearly gone mad sitting around the house. Unable to do very much, I would drop over to Clare's to see Ma most days, which helped to kill a few hours for me. Other days I might drop down to Crumlin to see Carmel. There was always somebody dropping in through the day and plenty to talk about.

'Kathleen,' said Noel one day, 'did yeh hear Phil is not feelin' too well over there in Canada? I got a phone call off Joan the other day, tellin' me tha' he's goin' for some serious tests, brain scans and all sorts of things happenin' to him.'

Noel only had the words out of his mouth when I thought to myself, *I wonder did Phil know when he was home tha' there was somethin' wrong with him and never said?* When I look back now, he was so pale and tired-looking. I thought it was because of the grief and sadness he was feeling inside over Da.

As soon as I got home, I phoned Phil up straight away.

'Wha's all this I'm hearin' about yeh not feelin' the best? Why didn't yeh tell me when I was talkin' to yeh last?'

'Now why would I do tha', Kathleen? Yeh know you, I'd only have to listen to yeh whingin' all over the place. If my memory serves me right, as soon as there's anythin' wrong with any of us, yeh get yerself into a state. So I thought it best to wait until the final results come through. Anyway, it's probably nothin'. I think I'm just tired from workin' so hard over the years, Kathleen. I've been holdin' down two jobs for God knows how long. I suppose it's bound to take its toll in the end. Never mind, enough of all tha' shite talk, Kathleen. Fill us in on wha's happenin' with Ma, which is more important. How's she doin'? Give her a big hug and a kiss for me and say tha' as soon as I sort a few things out over here I'll be over to see her.'

The subject was changed so I left well enough alone and didn't keep on at him. I launched into all that was going on with Ma and the others, trying to throw a few laughs in, which was so hard to do at that moment.

* * *

Weeks and weeks went by. When I didn't hear back from Phil, I knew there was something wrong. I checked with the rest of the family; they'd also heard nothing.

Then the phone call came. I knew when I walked into the house in Crumlin that there was something up. They were all there and everybody was too quiet. First of all I thought something had happened to Ma, but when I looked into the kitchen she was sitting there with Clare, not a bother on her, having her lunch.

'There's somethin' wrong,' I said. 'Wha's after happenin'?' The girls all sat there not saying a word and I could see that they had been crying.

191

'Kathleen,' said Noel, 'Phil's after takin' a stroke. He's paralysed all down one side of his body. They found a brain tumour and they're operating on him as we speak.'

I couldn't believe what I was hearing. I half expected one of the them to jump up and say, 'Got yeh! Only jokin'.' I got such a pain in my chest with the fright that I thought I was going to faint.

'Sit down, Kathleen,' said Clare. 'We're all in just as much shock. None of us can get our heads around this.'

'How can this be happenin' again?' I said. 'I mean, look at Ma – she's only a couple of months over her brain operation. Why, why?' I was starting to scream at this stage. 'Phil's too young, it's not fair, it's not fair!'

I cried and cried for such a long time. I couldn't speak to anyone. I kept thinking about how frightened he must have felt when he went paralysed. Where was he when it happened? Was there anyone with him? And now, having to go through this, and none of us there with him. That's when I snapped out of myself.

'Some of us will have to go over to Phil,' I said.

'It's all arranged, Kathleen,' said Noel. 'Myself and Thomas are goin' to make our way over to him. We're goin' down to book the flights now.'

'And wha' about us? Can we not go with yiz?' I asked.

'I don't think any of yiz are in any fit state to be goin' over to Phil,' said Noel. 'I mean, look at yiz – yeh're all fallin' apart. Anyway, best tha' we go on our own to see wha' way things are and how he is after the operation.'

* * *

Noel and Thomas flew over to Canada within the next couple of days and it seemed to take forever before we heard back from them. When they did finally ring, the news sounded good. They said that they had been hanging around the hospital, waiting to see the doctor, trying to get as much information as they could before passing it on to us.

'Phil is fine,' they said. 'He's sitting up in the bed, talkin' away to us and throwin' the odd joke in here and there.'

I was over the moon when I heard what they had to say – that was, until they came home and told us the real truth.

We all gathered together in Crumlin to meet Noel and Thomas, so as we could find out the details. But I could see straight away how upset they both were. Noel's voice was shaking as he spoke. We listened in shocked silence.

'We didn't want to tell yiz this over the phone, but it's not lookin' too good for Phil. This wasn't his first brain operation. He's already had one previous to this. He didn't want anybody to know because in his mind he's convinced tha' this will pass and everythin' will be okay again. "Wha's the point in worryin' yiz all?" he said. "There's no need for it. This is just a bit of a blip, I'll be fine. Yiz all know me by now, I never let anythin' get the better of me."'

'Maybe Phil is righ',' I said. 'I mean, look at Ma, she's up and walkin' around and gettin' stronger by the day.'

'Kathleen, listen to me,' said Noel. 'Ma's tumour was on the outside of her brain and they were able to get at it easy enough. And another thing, it wasn't cancerous. Phil's is, and it's set down deep in his brain. They've tried to remove it a couple of times but they just can't get to the root of it.'

That's when everyone started chiming in together, all trying to find out what the future held for Phil. Noel wasn't able to hold it together any longer and made his way outside to the back garden, while Thomas carried on filling us in about what we should all do next.

'Phil hasn't worked in nearly nine months and any money tha' he had is gone. Joan has to keep workin' away to keep the house goin' and pay the bills. Now, there was a nurse comin' in every day for a few hours to take care of Phil, but tha's all stopped now because his insurance has run out. So the bottom line is, we'll have to take care of him for as long as we can ourselves.'

I left them all talking and made my way out to Noel.

'Noel, are yeh all righ'?' I asked.

'Well, Kathleen, let's just say I've been better. I can't get Phil's face out of me mind. It was so hard lookin' at him like tha', not bein' able to move. He was such a strong big fella. It's terrible. And de yeh know somethin', after a couple of days he was still tryin' to put a front up. Crackin' a joke here and there – when he wanted one of us to help him sit up or turn him around, he'd come out with the likes of, "Tha' bloody arm of mine is gone asleep again, will yeh give us a lift up there till it comes back?"'

'I know, Noel, tha's Phil, always the joker, and tha's how he always got through everythin' in his life. Maybe tha's wha' will get him through this. I hope.'

'De yeh know wha' else he said to us, Kathleen? And I swear, it nearly killed me. "Don't go," he said. "I do be very lonely here on me own. I miss yiz all so much." Thomas had to leave the room, he got tha' choked up. He couldn't even answer him. I don't know how I held it together.

'"Jaysus, Phil," I said, "yeh know we'd stay if we could, but we have to get back to work."

'"Ah for fuck sake, Noel, if tha's all yeh're worryin' about, sure I'll pay yiz yer wages."

'God love him, Kathleen, and him with not a shillin' left in his pocket. "It's not only the job, Phil, it's Breda," I said. "She's only after havin' a baby a few weeks ago and she's not great in herself since then. I have to get back to give her a hand. Anyway, isn't the rest of them back home only goin' mad to come over to yeh." He just gave me one of his big smiles, showin' his pearly whites, and said no more on the matter. And tha's the way we had to leave him. Still in the hospital, sittin' there, wavin' to us and doin' his best tryin' to smile as we walked away. I swear, Kathleen, to the end of me days I'll never forget the lost look on Phil's face as we left him. Meself and Thomas hardly spoke to one another all the way home, it had tha' much effect on us.'

'Don't be worryin', Noel', I said. 'Phil will pull through this. He's not goin' anywhere. As he said, this is just a blip. Now, come on, let's go back into the house and see wha' plans they're all makin'.' I knew I was trying to convince myself. Noel just stood there and looked me straight in the eye. Before he could say another word, I went on in ahead of him. There was no way I wanted to hear anything more about Phil being sick.

'Righ' then, wha's happenin'?' I asked.

'Well, Kathleen,' said Patricia, 'we were just sayin', if you want to go over first to see Phil, and maybe take Ma with yeh. I'm sure he'd love to see her. Mano said tha' he'll go with yeh and when yiz come back, meself and Jacinta will make our way over next and whoever else can manage to go after us. Then we'll just have to take it from there and see wha' happens along the way.'

'Tha's grand, Patricia. I'm happy enough to go now.'

* * *

I hated leaving Alan and the kids for the next three weeks. We had never been apart this long before, but this was something I needed to do so much and each of them understood that. So I was sent on my way, with loads of hugs and kisses from all.

I thought I'd never get over to Canada to see Phil and take care of him, but part of me was also dreading having to see him so helpless, having to depend on everyone for practically everything. Knowing him, though, he'd gloss things over as always with a laugh and a joke.

The flight wasn't too bad. Mano and Ma slept all the way, while I got lost in my thoughts as usual. I was planning how I would handle things when I got there and at the same time hoping I wouldn't fall to pieces. Before I knew it, the plane was touching the ground and when I looked out I saw that the place was covered in thick snow, which looked really lovely.

Phil's wife Joan was there to meet us. We got plenty of hugs and kisses before we made our way outside to her car. I had never felt such cold in my whole life.

'I know Thomas and Noel told us to wrap up well, but I wasn't expecting anything like this. How in the name of God de yiz stick this weather, Joan?' I said.

'You get used to it and most of the time it doesn't be too bad. Now, having said that, Kathleen, January is one of the worst months for you to be coming out here. But I am so glad that you came because I really do need the help, and Phil is so happy that you're here. He can't wait to see all of you.'

The two of us chatted all the way to the house.

'How is he, Joan?' I asked.

'I won't lie to you, Kathleen, he has been through hell and back. But you know him; he's a fighter all the way. He tells me and everyone around him that he will be back out and about in no time at all. So, just go along with whatever he has to say. It's what keeps him going. Anyway, here we are now. But before we go in, if it's okay with you, Kathleen, I was going to try to work as many extra hours as I can while you're here to look after Phil, which will help out a great deal.'

'Tha' won't be a problem, Joan. You do wha' yeh have to. We'll look after Phil and the kids. Yeh can be sure of tha'. Now, let's go in before we freeze to death out here.'

I'll never forget the look on Phil's face when we walked into the house. He lit the whole room up with the biggest smile ever. I stood back and watched as he gave Ma such a hug with his one good arm. I could see the way he had himself covered up with a blanket, trying to hide how bad he was.

'Jaysus Christ, Phil,' I said, trying to gloss things over, 'how de yeh live in this Godforsaken place? Me face is nearly after fallin' off, it's tha' cold out there.'

'I see yeh're still rammagin' on as always, Kathleen. Now will yeh stop givin' out and give us a big hug.'

We held on so tight to one another and it felt good.

'Now, Mano, come on – yeh're next. Righ' here on the lips – a nice big juicy kiss, come on.'

'Would yeh ever fuck off, Phil,' said Mano. 'Yeh're not gettin' a kiss off me. I don't care wha' yeh have wrong with yeh!'

That was it; the ice was broken and we settled into our first night in Canada.

Phil was really proud showing off his three sons. The eldest, Philip, was a lovely quiet boy of eleven, J.J. was wild as they come, even at nine, and the baby of the family, Andrew, was almost seven. Phil kept talking about the sports they were into and how well they were doing.

Ma sat beside him the whole night, holding his hand. She knew there was something wrong, but never said a word. Every time Phil said something, even if it wasn't funny, Ma would roar laughing. We were all used to her behaviour since the hospital, but Phil couldn't get over it. He thought it was hilarious. He ended up laughing along with her, so much so that the tears rolled down his face.

'Yeh know wha', Kathleen,' he said, 'I haven't laughed this much in I don't know how long, and the thing is I haven't a clue wha's so funny.'

'I know, Phil. When Ma starts tha' at home, and especially if there's a few of us together in Crumlin, she does have us all at it with her. It does be like somethin' out of a funny farm.'

'Ah well, Kathleen, at least she's okay. Tha's the main thing,' said Phil. 'We could easily have lost her back then, but she's as tough as old nails, and tha's who I take after. So, the way I see it, if Ma can beat all them odds tha' was stacked up against her, well then, so can I.'

When Phil said those words, Ma bent over, put her two arms around him and wouldn't let go. I could see Phil was enjoying every minute of it. Talk about me trying to hold myself together – it took me all my energy to hold back the tears, looking at the pair of them like that.

* * *

Joan and the kids were gone from early the following morning. Mano was still asleep and so was Ma, which I was glad of. It gave me some time to spend alone with Phil. I made my way downstairs. As I walked into the room, I nearly died. Phil was crawling along the floor, trying to make his way to the toilet. He stopped dead in his tracks when he saw me standing there. Such a lost look he had on his face as he tried to turn away.

'Now, wha' are yeh doin' down there on the floor, Phil?' I said. 'Actin' the eejit as usual, I suppose.' I bent down on my hunkers. 'Are yeh righ'? Let's get yeh back up onto the chair.'

I needn't tell you, I was strangled, but I managed it in the end.

'Now, yeh know wha' we'll do, Phil? Get yer good arm and put it around me shoulder. I'll hold onto the other one and then we'll just drag yeh along. Wait and see, it'll be a piece of cake. Now, the only thing is, yeh'd better not piss all over me before we get there. I swear to Jaysus, Phil, I'll drop yeh if yeh do.'

'Will yeh stop messin', Kathleen, or I'll start laughin', and then I *will* piss all over yeh.'

It took me every bit of strength I had to walk that short distance. There I was, with my seven and a half stone, trying to carry Phil. Even with all his sickness, he was still one big fella. But I got him there in the end.

'Yeh know somethin', Phil?' I said as I stood outside the door and waited, 'we could kill two birds with one stone here. I'd be able to give yeh a grand wash down while I have yeh sittin' there.'

'No! It's hard enough havin' to let yeh bring me to the toilet, Kathleen, without washin' me as well.'

'Don't start gettin' all shy on me now, Phil. It wouldn't be the first time I saw yer arse. Remember years ago when we were teenagers, all them mooners yeh used to do on me when I would be sittin' on the end of the stairs with Alan? The two of us tryin' to have a wear behind Ma and Da's back. Yeh'd call down to us and all we'd see was this big hairy arse lookin' down at us. I used to get real annoyed, 'cause yeh were makin' a show of me.'

'Tha' was the best part, Kathleen, lookin' at yeh gettin' yerself into a state. And the gas thing was, Alan didn't give two shites wha' any of us did. He just cared about you and nothing was goin' to change tha'.'

'I know, Phil. I was a gobshite back then, tryin' to be Mrs Proper all the time when Alan was around.'

'All the same, Kathleen, we had some great times, the pair of us, when we were kids. We did some mad things together. Wouldn't it be great if yeh could go back in time, even just for a while, and forget about all tha's goin' on at the minute. And yeh know wha'? As poor as we were, I wouldn't change a thing. How about you, Kathleen?'

'Not one single minute, Phil. Anyway, don't be changin' the subject on me. I'm standing out here with a basin full of warm water. Now, hurry up and let me come in and wipe yer arse and I'll have yeh done and dusted before Ma or Mano wake up, and nobody will be wiser.'

I could see he was embarrassed, but he sat there and let me get on with what I had to do.

'Kathleen, did yeh ever think tha' yeh'd be doin' the likes of this for me?'

'Sure, wouldn't yeh do it for me, Phil, if yeh had to?'

I kept rammaging on as I do when I get nervous, and before he knew it I had him back sitting on his chair, as fresh as a daisy.

'Now, tha' wasn't too bad, Phil, was it?'

'Yeh're still a bossy bitch, Kathleen, but thanks, I feel a lot better.'

'I'm goin' to go in now and make yeh a good old Irish breakfast like the way Ma used to.'

'Will yeh stop, Kathleen. I was often sittin' here waterin' from the mouth, just thinkin' about the lovely fry-ups she used to make for us. Remember every Saturday night when she'd put the big pot on and fill it up with pigs' feet and ribs? We'd be sittin' there on the floor, suckin' on the bones for the night while we watched the telly.'

I cooked while Phil continued his trip down memory lane, which seemed to be helping to lift his spirits. I suppose not knowing what the future held for him, he felt it was better not to go there. So I left well enough alone for the moment.

* * *

Joan seemed to be coping well. She never talked about Phil's illness to us; maybe that was her way of handling things. The kids played around as normal, with not a notion of what was happening, and that's the way Phil wanted it; he didn't want them upset in any way. When I think back now, we were all doing the same thing; if you didn't say it out loud then you could pretend it wasn't happening.

I made it my business every day to cook all his favourite dinners. I would get such pleasure looking at him when he'd lick the plate at the end. He would be laughing his head off looking at the antics of Mano, after the kids came in from school. Mano would roll around the floor with them, acting the eejit, bringing himself down to their level – although that didn't take much, as Mano was just a big kid himself.

Mano was arm-wrestling with one of the kids one day when Phil turned around to him and said, 'I bet tha' I could still beat yeh, even with just me one arm.'

'Would yeh get away with yerself,' said Mano. 'I'd have yeh on the floor in seconds.'

Holy Jaysus, I thought I was hearing things. I was going cross-eyed trying to give Mano the look as I stood behind Phil. But as soon as Phil looked the other way, Mano gave me a wink.

He sat down in front of Phil. 'Come on now,' said Mano, 'let's see wha' yeh're made of.'

My heart was bursting, looking at Phil trying to steady himself for the big match.

'Kathleen, hold onto the back of the chair for me, just in case it slips, and I'll show this Mano fella wha' real strength is.'

Mano was great; he started banging the table and making all sorts of mad faces at Phil, like wrestlers do before a fight.

'Tha's not fair, Mano,' said Phil. 'Yeh're makin' me laugh and I can't do it now.'

'Righ' then, roar back at me, Phil. Come on, ROAR,' he shouted, making more crazy faces.

I thought I was going to die with the laughing, looking at the pair of them screaming into each other's face. Ma was clapping her hands and stamping her feet as she called out Phil's name. The kids were like lunatics, trying to make faces along with their Da.

Of course, Mano pretended to be struggling as he went on and let Phil win the match. Such a laugh we had that day.

It cheered Phil up so much that he turned around to me and said, 'Kathleen, I really feel good in meself since yiz all started comin' over to me. I think I'm gettin' stronger as the days go on. I mean, just look at the way I beat Mano, and he's nearly as big as meself. Yeh never know, I might beat this bloody thing yet.'

'Of course yeh will, Phil,' I said. 'This is just a blip, tha's all.' There was no way I would let myself think of anything else, so I changed the subject as fast as I could. 'Now, wha' would yeh like to eat for yer lunch? I have to make sure and keep tha' strength of yers up.'

'Jaysus, I'd love nothin' more than a few beans on toast.'

'I was lookin' for some the other day. I don't think there's any in the press, Phil. But it doesn't matter, I'll go down to the corner shop and get some.' I would have gone to the ends of the earth for any little thing that he wanted.

'Go away, yeh mad thing, Kathleen, there's no such thing as a corner shop here. They're all big malls.'

'Wha' the fuck is a mall, Phil?'

'Shops the size of the whole street out there, tha's wha' they are.'

'It's the same thing, Phil. They're just big corner shops.'

'Anyway, yeh can't go out in tha' weather. Yeh'd freeze.'

'I'll be grand, now will yeh stop fussin'. I'll be there and back before yeh know it. A bit of fresh air won't do me any harm either. I'm not used to being stuck in a house all the time like this. Now, just tell me, do I go righ' or left to find one of these "mall" places?'

'As usual yeh won't take any heed of wha' I'm sayin', Kathleen. So put my big jacket on and when yeh get outside turn righ' and keep walkin' straight ahead.'

I was glad to be getting a bit of break on my own so I could work out in my head how I was going to handle things when it came time for us to leave. It was going to be one of the hardest things I would have to do in my whole life – leaving Phil, knowing that we would never see each other again. I didn't think I'd be strong enough to do it.

I got so lost in my thoughts that I didn't realise how far I had walked or where I was. There wasn't a sign of anyone around – probably because they had more sense than me. It was so cold out and the snow had got really heavy. I could barely see in front of me. I walked and walked until finally I could see bright lights in the distance. There it was, the biggest corner shop you ever saw.

'Thank God,' I said to myself, because at that stage I was starting to panic a bit. I picked up a few tins of beans and made my way back.

Phil nearly fell off the couch from laughing so much when he saw me. I must have looked like a full-size snowman. The snow was actually starting to freeze on me. Mano quickly dried me off, then wrapped me in a blanket and put me lying on the floor beside the fire to thaw me out. All Phil kept saying was, 'I told yeh, Kathleen, but would yeh listen to me? No.'

When I finally stopped shaking and was able to talk again, the first thing I said was, 'Will yeh have them beans on toast now?'

Phil gave me such a smile it made everything worthwhile.

* * *

I started to sleep downstairs on the couch across from Phil. When everyone was gone to bed, the two of us would lie there, talking across to one another, mostly about the past and all the fun and happy times we spent together as a family. We never spoke about the future, not until it was coming to the end of our stay.

'Kathleen, I want to have a talk with yeh,' he said.

I didn't want to hear what he was about to say.

'Now, I'm only sayin', but if this all goes belly-up and goes against me, I want yeh to promise me tha' yeh'll all keep in touch with the kids through the years. Let them know tha' they always have a family there if they need yiz.'

I was in floods of tears and was barely able to answer him.

'The other thing is, I'd like for me ashes to be brought back to Ireland, because tha's where me heart was always. Yiz can put me in the little cabinet beside Da's ashes in Crumlin. Tha' way I'll be back amongst yiz all. So, will yeh make sure and do tha' for me?'

I couldn't speak; I just gave him a nod.

'Come on over here, Kathleen, and lie beside me and we'll pretend tha' there's nothin' wrong.'

He put his good strong arm around me and held me so tight, like he was never going to let go. As I lay there all I could hear was Phil sobbing through the night. It was so hard to take in, to try to understand why, why this was all happening.

* * *

I was up bright and early the next morning and knew I had to keep myself busy; otherwise I would fall to pieces. So I decided that, because it was our last day, I was going to cook a big Christmas dinner with all the trimmings. Joan had all the presses and freezer well stocked up with everything and anything I needed, so as soon as I had Phil and Ma washed and ready, I spent the rest of the day cooking. I have to say, when I finished, it was a spread fit for a king. Phil couldn't believe his eyes when we sat him down at the table.

'Holy Mother of God, Kathleen, de yeh think yeh're feedin' an army or wha'? Now, having said tha', I think meself and Mano will get through a fair share of this.'

'Are yeh on then, Phil?' said Mano. 'Let's see who can eat the most!' As always, Phil loved a challenge. Mano knew he was upset and was doing everything and anything he thought would make him happy. The pair of them stuffed themselves until they couldn't move. The result was a tie.

'Well, little brother,' said Phil, 'yeh're nearly as good as meself now.'

'And me answer to yeh, big brother, is tha's somethin' else comin' from you.'

I thought Mano was going to break down, but he held it together by jumping up and down and chasing the kids around, doing what he does best – acting the eejit, which I suppose is his way of coping with things. Ma sat there for the whole night holding Phil's hand while the rest of us told the kids all sorts of stories about times gone by.

Our flight was early enough the next day, so we had to be up from the crack of dawn. There was no way Phil was letting us go to the airport without him. I was hoping that this wouldn't happen. I felt it might be a bit easier on all of us to say our goodbyes in the privacy of his home. But he was having none of it.

'There's no way I'm sittin' here on me own,' said Phil. 'I want to spend every last minute with yiz before yeh go.'

He was starting to get upset, so I agreed with him. 'Yeh're righ', Phil,' I said. 'Anyway, Jacinta and Patricia's flight will be landin' around the same time tha' we're takin' off, so yeh'll be there to meet them when they come through. They're only dyin' to see yeh.' He seemed happy enough when I said that and calmed himself down.

There was loads of hustle and bustle as we all gathered ourselves into the car to head for the airport. We all sat there in silence as Joan rammaged on about how bad the snow was and hoped that we would get there in time. I wanted to talk but I knew that as soon as I opened my mouth I would break down and cry, and I could see Mano and Phil were feeling the same. As for Ma, well, she was lost in her own little world, and maybe it was better that way for her.

While I was checking us in at the desk and Joan was taking care of Ma, what was Mano doing? Only flying around the airport with Phil in the wheelchair, skidding all over the place. You'd want to see the laughs of the pair of them. Usually I would be giving out like shite and worrying what people might think, but not today. Phil was laughing, and that was all that mattered.

It finally came time for us to board. I was sick to the pits of my stomach and could feel myself start to shake as I watched Phil hug Ma and Mano. He held onto them so tight, as he broke down and cried. Ma touched his face softly, wiping his tears, before Mano took her by the hand and walked away.

I knelt down in front of Phil. He cried so hard as he spoke. 'This is so hard, Kathleen, I'm not ready to die. I don't want to leave everyone.'

'I know, Phil, I know.' I put my arms around him. The two of us held on to one another and neither of us wanted to let go. I could hear Joan's voice calling my name.

'Kathleen,' she said, 'you have to go; your flight's boarding now.'

'Remember wha' we said, Phil,' I whispered in his ear. 'Everythin's fine; there's nothin' wrong; this is just a blip. You just keep thinkin' like tha', de yeh hear me? Now come on and give me one of yer special smiles. Let's see those pearly whites.'

I was sobbing my heart out as I walked away. Just before I went through the gates, I turned around and there he was, waving and smiling as best he could. That was my last memory of Phil. We never saw or spoke to one another ever again.

Myself and Mano sat in silence through the whole flight, while Ma laughed away at the telly. I suppose at the end of the day it was best that she didn't know all that was going on around her. I don't think she would have been able to cope, knowing what was ahead for Phil.

I was so happy to see Alan when we landed. I knew if anybody was going to help me get through this, it would be him.

* * *

I had only been home a day or two after leaving Phil. I tried really hard to keep a front up for the kids' sakes but I found it so hard. I knew deep down in my heart that he wasn't going to make it and when I was leaving we had both pretended that he would.

Alan was so good; he was doing everything for me, but he knew in the end just to leave me and let me try to cope in my own way. For me, that meant keeping busy, busy all the time. That way I didn't have to think or face reality and maybe by some miracle the inevitable might not happen.

I was upstairs tidying around when young Alan, who was sixteen and a half at this time, came into my room and sat on the bed.

'Are yeh okay, Ma? I heard yeh cryin' last night.'

'I'm sorry, pet. I didn't mean for yeh to hear me, but don't be worryin'. I'll be fine.'

'I need to talk to yeh, but yeh're so upset about Phil and no time is goin' to be the righ' time. But I have to tell yeh, Ma, before somebody else does.'

'Alan, please don't tell me yeh're in trouble with the police. I haven't got the energy to take anythin' like tha' now.'

'It's nothing like tha', Ma. It's . . . it's . . . it's just . . . just . . . Donna's five months pregnant. There, it's out. I've said it. I'm sorry, Ma.'

I could feel the blood draining from me. I actually went down on my knees with the fright and broke down crying.

'Oh my God! I can't believe this is happenin' again. Wha' the hell is wrong with yiz all? Yeh're too young to be a father,' I screamed. 'Yeh're not capable of lookin' after yerself, never mind a child. I'm not able for all this at the minute, Alan McGrath. Just go. Leave me. I want to be on me own.'

I stared out of the window. My head was all over the place. I couldn't think straight. I didn't want to have to think or worry about anything else. This time in my life was supposed to be for me and Phil. That's all I wanted on my mind right now – nothing else. But, being a parent, that wasn't to be. So I carried on doing what I was supposed to do, which was, like most mothers, trying to fix the problems that are put before us.

When I told Alan, I could see that he wanted to lose the plot, just like I did, but he didn't. He held it together, as always. He was just as upset about Phil as we all were, as he'd been in my family since he was fifteen. They were like brothers.

After a few days, I got young Alan to bring Donna down to see us. The pair of them had been going out since they were both fourteen and I really was very fond of her. She was a lovely little one, which helped so much in this situation. The two of them stood in front of me. What I really wanted to do was to give them both a good box for being so irresponsible and stupid. But I knew that wasn't the way to fix things. So I just put my arms around them and said, 'Don't worry, we'll work things out. All tha' matters now is tha' yeh're okay, Donna, and yeh have a healthy little baby.'

'Thanks so much, Kathleen. I was afraid wha' way yeh were goin' to take things, with Martina only after havin' Danielle not so long ago.'

'Wha' did yer own Ma and Da say when yeh told them yer news?'

'They were in shock at first but, like yerself, they're being very good about it. Once the baby's okay, they'll be happy.'

It was only when she said that to me that I realised this was to be our second grandchild – coming a lot sooner than we thought or expected. It's difficult to take this kind of news in, especially when your own children are only children themselves. But – and I really mean this – after holding my first grandchild in my arms the day she was born, I knew in my heart that when the time came I would be ready to welcome this little baby into our family with open arms.

* * *

The next few weeks seemed to go by so fast and it was nearly time for Jacinta and Patricia to come home from Canada, and time for the next two of us to go over to take care of Phil. Alan was going, with my younger brother Paul.

'Alan, I wish so much tha' I was goin' back over with yeh.'

'I know tha', Kathleen, but yeh know tha' the money is just not there for both of us to go, and I really do want to see Phil meself. Anyway, one of us has to be here to take care of the kids. I promise, I'll phone yeh every day and keep yeh posted about all tha's goin' on. I'll tell yeh wha' – I'll even put Phil on the phone to talk to yeh.'

With that thought in my mind, I felt a bit better and was happy enough to send Alan on his way for the next three weeks. I never did get to talk to Phil again, because by the time Alan and Paul got there, Phil wasn't great. Then he took a turn for the worse and was taken into the hospital. But Alan didn't tell me that at the time. Every time I asked, he would say Phil was in hospital getting a few tests done. He would be telling me everything and anything but the truth so as not to upset me. He knew when the time came the devastating effect Phil's death would have on me.

He was gone less than a week when, early one morning, I woke up to the sound of the phone ringing. When I looked at my watch, it was only seven o'clock. I thought, *Jaysus, who could tha' be at this hour of the mornin'?* To my surprise, it was Alan.

'Howyeh, love,' I said. 'I wasn't expectin' yeh to ring me until later on.'

'Is there anybody there with yeh, Kathleen?' asked Alan.

As soon as he said that, I knew. I didn't give him a chance to say a word; I started rammaging on like I don't know what. I was in complete denial.

'Anyway, fill us in. Wha's happenin', Alan? How's Phil? Is he feelin' any better? When are they lettin' him home? I want yeh to make sure the first thing yeh do is put him on the phone to me. I've loads to tell him. Did yeh tell him I'm goin' to be a granny again? I can just see him now. I bet yeh he was breakin' his heart laughin' . . .'

'Kathleen, stop talkin', please. I've somethin' to tell yeh.'

'No! I won't stop talkin' and don't you dare tell me anythin'. De yeh hear me, Alan McGrath? Don't say it!'

By this stage I could hardly breathe. I was sitting at the end of the stairs with the phone up to my chest, screaming, crying, but I could still hear Alan calling my name. The three kids had made their way down and were sitting beside me with their arms around me.

'Kathleen, come on, love, pick the phone up, please.'

I kept thinking, if I didn't hear it, then it didn't happen. But it did happen and I knew I had to face up to the truth, but it was so, so hard. I slowly put the phone up to my ear and spoke.

'I'm here, Alan.'

'I know yeh are, love . . . I didn't want yeh to hear this over the phone. Thomas was supposed to come down last night and tell yeh. I'm so sorry to have to tell yeh this news. But Phil died last night.'

It was like a knife sticking into my heart, as I sobbed uncontrollably. The kids were getting so upset looking at me that I had to try to pull myself together.

'Please, Alan, tell me, at wha' time did it happen?'

'It was around nine o'clock our time. Why?'

'Because it was me Da's anniversary yesterday. He was a year dead, and it was nine o'clock to the minute when he died.'

At that moment I got a flashback of Phil at Da's bedside, just after he'd passed away, saying, 'Don't be afraid, Da. I'll be with yeh soon'. *Oh my God*, I thought, *I wonder did he know then what lay ahead for him and he never said.*

Just then there was a knock on the door. Martina opened it and let in Thomas.

'Alan, Thomas is here now.'

'Tha's good, Kathleen, because I'll have to go. Joan wants to ring around Phil's friends. Try and hang in there, love, until I get meself home to yeh.'

I was still crying and sobbing as I put the phone down. Thomas put his arm around me and I felt a bit better.

'I was goin' to come down last night, Kathleen,' he said, 'but then I thought I'd be only leavin' yeh on yer own afterwards. I felt it would be better to let yeh get a good night's sleep before breakin' the news to yeh. Meself and Noel phoned around the rest of the family so yeh don't have to do anythin', only get yerself ready. We're all meetin' up in Crumlin.'

The shock on everyone's faces as I walked into the room said it all.

* * *

At the time, none of us could afford to go back over to Canada, so it was left to Alan and Paul to represent the family. We all sent sprays and sprays of flowers, and the biggest bunch of red roses from Ma, making our presence felt.

We decided that it was best not to tell Ma. She had come on so well over the past year, we were afraid that the news of Phil's death would knock her back. Why put her through all that pain if we didn't have to? So, in Ma's eyes, her blue-eyed boy was working away in Canada and she was none the wiser.

It wasn't too long before Alan and Paul were back home and filling us in on all that went on. 'By the time we got there,' said Paul, 'Phil was very weak. Meself and Alan had a few days with him. He was trying to talk and give the odd smile, but you could see he wasn't able. It was so hard, seein' him like tha'. Then he took a turn for the worse and went into a coma. He didn't last long after tha'. I was sittin' there with Joan; both of us were holdin' his hands when he passed away. The doctor told us that he didn't suffer any pain.'

'Thank God for tha', Paul,' I said, 'at least he wasn't on his own and yiz were all there with him.'

'Poor Joan; she fell to pieces. Yeh'd want to hear the cries from her. Tha' was bad enough, but when we went back to the house and told the kids – oh my God, Kathleen, I never want to see the likes of tha' ever again. The cries from the three of them would break yer heart in two. Alan and meself had to get up and leave the room. It was too much. God help them, they were all in bits.'

We all sat there listening, trying to take it all in as Alan and Paul told us about the funeral and how they all tried to cope in the days that followed.

There was nothing but doom and gloom for such a long time afterwards. It was hard enough trying to cope with Da gone, then with so much happening to Ma, and now Phil. All in the space of a year. It was too much to take in.

I felt such a loss and emptiness inside of me, which I kept to myself. I grieved in silence, not wanting to worry Alan or my children. I would keep going over and over again in my head, thinking about the past, all the fun we had when we were growing up, the madness that went on. Not a day would go by without something crazy happening in Crumlin. My God, was it any wonder poor Ma ended up getting a brain tumour, with our carry-on?

* * *

One day in particular stood out. It makes me laugh now when I look back. Who was the culprit? Only Phil as usual, with Noel on the receiving end this time. Da always had half-cans of paint lying around in the back garden and Noel was forever at it. If he wasn't painting planks of wood, bits of bikes or the garden wall, anything he could get his hands on got a lick. He would always end up getting more of the paint on himself than anything else.

I was having a yap with Phil, when he turned around with a dirty big grin on his face. I could see the devilment in him straightaway.

'Phil, wha' are yeh schemin' there in tha' head of yers? I know tha' look. Come on, tell me.'

'Yeh'll know in a minute, Kathleen. Now would yeh have a look at tha' gobshite Noel, tryin' to paint tha' oul bike out there. How many times has Ma told him to keep away from it? But does the little fucker listen? No. So I think I'll teach him a lesson once and for all.'

When I looked out, there was Noel, as happy as anything, painting away, not minding anyone, when Phil went and grabbed him. I couldn't believe what he did next – he actually painted Noel all over, every bit of him. Green, white and orange. He only left his eyes out. Phil was falling around the place laughing while Noel was trying to get away from him. Phil thought this was the funniest thing ever.

'Would yeh have a look, Kathleen?' he said. 'I could hang him out of the line pole there and, yeh know wha'? He'd be like the Irish flag, flyin' in the wind.'

Poor Noel was crying his eyes out, not knowing what Phil would do next.

'For fuck sake, give it over, Phil,' I said. 'Jaysus Christ, yeh've really gone too far this time. How are we goin' to get this paint off him. Ma will be back soon. There'll be blue murder when she sees this.'

Phil wasn't taking any heed of me. 'Yeh'll think the next time, won't yeh, Noel, before yeh go near the paint again.'

'Don't mind him, Noel. Come on into the kitchen with me and let's see if there's any turps there. I'm sure Da would have some for his brushes.' He did, but only a drop. Then I found a bottle of methylated spirits. I was standing there, rubbing Noel's face like mad, when Ma walked in the door. Phil was gone like a light into the back garden, leaving me to face the music. Ma lost the plot altogether, and I mean really lost it. She made a mad run at Noel, who was trying to hide behind my back. She was tearing her hair out when she saw him.

'Yeh little fuck, Noel Doyle,' she screamed, over and over again. 'Wha' did I tell yeh? If yeh went near tha' paint again, didn't I say I'd kill yeh stone dead? Stand aside, Kathleen, and let me at him. I can't take any more of this. Lunatics, I'm after rearin' – fuckin' lunatics!'

'Ma, please calm down. It wasn't all Noel's fault. Phil had a hand in this too.'

I was edging Noel towards the front door, trying to get him off side.

'And wha' reason would Phil have to do such a thing? Don't start telling' fibs to me, Kathleen Doyle, or yeh'll get the back of me hand along with the Noel fella.'

I couldn't believe what I was hearing! To top it all, there was Phil standing at the kitchen window, laughing his head off, taking in all Ma was saying, knowing that he was in the clear. I knew I definitely had to get Noel out of the house, even if it was only for a couple of hours, until I got the paint off him and Ma calmed herself down.

It took her nearly three days to calm her down, with one of the neighbours holding onto Noel in the meantime. His skin was in a right mess for weeks afterwards. It was raw from all the turps we had to use.

Noel never went near the paint ever again. Well, not in the back garden anyway. He knew better. But as soon as he was old enough to work, guess what he became? A painter! And who did he end up working with, only the scourged Phil, who still played many tricks on him and everyone else over the years.

* * *

I think all my happy memories helped me get through those first few months after Phil died. I was trying to live in the past, not wanting to face the present or the future, and I was going around lost in my thoughts, so much so that I was not really looking at what my young son and his girlfriend were trying to cope with.

Here he was, going to be a father very soon. Though it was his own fault, nevertheless, I wasn't there for him. My little grandchild was coming into the world very soon. That thought helped me snap out of the very dark hole I had buried myself in and brought me back to reality.

As soon as Donna went into labour, the word was sent down to us straight away. I was into the hospital with young Alan in no time at all. Donna's Ma was in with her and came out to let Alan go in. We sat there talking for a while.

'Kathleen,' she said, 'would yeh mind if I went home. I'm not feelin' too good. Yeh know I'm a couple of months gone meself with twins.'

'So I believe, Cathy. Tha's no problem, you go ahead and I'll phone yeh as soon as there is any news.'

I have to say, young Alan made me laugh as I sat there for hours on end, with him running in and out of the labour ward, telling me every little thing that was going on – as if I didn't know. At one stage, he came out laughing his head off.

'De yeh know somethin', Ma? I'm after tryin' some of tha' gas – it's deadly!' Before I could say a word, he ran off again.

Then, when it was coming to the end of Donna's labour, he came bursting out the doors.

'Jaysus, Ma, there's really serious stuff goin' on in here now. I'm tellin' yeh, yeh'd want to see it.' I sat there listening to him, thinking there was no way on this earth he was grown up or mature enough for what lay ahead. What seventeen-year-old boy or girl is?

But I wasn't going to worry about that now. All that mattered at that moment was that Donna and the baby were safe, which they were. It wasn't long after that my lovely Jessica was born. My second granddaughter, who melted my heart straight away.

As I sat there holding her in my arms, I thought of Phil. Someone who had been so close and meant so much to me had been taken away so quickly, for whatever reason I'll never really understand. But they say God works in mysterious ways. As one precious life was taken away from me, I was handed another one just as quick, which helped me get through that very hard time in my life. In time, I was eventually able to move on. But never once did I ever forget my brother Phil.

* * *

It was about a year after Phil's death, when Ma was a bit stronger in herself, that we finally felt the time was right to tell her about Da and Phil. She was inconsolable and cried for days after, saying over and over again, 'I want to die, I want to go up to heaven to yer Da and Phil.' It took so much out of her that she didn't talk for weeks. We were all so worried, wondering if we had done the right thing in telling her or if we should have left her in her own little world, happy as Larry. But Ma was a very strong woman and in time she slowly came around, but she was never really the same again.

22

Shops and Robbers

It had been a good two years since I had first spoken about opening up my own salon. But with one thing and another happening within the family, no time ever seemed to be the right time. Then when I did start looking around, the salons were either too expensive or in the wrong location. But that didn't stop me looking. I was back on track now and more determined than ever that this was what I wanted.

Alan was reading the paper while I was pottering about, getting the dinner ready.

'Come over here, Kathleen,' he said, 'and have a look at this.'

'I'm in the middle of peelin' the potatoes, Alan. Just read it out to me.'

'Righ' yeh are then. "Prime hairdressin' salon for sale, leasehold, Rathfarnham area".'

My ears cocked up and I had the newspaper in my hands before Alan could blink an eye.

'I knew tha' would get yer attention fast enough, Kathleen.'

'Tha's not too far from here, Alan. Will yeh come down and have a look with me?'

'Sure don't yeh know I will. Come on, we'll go straight away. Leave wha' yeh're doin' there; yeh can finish tha' when we come back.'

I didn't think twice about it. I had my coat on and we were in the car heading for Rathfarnham in no time at all. As soon as we pulled up outside the salon, which was called Talking Heads, I fell in love with it straight away. It looked quite small from the outside and I couldn't see in because of the white net curtains. There was a chemist's and a post office either side of it, with a newsagent at the end and a garage around the corner. As I looked around, my brain went straight into overdrive.

'This is a great area, Alan. I mean, wha' more could yeh ask for only to be stuck right in the middle of two of the main shops tha' get used all the time, a chemist's and a post office. There'll be people around here all the time.'

'We'll sit here for a while and see how busy it gets. I know yeh're hell-bent on doin' this, but we have to make sure tha' we get it righ', because every penny we have will be goin' into this, or wha'ever shop yeh decide to go for.'

While Alan counted who was out and about, I went into the shop and asked about their prices, so I could have a quick gander around the place. I liked what I saw. It was certainly small, but it had everything you'd need – two dressing out mirrors and chairs, and two sinks. The waiting area had a couch with three hooded hairdryers attached to the back of it, with a glass coffee table to hold magazines and a long standing press against the wall, with a kettle on the top for a cup of tea. Oh yes, and a tiny – and I mean tiny – toilet. I thanked the girl and made my way back out to Alan, filling him in on all that I had seen.

'From wha' yeh're tellin' me, Kathleen, the place tha' I got built out the back garden for yeh is twice the size. To be honest with yeh, I can't get me head around why yeh want to do this.'

'I told yeh why, Alan. Didn't I say after me operation, when I couldn't work for a couple of months and me money stopped comin' in, how hard it was tryin' to get by on yer wages alone? No, I'm sorry, Alan, but I don't want tha' for us, no more than you do, scrimpin' and scrapin' from week to week. Tha's why if I have a shop and there's somebody workin' with me and somethin' happens, at least there'll be a wage there for me. Anyway, I have a plan.'

'Oh, here we go again. Wha' are yeh up to now, Kathleen?'

'I'll tell yeh in a minute, Alan. First of all, was there many people about when I was in?'

'There was. They were comin' and goin' all the time. It's a busy little area all righ'.'

'Good, tha's all I wanted to hear. Now, wha' I have in me mind is this: yeh know Thomas's wife, Trish? Well, with her bein' a hairdresser, I was going to ask if she would like to come in on the shop with me. Yeh know, be partners in business. Tha' way, me back will be covered at all times and we won't have to worry about money ever again.'

'If it's wha' yeh really want to do, Kathleen, I'll back yeh all the way. Yeh know me – anythin' to keep yeh happy.'

* * *

And that was it; I was full speed ahead. I asked Trish straight away.

'The only thing is, Kathleen,' said Trish, 'I only have two more months to go before I have me baby. Yeh'd be on yer own for a while.'

'Tha' won't be a problem, Trish, sure haven't I been workin' on me own for years. I'll look after things while yeh're out. Don't yeh worry about tha'. Come on, I promise yeh won't regret it.'

She said yes and within the month the two of us were standing outside the shop with the keys in our hand and fifty pounds worth of stock to start us off. The first thing we did as soon as we walked in the door was to take the net curtains down and brighten up the shop.

'We might be small,' I said to Trish, 'but from now on everybody will be able to see and know tha' we're here.'

I remember that first day so well; we were so excited. We took the place apart, scrubbing it from top to bottom. There wasn't much we could do in terms of moving things around to change it – even a little bit, just to put our own mark on it. But it looked and felt so fresh, with the kettle full and ready, new magazines on the coffee table and a nice big box of chocolates to make our first clients welcome. The only problem was, there didn't seem to be a sign of any clients around.

'I can't understand this, Trish,' I said as we sat there twirling our thumbs, looking out the window. 'When I was down here with Alan, there was a good few people in the shop.'

'I am a bit surprised, Kathleen, I thought tha' we might have had at least one or two clients in before this. I mean, the day is nearly half over.'

'I know, but we won't panic.'

Having said that, I was doing ninety inside my head, but I didn't let her know that. I had a pain in my face from smiling so much at anyone who passed our door.

All of a sudden, an elderly woman stopped outside the window and stood there for a minute, looking in at us. She looked very annoyed. There we were, smiling and nodding out at her, trying our best to look friendly, when she turned

221

on her heels and came straight in to us. The two of us jumped up together, delighted to see a client at last.

'Are you open today or not?' she asked. 'I'm after coming down here twice today already to get my hair done and all I can see is the two of you sitting there showing your teeth off and doing nothing. Now, I'll ask again, are you open for business or not?'

'Of course we are!' I said. 'We're open since nine o'clock.'

'Well, you have a fine way of showing it, because your closed sign is still up on the door.'

The two of us just looked at one another and all we could do was laugh. We must have looked like two gobshites, smiling out at everyone all day with the sign saying 'closed'.

The woman turned out to be very nice in the end and, being our first and only client of the day, we did her hair for free, which she was well pleased about.

That first day was the joke of the century with everyone inside the family for such a long time afterwards.

* * *

Although I was coming up to my fortieth birthday and Trish was only twenty-four, we got on very well together. It worked out even better with the clients; I looked after most of the older ones and Trish looked after the younger ones. It balanced out very well.

The salon went from strength to strength, so much so that we opened up our second 'Talking Heads' in Walkinstown after about two years. This shop had also originally been a hairdressing salon but was very run down and needed a good overhaul. But that wasn't a problem, because Alan and my brother Thomas got stuck in and did all the work, which saved us a lot of money. It took a few weeks to do but looked very well by the time it was finished.

Martina had just completed her apprenticeship, so she came on board, stepping into my shoes in the Rathfarnham salon and leaving me to get the other salon off the ground. This area was quieter, so it took me a bit longer to get the salon up and running. But I got there, eventually taking on a full-time stylist and a junior apprentice. And that was me on my way once more.

* * *

Everything was going well in Walkinstown until one Friday evening in winter, around half-past-four, just as it was getting dark. The rain was pelting down against the window. I always made it my business to lock the door. As Ma would say, 'better to be safe than sorry'. I was well sorry by the time that day was over.

We were finishing a few clients in the salon when there came a hard knock on the door. I looked over and saw a man standing outside.

'I'm sorry,' I called out, 'we're finished for the night.' He beckoned for me to come over to him, which I did, but I still didn't open the door.

'We're closed. I'll do yer hair tomorrow,' I said again. That's when he held up the umbrella. I noticed that he kept blinking his eyes.

'I just want to give this to me wife.'

What I did next was stupid; I went and opened the door, just enough to slip my hand out to take the umbrella off him. He then pushed the door in on top of me and at the same time dropped his other hand down, slipping an iron bar out of his sleeve. He lashed it on the reception desk, screaming, 'Where's the money? Get me the fuckin' money NOW!' I could feel the blood draining from my face as he screamed at me.

The clients all huddled themselves together in the corner while my two staff members dived under the work-top, hugging one another. I was shaking as I spoke.

'Please . . . please, give me a minute. I'll get it for yeh.' I didn't have a till at the time, only a cash box. When I gave him the money, he took one look at it and went crazy.

'Wha' the fuck is this? Where's the rest?' he kept roaring as he banged the bar down on the desk once more.

I was shitting myself at this stage, never mind the clients. 'Tha's all I have; there's no more, I swear.'

He made a swipe at me with the iron bar, missing my head by inches.

'I said, where's the fuckin' money? Where is it?' At this stage he was nearly frothing at the mouth as he made a dash for me. I started running around the reception desk, trying to get away from him, almost pissing in my knickers with the fright. Thank God he didn't catch me.

He gave the desk a few more bangs, taking lumps out of it, while he grabbed the cash box on his way out and ran. He jumped into a car parked outside the salon. I looked out, trying to get a quick glance at the registration, but it was covered over with black plastic. I was trying to calm myself down, as well as the clients and staff, when Alan walked in to collect me.

'Holy Jaysus, Kathleen, wha's after happenin' here?'

'Oh my God, Alan, I'm nearly after gettin' me brains bashed in by robbers. It's only after happenin'. Yeh must have passed them by when yeh were drivin' in.'

He didn't wait for me to say any more. He was on to the police right away and they were up to us in no time at all. They asked the clients and staff a few questions, but they were all too upset to talk and just wanted to go home – which they did, leaving me to fill the gardaí in. The thief's face was right there in front of me when I went to the door, so I had no problem in giving a description of what he looked like to the guards. As soon as I said that he kept blinking, the two guards looked at one another and smiled. They knew who he was, but they weren't telling me.

'You're not the only one who got hit tonight,' said the guard. 'There were two more premises robbed not too far from here, and by the sound of it by the same person.'

They had a quick look around the salon, checking the damage done. Just as they were leaving, they said, 'We will be in touch.' But that was the last I heard on the matter. I checked a few times with the guards to see if they'd been caught, only to be told 'there's still no progress'.

I was very shaken and nervous at work for a good while afterwards, but I soon got my act together. There was no way I would let the likes of your man – a thug – stop me moving forward to follow my dreams.

* * *

Amanda, my younger daughter, who wasn't far off seventeen, had just finished her Leaving Certificate and did very well. She didn't know what line of work she wanted to do, so she settled on a typing course.

I went along with that and didn't say a thing, but when she got six months work experience in the local school, getting paid nothing, I was up the wall. I knew I could give her a full-time job with a good wage to go with it; I kept my mouth shut, which is not an easy thing for me to do. Amanda had always helped me on weekends, just like Martina did, washing hair and tidying around for her pocket money. She was very thorough in everything she did and was great with the clients; I knew she had the makings of a good hairdresser. After a few weeks, I couldn't stand it any longer, so I finally decided to sit her down and have a chat.

'De yeh know wha' I'm goin' to do, Amanda? Now, tha's only if yeh agree; otherwise I'll say no more on the matter.'

'And wha's tha', Ma?'

'I was thinkin' of teachin' yeh how to put colour on and blow-dry hair. Tha' way yeh might be able to judge if yeh would like to go into the hairdressin' or not. Now I'm only sayin', it's up to you at the end of the day, but I think it's worth givin' it a try.'

She thought about it for a while and then came back to me.

'Righ' then, Ma, I'll give it a go. I'm actually lookin' forward to it.'

I was over the moon when I heard that. So over the next couple of months, I taught her every chance I got. I could see she was enjoying the classes more and more as time went on.

In the meantime I got the itch to open up another salon and there just happened to be one not too far from where I lived. It had been a hairdressing salon which had closed down a few years earlier and never reopened. Lately, every time I would go to the shops, I found myself looking at it, and then I'd think *No, no, forget about it, Kathleen. Yeh've enough on yer plate.* So, off I'd go about my business for another while, but it was in the back of my head all the time. I kept thinking it would be a great spot. Everyone in the area knew me from doing hairdressing from my home, so I wasn't worried; I knew I would have plenty of clients.

I spoke to Trish and her very words were, 'Yer instincts are usually very good, Kathleen, so we'll go with them.' And that was it; she was happy enough to go along with the plan, which fell into place straight away.

This salon was very big, but it was just a shell, so we had to start from scratch, which meant borrowing from the bank. We had built up a very good name since we first went into business, so we had a track record and there wasn't any problem getting the loan. It took a few months to get it up and running, but it was worth it in the end. It looked really classy when it was finished and did very well from day one, just like I knew it would.

To put the icing on the cake, Amanda made up her mind and came to work for us. I moved up to the new salon to get it off the ground, taking Amanda along with me, which worked out very well. The younger and older stylists worked side by side, again getting the balance right for the third 'Talking Heads'. We had a very good stylist in Walkinstown who was well able to take over managing that salon.

So I decided to stay working in Tallaght, since I lived just five minutes down the road. I was able to slip down to the house the odd time to do a few bits and bobs, and to pop in to my next-door neighbour, who was now Danielle's child minder.

I couldn't believe it; everything just seemed to have fallen into place for me. I was going around on top of the world.

* * *

One day, after we'd been open about a year, it was coming to the end of the day and we were having a meeting, talking about one thing and another. Thank God there were no clients in the salon. Next thing we knew, two young fellas were in on top of us, screaming and roaring their heads off, 'Give us the money!' I took one look and thought, *Holy Jaysus, here we go again.*

One of them wore a white mask like Hannibal Lecter in *Silence of the Lambs*, and he had a small gun in his hand. The other one had a nylon stocking on his head, covering his face, with a hatchet in his hand. He lashed it down on to the couch, taking lumps out of it, just to let us know the full force of their presence. The girls all started screaming. I wanted to scream with them, but I knew I had to try to keep it together.

'Don't hurt anybody,' I said. 'I'll give yeh the money.'

With that, the one with the mask put the gun up to Amanda's head, saying, 'Get the fuckin' money for me. I said GET IT!'

Amanda was sobbing, saying, 'Please don't hurt me', as she made her way over to the till and handed him the money.

I wanted to jump on top of him and bash his brains out for putting my child through that. But he was the one with the gun so I just bit my lip and said, 'Yeh have the money, now get out.' The other one gave the couch a few more bangs with the hatchet and then both of them ran.

I know I shouldn't have done this but I couldn't help myself. I ran out the door and screamed after them, 'I'll find out who yeh are and we'll see who'll be cryin' then! Yeh won't treat my child like tha' and get away with it – yiz pigs!'

All of this happened in broad daylight and it goes to show you that when these kids – and that's all they were – want money they don't care what they have to do to get it.

Sure enough, as soon as I asked around, within ten or fifteen minutes I was told their names and where they lived by a few of the local kids. When I told young Alan and his Da, they went ballistic and went straight to their houses. Of course, the young lads weren't there, and maybe at the end of the day this was for the best. With the temper everyone was in, God only knows what would have happened. But Alan told their parents what had happened, and let them know that they knew who had done it. There was no way they were going to get away with it.

When Amanda's boyfriend heard, he totally lost the plot, along with a couple of others in the family. That's when the hunt was on. They drove around every inch of the area, asking questions of anyone they could talk to. There wasn't a sighting of the two lads anywhere.

I didn't get much sleep that night. I kept reliving every minute of what had happened. All I could see was the look on Amanda's face and the fear in her eyes when he held the gun to her head. I broke out in a cold sweat just thinking about what could have been if it had all gone wrong.

It was well into the next day as I was tidying around, trying to keep myself busy, when there was a knock on the door. I didn't recognise the man standing on our doorstep.

'Hello,' he said, 'you don't know me but my friend wants to know can he come down with his son and talk to yiz about wha' happened in yer shop yesterday.' My ears cocked up when I heard that.

'Hold on a minute there 'til I get me husband,' I said.

Alan came out and we listened to what he had to say. We agreed to a meeting in our house that evening with both young boys and their fathers.

It turned out that one of them was only fifteen and was shitting himself and too scared to come down, so his father came alone. The other one was nineteen and came down with his father. I don't really know what I wanted or expected from this. The previous night, I wanted to kick the living daylights out of them, but now I think I wanted to see them face to face, with no masks on or gun, and to ask them how they would feel if it was their sister or mother that was put through such an ordeal. I wanted them to understand the trauma and upset that they had caused. I could see how nervous they all were as I brought them into the sitting-room.

We sat there and listened to both fathers talk about their sons' drug habits and how they were trying to get them into rehab and hopefully back on the straight and narrow. They offered to pay for any damage that was done and monies taken.

'Was the gun real?' Alan asked.

'No way, it wasn't a real one,' we were told.

In the middle of all this, Amanda walked into the room. The boy jumped when he saw her.

'Amanda,' I said as I made my way over to her, 'I think it's best tha' yeh not be here.'

'No, Ma, I'm sorry, but I want to see who it is tha' did this to me. I want to tell him how frightened I am now to go to work. All because of him. I need to say this.'

The boy had been sitting there with his head down, not saying a word, from the time he came in, until Amanda stood in front of him. She was in shock when she saw who it was.

'I can't believe it's you,' she said. 'Of all the people, how could yeh do such a thing? We were in school together, in the same class.'

'I'm sorry, Amanda. I'm really sorry. I never would have come into the shop if I'd known yeh were there. But when I saw yeh, it was too late.'

'Yeh shouldn't have come into the shop in the first place – no matter who was there.' She started to cry at this stage.

'I know, I know. I don't know wha' to be sayin' or doin'. I'm sorry. I didn't mean it.'

As I stood there, I could feel myself starting to soften watching my young daughter, so brave and grown-up for her years. Then I looked over at the father of the boy, with his hands up to his face, crying as he listened to his young son. That was hard to watch.

Only then did I realise how lucky we were with our three children, me and the girls working in the salons and our son working with his Da in the ice-cream van, each of them doing well for themselves.

They left a short while later, with the boy promising the sun, moon and stars that he would never bother us again, and no end of apologies from the fathers.

* * *

It took a while for Amanda and myself to settle back down to work without always looking over our shoulders, worrying and wondering if there could be a next time. That thought never really leaves you.

I was to learn in time that the older of the boys carried on in the world of drugs, but eventually over the years sorted himself out. But the younger one stayed in rehab and, when he got older, he became a counsellor himself. If nothing else, at least that bit of good came out of our ordeal. Thank God we never got robbed again.

The three salons did very well over the years and we all earned a very good living along the way.

231

23

The Hideaway

Alan was dropping me off to work one morning. It had been raining non-stop for the past few days, so the traffic was really heavy. We were just coming up to the lights in Tallaght village and I could see that there had been a bad crash on the opposite side of the road. A young woman was sitting in the crashed car with a baby in her arms. She was covered in glass, with cuts all over her face.

'Oh my God, Alan, de yeh see tha'? The poor girl, she's in an awful state. I hope tha' little baby is okay.'

'I wasn't mindin', Kathleen, I'm too busy tryin' to keep me eyes on the road.'

With that we got an unmerciful bang into the back of our little van. If I hadn't been wearing my seatbelt, I would have gone through the windscreen, the force was so strong. A sharp pain shot into my neck and down into my shoulder.

'Holy Jaysus, wha' was tha'?' said Alan. 'Are yeh okay, Kathleen?'

I didn't get a chance to answer. He jumped out of the van to see what had happened. All I could hear were horns beeping as other cars tried to get around us. As soon as I got myself together after the fright, I went out to Alan. He was talking to a man who looked just as shaken up as we were. He had crashed his truck into the back of us. Because the police were on the scene of the other crash, they were over to us straight away, letting the poor man know that they had seen everything. They left it to Alan to sort things out.

'I'm terribly sorry,' said the man. 'I only took my eyes off the road for a second or two, lookin' at tha' young girl and baby. Jaysus, missus, are yeh all righ'? Yeh're an awful bad colour.'

'Me neck and shoulder got a bit of a jerk, but I think I'm okay.'

I got back into the van and let Alan get on with the paperwork for the insurance, which would be needed badly, looking at the state the back of the van was in.

'Righ' then, Kathleen,' said Alan as he sat in beside me, 'now tha's sorted, I think we'd better go to the hospital and have yeh looked over.'

'Would yeh stop, Alan, I'm fine. I just got a bit of a fright, tha's all. Now, come on, I'm late for work as it is.'

* * *

I didn't feel great over the next few days but didn't say anything to Alan. That was, until I couldn't move my head and was finding it very hard to lift my right arm up. So I eventually had to give in and go to the hospital. They suspected that severe whiplash was probably causing the problem with my arm and told me it would take time to heal.

But it didn't heal. I spent well over a year going back and forth to the hospital, getting all sorts of tests done, before they finally discovered that part of my shoulder bone was stuck through a ligament. I ended up needing some major surgery, where they cut parts of the bone away. This left my right arm very weak. I was out of work once again for months on end, which is not a good thing for me, because that's when I start thinking and planning what I can do next. That's when I came up with the idea of buying a holiday cottage down the country.

'De yeh know wha', Alan, I was just thinkin' . . .'

'Oh, here we go again, Kathleen. I knew it. I said to meself only the other day, with all this time on yer hands, yeh'll end up schemin' somethin' in tha' head of yers.'

'Now, I'm only sayin', Alan, but see wha' yeh think anyway. I'd love to buy a little cottage down the country. Somewhere like Wexford. I always had a bit of a soft spot for the place since our honeymoon, and yeh know wha'? There'd be no problem for us to do it, with me gettin' a few bob from the accident. So wha' de yeh think? Are yeh on for it?'

'Yeh know somethin', Kathleen? Yeh always amaze me with tha' brain of yers. I get tired just listenin' to yeh.'

'Ah, go on Alan, it'll be like a new adventure for the pair of us, and we'll be able to spend a bit more time with one another.'

As soon as I said that, he was hooked.

* * *

We didn't go looking straight away because I still had to go to the hospital every day for a couple of months for physiotherapy, trying to get the strength back into my arm. I never really got the full power back, which limited what I could do at work. But I didn't let it stop me. I still carried on as best I could. Instead, I took on the role of teaching and training all the staff for the three shops, which I really enjoyed doing.

Even though I had to cut back on some of my hairdressing, I was still kept very busy. Over the years since I had started the business, I had taught myself how to do the bookkeeping for the shops. I made plenty of mistakes in the beginning, but as time went on I got so good at it that the accountant said she would give me a job. I was well pleased to hear that.

So between cutting hair, doing the books and training staff, I seemed to be chasing my tail all the time, which made me even more determined to try and get a little hideaway for myself and Alan before we ended up becoming strangers, we spent so little time together.

We must have driven the length and breadth of Wexford before we found what we were looking for. It was a two-up, two-down cottage. I remember when we pulled up outside it with the young girl from the auctioneers. It was lashing rain and the whole place looked so dreary. My first thought was, *No way, this place is in bits*. The cottage looked as if it hadn't been painted in years. The gutters were hanging down the side of the roof; the gate was broken; it was overgrown with weeds. And that was the good part.

When we walked in the front door, there was a tiny hallway with a small room to the right, what we used to call a parlour. It had a small black-iron fireplace. The window was a good size, so plenty of sunlight was shining through, which gave it a warm feeling. On the left-hand side, you stepped straight into the sitting-room, where the first thing that hit you in the face was a huge open fireplace. I could actually stand inside it. Facing that was a press built into the wall. Being nosey, I had a little peep in. There were one or two old black pots and an iron pan to match. It looked like they hadn't been used in a long time. Just to the left was the staircase. An old cap hanging off a nail at the end of the stairs drew my eye.

Looking around, I said to Alan, 'This is like goin' back in time.'

'I know, Kathleen, isn't it great? Now, come upstairs and let's have a look.'

To my surprise, the two bedrooms were a good size but, by God, the cold didn't half hit me in the face as soon as I walked into them.

'Jaysus, Alan, it's freezin' up here. I'm shiverin' with the cold. There must never have been any heat put into these rooms.'

'Tha' wouldn't be a problem, Kathleen. I'd have tha' sorted out in no time at all.'

I looked at him and thought to myself, *Is he for real or wha'?*

As Alan made his way back down I stood there for a minute or two, looking around. There was a really old wardrobe which wasn't too bad, but the bed was riddled with woodworm. I was trying to get a picture in my head of what it could look like freshened up, with a few bits of new furniture about the place. Then I thought, *No, no, I'm not goin' to let meself go there.*

'Are yeh righ', Kathleen? There's more downstairs I want to show yeh. Hurry up, will yeh!'

I made my way down to Alan, who was in the extension at the back of the cottage, which I hadn't even realised was there. I couldn't believe it when I walked in. It was a fine-sized kitchen. Now there was nothing in it but a broken-down sink unit, with a nest of spiders stuck in the corner and a small wooden table. I could see as I looked out the window that there was a large yard out the back with a wire fence around it.

Then I saw the most beautiful sight you could ever see. Just beyond that there was a whole field full of sheep and lots of little baby lambs jumping around.

'Oh my God, Alan, did yeh see wha's out there?'

'I know, I know, Kathleen – and guess wha'? Tha' field, which is a half-acre of land, goes with this cottage. Can yeh believe it?'

'But who owns all them sheep, Alan?'

'The girl was just tellin' me tha' the man tha' lives across from here lets them in there to keep the grass down for the owners of this cottage. Anyway, leave tha' for the minute. Come over and have a look at this.'

Curious, I went and stood beside him.

'Well, wha' de yeh think, Kathleen? There's your shower and toilet.' He gave me a big smile. He pointed into what I can only describe as a disaster area. There was a big hole in the side of the roof. The water was pouring down the walls. The toilet had so many chips out of it that if you sat on it you'd cut the arse off yourself. I didn't get a chance to open my mouth. Alan got in there before me.

'Now, don't say a word, Kathleen, let me get me spoke in first. This is the place I think we should buy. The structure is good, tha's the main thing. Forget wha' the inside looks like now. Think beyond tha'. Yeh know me – once I put me mind to it, I'll have this brand new by the time I'm finished.'

'Okay, Alan, yeh're on.'

'Yeh mean yeh're agreeing with me, Kathleen? Yeh're not goin' to put up a fight?'

'I know the place is in bits, Alan, but I have a good feelin' about it. Anyway, after I saw them baby lambs dancin' out there, I knew this was the one for us.'

The young girl told us that a woman from England had put in an offer the previous week. I got a fright when she said that. We went ahead and put our own offer in. It was accepted straight away and a few weeks later, just before Christmas, we were handed the keys to our very own little cottage.

Alan thought that Christmas would never be over so that he could get working on the cottage.

'Are yeh right', Kathleen?' he said. 'Throw a few clothes in a bag there and let's head down to Wexford. There's no time like the present. I could get a lot done over the few days.'

'Alan, it's Stephen's Day. Everywhere is closed. It's freezin' down there. We've nothin' to sit on and there's no cooker.'

'Don't be puttin' obstacles in me way, Kathleen. Anyway, I have it all worked out. Yeh see tha' little two-seater couch there in the kitchen. Well, tha's comin' down in the van with us. I have the two-ring cooker tha' we use when we go campin' and I bought two sacks of coal and a couple of bags of logs durin' the week. I'll have the place pipin' hot in no time at all. Grab the two sleepin' bags from under the stairs so we can put them on tha' oul' mattress tha's there. Now, will yeh come on and let's hit the road.'

'Okay, Alan, don't be gettin' yer knickers in a knot! Give me a chance to rustle up a bit of food.'

While I was doing that, Alan loaded the van and soon after we were on our way. He never stopped talking the whole way down, rammaging on about all he was going to do as soon as we got there. The first thing he did was to light the fire. I know the cottage was in a bad way and needed a right going over, but after an hour or two with a bit of heat going through it, things didn't seem to look or feel too bad.

Everything that was moveable was thrown out into the back yard. The pair of us worked non-stop for hours on end, so much so that we actually forgot to eat. It was only when my stomach started grumbling and talking to me that I thought of food.

'Alan, I'm goin' to stop and make us somethin' to eat before we fall out of our standin'.'

'Okay, you go ahead, Kathleen. I'm tryin' to see if I can stop the water pourin' down the walls in the toilet. Otherwise we'll be drowned when we're usin' it.'

I was kneeling down at the fire, cooking away, when suddenly I heard a buzzing noise. I wasn't sure if it was coming from the chimney, but I thought at first it must be the wind. So I carried on with what I was doing, but after a while it got a lot stronger. I went in to Alan.

'Can yeh hear tha' noise in there? I'm not sure if it's up the chimney or up the stairs.'

'Maybe we have a ghost, Kathleen?' he said as he chased me around the kitchen and on up the stairs. I was laughing my head off as I ran into one of the bedrooms.

I ran right into a swarm of monster bees – each of them nearly half the size of your finger. I started screaming.

'Holy fuck! Alan, Alan!' Quick as lightning, he grabbed me by the jumper and pulled me back out, closing the door as tightly as he could behind us. The two of us fell down the stairs with the fright that we got.

'Tha's it, Alan, I'm not stayin' here. This is fuckin' mental. Did yeh see the size of them bees?'

'Will yeh calm down, Kathleen, and let me check to see if yeh got any stings.'

I started jumping up and down, rubbing myself all over in case there were still any of them on me. There weren't and thankfully I had no stings.

'De yeh know wha's after happenin' here, Kathleen? Them bees were hibernating, tha's wha' they were doin'. As soon as we lit the fire and the bit of heat got into the place, they came alive again.'

'Come on, let's go home, Alan. Please. I'll be shittin' meself if we stay here. I won't be able to sleep. Oh my God, can yeh hear them buzzin'? They're goin' mad so they are.'

'Will yeh just sit there and leave this to me, Kathleen.'

With that, he pulled the old lace curtains off the window, covered himself from head to toe with them and ran up into the room, banging the door behind him. I could hear him opening the window and hopefully letting all the bees fly away.

It took a while for every last one to be gone, but that didn't make any difference to me. There was no way I would go up the stairs that first night – no way, despite Alan reassuring me that the coast was clear.

I settled myself back down and made us a bite to eat. That night, we slept on the mattress in front of the blazing fire and I have to say it was nice and cosy. It reminded me so much of when I was a child, how we would all fall asleep every night on the floor in front of the fire before Da would carry us up to bed. With that happy thought in my mind, I fell asleep without a problem.

* * *

I had to laugh the next morning when I went into the toilet. Alan had pulled the gutter that was hanging off the side of the house through the hole in the roof, and had it sitting in a bucket catching the water. I thought to myself, *Isn't he a cute hoor, the things tha' he comes up with*? No matter what happens or goes wrong, Alan always finds a way to fix things.

Later on, both of us were working away. Alan was on the inside, tearing the place apart, while I was outside washing windows and sweeping around, when I heard a man's voice call out to me.

'Hello there,' he said, 'I'm Jim, from just across the road. Them's my sheep on yer land.'

I got a bit of a flutter in my stomach when he said that. *My land*, I thought. *Jaysus, wait till I tell Ma about this; she'll be well pleased.*

'Howyeh,' I said, 'I'm Kathleen. Come on into the garden. Alan, come 'ere,' I roared. 'Come out, will yeh, the man is here about his sheep.'

He was out in a flash, rubbing his hands all over his jumper, trying to get some of the dirt off before shaking hands with Jim.

'I wasn't expectin' yiz down over the Christmas,' said Jim, 'Otherwise, I would have had the sheep out. It's just that the last owner asked me to put them in there to graze and keep the grass down for her. If you like, I'll do the same for yourselves.'

'Tha'll be great, Jim,' said Alan. 'Sure, isn't tha' wha' sold the cottage for Kathleen? She melted as soon as she saw them out there in the field.'

I could see by Jim's face that he was happy with that. By the time we were all finished talking, we were getting on like a house on fire, so much so that we became the best of friends over the years.

It took us a good few days, but by the time we were finished, we had the upstairs ready for the first coat of paint. That was as much as we could get done before heading back to Dublin. Jim told us he'd keep an eye on the place for us. With that in our minds, we drove away happy.

I thought I'd never get home quickly enough to tell Ma and the kids how we had got on, and how I was nearly stung to death by thousands of bees. Well, maybe not thousands, but there really were loads, I swear.

* * *

Ma had come on so well over the previous three years. She was still living with Clare. I was on my way over to her, dying to tell her my news, but at the same time I knew she was going to lash me off for not turning up for the yearly reunion in Crumlin with the whole family on St Stephen's Day. It was a very important occasion for Ma, having us all together under the same roof at the same time. But I had to think about what Alan wanted too. It wasn't very often that he would ask for much and he thought he'd never get started on the cottage.

As soon as I walked in I got the famous look.

'Hmm,' said Ma, 'so yeh've turned up now, have yeh, Kathleen Doyle? Where the hell did yeh get yerself to? The one day of the year tha' I look forward to, when me whole family is all around, yeh went and got yerself missin'.'

'I know, I know, Ma,' I said, putting my arms around her. 'I should've told yeh. I'd no intentions of goin' anywhere. I'm sorry, it's just the way things went.'

I told her about the house, how excited Alan was and all the work we'd got done. She had to give in and laugh when I told her about Alan running around with the lace curtains over his head, chasing the bees.

'Well, I suppose when yeh put it like tha', Kathleen, I can make allowances. But make sure it doesn't happen again, de yeh hear me now?'

I stayed there most of the day with Clare and Ma, the three of us yapping away about everything and anything. Suddenly, Clare's older son Dominic, who was now around sixteen years old, came barging in through the back door, flying past us into the kitchen, nearly knocking me and Clare onto the floor.

'Quick, Ma,' he shouted, 'they're after me.'

Of course, Clare knew what this meant straight away and roared out, 'Quick, Dominic, head for the attic.'

'Holy Jaysus, Clare, wha' the hell is goin' on?'

'Shut the fuck up, Kathleen, and if anybody comes in here, say nothin'. Just zip yer mouth up.'

Ma didn't even blink an eye to what was going on. Then these two fellas came charging into the kitchen, screaming, 'Where is he?' They only had the words out of their mouths when Ma picked up the sweeping brush and lashed one of them across the head with it. He lost his balance and fell against the cooker. The other one grabbed the brush off Ma. My immediate instinct was to stand in front of Ma.

'Don't you dare touch her, de yeh hear me?' I roared.

'Stand aside,' he said.

'No, I won't,' I roared again.

That's when Clare stepped in. 'Kathleen, I told yeh to keep tha' mouth of yers shut. But yeh never listen. Them's the police.'

I stood there and nearly shit a brick with the fright I got. When the policeman Ma had hit got himself off the floor, he said he was going to arrest her for assault.

'Yeh can't do tha',' said Clare. 'Me Ma has brain damage; she doesn' know wha' she's doin' half the time.'

That's when Ma got her spoke in and, like me, should have kept quiet. 'I thought yiz were robbers comin' in to attack us. I was only takin' care of meself and me daughters. Anyway, how was I supposed to know? Yeh should be dressed like proper policemen.'

Now, while this was all going on, from the corner of my eye I could see Dominic jumping through the hole in the ceiling of the sitting room – which had been caused some time before by Romano falling through it. Clare had never got it fixed. Anyway, Dominic slipped out the side door, jumped onto the horse, Goldie, and charged past the kitchen window.

The two policemen fell out of the house, trying to get into their car as quickly as they could. They skidded out, nearly on two wheels, onto the road after him. Just as I was running out to the garden with Clare to see what was happening, Romano was making his way in. He started jumping up and down with excitement.

When I looked, to my amazement I saw Dominic flying through the fields, bareback on Goldie, with his dark brown skin and coal-black hair flying in the wind. He was like a young Indian on the chase. Of course, the police couldn't follow him through the fields in their car. But they weren't long about making their way back to Clare. One of them came in and told her Dominic had been seen joyriding in the area.

'I'm sorry, guard,' said Clare. 'I'll give him a righ' box when I get me hands on him, yeh can be sure of tha'. And don't mind me Ma – yeh'll have to make allowances for her. As I've said, it's her oul' brain.'

'Hmm,' he said, looking over at Ma, who was sitting there smiling and giving him a wink. He just shook his head and made his way over to the door, telling Clare, 'I'll be back up to talk to Dominic. The next time, don't be hiding him on us, because at the end of the day, Clare, you're not doing him any favours.'

'Holy Jaysus, Clare,' I said as soon as they were gone, 'I'll be half afraid to come here in future. I mean, it's bad enough when them lunatic sons of yours are together. I do be lookin' over me shoulder as it is, not knowin' wha' they're goin' to get up to. Now there's the police on top of all tha'.'

'Ah, will yeh ever give it over, Kathleen. I keep sayin' it over and over again, yeh worry too much.'

I got myself all worked up and started giving out like shite. 'Yeh wouldn't be sayin' tha' now, Clare, if Ma had been taken out of here in handcuffs. Wha' would yeh have done then, seein' tha' yeh're all so easy-goin' and worry about nothin'? Go on, tell me – wha' would yeh have done?'

'There's only one thing I could have done, Kathleen, and tha' would be to go down and sit in the cell with her. I mean, yeh couldn't let her go on her own now, could yeh?'

'Ah, for fuck sake, Clare, yeh're really pissin' me off now. I'll burst a blood vessel in me brain in a minute if yeh don't stop.'

'Don't be such a gobshite, Kathleen. There's no way Ma was goin' out of this house – because, in the first place, them policemen shouldn't have set one foot inside my house without a warrant, and they knew tha' as soon as they did it. But they were all fired up and forgot the rules for a minute or two. Just like wha' happened Ma in the heat of the moment. So, if they had pushed it over Ma, then I'd have had them, and they knew tha' at the end of the day. Anyway, they are righ', Kathleen, Dominic is a little fuck; he's gettin' up to all sorts of trouble out there and I don't know how many times I've had the police here. Believe me, it's not easy. Me mind does be in hell at times, but the only way I know how to cope is to keep calm and switch off from all the madness tha's around me. Otherwise, I'd end up being a hyper-hole like you, and I don't think me body or mind would have the energy for all tha'.'

'Yeh can say tha' again, Clare,' I said. 'But seriously, yeh'll have to keep an eye on Ma and make sure she doesn't do anythin' like tha' again. Or they really will lock her up the next time.'

'I will, Kathleen. Now, let's get back to talkin' about yer cottage and them lovely sheep with the baby lambs. I'd say tha' was a sight for sore eyes. Yeh'll have to bring me down with yeh some day.'

'Of course I will, both you and Ma – but yeh can leave yer mad kids behind.'

And that was it; Clare carried on like nothing happened. For her, that would be just another ordinary day. Looking at Ma's face, she was loving every minute of it. She was in her element living with Clare.

* * *

Over the next couple of months, myself and Alan were down in Wexford every chance we got, trying to get as much work done as possible. I grew to love the place and couldn't wait for the weekends to come. After all the hustle and bustle of the week, to get down to the peace and quiet was great.

Alan would be working on the inside of the cottage while I tidied around the garden. I absolutely love flowers and wanted to have every colour of the rainbow planted around me. I seemed to have been raking away for hours and wasn't getting anywhere, when Jim made his way over to me.

'Move over there, Kathleen,' he said, 'and I'll give you a hand, or it will be well into the middle of next year before you get anywhere.'

We had become very good friends with Jim over the months. I always made sure to bring him down a bottle of whiskey for keeping an eye to the place for us, and when I cooked dinner, there was always extra put on for him. He was a very private man who lived alone, but from day one we just seemed to hit it off so well. He was there for every hand's turn when we needed a bit of help.

I remember one day in particular; we had just got a television aerial on the roof a few weeks earlier, but we still couldn't get any of the channels. I wanted to get the man who had put it up to fix it, but Alan wasn't having any of it.

'Will yeh give it over, Kathleen,' he said. 'Wha' de yeh want to be bringin' the man back for when I can fix it meself?'

'Tha' roof is very high, Alan. I don't think yeh should get up on it. I mean, wha' if yeh fall?'

He just laughed and carried on with what he was doing.

'I'm serious, Alan, yeh could fall, and wha' would I do if yeh were lyin' there dead in front of me? Tell me, wha' would I do here on me own?'

'Well, I'd be dead so there wouldn't be much I could do for yeh, so I guess yeh'd have to go over and get Jim.'

'There's no talkin' to yeh, Alan McGrath.' I chased him around, trying to give him a swipe of the teacloth.

'Righ' then, Kathleen, if it keeps yeh happy, I'll go over and get Jim to give me a hand.'

But Jim wasn't there, so Alan went ahead anyway, taking no heed of anything I had to say. I watched him inching his way up along the slates, which he seemed to manage well.

'There yeh are, Kathleen,' he said, 'wha' did I tell yeh? Piece of cake. The only thing is, I still can't reach the aerial. I'll have to get up onto the chimney pot.'

'Holy Jaysus, Alan, are yeh tryin' to kill me with worry? Don't go up any higher. Please.'

But did he listen to me? No. I covered my eyes with my hands and peeped out through my fingers, cringing, looking at him stretching out to turn the aerial. Suddenly a couple of bricks on the chimney broke away, sending Alan flying through the air. Well, you'd want to hear the screams of me as I watched him bounce down onto the roof of the extension and then onto the cobbled stones on the ground. He landed flat down on his face. As I tried to help him up off the ground, all I could see was blood; it was all over his face and down his shirt.

'Oh my God, Alan, where's all this blood comin' from?'

He couldn't even speak and was weak at the knees as I tried to get him into the kitchen. It was only then that I realised there was a piece of an old pen struck through the palate at the top of his mouth. I was screaming inside my head with panic as I watched him pull it out. The blood sprayed out of his mouth, everywhere. I grabbed some cotton wool and tried to plug it as best I could until we got to the hospital.

We were seen to straight away. Alan was given a few stitches to his mouth and told that he had a couple of broken ribs to go along with it. His body was black and blue. His face and hands were cut to bits. He really looked bad.

I wanted to say I told you so, but then I thought better of it, so I zipped my mouth up and we headed back to the cottage. But Jim wasn't long about letting him know the truth.

'I'm surprised at you, Alan, doing something stupid like that. I mean, that's a mighty height to be climbing and with not a bit of help. Maybe you'll think the next time and wait until I am here to give you a hand.'

'Yeh can be sure of tha', Jim,' said Alan, struggling to get the words out.

There wasn't much Alan could do with the state he was in, so we headed back home to Dublin and what he had to listen to from everybody who saw him. The slagging was mighty, with everyone saying I must have given him a few digs. So between the pain that he went through and all he had to listen to, there was no way he ever took a chance like that again. Not unless Jim was around.

* * *

It was a week or two before Alan was feeling okay again. We thought we'd never get back down to the cottage. I was dying to show it off, so I asked Clare and Ma to come with us.

Clare fell in love with it straight away, which I knew she would. As soon as she saw the sheep, she was hooked, and that was before I brought her across to Jim's yard, where he kept his other animals – a couple of pigs, a cock, loads of hens and ducks, and he nearly always had one or two baby lambs that needed a bit of extra care, that he would be feeding from a bottle. Clare thought she was in heaven when Jim handed her one of the baby pigs to hold. I left her there talking away to Jim, while I made my way back over to Ma, who was happy enough sitting beside the blazing fire watching the telly.

'Well, wha' de yeh think, Ma?' I asked her.

'If yeh want me to give yeh the God's honest truth, Kathleen, it looks grand, and if I know Alan, by the time he's finished it'll be massive. But it wouldn't be my cup of tea. No way. Stuck out here in the arsehole of nowhere, with not a shop to be seen anywhere. But if it's wha' yeh want, tha's all tha' matters.'

* * *

That was Ma's one and only visit to the cottage. Clare came down with me a few times and enjoyed every minute. The rest of the family, as well as our own kids, dropped down to see what we were raving about and, just like Ma, for them it was too quiet.

Because we were only able to go down on weekends and the odd holiday, it took us a couple of years to finish the cottage off the way we wanted it. But I have to say, by the time it was done, it was like something out of a picture postcard. It became our very own hideaway – just for us.

We had some great times and many happy years down in the cottage before selling it on. It was much later that we bought the apartment in Portugal. Which brings me back to where I started . . .

Epilogue

'Tha' water was really nice, Kathleen. Yeh should've got in and had a swim with me.'

'I enjoyed lyin' here in the sun, gettin' lost in me thoughts for a while.'

'Jaysus, Kathleen, de yeh ever give tha' brain of yers a rest?'

'Well, I tell yeh one thing for nothin', Alan, the day tha' happens, yeh'll have somethin' to worry about, because tha's when I'm happy plannin' away in me head, thinkin' wha's next out there tha' I can do. Anyway, it's time we started makin' a move.'

As we made our way along the beach up to our apartment, I was bursting inside, thinking about the night I had planned ahead for us. As usual, I couldn't keep my mouth shut.

'Yeh know wha' today is, Alan.'

'Sunday, of course – why?'

'It's our anniversary, we're forty-eight years together and forty-three years married today.'

'Good shite, Kathleen, I forgot all about it.'

'I know yeh did, but never mind. Sure, hasn't it slipped my mind many times over the years. All the same, Alan, the years are really startin' to creep up on us now. Do yeh feel like we're gettin' old?'

'Not at all, Kathleen, yeh're only as old as yeh feel. I certainly don't feel me age and I know tha' you definitely don't, with the carry-on of yeh half the time. If yeh had yer way, yeh'd be out there tryin' to rule the world with the energy tha' yeh still have.'

'I know, Alan, I'm an awful fidget. I can't keep meself easy. But yeh're so right; it's only a number, and I feel great! Now wait till l tell yeh wha' I have planned out for us tonight. We're gonna have the best fun ever. I've booked a table at tha' fancy new restaurant in the old town and then we'll head up to Marco's place for a bit of dancin' afterwards. There's a big '60s night on there later on. We'll be able to have an oul' jive. So are yeh on for it?'

I got the biggest smile off Alan as he put his arm around me.

'Tha's my girl.'

On we went, walking along the beach, with me rammaging on as I do and at the same time thinking to myself:

This is the life!